THE CAMBRIDGE COMPANION TO
KARL BARTH

This authoritative book introducing Karl Barth is written by leading scholars of his work, drawn from Europe and North America. They offer challenging yet accessible accounts of the major features of Barth's theological work, especially as it has become available through the publication of his collected works, and interact with the very best of contemporary Barth scholarship. The contributors also assess Barth's significance for contemporary constructive theology, and his place in the history of twentieth-century Christian thought. The *Companion* both sums up and extends recent renewed interest in Barth's theology, especially among English-speaking theologians, and shows him to be once again a major voice in constructive theology.

JOHN WEBSTER is Lady Margaret Professor of Divinity and Canon of Christ Church, University of Oxford, and is author of *Eberhard Jüngel* (1991), *Barth's Ethics of Reconciliation* (1995), and *Barth's Moral Theology* (1999).

CAMBRIDGE COMPANIONS TO RELIGION
A series of companions to major topics and key figures in theology and
religious studies. Each volume contains specially commissioned chapters
by international scholars which provide an accessible and stimulating
introduction to the subject for new readers and non-specialists.

Other titles in the series
THE CAMBRIDGE COMPANION TO CHRISTIAN DOCTRINE
edited by Colin Gunton (1997)
ISBN 0 521 47118 4 hardback   ISBN 0 521 47695 8 paperback

THE CAMBRIDGE COMPANION TO BIBLICAL INTERPRETATION
edited by John Barton (1998)
ISBN 0 521 48144 9 hardback   ISBN 0 521 48593 2 paperback

THE CAMBRIDGE COMPANION TO DIETRICH BONHOEFFER
edited by John de Gruchy (1999)
ISBN 0 521 58258 x hardback   ISBN 0 521 58751 6 paperback

THE CAMBRIDGE COMPANION TO LIBERATION THEOLOGY
edited by Chris Rowland (1999)
ISBN 0 521 46144 8 hardback   ISBN 0 521 46707 1 paperback

THE CAMBRIDGE COMPANION TO KARL BARTH
edited by John Webster (2000)
ISBN 0 521 58476 0 hardback   ISBN 0 521 58560 0 paperback

THE CAMBRIDGE COMPANION TO CHRISTIAN ETHICS
edited by Robin Gill (2001)
ISBN 0 521 77070 x hardback   ISBN 0 521 77918 9 paperback

THE CAMBRIDGE COMPANION TO JESUS
edited by Markus Bockmuehl (2001)
ISBN 0 521 79261 4 hardback   ISBN 0 521 79678 4 paperback

THE CAMBRIDGE COMPANION TO FEMINIST THEOLOGY
edited by Susan Frank Parsons (2002)
ISBN 0 521 66327 x hardback   ISBN 0 521 66380 6 paperback

THE CAMBRIDGE COMPANION TO MARTIN LUTHER
edited by Donald K. McKim (2003)
ISBN 0 521 81648 3 hardback   ISBN 0 521 01673 8 paperback

THE CAMBRIDGE COMPANION TO ST PAUL
edited by James D. G. Dunn (2003)
ISBN 0 521 78155 8 hardback   ISBN 0 521 78694 0 paperback

THE CAMBRIDGE COMPANION TO POSTMODERN THEOLOGY
edited by Kevin J. Vanhoozer (2003)
ISBN 0 521 79062 x hardback   ISBN 0 521 79395 5 paperback

THE CAMBRIDGE COMPANION TO MEDIEVAL JEWISH PHILOSOPHY
edited by Daniel H. Frank and Oliver Leaman (2003)
ISBN 0 521 65207 3 hardback   ISBN 0 521 65574 9 paperback

THE CAMBRIDGE COMPANION TO JOHN CALVIN
edited by Donald K. McKim (2004)
ISBN 0 521 81647 5 hardback   ISBN 0 521 01672 X paperback

THE CAMBRIDGE COMPANION TO HANS URS VON BALTHASAR
edited by Edward T. Oakes, S. J. and David Moss (2004)
ISBN 0 521 81467 7 hardback   ISBN 0 521 89147 7 paperback

THE CAMBRIDGE COMPANION TO REFORMATION THEOLOGY
edited by David Bagchi and David Steinmetz (2004)
ISBN 0 521 77224 9 hardback   ISBN 0 521 77662 7 paperback

Forthcoming

THE CAMBRIDGE COMPANION TO AMERICAN JUDAISM
edited by Dana Evan Kaplan

THE CAMBRIDGE COMPANION TO KARL RAHNER
edited by Declan Marmion and Mary E. Hines

THE CAMBRIDGE COMPANION TO FREIDRICK SCHLEIERMACHER
edited by Jacqueline Mariña

THE CAMBRIDGE COMPANION TO THE GOSPELS
edited by Stephen C. Barton

THE CAMBRIDGE COMPANION TO ISLAMIC THEOLOGY
edited by Tim Winter

THE CAMBRIDGE COMPANION TO THE QUR'AN
edited by Jane Dammen McAuliffe

THE CAMBRIDGE COMPANION TO EVANGELICAL THEOLOGY
edited by Timothy Larsen and Daniel J. Treier

THE CAMBRIDGE COMPANION TO
KARL BARTH

John Webster
University of Oxford

CAMBRIDGE
UNIVERSITY PRESS

PUBLISHED BY THE PRESS SYNDICATE OF THE UNIVERSITY OF CAMBRIDGE
The Pitt Building, Trumpington Street, Cambridge, United Kingdom

CAMBRIDGE UNIVERSITY PRESS
The Edinburgh Building, Cambridge, CB2 2RU, UK
40 West 20th Street, New York, NY 10011-4211, USA
477 Williamstown Road, Port Melbourne, VIC 3207, Australia
Ruiz de Alarcón 13, 28014 Madrid, Spain
Dock House, The Waterfront, Cape Town 8001, South Africa

http://www.cambridge.org

First published 2000
Third printing 2005

Printed in the United Kingdom at the University Press, Cambridge

Typeset in Celeste 10/13pt [VN]

A catalogue record for this book is available from the British Library

Library of Congress cataloguing in publication data
The Cambridge companion to Karl Barth/[edited by] John Webster.
    p.   cm. – (Cambridge companions to religion)
Includes index.
ISBN 0 521 58476 0 – ISBN 0 521 58560 0 (pbk.)
1. Barth, Karl, 1886–1968.   I. Webster, J. B. (John Bainbridge), 1955–   II. Series.
BX4827.B3 C26 2000
230'.044'092 – dc21   99-056882

ISBN 0 521 58476 0 hardback
ISBN 0 521 58560 0 paperback

Contents

Notes on contributors

NIGEL BIGGAR is Professor of Theology, University of Leeds. An expert on Barth's ethical thinking, he has written *The Hastening That Waits. Karl Barth's Ethics* (Oxford: Clarendon Press, 1993, 1995) and edited a centenary collection of studies of Barth, *Reckoning with Barth* (Oxford; Mowbray, 1988).

JAMES BUCKLEY is Professor of Theology, Loyola College in Maryland, and an editor of *Modern Theology*. Among his publications is an important study of themes in Barth's doctrine of the church, and *Seeking the Humanity of God* (Collegeville, Minn.: Liturgical Press, 1992).

J. AUGUSTINE DI NOIA is Professor of Theology, Dominican House of Studies, Washington, DC, and has written widely on doctrinal and inter-religious topics. He is the author of *The Diversity of Religions: A Christian Perspective* (Washington: Catholic University Press of America, 1992), and editor of *The Thomist*.

COLIN GUNTON is Professor of Christian Doctrine, King's College, University of London. One of the most prominent British doctrinal theologians, he has written many books on systematic theology, especially on the place of the doctrine of the Trinity in Christian thought. He has also published widely on Barth's thought, notably in *Becoming and Being* (Oxford: Oxford University Press, 1978).

TREVOR HART has taught theology in Aberdeen and is currently Professor of Divinity, University of St Andrews. He has edited and contributed to volumes on modern theologians such as P. T. Forsyth and Jürgen Moltmann, and has published a series of studies of Barth entitled *Regarding Karl Barth* (Carlisle: Paternoster, 1999).

ALASDAIR I. C. HERON has held posts in Tübingen, Dublin and Edinburgh, and is Professor of Reformed Theology, University of Erlangen. A notable ecumenist and historian of modern theology, he is the author of *A Century of Protestant Theology* (Guildford: Lutterworth, 1980), *Table and Tradition* (Edinburgh: Handsel, 1983) and *The Holy Spirit* (London: Marshall, 1983). In 1999 he delivered the Hensley Henson lectures at Oxford on the theology of Barth.

GEORGE HUNSINGER is Director of the Center for Barth Studies, Princeton Theological Seminary. A leading interpreter of Barth's theology, he edited *Karl Barth and Radical Politics* (Philadelphia: Westminster, 1976) and has published *How to Read Karl Barth* (Oxford: Oxford University Press, 1991), and *Disruptive Grace* (Grand Rapids: Eerdmans, 2000).

WOLF KRÖTKE is Professor of Systematic Theology, at the Humboldt University of Berlin, has written widely on the situation of Christian theology in Europe and the theological legacy of Barth and Bonhoeffer. He is author of *Sünde und Nichtiges bei Karl Barth* (Berlin: Evangelische Verlag, 1970).

BRUCE MCCORMACK is Frederick and Margaret L. Weyerhauser Professor of Systematic Theology, Princeton Theological Seminary. His highly-acclaimed study *Karl Barth's Critically Realistic Dialectical Theology. Its Genesis and Development 1909–1936* (Oxford: Clarendon Press, 1995) revised much previous thinking on the development of Barth's thought. He was awarded the Karl Barth Prize in 1998.

CHRISTOPH SCHWÖBEL has previously taught in London and Kiel, and is now Professor of Systematic Theology and Director of the Ecumenical Institute, University of Heidelberg. He has written widely on constructive Christian theology, as well as on German theology of the earlier twentieth century, and has edited the correspondence of Barth and Martin Rade (Karl Barth – Martin Rade, *Ein Briefwechsel* (Gütersloh: Mohn, 1981)).

KATHERINE SONDEREGGER is Professor of Religion, Middlebury College, and the author of *That Jesus Christ Was Born a Jew: Karl Barth's "Doctrine of Israel"* (University Park, Pa.: Pennsylvania State University Press, 1992).

KATHRYN TANNER is Associate Professor of Theology, University of Chicago Divinity School, having previously taught at Yale. As well as articles on issues in modern Christian thought and its relation to critical and social theory, she has written *God and Creation in Christian Theology* (Oxford: Blackwell, 1988), *The Politics of God* (Minneapolis; Fortress, 1992) and *Theories of Culture* (Minneapolis: Fortress, 1997).

ALAN TORRANCE is Professor of Systematic Theology, University of St Andrews, having previously taught in Aberdeen, New Zealand and London. His book *Persons in Communion* (Edinburgh: T. & T. Clark, 1996) offers a reading of Barth's earlier doctrine of the Trinity.

GRAHAM WARD is Professor of Contextual Theology and Ethics, University of Manchester, and formerly Dean of Peterhouse, Cambridge. He is especially interested in the relation of Christianity and postmodernism, and has written *Barth, Derrida and the Language of Theology* (Cambridge: Cambridge University Press, 1995).

FRANCIS WATSON is Professor of New Testament Exegesis, University of Aberdeen; he previously taught in London. An important figure in the recent renewal of theological interpretation of Scripture, his published work includes *Text, Church and World* (Edinburgh: T. & T. Clark, 1994) and *Text and Truth* (Edinburgh: T. & T. Clark, 1997).

JOHN WEBSTER is Lady Margaret Professor of Divinity and Canon of Christ Church, University of Oxford; he previously taught in Durham and Toronto. He has written widely on modern systematic theology, especially the work of Eberhard Jüngel; his work on Barth includes *Barth's Ethics of Reconciliation* (Cambridge: Cambridge University Press, 1995) and *Barth's Moral Theology* (Edinburgh: T. & T. Clark, 1998). He is an editor of the *International Journal of Systematic Theology*.

WILLIAM WERPEHOWSKI is Associate Professor of Christian Ethics and Director of the Center for Peace and Justice Education, Villanova University. He has published important articles on the interpretation of Barth's ethical and political thought, and co-edited *The Love Commandments* (Washington, DC: Georgetown University Press, 1992) and *The Essential Paul Ramsey* (New Haven, Conn.: Yale University Press, 1994).

Preface

The work of Barth is central to modern Western theology, both historical and constructive. Although in German-speaking theological circles Barth's significance has rarely been denied (even when his theological convictions have been vigorously disputed), it has suffered from some neglect in English-speaking theological circles until fairly recently. Yet over the last twenty years or so, interest in Barth's work has begun to flourish here, and a considerable number of significant studies of his theology have appeared, often in dialogue with the best leading Barth scholarship in Germany. As a result, Barth is once again a major voice in contemporary systematic theology; indeed, the revival of constructive doctrinal thinking in English-language theology often owes a good deal to the stimulus of Barth's work.

Taken together, the essays in this *Companion* seek to map out and assess Barth's contribution to Christian thinking, especially with the perspective on his theology which can now be gained just over thirty years after his death. They are written by scholars who not only have established reputations as commentators upon and interpreters of the work of Barth, but also have an interest in promoting the kind of constructive engagement with the doctrinal legacy of the Christian church which he himself exemplified in magisterial fashion. After an introduction to Barth's life and the character of his work, the various chapters identify key themes in his theology, offering an analytical account of his writing in each area, and alerting the reader both to the main lines of critical conversation with Barth's thinking and to the resources he offers for contemporary Christian thought. The themes of the chapters cover most of the major doctrinal topics which Barth handled in the *Church Dogmatics* and, in addition, draw together his thinking on such topics as religion and politics, as well as looking at him in relation to specific modern preoccupations such as feminism and postmodernism. Though the authors are diverse in their interpretation of Barth's writings, in their assessment of his significance, and in the critical judgments they bring to bear on him, they are all convinced that time spent pondering his writings is amply rewarded.

The editor's thanks are due to all the contributors, as well as to successive editors at Cambridge University Press: Alex Wright, who originally conceived the project; Ruth Parr, who oversaw its growth; and Kevin Taylor, who brought it to completion. Thanks are to be recorded to them all for their enthusiasm, professional expertise, and polite goading; gratitude is also due to Patricia and Peter Anders, who gave valuable assistance with the production of the manuscript.

Abbreviations

CD   K. Barth, *Church Dogmatics* (Edinburgh: T. & T. Clark, 1956–75).

ChrL K. Barth, *The Christian Life. Church Dogmatics IV/4. Lecture Fragments.* (Edinburgh: T. & T. Clark, 1981).

GD   K. Barth, *The Göttingen Dogmatics. Instruction in the Christian Religion*, vol. I (Edinburgh: T. & T. Clark, 1991).

KD   K. Barth, *Die Kirchliche Dogmatik* (Zürich: TVZ Verlag, 1932–67).

PT   *Protestant Theology in the Nineteenth Century. Its Background and History* (London: SCM, 1972).

R   K. Barth, *The Epistle to the Romans* (Oxford: Oxford University Press, 1933).

1 Introducing Barth

JOHN WEBSTER

'As a theologian one can never be great, but at best one remains small in one's own way': so Barth at his eightieth birthday celebrations, characteristically attempting to distance himself from his own reputation.[1] Nonetheless, Barth is the most important Protestant theologian since Schleiermacher, and the extraordinary descriptive depth of his depiction of the Christian faith puts him in the company of a handful of thinkers in the classical Christian tradition. Yet firsthand, well-informed engagement with Barth's work remains – with some notable recent exceptions – quite rare in English-speaking theological culture. His *magnum opus*, the unfinished thirteen volumes of the *Church Dogmatics*, is not always studied with the necessary breadth and depth, and his theological commitments are still sometimes misconstrued or sloganized. The significance of Barth's work in his chosen sphere is comparable to that of, say, Wittgenstein, Heidegger, Freud, Weber, or Saussure in theirs, in that he decisively reorganized an entire discipline. Yet Barth's contribution to Christian theology is in many respects still only now beginning to be received.

Barth's life and work are inseparable, and his writings need to be read in the light of his biography and vice versa. He was at or close to the centre of most of the major developments in German-speaking Protestant theology and church life from the early 1920s to the early 1960s, and even his academic writings are 'occasional', emerging from and directed towards engagement in church life and theological teaching. At least part of the cogency of his writing derives, therefore, from his sheer urgent presence in what is said. No critical biography of Barth exists, though his last assistant, Eberhard Busch, assembled a great array of raw material in what is so far the standard account.[2] A projected autobiography started by Barth towards the end of his life was quickly abandoned; but a good deal of incidental autobiographical material is available in letters, published writings, and other forms. Barth was highly self-conscious about the course of his life, and especially about his intellectual development. In his mature writings, he often traced the history of nineteenth- and twentieth-century theology by describing his relationship to it and his own role in bringing to a close the era of Liberal Protestant high culture. Moreover, his theological concern not to drift away from hard-won conviction about the true nature of the Christian confession disposed him to keep revisiting the question of the continuity of his own work, and on fairly frequent occasions to look back over the course of his development. All of this means that, though much remains unknown about Barth's inner life, much can be said at the biographical level.

BARTH'S LIFE

Barth was born on 10 May, 1886, in Basel, Switzerland; his family background placed him at the centre of Basel religious and intellectual life. His father, Fritz Barth, taught at the College of Preachers, but when Barth was young moved to teach at the University of Bern. In later life, Barth came to regard his father as '[t]he man to whom I undoubtedly owe the presuppositions of my later relation to theology', and as one 'who by the quiet seriousness with which he applied himself to Christian things as a scholar and as a teacher was for me, and still is, an ineffaceable and often enough admonitory example'.[3] Barth records that his confirmation instructor 'brought the whole problem of religion so closely home to me that at the end of the classes I realized clearly the need to know more about the matter. On this rudimentary basis, I resolved to study theology.'[4] He began theological studies in Bern in 1904, finding much of the teaching a dull though (as he later saw it) effective inoculation against the excessive claims of historical criticism.[5] Bern did introduce him to Kant, whose *Critique of Practical Reason* he called '[t]he first book that really moved me as a student',[6] and also to the lively excesses of student society life. From here Barth went to Berlin, then one of the great centres of Protestant liberalism, where he heard Harnack with unbounded enthusiasm. After Berlin, Barth studied briefly back in Bern and then in Tübingen, until finally he went to Marburg in 1908.

One thing drew him to Marburg: Wilhelm Herrmann, then at the height of his powers as dogmatician and ethicist. 'I absorbed Herrmann through every pore.'[7] And his influence on Barth, both immediate and long term, was profoundly formative. Partly, he offered a commanding example of lived theological vocation; partly, he articulated a coherent account of Christianity which took Kant and Schleiermacher with full seriousness. No less importantly, he also enabled Barth to set a limit to his liberalism: Herrmann's stress on the autonomy of the life of faith (*autopistia*) signified to Barth that, for example, Ernst Troeltsch's subsuming of Christianity under the history of moral culture was a point at which 'I must refuse to follow the dominant theology of the age.'[8] After finishing his studies, Barth deepened his immersion in the Marburg theological scene by working there for a year as an assistant editor for the journal *Christliche Welt*, edited by a leading liberal, Martin Rade. From here Barth went on to pastoral work in Switzerland. After a brief period as suffragan pastor in Geneva (where he was led 'to plunge into Calvin's *Institutio* – with profound impact'),[9] he began his work in 1911 as pastor in the small town of Safenwil in the Aargau.

The ten years Barth spent as a pastor were a period of intensely concentrated development, and most accounts of his work (including those from Barth himself) make much of how the realities of pastoral work, which were brought home to him during this decade, led to his abandonment of theological liberalism and his adoption of a quite different set of commitments. Barth's liberal assurances were initially undermined by his exposure to the Swiss social democratic movement, then at its height. His immersion in local social and political disputes, fed by the writings of Christian social thinkers such as Kutter and Ragaz, not only made his early years in the pastorate highly conflictual but also began to eat away at his confidence in the bourgeois religious ethos of his teachers. The outbreak of hostilities in 1914 further disillusioned him, especially because of what he saw as the collusion of mainstream theology with the ideology of war. At the end of his life, Barth described the crumbling of liberal Protestantism which this represented to him: 'An entire world of theological exegesis, ethics, dogmatics, and preaching, which up to that point I had accepted as basically credible, was thereby shaken to the foundations, and with it everything which flowed at that time from the pens of the German theologians.'[10]

In the crisis brought about by the loss of his operative theology and the apparent impossibility of pastoral work which this entailed, Barth began to search for illumination. Above all he immersed himself in an amazed rediscovery of the biblical writings, and especially of the Pauline corpus: '[B]eyond the problems of theological liberalism and religious socialism, the concept of the Kingdom of God in the real, transcendent sense of the Bible became increasingly more insistent, and the textual basis of my sermons, the Bible, which hitherto I had taken for granted, became more and more of a problem.'[11] In the summer of 1916 he began intensive study of the epistle to the Romans: 'I read and read and wrote and wrote.'[12] From his working notes there emerged the first edition of the Romans commentary, published early in 1919, in which he offered an extraordinarily vivid and insistent characterization of Christianity as eschatological and transcendent.

Toward the end of his pastorate, Barth was consumed by the task of reconstructing his account of the Christian faith, as lectures from the time (collected in English as *The Word of God and the Word of Man*) indicate. As a result of a lecture in Germany in 1919, Barth discovered himself at the centre of a new theological movement. 'I suddenly found a circle, and the prospect of further circles, of people to whose unrest my efforts promised answers which at once became new questions in the fresh contacts with these German contemporaries.'[13] One unexpected consequence of this new fame was that in 1921 Barth found himself appointed as Honorary Professor of Reformed Theology in Göttingen. Deeply aware of his own lack of preparedness for the role – 'at that time I did not even possess the Reformed confessional writings, and had certainly never read them'[14] – he began the work of theological teaching which was to occupy him for the rest of his life.

'These were, of course, difficult years, for I had not only to learn and teach continuously but also, as the champion of a new trend in theology, I had to vindicate and protect myself in the form of lectures and public discussions of every kind.'[15] In his teaching in these first years as professor, Barth was buried beneath the task of reacquainting himself with the classical and Reformed Christian tradition, largely under the pressure of the classroom. He took his students through texts like the Heidelberg Catechism or Calvin's *Institutes*, as well as offering theological exegesis of a variety of New Testament books, and eventually teaching a full-scale cycle on dogmatics (published posthumously as the so-called *Göttingen Dogmatics*). Barth also positioned himself more clearly vis-à-vis his liberal heritage, notably in a lecture cycle on Schleiermacher (which gave a remarkably mature and sympathetic critique of its subject), but also in external lectures, some of which can be found in the early collection, *Theology and Church*.[16] Barth's central role in the new trend which came to be called 'dialectical theology' demanded much of his energy and took him all over Germany, bringing him into alliance with figures such as Bultmann, Brunner and Gogarten. The journal *Zwischen den Zeiten*, founded in 1922, became the chief organ of the group.

Barth moved to teach at Münster in 1925 where he remained until 1930. During these years Barth consolidated the theological positions forged in the early part of the decade, and became more deeply acquainted with the Catholic tradition, notably through contact with the Jesuit theologian Erich Przywara. Above all, Barth devoted himself to lecturing and writing on dogmatics, publishing the first volume of his *Christian Dogmatics* in 1927 (the project was later abandoned in favour of the *Church Dogmatics*). Around this time Barth also gave a lengthy series of lectures on ethics (which he already understood as intrinsic to dogmatics), published only posthumously: some of the material found its way into the *Church Dogmatics* in a revised form.[17] Barth's immersion in dogmatics was one of the chief causes of friction with other leading figures in the circle around him. Bultmann, for example, suspected Barth of relapsing into arid scholasticism; Barth's increasingly profound internalization of the thought structure of classical dogmatics pushed him to judge his associates to be clinging to the wreckage of theological liberalism, whether in apologetic, anthropological, or existential form. By the end of the 1920s the group had all but dissolved (*Zwischen den Zeiten* lingered on until 1933), not without some personal bitterness on all sides. Looking back on the episode shortly before the Second World War, Barth reflected on 'the loss of a host of theological neighbours, co-workers, and friends . . . they and I, little by little or all at once, found ourselves unable to work together any more in the harmony of one mind and one spirit. We quite definitely got on different roads.'[18]

This distancing of himself from his 'theological neighbours' was part of a larger process whereby Barth rid himself of vestiges of his theological inheritance, and articulated a theological identity formed out of biblical and dogmatic habits of thought with rigorous consistency and with a certain exclusiveness. This process had begun, of course, during the writing of the *Romans* commentary and was continued during his first two professorships. However, with the publication of the first part-volume of the *Church Dogmatics* in 1932 (two years after Barth moved to teach in Bonn), Barth demonstrated more than hitherto a calm and unapologetic confidence about his theological commitments which gave his writing its characteristic descriptive richness and depth. He himself identified his study of Anselm at the beginning of the 1930s as an important intellectual episode in the gradual evolution towards the *Church Dogmatics*. In the book which resulted from this study, Barth noted 'the characteristic absence of crisis in Anselm's theologizing',[19] and the phrase says much of the theological style which became increasingly characteristic of his own work. The confidence had many roots: the fact that Barth felt that he had divested himself of 'the last remnants of a philosophical, i.e., anthropological . . . foundation and exposition of Christian doctrine';[20] the fact that by now he was thoroughly familiar with great stretches of the history of Christian theology – Patristic, Medieval, and Reformation – which made available to him compelling examples of theology done in other than a modern mode; and Barth's personal self-assurance as the leading Protestant thinker in Germany. Above all, Barth discovered in the course of the preparation of the early volumes of the *Church Dogmatics* the freedom to think and write confessionally without anxiety about securing extra-theological foundations for the possibility of theology. 'I can say everything far more clearly, unambiguously, simply, and more in the way of a confession, and at the same time also much more freely, openly, and comprehensively, than I could ever say it before.'[21]

Barth remained a sharply critical thinker, of course, even when he settled into a more confessional and descriptive manner. His repudiation of the hospitality to natural theology shown by his former associate, Emil Brunner, in a rather savage occasional piece entitled 'No!'[22] not only sealed the grave of the former dialectical theology group, but also provided evidence to generations of North American readers that Barth was at heart a polemicist (and a rude one at that), rather than a constructive church theologian. For Barth, a much more important critical task lay to hand in articulating a theological basis for the church's action in response to the Nazi takeover of Germany. In the early 1930s Barth found himself occupying a key role in church politics, in the face of 'a gigantic revelation of human lying and brutality on the one hand, and of human stupidity and fear on the other'.[23] His leadership, both in a stream of writings–most of all *Theological Existence Today*[24] – and in active participation in the nascent Confessing Church – symbolized in his major role in drafting the Barmen Theological Declaration in 1934 – was of critical significance. More, perhaps, than any other Protestant leader in Germany at the time, Barth was free of the desire to retain the social and cultural prestige of the church at any price, and could bring to bear on the events of the Nazi takeover a startlingly clear theological position in which the church was wholly defined by its confession of Jesus Christ as 'the one Word of God which we have to hear and which we have to trust and obey in life and in death'.[25]

His leadership in German church life was cut short by his dismissal from his teaching position and his return to Switzerland in 1935. Barth taught at Basel for the rest of his teaching career. His main task there was the production of the *Church Dogmatics*, first as lectures to ever-increasing crowds of students, and then in volume after volume of the final text. '[D]ogmatics has ever been with me,' he wrote in the middle of World War II, 'giving me a constant awareness of what should be my central and basic theme as a thinker' (*CD* II/2, p. ix). The task was utterly absorbing for Barth, and massive enough to be a compelling object both for his intellect and his will. As he wrote, the bulk of the project increased. He found himself reworking the biblical and historical grounds for dogmatics; he felt driven to reconstruct some crucial tracts of Reformed teaching (the doctrine of election is a telling example), or to handle topics in a fresh way (the doctrine of reconciliation, for example, weaves together Christology, soteriology, anthropology, and ecclesiology in a wholly unprecedented fashion). Above all, he discovered that the portrayal of the Christian confession upon which he had embarked could not be done 'except in penetrating expositions that will necessarily demand both time and space' (ibid.). As early as the end of World War II, Barth was expressing frustration with his slow progress and wishing that he 'could run his trains on two or more parallel tracks' (*CD* III/1, p. 10), and the work remained unfinished at his death, largely laid aside after retirement as he and his long-time assistant, Charlotte von Kirschbaum, became ill and the stimulus of teaching no longer goaded him to produce.

For all its demands upon Barth's energies, the *Dogmatics* did not eclipse other activities. He was constantly in demand as lecturer and preacher; he played a leading role in the ecumenical movement in the late 1940s, particularly the Amsterdam Assembly of the World Council of Churches; he had wide contact with others through correspondence and personal meetings; he devoted a great deal of time to the many students who came to Basel to write theses under his direction; and he kept up a constant stream of less major writings. Moreover, Barth never entirely avoided controversy on some front or other. He often found himself at odds with the Swiss political establishment; he spoke out vigorously in the 1950s against American and European anti-Communism and against German rearmament, to a storm of protest. As retirement approached, he became embroiled in a tangle about his successor, and at the end of his last semester of teaching was publicly criticized by the pro-Rector of the University for his political views. Even after his retirement he evoked considerable church controversy by his opposition to infant baptism in the final fragment of the *Church Dogmatics*, observing wryly that the book left him 'in the theological and ecclesiastical isolation which has been my lot for almost fifty years' (*CD* IV/4, p. 12).

After retiring at the end of the winter semester 1961–2 (his swan song was the series of lectures published as *Evangelical Theology*),[26] Barth undertook a lecture tour in the United States, and kept up a full schedule of writing, speaking, and informal teaching until his health broke down early in 1964. For much of the next two years he was in hospital or convalescent at home, and the long illness left him unable to work at major tasks for the rest of his life. He did travel to Rome in 1966 to talk with those involved in the Second Vatican Council, and prepared a last fragment of the *Church Dogmatics* for publication, along with a number of minor pieces. But Barth's closing years were often clouded by feelings of 'vexation, anxiety, weariness, humiliation, and melancholy',[27] especially in view of the constrictions imposed on him by old age: 'in every respect my feet can now move only in a small compass. Gone are the trips and runs and walks and rides of the past, gone the addresses to large groups, gone the participation in conferences and the like. Everything has its time, and for me all that kind of thing, it seems, has had its time.'[28] Barth felt the loss of his professional life with great acuteness; yet at times he was able to express a kind of mellow calm and simplicity, along with an untroubled freedom in limitation, as in the little collection of his writings from the months before his death, *Final Testimonies*.[29] He died on 10 December, 1968.

Barth was a powerful, complex personality. His life, as well as his literary work, demonstrates a highly developed attentiveness and curiosity: he found people, places, events, and ideas utterly interesting and absorbing. He was fascinated by all the different manifestations of the secular world. He took great delight in the international student body in Basel, and students often experienced his teaching in seminars and lectures as something in which they could 'witness the dynamics of newly-created thoughts'.[30] Barth was able to sustain at one and the same time a vigorously active public life and the continuous interior concentration and focus required to produce his writings, above all the *Dogmatics*. He experienced intense fulfilment in what he once called 'the necessity and beauty of serious and regular intellectual work'.[31] 'How fine a thing it is to be occupied with this great matter,' he wrote in the preface to *Church Dogmatics* IV/2 (p. ix). And yet he did not resist public activity; however much he felt harassed by the demands made of him, he appeared to need an external counterpoint to the intellectual. These two strong aspects of Barth, the internal and the external, coalesce in the fact that his personal identity was strongly defined in vocational categories. He thought of himself in terms of the tasks – intellectual, political, and so forth – which he felt called to undertake and which sustained his very firm sense of his own identity, rooted no doubt in the particular cast of his personality, but reinforced by his inhabitation of a broad imaginative space peopled with the figures and texts of classical Christian (and European) culture, and maintained by a commanding sense of calling to an engrossing set of tasks. This combination of interior breadth and highly focused vocation afforded him both a rootedness in his particular context and a freedom from its potential inhibitions.

There was also a certain alienating effect to Barth's personality. He could be devastatingly critical of people, views and institutions, and in both public and private life he experienced relationships which were strained or which ended in estrangement. Experiences here often led Barth to cast himself in the role of outsider, explaining his isolation to himself and others in terms of his sense that the primary ideas which drove his work had not been grasped or heeded or were contravened by the teachings and actions of others. At other times, his defence lay in irony and humour, through which he not only evaded his critics but also softened the negative impact which the weight of his own personality could have.

It is this restless, many-sided personality which lies behind Barth's writings. This does not, of course, mean that his theology should be read as a sort of encoded autobiography, for he was a sternly objective thinker. But there is an intensely personal aspect to all that he wrote (he wrote almost nothing in the way of pure 'detached' scholarship), precisely because his thinking and writing were who he was.

READING BARTH

Reading Barth is no easy task. Because the corpus of his writing is so massive and complex, what he has to say cannot be neatly summarized. Moreover, his preferred method of exposition, especially in the *Church Dogmatics*, is frustrating for readers looking to follow a linear thread of argument. Commentators often note the musical structure of Barth's major writings: the announcement of a theme, and its further extension in a long series of developments and recapitulations, through which the reader is invited to consider the theme from a number of different angles and in a number of different relations. No one stage of the argument is definitive; rather, it is the whole which conveys the substance of what he has to say. As a result, Barth's views on any given topic cannot be comprehended in a single statement (even if the statement be one of his own), but only in the interplay of a range of articulations of a theme.

Moreover, many readers of Barth find in him an unpalatable assertiveness, what Tillich called 'a demonic absolutism which throws the truth like stones at the heads of people not caring whether they can accept it or not'.[32] There are certainly traces of this in Barth (they are not simply restricted to his occasional writings), and there are plenty of places where he is polemical. But this aspect of his work is best read as a way of making a case for strong (and, judged by the canons of the theological establishment, deviant) views by severely critical attention to other voices. Like, for example, some feminist writers, Barth often feels the need to undermine dominant intellectual traditions which stand in the way of a proper appreciation of his own convictions. But it should also be noted that critique is usually subordinate to description, especially in Barth's later work. Nor should it be forgotten that Barth is capable of finely drawn and generous readings of those from whom he is theologically distant, and that the thinker whom he studied most critically and with the greatest disagreement – Schleiermacher – is also the thinker whom he read with the greatest deference and sensitivity.

Barth was emphatically a *church* theologian. He devoted his very considerable intellectual and literary gifts to articulating the great themes of the church's faith and practice, and the primary public for his writing was the Christian community (not the academy). But, more than this, Barth understood the activity of theology itself as a church exercise – as a spiritual undertaking which in the end can only be described by talking of God. Theology was not, for Barth, simply one more academic discipline, but an aspect of the holiness of the church, the sanctification of its speech and thought. As a church theologian, Barth was a 'positive' rather than a 'speculative', 'apologetic' or 'critical' thinker. He did not consider it the task of church theology to follow paths other than those indicated by the Christian gospel, or to identify common ground between Christian faith and other views of life, or to look for reasons for faith other than those already established in God's revelation. As a 'positive' theologian, he considered that Christian theology is called to govern itself by the given reality of Christian truth, and thereby to exemplify the obedience of faith to which the whole church is committed. And it was on precisely this basis that Barth was so often vigorously critical of the church: the theological task is to measure the church's speech and action against the gospel, not out of hostility towards the church, and certainly not from a safe distance, but as a modest instance of self-critical utterance in the Christian community.

For many readers, this churchly orientation means that the first encounter with Barth is fraught with obstacles. He seems remarkably assured where many others have not even begun to establish their certainties; he is immersed in the culture of Christian faith, intimately familiar with its great texts, themes, and episodes; his rhetoric is addressed to those whose minds are shaped by the architecture of Christian, and especially Protestant, dogmatics. Contemporary readers rarely find such a theology accessible, and so reading him makes quite heavy demands: neither its content nor its procedures make much sense to those schooled to think that one best approaches Christian theology by first putting in place an understanding of religion, or by establishing universal criteria of rational inquiry.

But this unfamiliarity of Barth's world of thought is an aspect of a larger issue which faces readers of his work. He persistently goes against the grain of some of the most settled intellectual habits of modernity. In his early writings this comes across in, for example, his refusal to allow that 'history' is a more comprehensive and well-founded reality than 'revelation'. In the *Church Dogmatics*, it expresses itself, for example, in his rejection of modern understandings of human moral selfhood which focus on ethical consciousness, deliberation, and choice as axiomatic. At key points, that is, Barth distances himself, sometimes dramatically, from the idealist and subject-centred traditions of modern intellectual culture. Those traditions still enjoy considerable authority in Western Christian theology, both in its liberal Protestant and its revisionist Catholic expressions, and still make Barth's work difficult to assimilate. And, it might be added, where they have waned – as in some recent 'post-liberal' theology – a recovery of Barth's thought has often been either a precipitating cause or a significant consequence.

Because of this, one of the most fruitful ways of reading Barth is to look at his thought in the more general context of the breakdown of 'modernity' – the decline, that is, of idealist metaphysics and of the philosophical, moral, and religious culture of subjectivity. Barth's relationship to modernity is very complicated, and it is too easy to reduce the complexities by making him appear to be either merely dismissive and reactionary or a kind of mirror image of modernity who never shook himself free of its grip. Barth is certainly a central figure in the break up of the modern tradition in its theological expression: for forty years he mounted a vigorous critique of that tradition, exposing what he took to be its fatal weaknesses and articulating a quite different way of doing Christian theology. What is less often discerned is that Barth was also in important respects heir to that tradition, and that even when he argued vociferously against it, it sometimes continued to set the terms of the debate. Barth was referring to much more than his age when he wrote at the end of his life: 'I am a child of the nineteenth century.'[33] One of the major ways in which Barth was in conversation with his nineteenth-century heritage was in his preoccupation with giving an account of the relation of God to humanity. In early work, the preoccupation expressed itself in urgent attempts to find a satisfactory answer to the question: How is God *God* for us? In the mature dogmatic writings, it came across in the centrality of the notion of 'covenant', through which Barth phrased his answer to a slightly different question: How is God God *for* us? Barth's answers always involved him in denying some of the basic premises of nineteenth-century theology – the priority of religious subjectivity and experience, the identification of God with ethical value, and the presentation of Jesus as archetypal religious and moral consciousness. And, as his thought developed, Barth became increasingly confident that no answer to the question of God's relation to humanity can be considered satisfactory which abstracts from the axiomatic reality of God's self-presence in Jesus

Christ. The brilliance of Barth's account of that reality was enough to bring large parts of the edifice of nineteenth-century liberalism crashing to the ground. Yet even so, it must not be forgotten that there is substantial continuity, in that, as Barth put it, 'the nineteenth century's tasks remain for us, too'.[34] In Barth, then, we will encounter a thinker who was both deeply indebted to the intellectual traditions of modernity and also their rigorous critic. If Barth dismantled modern Protestant theology as it developed in Germany in the eighteenth and nineteenth centuries, he did so from the inside.

INTERPRETING BARTH

The landscape of Barth studies has changed dramatically over the last two decades. In English-speaking theology, this is one fruit of a somewhat more hospitable attitude to Christian dogmatics, as liberal or revisionist theology has in some measure waned and more constructive engagement with Christian orthodoxy has gained momentum. Partly, again, it is because in the decades after Barth's death it has proved easier to reach more considered judgments about his project, informed less by partisanship (for or against) and more by close reading of his writings. Above all, however, the landscape now looks very different because the ongoing Swiss *Gesamtausgabe* (collected edition) of Barth has made available a good deal of unpublished material, making the corpus of Barth's writings a good deal more extensive than hitherto. This includes not only a large bulk of materials more peripheral to his academic writings (sermons, letters, confirmation addresses, and so forth), but also major lecture cycles, especially from the first decade of his work as theological professor. These include the already mentioned Göttingen dogmatics lectures from 1924–5; the cycle on theological ethics; an exegetical course on the first chapters of the Gospel of John; lectures on Calvin, Schleiermacher, and the Reformed confessional writings; and a volume of lecture texts from the end of Barth's career which substantially amplifies the published material on the ethics of reconciliation on which he was at work when he retired.

The effect of this new material, when read alongside what Barth published in his own lifetime, can be felt at a number of levels. Perhaps most strikingly, it has led to a substantially revised narrative of Barth's development, especially in his early years. What has established itself as the conventional picture of Barth (one with which Barth himself at times agreed) was that his theology changed gear twice: once when he moved away from theological liberalism, and once more when he moved beyond 'dialectical' theology into his mature dogmatic work. The more precise analysis of the genetic questions surrounding Barth's work that is now possible on the basis of the early lecture cycles and other published work shows that this map of Barth will not quite fit. On the one hand, 'dialectic' is a permanent feature of Barth's theology, not a temporary phase left behind in the 1930s. On the other hand, Barth's dogmatic interests start very early (within two years of the first commentary on Romans). As a result, the continuity of Barth's work after his break with liberal Protestantism is now much more evident, however much in later work he may have retracted or modified one or other early position.

Moreover, it is now clear that the driving force of Barth's development before the *Church Dogmatics* was specifically theological; his mind was shaped by his reading of the Bible and by his intense scrutiny of the classical traditions of Christian theology and their modern offspring. From the beginnings of his work as theological teacher, it was theology which afforded Barth the projection through which he mapped the world. At first, this task was performed by the great texts of the Reformed tradition: the Heidelberg Catechism and other confessions, Zwingli, and above all, Calvin. But soon it became a great store of Patristic, Medieval, Reformation and post-Reformation materials which drove his thought, always alongside the text of Scripture. Whatever else absorbed his attention, the decisive impulse was always theological. If those accounts of Barth which see him as, for example, a religious equivalent of Weimar expressionism or a Christian socio-political critic fail now to carry much weight, it is because they rest on an incomplete reading of Barth's work.

Beyond this, the materials now available demonstrate the crucial importance of two areas of Barth's theology which have not always been factored into accounts of his theology, but which are now claiming more attention. The first is biblical exegesis. In the 1920s, Barth lectured as much on biblical texts as he did on dogmatic and historical theology; moreover, the *Church Dogmatics* itself contains massive tracts of exegetical material. Not only is there renewed interest in Barth's exegetical practice and hermeneutical principles, but also a growing awareness that Barth's *magnum opus* is itself to be read as (like Calvin's *Institutes*) a guide to, rather than a speculative replacement for or improvement upon, Scripture. The second is Barth's interest in ethics, long left largely unnoticed but now coming to light as one of the clues to understanding his project as a whole. The posthumous ethical materials from the 1920s and the late 1950s (whose similarity of tone and content offers further evidence for the continuity of Barth's thinking), and the light they shed on the lengthy ethical reflections which round off each volume of the *Dogmatics*, show that Barth's theology was unified around a twofold concern: for God and humanity, agents in covenant, bound together in the mutuality of grace and gratitude. If one wishes to discover the sheer humanity of Barth's thinking, one need look no further than his writings on ethics.

In the end, however, it was as dogmatician that Barth's contribution to the history of church and theology was made; the best scholarship on his work will always be that which takes very seriously his dogmatic intention, and reads, argues with, and criticizes him as such. Most of the chapters in the present volume are given over to the analysis of and critical conversation with the major dogmatic themes to which Barth gave his attention with such vigour and constructive power. The best interpreters of Barth have also been and continue to be those who not only take the time to read and reflect upon his work with the respect and readiness for surprise which we are to adopt towards the classics, but also are themselves engaged in the task of church theology, whether they may find themselves agreeing or disagreeing with this vivid, provocative, at times infuriating but never dull pupil of the Word:

> Th[e] source of theology (which can also be called Gospel) is also its subject-matter, to which it is tied just as all other branches of knowledge pursued at the university are tied to their subject-matter. Without it theology could and would dissolve into amateurish excursions into history, philosophy, psychology, and so on . . . Bound to its subject matter though it is in this way, it enjoys complete freedom of inquiry and doctrine . . . and it accepts no instructions or regulations from anyone; it even serves the Church in the independence of its own responsibility. And since the God from whom it takes its name is no dictator, it cannot behave dictatorially. Bound only to his subject-matter, but also liberated by it, the teacher of theology can have and desires to have only pupils who are free in the same sense.[35]

Notes

1 'Karl Barth's Speech on the Occasion of his Eightieth Birthday Celebrations', in *Fragments Grave and Gay* (London: Collins, 1971), p. 112.
2 E. Busch, *Karl Barth. His Life from Letters and Autobiographical Fragments* (London: SCM, 1976).
3 Barth's entry in the Münster Faculty Album: text in K. Barth, R. Bultmann, *Letters 1922–1968* (Edinburgh: T & T Clark, 1982), p. 157.

4 *Ibid.*
5 K. Barth, 'Concluding Unscientific Postscript on Schleiermacher' in *The Theology of Schleiermacher* (Edinburgh: T & T Clark, 1982), p. 262.
6 Münster Faculty Album, p. 152.
7 Ibid.
8 Ibid.
9 Ibid., p. 154.
10 Barth, 'Concluding Unscientific Postscript', p. 264.
11 Barth, Münster Faculty Album, p. 154.
12 Barth, 'Concluding Unscientific Postscript', p. 265.
13 Münster Faculty Album, p. 155.
14 Ibid., p. 156. See also Barth's 'Foreword' to H. Heppe, *Reformed Dogmatics* (London: George Allen and Unwin, 1950), pp. v–vii.
15 Münster Faculty Album, p. 156.
16 K. Barth, *Theology and Church* (London: SCM, 1962).
17 K. Barth, *Ethics* (Edinburgh: T & T Clark, 1981).
18 K. Barth, *How I Changed My Mind* (Richmond, Va: John Knox Press, 1966), p. 41.
19 K. Barth, *Anselm. Fides Quaerens Intellectum* (London: SCM, 1960), p. 26.
20 Barth, *How I Changed My Mind*, pp. 42f.
21 Ibid., pp. 43f.
22 K. Barth, 'No! Answer to Emil Brunner' in *Natural Theology* (London: Geoffrey Bles, 1946), pp. 67–128.
23 Barth, *How I Changed My Mind*, p. 45.
24 K. Barth, *Theological Existence Today* (London: Hodder and Stoughton, 1933).
25 Article 1 of the Barmen Theological Declaration, in A. C. Cochrane, *The Church's Confession Under Hitler* (Philadelphia: Westminster, 1962), p. 239.
26 K. Barth, *Evangelical Theology* (London: Weidenfeld and Nicolson, 1963).
27 K. Barth, *Letters 1961–1968* (Edinburgh: T & T Clark, 1981), p. 295.
28 Ibid., p. 254.
29 Grand Rapids: Eerdmans, 1977.
30 D. Ritschl, 'How to Be Most Grateful to Karl Barth without Remaining a Barthian', in D. McKim, ed., *How Karl Barth Changed My Mind* (Grand Rapids: Eerdmans, 1986), p. 87.
31 Barth, *Letters 1961–1968*, p. 167.
32 P. Tillich, *Systematic Theology* III (Chicago: University of Chicago Press, 1963), p. 186.
33 K. Barth, *A Late Friendship* (Grand Rapids: Eerdmans, 1982), p. 3.
34 K. Barth, 'Evangelical Theology in the Nineteenth Century', in *The Humanity of God* (London: Collins, 1967), p. 12.
35 K. Barth, 'The Faculty of Theology', in *Fragments Grave and Gay*, p. 23.

Further reading

Balthasar, H. U. von, *The Theology of Karl Barth* (San Francisco: Ignatius, 1992).
Berkouwer, G. C., *The Triumph of Grace in the Theology of Karl Barth* (Grand Rapids: Eerdmans, 1956).

Busch, E., *Karl Barth. His Life from Letters and Autobiographical Texts* (London: SCM Press, 1976).

Erler, R. J. and R. Marquard, eds., *A Karl Barth Reader* (Edinburgh: T. & T. Clark, 1986).

Hunsinger, G., *How to Read Karl Barth. The Shape of his Theology* (Oxford: Oxford University Press, 1991).

Jüngel, E., *Karl Barth. A Theological Legacy* (Philadelphia: Westminster Press, 1986).

Thompson, J., *Christ in Perspective. Christological Perspectives in the Theology of Karl Barth* (Edinburgh: Saint Andrew Press, 1978).

Webster, J., *Barth* (London: Cassell, 2000).

Wildi, M., *Bibliographie Karl Barth*, 3 vols. (Zurich: TVZ, 1984–92).

2 Theology

CHRISTOPH SCHWÖBEL

However highly one values Barth's material contributions to theology, one could argue that his main significance lies not so much in what he contributed to the 'scientific self-examination of the Christian Church with respect to the content of its distinctive Talk about God' (*CD* I/1, p. 3), but in the way in which he taught his readers to conceive the task of theology and its presuppositions and procedures. One could even claim that the presentation of Barth's theology and its continual revision is a consequence of the new conception of the task of theology which shapes his theological 'forms of thought'. What makes Barth's material contributions to theology so significant is that they are part of a new way of understanding the task of theology which can be most clearly seen by contrasting it to what was taken for granted in the 'forms of thought' of modernity and its theology. Today those 'forms of thought' are no longer taken for granted, neither in theology nor outside theology. This provides a new stimulus for engagement with Barth's understanding of theology, its development, its elaboration, its problems and its promises in a situation which is no longer self-consciously modern, but is characterized by an uneasy oscillation between seeing itself as postmodern and/or late modern.

CONCEIVING THE TASK OF THEOLOGY: BEGINNINGS, ENDS, AND NEW BEGINNINGS

How the task of theology is to be conceived and how this shapes the practice of theology was a continuing concern for Karl Barth, from his earliest to his latest writings. His first book review was a discussion of a proposal for the reform of the study of theology, his last series of lectures entitled, 'Introduction to Evangelical Theology'. Between these starting and finishing posts there is a stretch of almost fifty-five years of reflection on theology. The early review, written when Barth was editorial assistant at Martin Rade's journal *Die Christliche Welt*, has as its central concern the 'bringing together' of Christianity and 'empirical reality'.[1] Against the programmatic appeal to relate these 'given entities', Barth asks: 'What else do we do in studying dogmatics and ethics than just "bring together" Christianity and empirical reality?' (*CD* I/1, p. 319). Barth chastises the author of the reform proposals, G. Mix, for seeing Christianity as a 'given entity'. Rather it is, as he says in the parlance of his teacher Wilhelm Herrmann, 'individual certainty'. Therefore the real question is: 'How do I mediate a personal certainty whose peculiar grounding on history and whose relationship to present reality has become theoretically clear to me, practically to others?' Barth is absolutely convinced that 'a student who has attended the school of historical and systematic theology with enthusiasm and love' will 'not make the transition to working in the church without some guidelines'. Barth, at that time an enthusiastic follower of Albrecht Ritschl's pupils Wilhelm Herrmann, Adolf von Harnack and Martin Rade (the main representatives of 'modern theology'), is optimistic about bridging the 'hiatus of theory and practice', of mediating between academic theology and work in the church.

A similar enthusiasm can be felt in Barth's first article for a major theological journal, the *Zeitschrift für Theologie und Kirche*, at that time edited by Wilhelm Herrmann and Martin Rade, the main forum of the theology of Ritschl's pupils. Barth's article, entitled 'Modern Theology and Work for the Kingdom of God'[2] starts with the observation that it is 'far more difficult to go from the lecture halls of Marburg or Heidelberg [the academic centres of 'modern theology'] to the ministry in the pulpit, to the sickbed and to the meeting-hall, than from those of Halle or Greifswald [the strongholds of the so-called 'positive' theology]'. Why should that be the case? Barth characterizes (approvingly) the character of modern theology as 'religious individualism' and 'historical relativism'. Inevitably, this makes the students of 'modern' theology less 'mature' than their positive counterparts, because they are aware that they have to steer a course between the Scylla of clericalism and the Charybdis of agnosticism. They apply the view of historical relativism also to their own theology and regard it as 'a form of appearance of the Gospel alongside others', which they employ to express the 'inexhaustible forces of the Christian religion' in those aspects which have specifically impressed them. 'Religion is for us in the strict sense individually conceived experience, and we regard it as our duty to engage clearly and constructively with the universal human consciousness of culture in its academic aspect. This is both our strength which we enjoy and our weakness which we acknowledge but do not regret, because we cannot do differently' (*CD* I/1, p. 347).

When the article was published it elicited angry responses from two of the leading 'modern' practical theologians of the day, Ernst Christian Achelis[3] and Paul Drews,[4] to which Barth responded,[5] before Rade closed the debate with a few remarks of his own. When Barth's counter-response was published, he had already made the transition to the ministry in Safenwil. Perhaps one must have drunk as deeply as Barth at the wells of modernity in order to reject it as fiercely as he did.

The process of Barth's distancing himself from the understanding of theology which he had taken over from his teachers and which he had defended in such a spirited manner, started gradually and then came to an abrupt climax. At first he sought orientation from the Religious Socialists in Switzerland, Leonhard Ragaz and Heinrich Kutter, who had taken up the challenge of the social situation created by the industrial revolution, which Barth could experience in his own parish in Safenwil by 'bringing together' Christianity and empirical reality in a strategy, not of mediation, but of conscious conflict. God must be understood from the revolutionary event of the coming of the Kingdom of God, which is not the joint product of God's realizing his goal for the world and the ethical activity of the Christian community as the Ritschlians had thought, but the catastrophe by which God challenges the structures of worldly reality, concretely the capitalism that had prospered through the industrial revolution. If theology wants to remain true to Jesus' message of the Kingdom, it cannot think theologically from the human standpoint towards God, but must learn to think from God towards the world. There is still much continuity here between the social engagement of the younger Ritschlian school exemplified in theologians like Martin Rade and the social theology of the Religious Socialists, but the optimism that 'modern theology' will provide the guidelines for the ministry of the church has already been shaken. At Safenwil, Barth's theology became a theology of a preacher for preachers, challenged by the task of being minister of the Word of God.

The task of preaching and the task of a theology focused on the task of preaching came to a crisis at the outbreak of the First World War. It is hard to exaggerate the effect the outbreak of the war had on Barth. For him the collapse of German academic theology into an instrument for legitimizing German war policies did not mean that a particular way of doing theology, the 'modern' theology of religious individualism and historical relativism, had been compromised; it meant that the possibility of doing theology at all had become questionable. It became impossible for Barth to continue doing theology as if nothing had happened. And the collapse of German social democracy by its support of the war had taken away the possibility of reorienting theology towards social tasks in the way the Religious Socialists had recommended. After theology had come to an end, where could it find a new beginning?

The experience of the war had for Barth become the crisis of all Christian theology. In consequence, where else could one start than in taking this crisis – the conflict between the world and God – seriously? For Barth the war had revealed the character of the world as a whole as being godless and evil. It is confronted by Jesus also as a whole, totally different from the world. Is it not necessary that Christian faith distance itself completely from the world, from all attempts to come to a compromise with its structures, and seek orientation in the 'new world' we encounter in Jesus in whom the human conditions of life are confronted with the totality of the divine conditions of life?[6] From 1916 Barth and Thurneysen discussed where they should start in finding a new beginning for theology, and they decided to start from the Bible. The result is *The Epistle to the Romans*. The first edition (1919) still explored the idea that the 'world of Jesus' is present in the world whose character had been disclosed by the war as godless and evil, and that it grows somehow organically from small beginnings to conquer godlessness and evil, similar to the way in which the Spirit transforms the materiality of existence. In the second edition (1922), on which we shall focus here, this organic model is relinquished and replaced by the radically dialectical character of the 'theology of crisis'.

The *Epistle to the Romans* is a disturbing book. Its disturbing character is, not least, rooted in the fact that its author communicates the disturbance he himself had experienced when he understood the First World War as the catastrophe of a way of doing theology from which he had hoped to find the guidelines for serving as a minister of the Word of God. The disturbance consists in the recognition that there is between God and the world a contrast, even a contradiction, that cannot be resolved from the human side by appeals to religious experience. But where does that leave theology? Is theology still possible? And if so, what are the conditions for its possibility?

Much of the expressionistic rhetoric of *Romans* is intended to emphasize the absolute distinction between God and the world. Famous is Barth's appeal to Kierkegaard in the preface to the second edition: 'If I have a "system" then it consists in the fact that I keep what Kierkegaard has called the "infinite qualitative difference" between time and eternity consistently in mind. God is in heaven and you on earth.'[7] The last sentence is perhaps the most famous from *Romans*. But what does it mean apart from a trivial insight which even the most modern of 'modern' theologians would not deny? Barth employs the statement of 'God in heaven and you on earth' in the context of his interpretation of Romans 8:22: 'Up to the present, we know, the whole created universe groans in all its parts as if in the pangs of childbirth.' He interprets the 'we know' as our not-knowing what God knows and precisely this he claims is our knowing of God. God knows what the universe is apart from and beyond its groaning to be freed from the shackles of mortality. We do not. But in this not-knowing we know God as the one who knows what our ultimate destiny will be.[8] If we presumed to know what God knows, we would abuse God by instrumentalizing God for our interests – exactly what Barth accuses the German war theology of having done. There is, then, a sense in which God is known as the one who is unknown, because God is not a metaphysical essence alongside other such essences, not an 'other' alongside what is not God, but the pure origin of everything that is not God.[9] The absolute difference between God and the world is expressed with astounding dialectics when Barth says that the 'line of death' that separates what God is and does from human being and action cannot be transcended, but then goes on to say that it is also the 'life-line', the end which is the beginning, the 'No' which is 'Yes'. No wonder Barth quotes Tertullian's *credo quia absurdum* in order to underline the paradoxical claim that the negation is also the affirmation.[10] Viewed from the human side God is the 'impossible possibility' (an expression Barth later employed to talk about sin), but from God's side the humanly impossible has entered the realm of the possible. In this sense, God's revelations are to be understood as 'conceivable testimonies of the inconceivable'.

But what of theology? Is it possible on such dialectical foundations? Barth concedes that the concern of theology is justified. He even spells that out for all the theological disciplines.[11] There is a concern for theology to be taught by the Bible about the meaning of the Word of God as it passes from its source and becomes a human word. There is a concern for historical theology to disclose the contradiction of 'Christianity'; i.e., the Word of God as it becomes a human word, against all other human culture or perversions of culture. There is even a concern for systematic theology to explore the boundaries defined for human beings and to state the question of God that is posed by the human witness to the Word of God and by the fact of human limitation. And there is a legitimate concern for practical theology to warn those aspiring to the ministry of illusions, securities, and service to humans instead of to God, and to admonish them to maintain strict 'objectivity'. Barth even says that theology should be not only one but the only ethical possibility, and this in the context where the criterion of all ethics is its radical critique by the Word of God, so that 'ethical' means nothing other than listening to the Word of God, leaving space for the work of God; it means nothing other than repentance.

THE WORD OF GOD AND THE POSSIBILITY OF THEOLOGY

When the second edition of *Romans* was published, Barth had already left Safenwil for the chair in Reformed theology at the University of Göttingen to which he was called in 1921. This meant that his 'theology' had to develop in the context of academic theology within a secular university. Much of the attraction of Barth's approach to theology consists in the fact that he does not submit the theological task to criteria derived from its academic context. He seeks a *theological* understanding of theology. This is most clearly developed in a paper that he gave – on the invitation of Martin Rade – to the 'Friends of The Christian World', the very group from which *Romans* had distanced him. This paper, 'The Word of God and the Task of the Ministry', is one of the classics of twentieth-century theology.[12]

The theologian's predicament is presented here with paradoxical clarity: 'As ministers we ought to speak of God. We are human, however, and so cannot speak of God. We ought therefore to recognize both our obligation and our inability and by that very recognition give God the glory. This is our perplexity. The rest of our task fades into insignificance in comparison.'[13] When explaining the statement, 'we ought to speak of God', Barth makes it quite clear that theology has not the task of responding to the many questions and problems that people encounter in their lives. The theological problem appears at the borderline of humanity. The problem is humanity itself in its state of being separated from God. Therefore, theologians are not called to answer the many questions of human existence, but the one question which *is* human existence and which points beyond human existence to God. As a faculty of the university theology is an 'alarm signal', an indication that something is not in order. There is no *a priori* justification for the presence of theology in the university; it is a permanent exception to the rule. Barth goes even further to say that as an academic discipline in the sense of the other disciplines, theology has no right to exist in the university; it exists beyond the boundary of scientific possibilities as a reminder of something that needs to be said by all disciplines but which, things being as they are, can only be said by such an emergency measure as the presence of theology in the university. What is it that makes theology both necessary and exceptional? It is its task of talking about God and nothing but God.

The problem, however, is that this is precisely what we cannot do, since we are humans and as such cannot talk about God. Talking about God would mean to talk on the basis of revelation and faith; it would mean to speak the Word of God, but that is beyond us: we are human beings and as such cannot talk about God. Barth presents three ways in which the impossible attempt is made to talk about God, but they all only demonstrate what we cannot do. The first is the dogmatic way, the way presenting the Word of God in the biblical witness and in the dogmas of the church as a normative way of talking about God. However, in this approach, the Word of God, the ground of faith, is presented as a collection of articles of faith. And if these are set before people, they cannot believe since they can only believe what has been disclosed to them – even dogmatic theology cannot make this happen. The second way, the critical way, responds to the human question, not by affirmations about God, but by confronting humanity with its negation, by trying to demonstrate that any human attempt to reach out to God is futile because humanity is what must be overcome. However, Barth says that this mystical way of approaching God by saying 'No' to humanity, necessary as it may be, does not reach its goal since all negations that could be offered from the human side seem irrelevant to the one negation which is God. It is only God who could fill the void of human emptiness. The critical way intensifies the question which humans *are*, but it cannot provide the answer. The third way, the dialectical way, is according to Barth by far the best. It relates the dogmatic affirmation and the critical negation, and in doing so creates a space in which the Word of God can be heard. The effect of relating affirmation and negation in this way is that both dogmatics and mysticism are relativized. Theological discourse becomes *witness*, which has its authority in pointing beyond itself to something that it can neither create nor control, that can only happen contingently. Barth indicates this when he says that theology's task of speaking about God can only be fulfilled if God himself speaks. Therefore, its very task is the certain defeat of all theology and all theologians.[14]

This approach to theology had to provoke criticism from the academic establishment and it came from Adolf von Harnack, one of Barth's former teachers, whose *Essence of Christianity* (1900) had summarized the content of the gospel distilled by historical reconstruction as the dynamic core of the history of Christianity. Harnack directed 'Fifteen Questions to the Despisers of Scientific Theology'[15] in the *Christian World* to which Barth, surely not the only target of Harnack's criticisms, responded. For Harnack, the academic respectability of theology resides in its character as *historical* discipline. For Barth, this deprives theology of its *theological character*.[16] Any science is determined by its subject-matter. In the case of theology, this subject-matter cannot be conceived as object, but as subject, and this changes all the rules of ordinary academic disciplines. Therefore, the place where God and world come together is not the harmony of the experience of

God with the experience of Truth, Beauty, and Goodness. God and world come together in the cross of Christ, they come together as they clash. The task of theology and the task of preaching are one. Harnack replies in an 'Open Letter'[17] to Barth that theology can only claim a place in the *universitas litterarum* if it conforms to the house rules; i.e., if it is itself an academic discipline so that the lectern in a lecture hall is not confused with a pulpit in a church. He accuses Barth of, like Marcion, cutting the links between faith and the human. In his counter-reply, Barth offers an extensive account of the understanding of theology he had reached at that time. What he criticizes in modern historical-critical theology is that it has placed so much weight on the normative character of its *method*, it has lost the sense of the normative *subject-matter* of theology. Instead of the Word of God, understood in the correlation of Scripture and the Spirit, modern historical-critical theology concentrates on a 'simple Gospel' that is placed beyond Scripture and gained apart from the Spirit.[18] Barth insists that the theme of theology can be nothing other than the theme of preaching, and that is the Word of God. It is the Word of God which according to the gospel secures its content; God's Word has primacy over the human act of hearing. Harnack's comment that he finds Barth's concept of revelation 'wholly incomprehensible'[19] necessitated an extended reply from Barth. Revelation is not the name for the highest or deepest possible human discovery. God's revelation occurs as a fact outside the normal correlation of words and events; it is God's possibility of acting under the guise of the humanly possible in reality. God became a human and a historical reality in the person of Christ. What can be known about Jesus by means of the possibilities of human historical reconstruction is not revelation. Revelation can only be known where God makes himself known through creating faith. Therefore, Barth distinguishes faith as God's work with regard to us from all 'known and unknown organs and functions', even from all religious experiences.[20] Here Barth's theology is programmatically presented as a theology of revelation and Barth's critic, Harnack, serves as midwife in this process. The reality of God's revelation in Christ is the ground of the possibility of knowing God.

THE NEED FOR CHRISTIAN DOCTRINE

The dispute with Harnack signals a turning point in Barth's understanding of theology. Whereas *Romans* emphasized that God cannot be grasped, Barth now turns to the way in which God, as the 'subject-matter' of theology, and in this sense its 'object', provides the basis for a theological 'objectivity' that distinguishes it sharply from the emphasis on human subjectivity in modernity. This notion of 'theological objectivity' is developed in the context of emphasizing the need for doctrinal theology. This doctrinal theology is not based on received truths of traditional doctrine, but on the truth of God which is made self-evident in revelation, and which is the ground for the formulation of doctrine. With this notion of the objectivity of God, Barth directly confronts all modern conceptions of reality and knowledge based on human subjectivity, and he claims that theology cannot be made to conform to the axioms of modern science. Indeed, it is a science in that it conforms to its subject-matter and the axiom entailed in seeing God as the subject-matter and, therefore, the only true subject of theology: God is only known by God. If humans are to know God, there is therefore no other way than to turn to the point where God makes his knowledge evident: in his self-revelation.

This line of thought, already indicated in the exchange with Harnack, is first enunciated in an address Barth gave in Emden in 1923 on 'The Doctrinal Task of the Reformed Churches'.[21] It is further developed in his lectures at Göttingen (*GD*), for which he chose the title, 'Instruction in the Christian Religion' ['Unterricht in der christlichen Religion'], the German translation of Calvin's classic *Institutio Religionis Christianae*, which is already an indication of the doctrinal turn in Barth's theology. In 1927 – meantime he had moved to a chair at Münster – Barth surprised the theological public with the first volume of the *Christian Dogmatics in Outline: The Doctrine of the Word of God.*[22] The astonishment this caused can only be understood against the background of Barth's polemic against a theology that claims to grasp God and, in this way, instrumentalizes God for its own needs and purposes. And now this magisterial work which by itself claims that there is a way to go beyond the incomprehensibility of God in developing a doctrinal theology. Has the critic of 'modern' theology turned to a 'pre-modern' way of doing theology?

Barth starts, after defining dogmatics as the 'effort for knowledge of the appropriate content of Christian discourse about God and humanity',[23] with the doctrine of the Word of God which is introduced by a chapter on the reality or actuality of the Word of God. The second chapter on 'The Revelation of God' begins with a section on the triune God. It is followed by a discussion of the Incarnation of the Word, starting with the 'objective possibility of revelation' (introduced by reflections on the 'necessity of the Incarnation'), and is continued by the 'Outpouring of the Holy Spirit'. This is introduced by a paragraph on the 'subjective possibility' of revelation. After that, Holy Scripture and the proclamation of the church are discussed. The programme of this work is implied in the modal terms – reality/actuality, possibility, necessity – that are being employed. Had Barth found a solution for the theologians' 'predicament' that he had described five years earlier, that we *must* speak of God but *cannot*?

THE FORBIDDEN SYNTHESIS

Barth further explored the dilemma he had described in 1922 in a lecture he delivered under the somewhat ominous title, 'Schicksal und Idee in der Theologie' (Fate and Idea in Theology) at Dortmund in 1929.[24] The lecture deals with the problem of how a theology of the 'proclaimed God' should relate to the fundamental and perennial philosophical problem of realism and idealism. Contrary to the often repeated opinion that Barth's theology is anti-philosophical, he states clearly that theologians operate in the 'framework of philosophy'[25] because they have no other than *human* categories, concepts, and modes of discourse in trying to talk about the Word of God. Theology, therefore, has to reflect on its 'nearness to philosophy – a nearness as necessary as it is perilous'.[26]

The structure of Barth's lecture is exactly parallel to that of the paper of 1922. What he contrasted there as the 'dogmatic' and the 'critical' ways are now discussed under the headings of 'realism' and 'idealism'. Every authentic theology, Barth argues, must acknowledge realism's concern for reality which mirrors its own concern for the reality, or better, the actuality, of God. However, this concern for realism becomes fatal if it is seen as grounded in some prior capacity of the human *logos* to apprehend reality.[27] If theological realism becomes a theological version of a realist philosophy, it overlooks the fact that the reality of God confronts us as sinners, so that God's reality cannot be abstracted from the way God becomes real for us in judgment and grace.

In Barth's view, it is precisely the strength of idealism that it questions the 'givenness' of given reality and so reminds theology that, in contrast to all other being, the being of God is not given and therefore 'non-being'. A theology that is completely purged of all idealism, Barth says, could be nothing but a 'pagan monstrosity'.[28] Yet, against the idealist, Barth maintains that the transcendence of God is not to be confused with the transcendence of the human mind. The 'beyond' of God is not the 'beyond' of the mind.[29] Therefore, it must be maintained with the Reformers that knowledge of God is solely God's work constituted for us passively in faith. The antithesis of the receptivity and spontaneity of reason has a merely regulative, not a constitutive, function. In faith's knowledge of God, both are grounded in the passivity which reflects that knowledge of God is God's work alone.

However, Barth's sharpest criticism is directed neither against realists nor idealists – be they philosophers or theologians – but against those who claim that there is a third way, a synthesis that somehow sublates the antithesis of reality and truth, of realism and idealism. This is an impossible possibility for any human project of thought. Therefore, Barth maintains that the relationship between theology and philosophy – a philosophy that strictly remains philosophy – is, at least for theology, 'a rich and instructive community of work'.[30] However, if philosophy becomes theosophy, if it claims to find God on the way of thought as the synthesis that resolves the dialectic of realism and idealism, of reality and truth, the relationship turns into 'war . . . and indeed war to the knife' ('Krieg bis aufs Messer').[31] Why? Because the reality of sin, our estrangement from God, prevents us from finding God apart from where he wants to be found – in the gracious address of the Word of God. What must be said critically with regard to a philosophy that turns into theosophy must be stated no less forcefully in self-criticism of theologies that claim to resolve the dilemma by positing a *concept* of God in the place of the reality of God's revelation. For Barth, it is therefore a practical criterion of a theology that is aware of its own relativity over against the Word of God, that it is patient with other theological conceptions.[32] Yet behind this criterion there is a second, theoretical, criterion. A theology which respects the impossibility of devising a synthesis between reality and truth, and so between realism and idealism, must speak of predestination. God's grace, Barth states, must stand at the top of the theological agenda. This, however, does not mean beginning with an eternal distinction between the elect and the reprobate, but – as Barth says in an interesting juxtaposition of Calvin and Luther – beginning where Christ began: in the manger.[33] And so Barth can conclude: theology would be truly a theology of the Word, of election, and of faith, when it is fully and truly Christology.

Does this resolve the dilemma of 1922? The truthful answer would have to be 'not yet', at least not completely. How are the two concerns to be integrated, the question of how the prolegomena of dogmatics are to be conceived and the emphasis on Christology which now seems to indicate how theologians *can* speak of God? Before Barth could publish the first volume of the *Church Dogmatics*, five years after the *Christian Dogmatics*, two more related sources of inspiration were needed to give Barth's view of theology the shape in which it is presented in authoritative form.

THE SCIENCE OF THEOLOGY AND ANSELM

The first was a challenge by Barth's friend and colleague at Münster, Heinrich Scholz, who gave the question of theology as a science a sharp profile.[34] There are for Scholz three uncontested minimal conditions for an intellectual pursuit being understood as science. These are that it be expressed in propositions which make truth-claims; that it have the coherence which defines the extension of a science; and that it have controllability: there must be criteria to test the truth-claims of scientific propositions. There are two more contested requirements, the demand of research without prejudice and what Scholz called the requirement of 'concordance', stating that scientific propositions must be coherent with that which is biologically or physically possible. And there is the maximal requirement that science contain only two kinds of propositions: axioms and theorems that can be derived from these axioms. Barth's response is clear: this notion of what it means to be scientific is unacceptable for theology.[35] The criterion of being free of contradiction implied in Scholz' first requirement can only be fulfilled in the sense that the 'propositions' in which theology resolves its 'contradictions' are propositions about God's free action. In contrast to Scholz, Barth sees the foundation of what it means to be 'science' in the one criterion of the adequacy of a discipline to its subject-matter.

What does it mean for theology to be adequate to its subject-matter, that is, what makes theology 'scientific'? Here Barth, by now professor at Bonn, draws on the help of Anselm of Canterbury. In *Anselm. Fides Quaerens Intellectum*, Barth offers a 'reconstruction' of the proof for the existence of God in the *Proslogion* in order to set out Anselm's understanding of theology and to develop his own understanding of theology in conversation with Anselm. The 'necessity' of theology is for Barth-Anselm the very nature of faith. Faith itself is necessarily ordered towards knowledge. We cannot have faith in God if God is not the cause of truth in the process of thought. If faith is the love of God, then this love necessarily includes knowledge. Furthermore, if faith means that the image of God is restored and actualized in humans, this must include the dimension of knowledge. Through the knowledge of faith, the believer is on the way towards the eschatological vision of God. For these theological reasons, Barth affirms with Anselm that faith is *necessarily* faith seeking understanding.[36] The *possibility* of theology is the 'Word of Christ' as it is encountered in the word of those who proclaim Christ. The 'subjective' credo of the individual believer is therefore unavoidably related to the 'objective' Credo of the church which includes the Bible and the ancient creeds.[37] If we have in this way understood the necessity and the possibility of theology, what is the *reality* or *actuality* of the subject matter of theology? Barth says that with Anselm everything depends on the fact that God does not only give the grace to think appropriately of him, but also gives himself as the subject-matter of this thinking. God must 'disclose' himself to the theologian, so that God is not only the 'object' of theological thought, but the 'subject' who makes himself real for theological thinking by disclosing himself (*CD* I/1, p. 40). In brief: the *reality* of the Word of Christ, understood as God (as subject) giving himself as the object of thought through faith, is the ground of the *possibility* of theology, and where this has happened in faith, theology becomes a *necessity*.

OVERTURNING THE MODERN PARADIGM

In his reconstruction of Anselm, Barth is effectively attempting to overcome the paradigm of modernity in conversation with a pre-modern theologian. Under the guise of interpreting a pre-modern conception he deals with a typical modern problem, the constitution of an 'object' of knowledge, and in doing so shatters the foundations that characterize the enterprise of modernity. What characterizes the modernity which is the target of Barth's critique?

The first is the inversion of the order of being and knowing, of ontology or metaphysics and epistemology. In pre-modern times, the question of the being (or the essence) of something had primacy over the question of how it can be known. The leading questions are whether something is (*an sit?*), what it is (*quod sit?*) and how it is (*qualis sit?*). Being comes before knowing, because what something is determines how it can be known. In modernity there is an inversion of the order of priority. The question of knowledge gains primacy over the question of being, and epistemology becomes the gateway to the real.

The second characteristic is the inversion of the order of actuality and possibility. In pre-modern times the actual reality (understood in the horizon of its ontological possibilities) came first and possibility second. Modernity is characterized by the primacy of the possible. This has much to do with a different approach to time. Whereas for pre-modern times where we come from determines who we are, so that tradition and custom play the leading role in organizing the universe of meaning, modernity interprets itself as liberation from tradition and as turning towards an open future. The advent of possibility as the leading category for interpreting the world is a feature that combines the Enlightenment's protest against the authority of tradition and the optimistic vision of the future as a realm of endless possibilities, which characterizes so many strands of modern self-understanding from the industrial to the technological revolution.

In the horizon of these two inversions, the further marks of modernity gain their specific weight. The much quoted modern 'turn to the subject' is only recognized in its significance when the subject of knowledge is the 'place' where the answer given to the question about the possibility of knowledge decides on the actuality of being. Only that which is real can possibly be known by the human subject. Not least, that also applies to the subject: its own being is determined by its possibilities of knowing. Therefore, the epistemological question is radicalized to become the question of the constitution of subjectivity: the privileged subject-matter of knowledge is not the external world, but the subject in the process of knowing the external world, or rather the subject which in itself must possess the conditions for the possibility of knowing the external world. This also explains the modern preoccupation with matters of method: one must have clear and distinct foundations of knowledge in order to proceed on the way to knowledge. The possibility of proceeding on this path determines the reality of the world. Engagement with this cluster of foundational assumptions, which are almost tacitly accepted in modernity, determines the way of theology in modernity.

Against this backdrop, we can appreciate the severity of Barth's attack against 'modern' theology. On his account, proper theology as *fides quaerens intellectum* can be done only if it inverts the two modern inversions. First of all, the being of God must be understood as the ground for knowledge of God. Secondly, the actuality of the Word of God determines the possibility of theology. Barth breaks out of the modern paradigm by challenging its two foundational assumptions. The knowing subject does not determine the reality of the object of knowledge through the conditions for the possibility of knowledge. The reality of God determines the necessity and the possibility of knowing God – 'ontically and noetically', as Barth is fond of saying with regard to being and to knowing, and in this order. The *Church Dogmatics* is the execution of this programme.

HOW TO DO THEOLOGY: *CHURCH DOGMATICS*

The *Church Dogmatics* develops the understanding of theology that Barth had reached at this point. Barth's view of theology is the guideline for the structuring and the presentation of the material. Barth's understanding of 'dogmatics' is now no longer focused on 'Christian discourse', but on the church: 'As a theological discipline dogmatics is the scientific self-examination of the Christian Church with respect to the content of its distinctive talk about God' (*CD* I/1, p. 3). Theology is a function of the church. Barth demands the correspondence of the church's talk of God (a noetic concept) with the being of the church (an ontological concept), since the being of the church is 'Jesus Christ: God in His gracious revealing and reconciling address to man' (*CD* I/1, p. 4). With this, Barth makes a twofold distinction both from neo-Protestantism in the tradition of Schleiermacher and from Catholicism. Against neo-Protestantism, which starts from 'modern man' and his pre-understanding, Barth states: '[T]he being of the church is *actus purus*, i.e. a divine action which is self-originating and which is to be understood only in terms of itself and not therefore in terms of a prior anthropology' (*CD* I/1, p. 41). Against Roman Catholicism he asserts: 'The being of the church is *actus purus*, but with the accent now on *actus*, i.e., a free action and not a constantly available connexion, grace being the event of personal address and not a transmitted material condition' (literally: not a substantial state that could be transferred) (*CD* I/1, p. 41). That means: the Word of God is not a 'given' in the quasi-substantial objectivity of ecclesial doctrine, but only in the event of its 'being given' in the unity of discourse and act. This is the 'nature' of the Word of God (an 'ontic' description) which is the ground of its (noetic) 'knowability' (paragraph 5). It is the reality of the Word of God which is the ground of its possibility of being known. The Word of God, however, is nothing other than 'God in his revelation', which, in turn, is the trinitarian self-correspondence of God as Father, Son, and Spirit. The 'object' of theology is God's self-presentation, which is the basis for the unity of content and event in Christian theology. The subject-matter (*der Gegenstand*) of Christian faith, which is disclosed in the event of the self-objectivation of the trinitarian God in revelation, is also the content (*der Inhalt*) of faith. The task of theology is, therefore, the explication of the content and event of the self-presentation of God as the ground of created reality and as the realization of its reconciliation.

The systematic structure of the *Church Dogmatics* is the resolution of the dilemma posed in 1922: as theologians we must speak of God, but as human beings we cannot. The resolution of this dilemma lies not in a 'third option' that could somehow transcend the 'contradiction' between 'must' and 'cannot'. It is to be found in God's free action and can be expressed only in sentences about God's free action. The *Church Dogmatics* tries to formulate these propositions, and tries and tries again in the ever new attempt to start at the beginning.

Starting at the beginning does not mean starting, according to the first dogma of modernity, with the question of whether we can *know* anything about God. It means starting with the being of God. Therefore, the doctrine of the Trinity acquires a crucial place in the prolegomena of dogmatics. It explains why we can know anything at all about God. Barth's thesis that God's Word is God himself in his revelation in the unity and distinction of being Revealer, Revelation, and Revealedness locates the possibility of knowing God in the immanent Trinity, in the unity-in-distinction of Father, Son, and Spirit. Their unity in distinction is precisely their relationship in revelation. In this sense, God *is* his revelation and so also his knowability. Similarly, starting at the beginning does not mean to start, according to the second dogma of modernity, with the *possibility* of knowledge and being. What are the conditions for the possibility of doing theology? It means starting from the reality of the Word of God and then gaining insight into its possibility. Barth does not simply skip the transcendental question about the conditions of the possibility of being and knowledge. He answers it with the astonishing thesis that the triune being of God, God in his Word, is the condition for the possibility of knowing God. However, this condition for the possibility of knowing God is given only in the reality or actuality of God in Jesus Christ; this is the concrete universal from which all theological reflection must start.

From this perspective, we can also understand Barth's constant polemics against natural theology which reached a high point at the time when the first volume of the *Church Dogmatics* was published. If the triune being of God (God in his revelation) is the possibility of knowing God, indeed the *only* possibility of knowing God, natural theology, the attempt to reach God by the powers of 'natural' reason, becomes an impossibility. It attempts to gain knowledge of God *actively* by the powers of human reason, whereas for humans it can only be *passively* received because it is *actively* disclosed by the self-revelation of the triune God to us. Natural theology confuses what is constituted *by* human beings with what is constituted *for* human beings, and in this way consistently conflates what human beings can do and what only God can do and has done. Trying to know God apart from God's revelation is to attempt the impossible, because it ignores the fact that God's self-revelation is the only condition for the possibility of knowing God. And since God's revelation is God's 'being in act' – 'God is who He is in the act of His revelation' (*CD* II/1, p. 257) – natural theology is, quite contrary to its intentions, the denial of God. To attempt to know God apart from God's revelation is to deny God, because God *is* his revelation. Natural theology, therefore, is for Barth the futile attempt to erect a Tower of Babel through which humans might aspire to knowledge of God alongside the Jacob's Ladder on which God comes to meet us in his revelation.

This is the reason why Barth consistently and annoyingly connects natural theology with the failure of the church in Germany to perceive the true character of Hitler's totalitarian regime, to recognize it for what it was and to act upon such a recognition. The denial of the God who can only be known through his revelation in Christ and not in the 'national revolution' is, for Barth, the common denominator of natural theology, the theology of the *Deutsche Christen* and the ideology of the National Socialist regime. Therefore, Barth insisted, the form of resistance both to the totalitarian regime and to the *Deutsche Christen* must be *theological*, because underlying the political perversity is a theological perversity. Barth's understanding of *theology* as grounded in the self-revelation of the triune God has political implications. At the beginning of the First World War, Barth had protested against conflating the things of the world and the things of God, because they were two 'worlds' that must be kept apart. In the time leading up to the Second World War Barth protested against conflating the things of the world and the things of God, because there is only one 'world' since there is only one Word of God: Jesus Christ.

THE CHALLENGE OF BARTH'S UNDERSTANDING OF THEOLOGY

Barth's understanding of theology remains a challenge in today's theological situation. It questions the tacit assumptions of ways of doing theology that, in some places, have quietly returned to doing theology as if Barth's challenge had never happened. It also questions the tacit assumptions of doing theology by imitating Barth's theology, because the challenge lies as much in the way in which Barth worked out his understanding of theology as at the 'position' at which he arrived. If Barth's understanding of theology points in the right direction, then there is no position that could somehow save us from starting at the beginning, from critically questioning – as Barth did – what is taken for granted in ways of doing theology and testing them with the question whether they can be appropriate to their subject-matter, if this subject-matter is indeed God. To imitate Barth's theology would mean to deprive it of the challenge it presents.

The widespread questioning of the paradigms of modernity has created a climate in which it seems particularly interesting to engage with Barth again. However, one should not too easily see Barth as a postmodern theologian, perhaps even the first postmodern theologian.[38] There is no doubt that Barth would have agreed with much of postmodernism's criticism of modernity, especially with the critique of foundationalism, and he would have been right in seeing his own work in many ways as a theological anticipation of this critique. However, it remains doubtful whether Barth would have found it easy to come to terms with the plurality of paradigms, the celebration of difference, sometimes the sheer arbitrariness of positions, that seem to be by-products of the self-congratulatory attitudes of post-modernism. Would he not have insisted that the necessity of talking about God questions not just the classical modern paradigms, but all paradigms (even the postmodern paradigm of the loss of all paradigms), and would he not have underlined that the impossibility of talking about God does not become any easier to bear in a postmodern culture?

The challenge which Barth's understanding of theology presents is to conceive of theology in one sense as an independent discipline that cannot be subjected to criteria drawn from other areas of intellectual inquiry. However, this independence is precisely not autonomy as a capacity for self-legislation, but faithfulness to its proper object of inquiry – the true subject-matter of theology, the triune God. The reality of the self-disclosure of God as the condition of the possibility of theological knowledge gives theology freedom as an intellectual inquiry by disclosing the service of God as the ground of that freedom. Independence, however, is not enough! What if Barth is right that the reality of God's revelation is the condition for knowledge, not just for theological knowledge, but for all knowledge? If God reveals himself as the Lord, it would be blasphemous to reduce God's Lordship to God being the Lord of theology and of the church only. If, therefore, the independence of theology is grounded in the self-disclosure of the triune God, it would have to be balanced by an equally strong emphasis on the interdependence of theology with all other modes of inquiry which are also grounded in the universality of the truth-claims of God's self-disclosure. Would this mean that not only theological knowledge but all knowledge is grounded in revelation? Calvin at least was of this opinion when he wrote: 'If we believe that the Spirit of God is the only fountain of truth, we shall neither reject nor despise the truth itself, wherever it shall appear, unless we wish to insult the Spirit of God.'[39] Could it be that a general theology of revelation – not a theology of general revelation! – is a necessary complement of the theology of God's special revelation in Christ, if that is to be understood as the self-revelation of the triune God? If so, Barth's understanding of theology would point beyond theology to all sciences. This is the reason why Barth insisted that theology 'may not regard its separate existence as necessary in principle. . . . This is the very thing which it cannot do' (*CD* I/1, p. 10). Barth's adamant emphasis that the separate existence of theology 'can have no epistemological basis' seems to indicate that the theological task is by no means reserved for theology alone: 'The other sciences, too, might finally set themselves this task, and this task alone, submitting all other tasks to it' (*CD* I/1, p. 7). It is the very ground of theology, the reality of the self-disclosure of the triune God, that necessitates seeing the independence of theology as an 'emergency measure' and which must be balanced by its interdependence with all other sciences. This would bring Barth close to his antipode in the nineteenth century, who in his *Dialectics* had claimed that God is the only ground of *all* knowing and willing. A horrifying thought for some followers of Barth, but not so for Barth who said – with the sense of humour that is one of the distinctive marks of his theology – that he looked forward to his conversations with Schleiermacher in heaven.[40] Perhaps this is one of the topics they might talk about.

Notes

1 Review of G. Mix, *Zur Reform des theologischen Studiums. Ein Alarmruf* (Munich: 1908), in *Die Christliche Welt* 23 (1909), pp. 116f.
2 'Moderne Theologie und Reichsgottesarbeit', *Zeitschrift für Theologie und Kirche* 19 (1909), pp. 317–21.
3 E. C. Achelis, 'Noch einmal: Moderne Theologie und Reichsgottesarbeit', *Zeitschrift für Theologie und Kirche* 19 (1909), pp. 406–10.
4 P. Drews, 'Zum dritten Mal: Moderne Theologie und Reichsgottesarbeit', *Zeitschrift für Theologie und Kirche* 19 (1909), pp. 475–9.
5 K. Barth, 'Antwort an D. Achelis und D. Drews', *Zeitschrift für Theologie und Kirche* 19 (1909), pp. 479–86.
6 K. Barth, letter to Rade, 19.6.1915, in C. Schwöbel, ed., *Karl Barth–Martin Rade. Ein Briefwechsel* (Gütersloh: Mohn, 1981), pp. 132f.
7 *R* XIII.
8 Ibid., p. 294.
9 Ibid., p. 52.
10 Ibid., p. 86.
11 Ibid., p. 433.
12 K. Barth, 'The Word of God and the Task of the Ministry', in *The Word of God and the Word of Man* (London: Hodder and Stoughton, 1928), pp. 183–217.
13 Ibid., p. 186.
14 Ibid., p. 214.
15 A. von Harnack, 'Fifteen Questions to the Despisers of Scientific Theology', in H.-M. Rumscheidt, ed., *Revelation and Theology. An Analysis of the Barth–Harnack Correspondence of 1923* (Cambridge: Cambridge University Press, 1972), pp. 29–31.
16 K. Barth, 'Fifteen Answers to Professor Adolf von Harnack', in Rumscheidt, ed., *Revelation and Theology*, pp. 31–5.
17 A. von Harnack, 'Open Letter', in Rumscheidt, ed., *Revelation and Theology*, pp. 35–9.

18 K. Barth, 'An Answer to Professor von Harnack's Open Letter', in Rumscheidt, ed., *Revelation and Theology*, p. 42.

19 Ibid., p. 36.

20 Ibid., p. 47.

21 K. Barth, 'The Doctrinal Task of the Reformed Churches', in *The Word of God and the Word of Man*, pp. 218–71.

22 K. Barth, *Die christliche Dogmatik im Entwurf. Erster Band: Die Lehre vom Worte Gottes. Prolegomena zur christlichen Dogmatik*, new edn, G. Sauter, ed. (Zurich: Theologischer Verlag, 1982).

23 Ibid., p. 13.

24 K. Barth, 'Fate and Idea in Theology', in H.-M. Rumscheidt, ed., *The Way of Theology in Karl Barth. Essays and Comments* (Allison Park, Pa.: Pickwick, 1986), pp. 25–61.

25 Ibid., p. 27.

26 Ibid., p. 32.

27 Ibid., pp. 39f.

28 Ibid., p. 47.

29 Ibid., pp. 48f.

30 Ibid., p. 54.

31 Ibid.

32 Ibid., p. 58.

33 Ibid., p. 60.

34 H. Scholz, 'Wie ist eine evangelische Theologie als Wissenschaft möglich?', in *Zwischen den Zeiten* 9 (1931), pp. 8–35, reprinted in G. Sauter, ed., *Theologie als Wissenschaft* (Münich: Chr. Kaiser, 1971), pp. 221–64.

35 Cf. Barth's brief but concise reply in *CD* I/1, pp. 8f.

36 Cf. the section on 'The Necessity of Theology', ibid., pp. 14–20.

37 Cf. the section on 'The Possibility of Theology', ibid. pp. 20–4.

38 For a discussion of the relationship of Barth and postmodernity, cf. W. S. Johnson, *Karl Barth and the Postmodern Foundations of Theology* (Louisville, Ky.: Westminster John Knox Press, 1997).

39 J. Calvin, *Institutes of the Christian Religion* II.ii.xv.

40 K. Barth, 'Concluding Unscientific Postscript on Schleiermacher', in *The Theology of Schleiermacher* (Edinburgh: T & T Clark, 1982), p. 277.

Further reading

Dalferth, I. U., 'Karl Barth's Eschatological Realism', in S. W. Sykes, ed., *Karl Barth. Centenary Essays* (Cambridge: Cambridge University Press, 1989), pp. 14–45.

Johnson, W. S., *The Mystery of God. Karl Barth and the Postmodern Foundations of Theology* (Louisville, Ky.: Westminster John Knox Press, 1997).

Pugh, J. C., *The Anselmic Shift. Christology and Method in Karl Barth's Theology* (New York: Lang, 1990).

Rumscheidt, H.-M., ed., *Revelation and Theology* (Cambridge: Cambridge University Press, 1972).

Torrance, T. F., *Karl Barth. An Introduction to his Early Theology 1910–1931* (London: SCM Press, 1962).

3 Revelation

TREVOR HART

The question of revelation in Christian theology is finally no less than the question of theology's own ultimate source and norm, of the conditions for the possibility of theology itself as a human activity. Insofar as theology is a matter of engaging *logos* and *Theos*, articulate human reflection and God, the question of the route to and conditions for such an engagement naturally arises. To answer this question by appeal to the category of revelation is at least to point to the inherent contingency of the circumstance and the knowledge arising out of it. There could be no procedure less fitting in an essay on Barth than that of seeking to establish some general definition of 'revelation' in terms of which to venture forth. Yet to reveal too much too quickly of the particular sense which this term bears in Barth's theology would make for an untidy chapter in which everything happened at once. For now, then, concerns of style and structure encourage the unveiling only of this: something *revealed* is something disclosed or given to be known to someone which apart from the act of revealing would remain hidden, disguised and unknown. What this means exactly for Barth will require the remainder of this chapter to help determine; but at this level the formulation has the advantage of being one which many quite different accounts of revelation within Christian theology might easily contain, even though in doing so they would read it in significantly different ways.

For the first eighteen centuries of the Christian era, while there were certainly different understandings of the precise nature and intermediate sources of revelation, and while revelation itself as a source and norm for theology was variously correlated with other relevant factors, there was nonetheless general agreement that 'revelation' was both a necessary and a central feature of the religious and theological encounter with God. God was to be 'known', that is to say, and subsequently spoken of only as and when God rendered the form and substance of such 'knowing', establishing humans in a knowing relation otherwise inaccessible to them. This was not, it should be stressed, an *a priori* judgment rooted in some general

anthropological or epistemological analysis, but the realization of those
who, believing themselves to have been the recipients of revelation, were
well aware that what they now 'knew' was something which, apart from
this encounter, they would and could not have known.

Barth's theology stands firmly within the mainstream of this way of
thinking. That it should do so is, however, no mere matter of the uncritical
reception of a venerable and uninterrupted tradition. On the contrary, in
the century and a half which preceded Barth's own theological formation
this tradition had undergone a considerable crisis and testing, and nowhere
more so than with respect to the questions of how far anything identifiable
as 'knowledge' of God might actually be said to be possible and, if it were,
what place the category of revelation might retain with respect to that
possibility. By the late nineteenth century the most significant streams of
Christian theological reflection had either quietly pushed the category aside
and substituted for it some other (more 'natural') basis for their endeavour,
or else had refashioned the concept in ways which served effectively (if not
intentionally) to relocate it within the sphere of human (natural) rather
than divine (supranatural) possibilities. Barth's own determined retrieval
and rehabilitation of the concept of revelation was certainly not an attempt
to ignore or skirt around the consequences and insights of this prolonged
struggle to come to terms with the distinctive spirit of modernity, but was
born out of its very midst. In other words, what he offers us is not an
anachronistic pre-critical but a properly post-critical version of the idea.

REVELATION AND BARTH'S THEOLOGICAL TURN
FROM THE SUBJECT

Among the many intellectual currents whose influence would have to
be acknowledged in a more substantial account, some may be picked out as
having had a particular impact on the early formation of Barth's theology.

First, there is the influence of the epistemological ground rules laid
down by Kant and modified in an even more markedly constructivist
direction by the neo-Kantian philosophers Cohen and Natorp.[1] For Kant the
'phenomena' which constitute the proper objects of human knowledge are
constructed in a synergistic transaction between the mind and what is given
to it from beyond itself. The mind (appealing to universal categories)
imposes form on the particular content perceived by our senses. Insisting
that the category of knowledge is confined to things which we know in this
manner, Kant concluded that God is not a legitimate object of human
'knowledge' at all but rather corresponds to 'faith', a disposition he located

within the sphere of the moral. From this there followed a widespread tendency in nineteenth-century theology to insist that real religion was essentially a matter of the heart and will rather than the head, and to identify the most obvious locus of contact with God in that moral sensibility to which we habitually refer as 'conscience'.

The neo-Kantians with whose thought Barth became familiar in his years as a student in Marburg pressed Kant's model to what seemed to be its logical conclusion, insisting that no account at all need be offered of a pre-cognitive 'given' which supplies matter for the mind subsequently to fashion into coherent objects. Thought, they suggested, is self-originating and creates its own objects *ex nihilo*, supplying them with both form and content. Reality, in other words, is entirely constructed by the knower in the knowing process. In addition, each in his own way embraced the final consequences of this constructivist logic and, while positing 'God' as a necessary or valuable human idea, he finally abandoned any suggestion of God being a supracognitive personal reality impinging on human existence.

As a student Barth read the works of Schleiermacher with great enthusiasm, and a somewhat ambiguous relationship to the latter's theology was eventually to shape Barth's own work quite decisively. Schleiermacher, having learned from Kant that theology could not properly be a matter of knowledge, preferred nonetheless to trace religion and to root theological reflection not in the moral sphere, but in another dimension of human existence, the capacity for what he describes as a 'sense of absolute dependence' or, more theologically, 'God-consciousness'. What this amounts to is a claim that all humans (whether or not they are aware of the fact) are naturally fitted for an encounter with Infinity. As humans we possess the capacity for our experience of, engagement with and activity in the world to be shaped by a fundamental intuition of the determination of our being by that which lies beyond it – what Schleiermacher refers to variously as the All, the Universe, the Whole, and God. Such an intuition grants a qualitative difference to our knowing and acting. Religious experience, therefore, is not a particular type of experience, or experience of a particular sort of reality: it is a way of experiencing the whole of life as lived, as it were, in the presence of the Absolute. This 'sense' is supracognitive and comes to expression in the various symbolic forms of positive religion. While Schleiermacher insists that in the Christian religion this general human capacity is decisively modified through contact with the personality of Jesus and his redemptive work, his model for theology does not easily accommodate the idea of revelation in the sense we have identified above; namely, a particular and peculiar manifestation which is in some sense additional to, inexplicable in terms of, and even an interruption of, the ordinary ('natural') sources and patterns of our knowing. While Schleiermacher (in his guise as an explicitly ecclesial theologian) can describe revelation as a divinely caused original intuition arising in the sphere of self-consciousness,[2] his wider comments reveal that he is thinking of something to be placed in the same category as the inspiration which springs up within the artist through engagement with the world. The originality is thus nonetheless a perfectly 'natural' phenomenon insofar as it derives from the God-consciousness proper to human nature. Indeed, every event and every object is potentially a locus of revelation in this sense. 'Every finite thing . . . is a sign of the Infinite.'[3] Religion, as Schleiermacher observes in one of his earliest writings, far from involving a source which disrupts the natural, actually leaves both physics and psychology untouched.[4] Meanwhile, theology is a matter of critical reflection on the symbolic forms in which God-consciousness comes to expression in a particular community. It is, in other words, a matter of taking stock of the shape of our experience and, whatever Schleiermacher may or may not assume about that which evokes this sense of absolute dependence, his theology lays no claim to do any more than sketch the contours of the imprint it leaves in the human soul.

The Ritschlian school, to which most of Barth's theological teachers belonged, eschewed any notion of the Christian religion being rooted in some general human capacity (intellectual, moral or experiential) and insisted rather upon the positive and particular revelation of God in the historical person of Jesus. In doing so it tended to identify the content of that revelation directly with historically locatable phenomena (the teaching, or the moral and spiritual example, of the Jesus of history) and thereby to place this content at the immediate disposal of any who cared to equip themselves with the relevant historical-critical tools and methods. In doing this, of course, it also left the faithful majority of Christians (who lacked such training) waiting on the results of the endeavour to see what might emerge. Faith became contingent on the knowledge mediated by a priesthood of academics. 'Revelation' (whatever its ultimate source) was effectively reduced to those this-worldly phenomena from Jesus' life which remained once the scholars had done their work on the text of the Gospels.

As a mature teacher of theology Barth adopted the habit of having his students begin by reading Feuerbach; for, in Feuerbach's accusation that talk about God is in the end only talk about humanity, Barth identified the most complete and telling judgment on the nineteenth-century theological project. For all the varied emphases which may be identified, the chief characteristic of that project was in one way or another to seek to found religion, and the theological reflection which attaches to it, on some aspect of a human nature and experience which belongs to history and may be understood within its terms. We should note that the largely pre-critical appeal of Protestant orthodoxy to possess an inspired and inerrant biblical text and of Roman Catholicism to an infallible human magisterium fared little better in this respect. In all these ways, Barth believed theology had effectively already capitulated to Feuerbach's charge and had left itself no way of locating its final source in a God whose reality and activity utterly transcends the sphere of the human.

The only way to secure what must be secured here, Barth insisted from his earliest writings, was to be unequivocally clear from the outset about the proper logic of theological statements (i.e., their claim to speak about God and not about some dimension or feature of the human), and this in turn would mean being quite clear about the conditions alone within which such speech is possible. Christian faith and speech are essentially response and not essentially source. God produces faith and not vice versa. It is this concern which lies behind Barth's relentless appeal to the category of revelation and his particular way of interpreting what is involved in revelation.

REVELATION AS MIRACLE

Theology, which is itself contingent on faith and proclamation while it is a human activity, is, Barth urges, one which is only possible at all because God has first spoken and given himself to be known: 'Theologians are people who speak about God' (*GD*, p. 46). But they dare (and find themselves compelled) to do so precisely and only because of this prior divine address apart from which knowledge of and speech about God is an impossibility for humans. Again, this must be seen as an *a posteriori* judgment: there are plenty of people who speak about 'God' and sense no presumption in doing so; but for the person who actually knows God, who has been drawn into the circle of God's presence, who has some sense of the reality to whom the word 'God' properly refers, the paradoxical impossibility and necessity of human speech about God is all too apparent.

Barth identifies two distinct but related reasons for the impossibility of human knowing of God. First there is that circumstance which the tradition has spoken of as God's holiness and the alienation or contradiction of the post-lapsarian creature with respect to it. God's holy majesty is something our sinful and darkened minds are incapable and unworthy of contemplating. Revelation occurs, therefore, to reverse the epistemic consequences of the Fall. (So, e.g., *GD*, p. 155.) To the extent that this is true, Barth suggests, revelation itself has a limited remit and will end once God's work of redemption is finished (*GD*, p. 156). Elsewhere, though, Barth insists that human knowing of God through revelation 'will remain a miracle to all eternity of completed redemption' (*CD* I/2, p. 245). The need for it will and could never disappear whenever the distinction between God's existence and human existence is taken seriously, because (secondly) what faith discovers in its encounter with the living God is that this God is wholly other than the creature and confronts it as such in absolute mystery. God does not belong to the world of objects with which human apprehension and speech ordinarily have to do and to which they are fitted to pertain. God's reality transcends this realm in such a way that human knowing could never aspire to lay hold of it and render it into an 'object'. God is beyond human classification, understanding and description. At this point Barth is at one with his Kantian heritage in its refusal to treat God as if he were just another phenomenon within the world of human experience.

The conclusion to be drawn from all this, for Barth, is that 'we have no organ or capacity for God' (*CD* I/1, p. 168), and that this lack is not partial but total (see *CD* I/2, p. 257). There is, in other words, no natural propensity or aptitude for God in humans; it is unbelief and ignorance rather than faith and knowledge which are the most natural manifestations of humanity with respect to God (*GD*, p. 456). We cannot even be said to be neutral with respect to God; we are naturally antagonistic and resist the approach of God when he draws close to us, so that even talk of a passive 'capacity for revelation' is dangerously misleading and must be eschewed. There is a principle within us which must first be overcome, a breach which must be healed before God can draw us into the circle of his own self-knowing. For the 'knowledge' which Barth insists can and does take place, even though it is impossible that it should, is not an objectifying 'knowledge about'; even though it exists within a precise conceptual and verbal matrix, it is above all a self-involving and self-transforming communion with God as personal Other. For Barth, therefore, revelation and reconciliation/atonement are two aspects of the same reality: they are both ways of referring to what happens and what must happen in order for humans to be drawn into a personal knowing of God.

Knowledge of God is an impossibility for humans. Barth's conclusion, however, is not that God can thus never be 'known' and may be encountered only in some essentially non-cognitive relation. To move in this direction would be entirely false to the logic of God's actual revelatory engagement with us and would thereby let go of the proper objectivity of theological statements. We must recall that while this alleged impossibility has profound implications for a theological anthropology it is not itself rooted in any general anthropological consideration. Paradoxically, for Barth, it is only within a context where human knowing of God is joyfully affirmed as a reality that such a statement can be made with any degree of confidence at all. The impossibility of humans knowing God must be placed alongside the impossibility of resurrection from the dead to which it is formally similar within the logic of Christian faith. If we ask what is possible within the general terms and potentialities of the 'natural' circumstance, then in both instances we must face the dark truth that we are entrapped within the limits of our sinful finitude and have no basis for hope. But the characteristic of Christian faith is precisely to look away from itself and from its own natural capacities, and to consider instead the capacities and possibilities of the God who raised Jesus from death and who has given himself to be known to us. The fact that God is known does not invalidate the truth of this claim that such knowledge is impossible: rather it transcends and brackets that claim by introducing into the frame a wholly different sort of possibility (*CD* I/1, p. 238). In other words, revelation is – when we consider the broader context for it – to be understood precisely as a miracle, the restoration of life to that which otherwise was doomed to corruption. It is not an inherent human possibility or capacity which simply needs to be realized and embraced, fertilized and nurtured, or tweaked and reconfigured.

If the impossibility of human knowledge of God is a negative inference drawn from the positive fact of revelation, it is nonetheless an important inference. It means, for example, that there can be no question of human beings strategizing or devising systematic methods for acquiring such knowledge which, when it arises within the human sphere, does so necessarily as a result of God's own particular choosing and activity (*CD* I/1, p. 183). This admission renders any approach to Christian religion and theology which begins with talk about general or natural human phenomena, as if the former were simply a particular manifestation or modification of the latter, frankly irrelevant. Hence the proper sphere for talk about God which *really is* talk about God (and not, as Feuerbach suggested, talk about something else) will be the sphere of faith; wherever, that is to say, faith and obedience as the legitimate responses to God's self-revealing initiative are to be identified. This is not because the 'faithful' are in some sense to be deemed especially privileged or equipped by comparison with those who do not have faith. To think thus is to miss the point. Rather, faith and obedience *are themselves* one pole of the knowing relation within which such speech is possible. They are by definition the point within the created sphere where God turns an epistemic and moral impossibility into a possibility, calling forth out of non-existence (as only God can) an appropriate human response to his own Word. This Word or speaking is the objective condition for the possibility of revelation: God, who cannot be 'objectified', nonetheless renders himself a possible object of human knowing in an act of supreme divine condescension, entering into the world of our conceptuality and experience and somehow giving himself to be known within its terms (*GD*, p. 359). As we shall see, this is a claim which is itself hedged around with difficulties. But for now we need note only that this initial self-objectifying is not in itself the full reality of revelation, but only one vital pole of it. In order for revelation to be actual, there must be a reception, a hearing and a response within the human sphere (*GD*, p. 168; *CD* I/2, p. 204). Otherwise, we might say, nothing is actually revealed to anyone; that hearing and responding are to be identified in the faith and obedience which occurs solely through the creative presence and work in us of God's Spirit.

Faith and obedience, as the form of all true human knowing of God, are thus a gift given by God. But, vitally, the gift is not that of a 'capacity' to know God which, once bestowed, remains within our possession like a skill acquired or a piece of knowledge which once learned may be stored away for subsequent retrieval and use. Faith is a loan (*CD* I/1, p. 238), a capacity granted to the incapable (*CD* I/1, p. 241) which, as and while it is actualized, lifts us up beyond the limits of our own incapacities into the self-transcending circle of knowledge of God. Faith and obedience are thus the particular form God's self-giving takes within the human sphere as it occurs. Like the glow in which a winter's afternoon is bathed while the sun shines, they have no endurance or reality apart from the event itself. Thus faith is not a capacity which we bring to and with which we meet and respond to God's revelation, as if these two were separable things. It is the form that revelation itself assumes within the reality of human life, a form which is just as surely the result of God's own self-giving as the various objective loci of God's speaking towards which it is properly directed. Faith, that is to say, is itself part of the miracle of revelation, a miracle which must constantly and continuously be wrought if God is to be known and spoken of in the human sphere. It is *in* history, but it is not *of* history. No satisfactory account can be given of its possibility in purely human or historical terms. Apart from God's creative and redemptive act, it has no existence. It is anhypostatic and enhypostatic in God's revelatory drawing of people to himself.

REVELATION AS EVENT

From all this it will already be apparent that when the word 'revelation' occurs in Barth's writings, we are being referred to a reality which is essentially dynamic rather than static. Revelation, as Barth never tires of reminding his readers, is an event: it is something which happens, something which God does, and something in which we are actively involved. The habitual use of the noun form tends inevitably to direct our thinking instead toward the abstract, and to suggest some commodity (textual, historical or whatever) which represents the abiding deposit of a prior act of 'revealing'. But every such deposit may as such legitimately be identified within and dealt with in terms of the sphere of the human. If we identify 'revelation', that is to say, with a set of texts, a particular human person, a series of historical facts, a body of ethical and spiritual teaching or with some other phenomenon, we locate it firmly within the sphere of that which is *of* history as well as *in* it. Thus we inevitably bracket God himself out of consideration, for God is certainly not of history in this sense and cannot be either located within or dealt with in terms of the categories we ordinarily apply to it. Further, we risk falling under the dangerous illusion that God's 'Word' (the biblical category most closely corresponding to that of revelation) is something which has, as it were, become an earthly commodity and been handed over into human custody and control, domesticated and packaged for responsible human use (*CD* I/1, p. 214). But, Barth reminds us, this is very far from the picture of the living Word of God known to the prophets and to the apostles. This Word is a sovereign and free power which could never be domesticated, never contained or controlled under any created form (however closely associated with certain created phenomena it may be or become): the Word of God is God himself speaking in his uncreated sovereign freedom. A dogmatics which has as its basis a tame and humanly useful 'Word', Barth suggests, will in reality only be manipulating the this-worldly (textual, fleshly and other) coordinates, forms or means of God's free self-revealing activity. All that matters, all that makes revelation genuinely revelatory, he insists, will thereby necessarily be absent from its sphere of jurisdiction; for God cannot be confiscated or put to work even by the church, and revelation is precisely the event in which (by entering into a particular relation with certain created forms or media) God acts and gives *himself* to be known (*CD* I/1, p. 321).

Just as the capacity to know God is something granted to humans only in the event of revelation itself (*CD* I/1, pp. 193f.) so too, Barth insists, the efficacy of the media in and through which God gives himself objectively to be known (God's 'secondary objectivity' as Barth calls it) is equally contingent on this same dynamic action of God. In other words, neither we as the recipients of revelation nor the chosen vehicles of God's continual self-revealing are possessed of any natural correspondence to God, any abiding 'capacity for revelation'. God, as we have already noted, is 'wholly other' with respect to the world; he 'does not belong to the series of objects for which we have categories and words by means of which we draw the attention of others to them, and bring them into relation with them' (*CD* I/2, p. 750). Thus there is nothing in this world, not even in the realm of our words and ideas, which may serve naturally as the vehicle for God's self-objectification by means of which he draws attention to himself and brings us into relation with himself. There is no *analogia entis*, no natural correspondence between the created and the uncreated (see *CD* I/1, p. 166). If revelation is to occur, therefore, then this occurrence will necessarily be one in which God takes objects, events, words, ideas and other this-worldly entities and bestows upon them a capacity which in and of themselves they do not possess.

This, Barth suggests, is precisely what happens in the event of revelation. Objects which in and of themselves serve only and precisely to veil God (for they are, in themselves, not God) are taken up into a relationship with God where their natural capacities are wholly transcended and where they are rendered transparent with respect to God. The particular media to which the church is bound are the humanity of God in the life, death and resurrection of Jesus (Barth places particular emphasis upon the resurrection, especially in his earliest theology), Scripture as the prophetic and apostolic witness to God's action in Christ, and the proclamation of the Christian church.[5] Barth insists, though, that God cannot be bound to these media and that other vehicles for his speaking must be supposed effective for those who, by accident of history, are excluded from the sphere where these media operate. In such cases, however, we should be clear that it is the God known pre-eminently as Jesus Christ who acts and makes himself known in these other places (we are certainly not dealing with a form of natural theology), and the significance of any such signs could thus only fully and finally be understood by bringing them into alignment with this primary locus of God's revealing (see *GD*, pp. 50f., 324; *CD* IV/3, pp. 38–165). Whatever the particular created locus, though, an unnatural or supranatural correspondence between the media of revelation and of God is established in the event of revealing, a correspondence which faith is given to apprehend. This, then, is the force of the so-called 'analogy of faith' of which Barth was so fond of speaking. In the event of God's own self-revealing, both the recipient and the medium of revelation are lifted up beyond the limits of their own natural capacities and drawn into an epistemic triangulation, the third term in which is God himself. A person, an event, a text which in itself is not God and veils God nonetheless becomes transparent to faith and refers faith beyond itself appropriately to God (*GD*, p. 175; *CD* I/1, pp. 165f., 227–47). The nature of this 'reference beyond' cannot be subsequently captured precisely in words or in ideas (if it could, the analogy itself would be unnecessary) but is known intuitively and undeniably by faith in the event in which it indwells the relation. The veil is pierced. God is known. But in the knowing, God remains mysterious (*GD*, p. 446; *CD* I/1, p. 174). The mystery is never fathomed but rather indwelt in the relation of faith. Revelation, therefore, is not a matter of the replication or 'imaging' of the divine on a this-worldly scale, but rather of the opening up of this-worldly phenomena and human minds/wills/hearts to a level of self-transcendence in which God is corresponded to in an appropriate creaturely manner and thereby 'known' in relation.

Barth insists that in this event of revelation God is the Subject from first to last (*GD*, pp. 11, 57; *CD* I/1, p. 296; *CD* I/2, p. 1). What this means is that God acts 'from above' (*CD* I/1, p. 242) to secure what must happen on both sides of the knowing relation. 'The Word', Barth writes, 'creates the fact that we hear the Word . . . Up there with Him it is possible for it to be possible down here with us' (*CD* I/2, p. 247). God is the one who (as a personal rather than an inanimate object) opens himself to others in order to be known as only persons can and must. He is also (as the Creator God who wholly transcends this world) the one who adopts and adapts both the recipients and the media of revelation, establishing the analogy through which faith is enabled to participate in this knowing relation. Several further important points arise out of this claim.

First, God's self-revealing is particular rather than general (*CD* I/1, pp. 140, 329; *CD* I/2, p. 209). God makes himself known to some rather than to all in the economy of revelation and redemption. As in the Gospel narratives it is those who are granted 'eyes to see and ears to hear' who are compelled to confess Jesus as Christ, Lord and Son of God, so more generally it is only where faith is created in the event of God's speaking that revelation occurs. God chooses to whom he will make himself known. His self-disclosure is apparent to some and remains wholly hidden from others. To these others, to whom the gift of faith is not yet granted, the media or vehicles of God's self-objectifying remain opaque, veiling God rather than disclosing him. Revelation is thus closely allied to election in Barth's thought (*GD*, pp. 451–2).[6] It is not just an event but precisely a decision (*CD* I/1,

p. 156), a decision corresponding to God's gracious decision for the human race in Jesus Christ. What is decided in the event of revelation, in other words, is 'not whether the individual is elect or not, but whether she will respond to her election in faith and obedience; whether, in other words, she will live as one who is elect (and, therefore, on the basis of the truth of her existence) or as one who is reprobate (and, therefore, on the basis of a lie)'.[7]

Second, revelation takes the form of personal address. It is the event in which God speaks to particular people at particular times and in particular circumstances (*CD* I/1, pp. 140, 329), and in speaking calls forth a response either of faith and obedience or of unbelief. It is an event in which our particular existence is 'determined' (*bestimmt*) by God's gracious decision and action with respect to us (see *CD* I/1, pp. 198f.). Normally this occurs through the mediation of certain familiar and identifiable this-worldly forms (Scripture, the preaching and other forms of life of the Christian community); but, Barth reminds us, while these media or 'signs' are tied to God, God is not tied to them, and we cannot be prescriptive with respect to how and where and when God may disclose himself (*CD* I/2, p. 224; cf. *GD*, pp. 150f., 342). Conversely, while the community of faith is the normative social context for God's self-disclosure (*CD* I/2, p. 211), participation in the life of this community is no surety of being or becoming a recipient of God's self-disclosure. When God speaks, however, those to whom he speaks, who are drawn into the circle of his self-knowing, can be and are left in no doubt about the matter. The Holy Spirit, Barth assures us, 'kein Dialektiker ist!' (*KD* I/2, p. 268). God is not a dialectician, does not dispute or debate with us; but he draws us in a supremely self-involving way into the presence and knowledge of a wholly and holy Other whose reality and claim upon us are self-authenticating within this encounter. Hence, 'in the Holy Spirit we are confronted by what we cannot deny even if we wanted to do so' (*CD* I/2, p. 246). In order for revelation to be thus, we should note, there must be no false polarizing of the personal/moral over against the cognitive/conceptual. Barth holds these together in a manner which transcends the respective tendencies of his forebears to emphasize one at the expense of the other. The event of revelation is one in which we meet with God and know that we have met with God: but this meeting is, as we have seen, through God's appropriation and adaptation of verbal and conceptual (as well as other this-worldly) media; and the faith it creates is always faith *in* someone or something, not a bare and nebulous mystical encounter with numinousness. There is an indispensable cognitivity about our knowing of God, therefore, which is most appropriately characterized as a hearing of and obedient response to his Word who commandeers our words for the purposes of making himself knowable and known (*GD*, pp. 62f., 367; cf. *CD* I/1, p. 136). Revelation, then, is a personal, self-involving verbal event.

Finally, revelation is not just an event but an action. It involves action, that is to say, not just on God's part but also on ours. We are called to respond when God speaks to us and this response is itself an integral part of 'revelation'. The fact that God himself creates this response where there is otherwise no capacity for it on our part, the fact that Barth will speak of a 'determination' of our existence in the event of revelation, none of this should be taken to imply any essential passivity or any loss of freedom and responsibility on our part (*CD* I/2, p. 266). On the contrary, here as throughout Barth's theology, freedom and responsibility are not eroded or undermined but precisely established and undergirded by the creative and gracious action of God who sets us free to do and to be what otherwise we could never be in any position to do and to be. That God's gracious action in the Word and in the Spirit wholly envelops and penetrates our action (and makes ours possible in so doing) does not, therefore, imply any loss of the difference between human and divine, created and uncreated. We do not become divine as we are drawn into God's presence, but we are established as those creatures whose existence and action corresponds (for now in part and under the form of eschatological prolepsis) to God's own. The event of revelation, then, is both a fully divine and a fully human event; it is an event in which both God and humans are wholly free in their mutual correspondence: yet their respective freedoms and activities are certainly not symmetrical (*CD* I/1, pp. 200f.). It is God who establishes the possibility of both 'from above' (*CD* I/2, p. 204).

REVELATION, INCARNATION AND TRINITY

That revelation is a trinitarian event should already be apparent from the preceding account. God speaks his creative Word, which is heard and returns to him in the achievement among humans of faith and obedience in the power of the Holy Spirit. The Father sends his Son into the world and creates a community of response in the power of the Spirit. Thus the event of revelation is trinitarian in form as well as in content. It is not simply that God is revealed to be a triune God, but that the event of God's self-manifestation is itself triune in structure. In this event the same God is present (and known) thrice: as the one who takes form (the Son), as the one who enables our recognition of and response to this form (the Spirit), and as the one who does not take form (the Father). In Barth's language, 'God, the

Revealer, is identical with His act in revelation and also identical with its effect' (*CD* I/1, p. 296).

We have already seen the reasons for this insistence in Barth. It leads him to inquire what this God must be like who is able to make himself known in this particular way. The answer he arrives at is a doctrine of the immanent Trinity. In other words, God's self-revealing in this differentiated threefold form is not itself the occasion for the self-differentiation (God does not become his own 'alter ego' only with the conception in Mary's womb); it is rather the unveiling of a logically and ontologically prior self-differentiation in God in which his freedom to be for us in this way is grounded. 'Because God in His one nature is not solitary but different (*verschieden*) in His modes of existence, because He is the Father who has an only-begotten Son, therefore the fact that He can be free for others, that He can be free for a reality different from Himself, is eternally grounded within God Himself' (*CD* I/2, p. 34). In other words, God is able to be his own 'alter ego' in Christ and in the Spirit ('for us' and 'in us'), is able to enter history without ceasing to be what eternally he is, precisely because there is already hypostatic differentiation within the Godhead. Thus the form and content of revelation are utterly integrated. What is 'known' is the pattern indwelt by participants in the event of revelation, a pattern which is itself grounded in the mystery of God's eternal triune identity.

In a related vein, Barth reminds us elsewhere that the Word which God speaks to humankind is the same Word which he speaks to himself eternally (*CD* I/1, p. 191). If the latter statement lends weight to the suggestion that Barth's single-minded deployment of the metaphor of speech in his doctrine of revelation leads him to understate the *reciprocity* of the trinitarian persons in their eternal communion,[8] the former can be read as pointing in a quite different direction: namely, as indicative that 'freedom for the other' (and the desire to be 'for' the other which the realization of this freedom manifests) *must be* an important dimension of God's own triune life and identity. The Spirit's role as Creator of free and obedient response to the Father in human persons might also be supposed to reflect an eternal prerogative of an analogous sort. It must be admitted, though, that the emphasis of Barth's model is ever against the danger of a neo-Arian relegation of the Son from the Godhead, and to that end often underplays the hypostatic diversity and correlation within the Trinity.

From the first edition of *The Epistle to the Romans* (1919) onward, a singular concern may be identified in Barth's writing on the theme of revelation: namely, to give an account of the reality of this event in which the proper (and vital) distinction between God and the world is maintained at every point. God is known in the midst of historical existence. That, as we have seen, is the miracle. But in the midst of this miracle God remains the one who is wholly other than us, and we, for our part, remain human (see *R*, pp. 10f.). The radical boundary between God's existence and ours, between the uncreated Lord and the creature, is, that is to say, in some sense transcended in the event of knowing, yet without any concomitant loss or compromising of either God's identity or ours. Furthermore, the one who does not and could never belong to the world of 'objects' locates himself within that world, giving himself over to us as an *Objekt* of our knowing, yet doing so (crucially) in such a manner that he remains in control (*das Subjekt*) of this knowing from first to last. How, then, are we to think of this? How can it be possible for God genuinely to be known in the world without yet being *of* the world?

The answer to these questions, Barth realized, lay in the insistence that in Jesus God himself has 'taken flesh' and entered into the sphere of creaturely existence. God, in other words, has become a part of the world of phenomena within which human knowledge ordinarily arises. In this sense the incarnation is the primary objective condition for the possibility of God's self-revelation in the world. The Word has 'become flesh'. Yet this unqualified profession of divine inhomination raises more questions than it answers, and Barth was well aware of the convoluted history of its interpretation, not least ways which would betray rather than secure the points he deemed so vital to a healthy reorientation of theology in the modern period. The nature and implications of the 'assumption' and the 'becoming' would need to be pinned down much more precisely.

As early as the Göttingen lectures in dogmatics (1924),[9] Barth came to see that this modern set of theological problems had its ancient counterpart, and that the classical doctrine of hypostatic union espoused at the Council of Chalcedon in AD 451 offered resources to enable him to make sense of the claim that in Jesus God 'becomes not-God as well' and, through this 'secondary objectivity', gives himself to be known by men and women of his choosing. The precise function of the 'two natures' doctrine (in the incarnation there is one 'hypostasis' to be discerned subsisting in two distinct 'natures') was to insist on the personal presence of God in a particular human life while yet differentiating the content of that life at every tangible point from God's own existence as God. This suited Barth's demands perfectly. God becomes the man Jesus, yet this becoming entails the addition of a human level of existence ('nature') to who and what God eternally is, an existence which remains distinct from his divine 'nature'. Thus God enters the world 'hypostatically' while yet remaining utterly distinct from it by nature. Furthermore, in apprehending the man Jesus, we do not as such and without further ado lay hold of God. We are, after all, beholding his *humanity* which serves as a created veil for the divinity as well as a door which, at God's own behest, may open for us. Since 'hypostasis' is a transcendental category rather than a predicate there is nothing of God's *nature* present phenomenally. It is not 'God', but rather God as 'not-God' who is present in the world and available to the normal channels of knowing. In order for this same human form to become transparent with respect to God's own being, the event of revelation must come to completion in the way we have described above.

This immediately raises a question about the relationship between these two distinct levels of God's hypostatically united existence (as God and as a human being). How does what we know of Jesus relate to the 'knowledge' granted us in the event of revelation? Barth insists that in the case of our knowing of God, the form under which we apprehend God is related to the content of that knowing not simply by distinction but (due to God's wholly and holy otherness) by contradiction (*CD* I/1, p. 166). Even though Jesus' life, death and resurrection constitute the primary objective locus or site of God's self-revealing (Barth admits others of course, chiefly Scripture and preaching; but these are themselves always held closely together with Jesus Christ to whom they bear witness), these pertain precisely to the human nature of the incarnate one; they are wholly other than God as such, and Barth is adamant that we should not confuse 'revelation' with anything we know or believe at this level. Nor can the relation between the two natures (or, correspondingly, the form and content of revelation) be entirely arbitrary or merely tangential: otherwise it would be a matter of sheer caprice for God to 'reveal' himself in the man Jesus rather than Ivan the Terrible or a dead dog. That God *could* do so is not really the point. To the extent that the Christian church wishes to make Jesus Christ the object of its worship and the central criterion of its belief and practice it indicates that it is not in fact thus. So Barth is quite clear that there can be no docetic indifference to the humanity of the Lord. Christian thought about God (and much else besides) must be decisively shaped by what it finds at this point, rather than importing preconceived notions (*CD* I/2, p. 17).

However, the fact remains that the vehicle of revelation, even when it is hypostatically united with God, is not itself God. Information about Jesus' life, character, actions, death and resurrection is not knowledge of God in the sense that Barth intends it and in the event of revelation it is precisely *God himself* who is known. For this to happen, the particular form of Jesus' humanity is necessary but not sufficient. The veil must become transparent.

Faith must be called into being, faith which travels through and transcends the veil of the flesh to a depth of reality to which the created form now points and corresponds, not in and of itself, but as God takes it up into his dynamic revealing activity. This happens as the story of Jesus is told and heard within and by the church. In telling of what we have 'known' of this event we are, of course, compelled to speak of and on the basis of this same story, allowing its particular content to continue to direct us beyond itself. There is no discarnate logos. We cannot skirt around the scandal of the humanity of God. Yet this objective human form is in itself merely the vehicle through which God encounters and lays hold of us. Knowledge of Jesus is not revelation as such. Theology, Barth concludes, must finally not be too Christocentric (*GD*, p. 91) but must be concerned with the God who is made known in and through Christ. That there is a positive relation between the humanity of Jesus and our knowing of God, between the form and the content of revelation, is something faith insists upon and knows to be true. But, '[t]o receive the Word of God does not mean . . . to be able to see and know and state the relation between the two sides, to be able to say why and how far the veiled Word now means unveiling . . . If we could know and state this, the Word of God would obviously cease to be a mystery' (*CD* I/1, p. 174). The correspondence of Jesus' humanity and of our words and thoughts about it to the reality of God in the *analogia fidei* is real: but precisely because the analogy is required, we cannot articulate that which lies beyond the level of the phenomenal; we cannot say precisely *how* the two sides of the analogy are related. That they are is the basic concern of the church's confession of Jesus, the man from Nazareth, as Lord and as Immanuel. That God is hypostatically present in this man means at least that in some sense God is like Jesus: but what this word 'like' connotes can be known only in the knowing relation itself and cannot be captured in conceptual or verbal form.

REVELATION AND RECONCILIATION

It has been argued by some that the theme of revelation so dominates Barth's understanding of the God–human relation as to obscure or even displace any adequate account of salvation. So, for example, Gustaf Wingren devotes an entire chapter to this point,[10] insisting that Barth consistently shifts the centre of gravity from the cross and resurrection to the virgin conception and incarnation in his theology – a shift which detracts from any serious consideration of the problems of human sin and guilt, the reality of evil, and the resultant conflict and struggle through which salvation is wrought. The human problem here, Wingren maintains, is that of ignorance rather than guilt and personal alienation, and the corresponding solution is the unveiling to men and women of the reality of their situation under God. This is presented in such a manner as to rob of significant force the themes of forgiveness and the need for the bestowal of a new righteousness.[11] More recently the same basic point has been rehearsed by Alister McGrath[12] who suggests, on the basis of 'the astonishingly frequent references to *Erkenntnis* (knowledge) and its cognates, where one might expect to find reference to *Heil* (salvation) or *Versöhnung* (reconciliation)' in Barth's approach to the death of Christ, that Barth regards 'man's predicament as being *ignorance of the true situation*' rather than '*bondage to sin or evil*'.[13]

This is clearly a profound charge if it can be made to stick. There is not space for a full evaluation of it here, but two rather obvious observations may fuel further reflection on the matter.

First, as we have seen, the issue of the possibility of knowledge of God and the proper sources of it was one which dominated the theologies of the late eighteenth and nineteenth centuries. McGrath's judgment that by focusing upon this question Barth aligns himself with the soteriologies of the Enlightenment (and, by inference, distances himself from the emphasis of Scripture) at least correctly identifies the post-critical nature of Barth's project (i.e., as a reaction to what he deemed to be the inadequate responses of his teachers to this problem). Unfortunately it also completely ignores the distinctiveness of his reaction, in particular his utter rejection of post-Enlightenment anthropological optimism, the radical seriousness he affords to the doctrine of the Fall from *The Epistle to the Romans* onward and his refusal to divorce the metaphysical from the moral. Barth is perfectly clear that to be human is to be a sinner in need of forgiveness and redemption, and otherwise deserving only rejection and judgment by God. The God–human relation is, for him, an ethical one captured helpfully in the central scriptural metaphor of covenant. It is not primarily an epistemic relation, although this leads neatly to our second point.

Second, while it might be possible to set up a polarity between the epistemic and the soteriological in some theologies, such a polarity is alien to the basic substance of Barth's understanding. This is not because he reduces salvation to the dispelling of ignorance through the bestowal of 'knowledge', but because he links these two themes together systematically in a way which broadens his model of salvation from a typically Western preoccupation with forensic and moral categories and integrates it more adequately with the doctrine of God as Trinity. Hence, to be the recipient of 'revelation', as we have seen, entails much more than the acquisition of hitherto unknowable data about God; it is actually to be drawn into fellowship with (reconciled to) the Father through the self-objectifying form of the crucified and risen Son and in the power of the Holy Spirit who now indwells one's life in a redemptive manner. The form this reception properly takes is faith manifest in repentance and obedience. In other words, the knowledge of God which, for Barth, is the heart of the God–human relation is not to be construed as some merely intellectual phenomenon, but is a self-involving transformative event in which the power of Christ's death and resurrection are realized in the lives of particular people, bringing those lives to a point of crisis and provoking ethical response. To refer to 'Barth's general lack of interest in soteriology'[14] on the basis that he talks rather often about 'knowing' God would thus seem to betray a profound misunderstanding of the meaning which the phrase bears in his theology. For Barth, as one contemporary theologian expresses the matter, God reveals himself in reconciling acts.

Notes

1 See S. Fisher, *Revelatory Positivism: Barth's Earliest Theology and the Marburg School* (Oxford: Oxford University Press, 1988), esp. pp. 7–122.
2 See F. Schleiermacher, *The Christian Faith* (Edinburgh: T & T Clark, 1928), pp. 50f.
3 See F. Schleiermacher, *On Religion: Speeches to its Cultured Despisers* (New York: Harper and Row, 1958), p. 88.
4 Ibid.
5 See, e.g., *CD* I/1, pp. 88–124, on 'The Word of God in its Threefold Form'. On the relationships between these three media see T. Hart, 'The Word, the words and the witness: proclamation as divine and human reality in the theology of Karl Barth', in *Tyndale Bulletin* 46.1 (1995), pp. 81–102.
6 See on this, B. L. McCormack, *Karl Barth's Critically Realistic Dialectical Theology* (Oxford: Clarendon Press, 1995), pp. 371–4, 458–63.
7 Ibid., p. 459.
8 See, most recently, A. J. Torrance, *Persons in Communion: An Essay on Trinitarian Description and Human Participation* (Edinburgh, T. & T. Clark, 1996), pp. 100f. Torrance's claim that Barth does not give sufficient account of Jesus as a hearer of and respondent to the divine Word is well taken. This, however, may be accounted for without positing a corresponding non-reciprocity at the level of trinitarian theology. Given the general psilanthropic shape of the nineteenth-century Christologies to which Barth was reacting, his Alexandrian (rather than Antiochene) emphasis is understandable enough. His fear of subordinationist or adoptionist trends, which would effectively sever the revelatory and trinitarian relation between Jesus and God, weighed more heavily more often than the need for a christologically balanced account of Jesus as a man who received God's

Word and responded to it in faith and obedience. Nor can 'a detrimental "anhypostaticism"' (Torrance, p. 104) be deemed responsible. The doctrine of the *anhypostasia* as such is concerned to deny the independent subsistence of Jesus' humanity; it makes no prescription concerning its particular shape or content. The organs of human response and reciprocity belong to the category of 'nature' rather than 'hypostasis'. The affirmation of a fully human experience and relation to God, therefore, is wholly compatible with 'anhypostaticism': the point of such a juxtaposition would simply be that in this particular case we have to do with *God's* fully human experience and relation to God. The suggestion that in Jesus we have to do with a human 'hypostasis' distinct from and independent of God's own hypostatically differentiated existence as Father, Son and Holy Spirit was one Barth was determined at all costs to avoid. An analogous point can be made with respect to any metaphorical extension of the term. In revelation, God is the Subject (hypostasis) from first to last; but this divine Subject is nonetheless manifest through a fully human existence.

9 For a discussion of the earlier writings, see McCormack, *Dialectical Theology*, esp. pp. 130f. and 207f.
10 See G. Wingren, *Theology in Conflict* (Edinburgh: Oliver & Boyd Ltd., 1958), ch. 6.
11 Ibid., p. 116.
12 See A. McGrath, *Iustitia Dei*, vol. II (Cambridge: Cambridge University Press, 1986), pp. 182–4.
13 Ibid., p. 183 (emphasis original, but English translations added).
14 Ibid., p. 178.

Further reading

Fisher, S., *Revelatory Positivism: Barth's Earliest Theology and the Marburg School* (Oxford: Oxford University Press, 1988).
Hart, T., 'The Word, the words and the witness: proclamation as divine and human reality in the theology of Karl Barth,' *Tyndale Bulletin* 461 (1995), pp. 81–102.
Hartwell, H., *The Theology of Karl Barth: an Introduction* (London: Duckworth, 1964), ch. II.
McCormack, B. L., *Karl Barth's Critically Realistic Dialectical Theology* (Oxford: Clarendon Press, 1995).
Rogers, E. F., *Thomas Aquinas and Karl Barth. Sacred Doctrine and the Natural Knowledge of God* (Notre Dame, Ind.: University of Notre Dame Press, 1995).
Thompson, J., *Christ in Perspective: Christological Perspectives in the Theology of Karl Barth* (Edinburgh: Saint Andrew Press, 1978), ch. 3.
Torrance, A., *Persons in Communion: An Essay on Trinitarian Description and Human Participation* (Edinburgh: T & T Clark, 1996).
Veitch, J., 'Revelation and Religion in the Theology of Karl Barth', *Scottish Journal of Theology* 24.1 (1971), pp. 1–22.
Wingren, G., *Theology in Conflict* (Philadelphia: Muhlenberg Press, 1958).

4 The Bible

FRANCIS WATSON

From beginning to end, Barth's *Church Dogmatics* is nothing other than a sustained meditation on the texts of Holy Scripture, in all the richness and diversity with which these texts elaborate their single theme: a divine-human action constitutive both of divine and of human being, a particular action that is nevertheless all-inclusive in its scope. There are, of course, many parts of the *Church Dogmatics* that practise an 'explicit' biblical interpretation or hermeneutics: from passing references to particular verses to extended expositions of whole chapters or books, from consideration of particular concepts such as 'witness' or 'saga' (or 'legend'), to the construction of what might be called an 'ontology' of Holy Scripture. This material can be roughly differentiated from other material where the biblical texts appear to be in the background, or are perhaps absent altogether. Yet to regard biblical interpretation as just one among a number of items on Barth's agenda would be to allow the seamless garment of his theology to be torn to pieces. Barth's biblical interpretation is not a particular item, but the foundation and principle of coherence of his entire project, and interpreters who overlook this biblical foundation, or who refer to it only in passing, will radically misinterpret that project. What will be lost or distorted is the 'ec-centric' character of Barth's theology, its orientation beyond itself towards scriptural texts that themselves point beyond, to the prior reality of the divine-human being-in-action. In failing to grasp that Barth's theology is from first to last *biblical* theology, one encloses it within itself and characterizes it instead as *Barth's* theology, centred now not on the biblical witness but on the impressive and problematic figure of the 'great theologian'.

It is (or so one would have thought) impossible to miss the foundational and central significance of biblical interpretation for Barth's theology. The transition from an initial liberal Protestant orientation to his own distinctive theological stance was occasioned (he himself believed) by a rediscovery of what he called 'the strange new world within the Bible'. Commentaries on

Pauline letters (Romans, but also Philippians and 1 Corinthians) indicate that, during the decade or so after the First World War, Barth's mature theology developed out of an intensive dialogue with the biblical texts. That dialogue continues in the *Church Dogmatics*; there is in no sense a vacillation between biblical interpretation and dogmatic theology in Barth's earlier work, finally resolved in favour of the latter. For Barth, what makes one a dogmatic theologian is ultimately not 'an education in the arts and a familiarity with the thinking of the philosopher, psychologist, historian, aesthetician, etc.', desirable and necessary though all that is, but simply an 'indemonstrable and unassuming attention to the sign of Holy Scripture around which the church gathers and continually becomes the church. By this attention, *and by nothing else*, the theologian becomes a theologian' (*CD* I/1, pp. 283–4; italics added). The task of dogmatic or systematic theology is to inquire into 'the agreement of church proclamation [i.e., contemporary Christian discourse with its focal point in the act of preaching] with the revelation which is attested in Holy Scripture' (ibid., p. 283). Barth never deviates from this understanding of theology. Towards the end of the *Church Dogmatics*, nearly thirty years after writing these programmatic statements, he considers the role of theology within the ministry of the church and again derives its rationale solely from the biblical texts. These texts, he claims, 'all put the question of the meaning and legitimacy of what they say as measured by the object presented, and each [theologian] in his own way, with a view to the community around and in dialogue with the better or worse theology pursued within it, gives his own answer and passes it on to his successors' (*CD* IV/3, p. 879). Theology is an attempt at an informed, timely response to the challenge posed by the biblical texts, which is to understand them as articulating not simply an authorial intention but above all a single, infinitely rich theological subject-matter. Theology should never be ashamed of its own foundation in biblical interpretation. It must assert the priority of Holy Scripture over all other human and Christian discourse, both in principle and above all in practice; it must not be deterred by the accusations of 'narrowness', 'biblicism', 'neo-conservatism', or indeed of 'Barthianism' that it will inevitably incur as it strives to hold its single theme in view and allows it to shed its light on the manifold realities of church and world. Underlying all the daunting complexity and prolixity of the *Church Dogmatics* is a simple, cheerful confidence that God speaks with us in and through the Bible in its testimony to Jesus. Of all modern theologians, Barth is the least inhibited by the fear of appearing to be naive, and it is precisely his willingness to speak naively about the Bible – with a directness and a clarity that are both the bestowal of the biblical subject-matter and the hard-won product of unceasing intellectual self-discipline – that gives life and warmth to his theological writing.

Why is it that the theologian is characterized as a theologian by an unceasing attentiveness to the biblical texts 'and by nothing else'? Does the insistent refusal to allow scriptural authority to be correlated with the authority of tradition, reason, or experience betoken an un-catholic, illiberal, merely Protestant narrowness? Barth has often been criticized along these lines. He is, it is said, a 'biblicist' – one who is excessively bound to the letter of the biblical text. But tradition, reason, and experience are not overlooked in this theology. Although they are not independent authorities in their own right, they do represent the context within which the Bible is read; and, granted a degree of theological discrimination, they are at least as likely to help our reading of the Bible as to hinder it. The Bible is not read, and must not be read, in a timeless, ahistorical vacuum. Nor is there much trace in Barth of conservative Protestant anxieties about biblical inerrancy, inspiration, non-contradiction, or historicity – although the legitimate concerns that underlie these anxieties are taken seriously. Barth's attitude to the Bible cannot be straightforwardly characterized as a 'conservative' one, and to understand it as such is to flatten out everything that is most distinctive to it.

Attentiveness to the biblical texts is required of the theologian because of the *particularity* of theology's subject-matter. If theology consisted in the study of the manifold phenomena of human religiousness, with the intention of tracing them back to their common roots in human experience of the world's transcendent limit, *then* the theologian's attentiveness to the Bible would be a matter of secondary rather than of primary importance. But to understand theology in this apparently more inclusive way would be to lose its specific subject-matter. It would be to construe God or ultimacy as the impressive but inert object of the human religious 'quest', overlooking or suppressing the fact that, for Christian faith, the one who is acknowledged as 'God' is disclosed as such only in an *action* in and towards the world that takes *particular* form. God is not God in general: God is 'the God and Father of our Lord Jesus Christ', and the name 'Jesus' and the person and the history to which it refers are therefore irreducibly necessary for the correct identification of 'God'. Without Jesus, God is not God. That which is ultimate and foundational for the world and humankind is actual only in and through the particularity indicated by this proper name. Conversely, in and through this particularity (and only here) we encounter not just the origin of a distinctive religious tradition, but that which is ultimate and foundational for our existence: being-itself. The 'narrowness' or 'exclusiveness' which distresses so many (non-)readers of the Bible is simply its insistence that the one it acknowledges as 'God' is no more an impersonal abstraction than we are. According to the Bible, divine universality is such as to embrace and comprehend the narrowness and exclusiveness of particular form, rather than being marked off from it and limited by it. The roots of Barth's alleged 'biblicism' lie in his assumption that the Nicene Creed and the universal church are right to speak of God in trinitarian and incarnational terms.

The Bible must be attended to because it *speaks of* this divine particularity, both in its content and in its form. But how does it come to do so? If it is simply a contingent historical fact that the biblical authors happened to speak and write about God as they did, then there is no reason to regard their speech as truthful and trustworthy. The truthfulness and trustworthiness of this human speech can be guaranteed not by subjecting it to general criteria of 'historical reliability' and the like, but only by showing it to be grounded in the truthfulness and trustworthiness of divine speech. What takes place in Jesus is God's *action*, the action in which God's eternal being is disclosed; and as such it is *communicative* action, a speech-act that intends not just the bringing about of a certain state of affairs in the world, but, specifically, an *addressee*. What takes place in Jesus is significant not for God alone, but also for the human being who is thereby constituted the object of the divine address. Since God's action intends communication, human beings are not excluded from its scope; they are not spectators but participants, drawn into the circle of the divine communicative action by the Word of God addressed to 'the world', to 'us', and also, irreducibly, to 'me'. Yet there is a distinction to be drawn among the addressees; there is an inner circle and an outer circle. The Word of God that is uttered at the centre must pass through the inner circle in its outward movement into the world; that is, it must be mediated by the Word of its first addressees. Because the content of the Word of God is the particular divine action constituted by the history of Jesus, in fulfilment of the prior history of the covenant with Israel, some people find themselves in more immediate proximity to the divine communicative action than others. Like Jesus himself, these people are Jews, Jesus' contemporaries and predecessors. Their hearing of the divine word entails a commission not only to hear but also to speak: to their own contemporaries, but also, through the medium of writing, to unborn generations and to the ends of the earth. According to the biblical etymology, to be a 'Jew' is to praise and confess God and God's action (cf. Gen. 29:35). 'Therefore I will praise you among the nations . . .' (Ps. 18:49, quoted in Rom. 15:9): in their written praise and confession of God-in-action, the biblical writers become an intrinsic part of the divine communicative action and so fulfil Israel's vocation to be a light to the Gentiles. The theological significance of the Bible is derived not from any of its immanent characteristics – its value as a historical source, its literary qualities, its religious insights, its influence on Western culture – but from the indispensable role assigned to it in the outward movement of the divine communicative action into the world.

The truthfulness and trustworthiness of the Bible are therefore guaranteed by its *intrinsic* relationship to the truthfulness and the trustworthiness of the divine self-disclosive speech-act that takes place in Jesus. For Barth, the Bible *is* 'the Word of God' in that the Word that God spoke once for all continues to address us in the word or testimony of the biblical writers. There is nothing artificial or arbitrary about the transmission of a word spoken at a particular time and place to quite different times and places – as though the word spoken was thereby deprived of its original and proper context, uprooted from its natural habitat and transplanted into an alien environment. *In* its spatio-temporal particularity, and not *in spite of* it, the Word made flesh is addressed to the world, and there is no environment that is alien to it; and, in a secondary and derived sense, the same is also true of the Bible. We cannot complain that our historical and cultural distance from the Bible's original context threatens to make it irrelevant to us, for its relevance is already ensured by Jesus' promise, 'I am with you always, to the close of the age' (Matt. 28:20). If the history of Jesus, from his birth to his death and resurrection, is God's address to the world, then this history cannot be contained and limited by its original time and place. Our own unfinished history becomes contemporaneous with this completed history, which therefore belongs to the present and to the future as much as to the past. 'Jesus Christ is the same yesterday and today and for ever' (Heb. 13:8): it is the living, contemporary Jesus of whom the Bible speaks in telling the story of a birth, a life, and a death that took place in a spatio-temporal location distant from our own. In the Word made flesh, God continues to speak with us, and the Bible attests and mediates this event rather than being 'the Word of God' of itself and in abstraction.

In this subordination to the Word made flesh which it attests and mediates, enabling the Word once spoken in the flesh of Jesus to be heard again now, the Bible is the Word of God. It is in and through the human words of the biblical writers that God continues to speak the Word that was once for all spoken in Jesus. In relation to the Word made flesh, the biblical writers are *witnesses* who confess: 'We cannot but speak of what we have seen and heard' (Acts 4:20). Silence is impossible for them. 'If I say, "I will not mention him, or speak any more in his name", there is in my heart as it were a burning fire shut up in my bones, and I am weary of holding it in, and I cannot' (Jer. 20:9). In their writing, their speaking is preserved and extended; the human technology of writing is made to serve the universal scope of the divine Word. The individualities of the witnesses are present in their writings, but only in a subordinate sense, for their commission is to 'preach not ourselves but Jesus Christ as Lord, with ourselves as your servants for Jesus' sake' (2 Cor. 4:5). They point to the event of God's self-disclosive and self-constitutive action, the action that makes God the God he is; and as they do so the event itself speaks, for the event is communicative action, the divine speech-act. The witness to 'what we have seen and heard' is therefore a witness not to an inert object safely located in the past, but to the *living* God, and it is his voice that sounds forth in the voice of the witnesses. Preceding and grounding the movement of the human word back to the event of the divine communicative action is the forward movement of the event itself to communicate itself in and through the human word of its witnesses. If the concept of 'witness' is detached from its context in a theology of the Word, then the Bible too will become static and inert, no more than a record preserving the traces of what was once said about what had been seen and heard. And we ourselves would no longer be the addressees of the divine communicative *action*, but the possessors of a holy but lifeless book. In the absence of the life-giving Holy Spirit who constitutes the book's true holiness, it is not surprising if its abstract holiness loses its credibility and the hermeneutical proposal to read the Bible 'just like any other book' comes to seem much more convincing. In its proper context within a theology of the divine communicative action, however, the Bible is fundamentally *unlike* every other book, and a biblical interpretation that is appropriate to its object will never forget this for a moment.

The biblical 'witnesses' fall into two categories: they are 'prophets' or 'apostles' (although Barth uses the latter term loosely enough not to entail any particular decisions about the authorship of individual New Testament books). These terms are derived from Greek verbs denoting speaking and sending respectively; the prophet speaks, the apostle is sent. Of course, the prophet is also sent and the apostle also speaks: it is common to all the biblical witnesses that they are sent to speak. Yet the difference between the terms is still significant. The term 'apostle' points back to a prior act and agent of sending. The term 'prophet' refers (at least in Christian usage) to a *fore*speaking, an articulation of that which is yet to be (cf. 1 Pet. 1:10–11). The New Testament, as the work of apostles or their followers, looks back to an act and an agent from which they and it derive. The Old Testament, as the work of prophets, looks forward and seeks from the future a fulfilment and a confirmation of that which at present and in itself is no more than empty words. In their different ways, both Testaments therefore derive from the event of the Word made flesh. They derive from this event in order that, in their different ways, they should point to it; and it is the task of a theologically oriented biblical interpretation to discern in the texts *this* gesture – that of the witness's outstretched index finger – and to look from the text to that which is indicated.

It might seem that the relationship between the Old Testament and the event of the Word made flesh is less direct and less important than in the case of the New Testament. We can study the Old Testament mainly 'for its own sake' because of its intrinsic historical, religious, and literary interest; and this can result in worthwhile, perceptive, and illuminating Old Testament scholarship. The only problem is that the writers of the Old Testament or 'Hebrew Bible' are no longer understood here as 'prophets', that is, as forespeakers of the Word made flesh. This view of the 'prophet' is often associated with a naive, superseded understanding of the fulfilment of prophecy in which direct, unambiguous correlations between Jesus and the prophetic text are held to *demonstrate* the truth of the Christian claim. Modern scholarship is right to hold that no such demonstration is available to us, but it is wrong to assume that the demise of a particular view of predictive prophecy means that the Old Testament can no longer be understood as forespeaking. This classical Christian understanding of the Old Testament originates in the New Testament's insistence that what takes place in Jesus takes place 'according to the scriptures' – in accordance with a prior script, an outline or pattern laid down in advance so that the Christ-event should be rightly interpreted. Even on Easter Day, the risen Jesus is not recognized by the disciples on the road to Emmaus until he has 'interpreted to them in all the scriptures the things concerning himself' (Luke 24:27); and Christian theology must similarly practise an Old Testament interpretation in the light of what has occurred in Jesus, for the sake of a more adequate understanding and acknowledgment of that occurrence – which is, as we must not forget, the event in which nothing less than the deity of the triune God is both disclosed and constituted. Such an event needs the broadest of interpretative horizons, encompassing creation itself; and early Christian preaching finds the interpretative framework it needs in 'the scriptures', whose previously concealed orientation towards this event is now brought into the clear light of day.

In this event, the witness of prophets and of apostles *converges*, and it is this convergence that establishes the unity of the Bible. Theological interpretation of the Bible presupposes a unity derived from the event on which the whole Bible converges, and not from any guaranteed non-contradiction between its individual assertions. In order briefly to illustrate how this convergence might affect the *practice* of biblical interpretation, we set out (as Barth characteristically does) from a particular theological problem. For example, a theological inquiry into the nature and significance of the human evil that resists the good that God intends for humankind might lead to a piece of biblical interpretation along the following lines.

According to the evangelists' rendering of the apostolic testimony, the putting to death of Jesus is an expression not simply of pragmatic political concerns (cf. John 11:47–50), but above all of hostility towards the beloved Son of Israel's God on the part of Israel's rulers (cf. Mark 12:1–8). Their action is evil, and yet it is also willed by God; for 'the Son of man *must* suffer many things, and be rejected by the elders and the chief priests and the scribes, and be killed . . .' (Mark 8:31), and it is God who calls him to accept this destiny and to drink this cup. But God does not will what is evil; God wills to use human evil in the service of the good that he intends for humankind, and the evil that befalls Jesus is therefore directed both to his own good and to the good of others. On the third day he is raised; and even his death partakes of the power of the resurrection for good, since he 'gives his life as a ransom for many' (Mark 10:45). Without ceasing to be evil, human evil is anticipated, encompassed, and transformed by divine good. It is not simply denounced and threatened from a safe distance, as though it were the problem of other people for which they alone will have to suffer the consequences. Its reality is acknowledged as lying at the very heart of human existence, even within God's chosen people; and it is the calling of the beloved son to endure it to the full for the sake of its assumption into the divine good. So there is no rendering of evil for evil, or cursing for cursing.

All this is said to take place 'according to the scriptures': in conformity not to scriptural 'predictions' in a narrow sense, but to scriptural patterns and archetypes – exemplified indeed in particular texts, but in texts that speak not only for themselves but for a broad range of scriptural material. Thus the peculiar relationship of human evil and divine good is classically articulated in the Joseph narrative, summed up at its conclusion in its protagonist's words of reassurance to his brothers: 'You meant evil against me, but God meant it for good, to bring it about that many people should be kept alive, as they are today' (Gen. 50:20). The transformation of human evil into divine good has involved the protagonist's humiliation at the hands of his own brothers and his subsequent exaltation; there has been a quasi-death and a quasi-resurrection; and this has all taken place for the benefit of the many. The correspondences between this story and that of the Gospels are of course imperfect and limited; but they are *there* – in the text, not just in the eye of the Christian beholder – and it is the task of a Christian Old Testament interpretation to bring such correspondence to light so that what takes place in Jesus is set within the broad interpretative horizons proper to it. Other interpretative concerns will be no more than preliminary to the theological task, and in some cases they can be safely overlooked. Source-critical analyses will lose their importance, since the text's capacity to shed its own distinctive light on the story of Jesus lies in its canonical form and not in its pre-history. The question of the 'historicity' of this and other pentateuchal narratives loses whatever urgency it once seemed to have, since the historical event that the text now attests is that of the 'forespeaking' in ancient Israel of the pattern of the Messiah's death and resurrection, in the form of this particular story.

On the other hand, careful reading of the text as a whole and on its own terms becomes more rather than less important, since it is only out of such a reading that the text's role as witness will come to light. This reading proceeds on the assumption that *all* scriptural texts are to be read with the same loving attention and patient expectation – however odd, alien, offensive, and theologically irrelevant they may seem on the surface. This theological hermeneutic is at the same time an ethic of reading. It does not sanction an uncritical reading that assumes the abstract perfection of the biblical texts, for the christological and trinitarian heart of Christian Scripture also functions as a critical principle; but the negative, critical dimension is subordinated to the overriding concern that the 'witness' of the text should be heard and that nothing should stand in the way of this. The goal of an interpretative practice along these lines is to show how the witness of apostles and prophets *converges* in what takes place in Jesus, and to do so in such a way that the *truth* that this witness intends is brought to light. Convergence does not mean identity. The distinctiveness of the Joseph story is preserved and not subverted when the story is reread in the light of the event at the heart of the scriptural testimony. The prophet does not cease to be a prophet and become an apostle instead; his testimony to Jesus retains its indirect character, since it is only *retrospectively* that his story can be read as testimony to Jesus. Yet, for Barth, there can be no theological interpretation of Christian Scripture except on the assumption of the convergent testimony of the apostles and the prophets.

In what has so far been said, the aim has been to identify some of the recurring themes and concerns of the *Church Dogmatics* as a work of scriptural interpretation, restating them where necessary in a language that is not Barth's own in order to bring out their underlying logic or theo-logic.

What, then, is the status of this logic? Is it simply *Barth's* logic, an exotic shrub for us to gaze at for a while in admiration or disbelief before moving on to contemplate some other plant in the theological garden? Or might this logic be not merely Barth's but also and to some degree a recovery or discovery of a logic intrinsic to Christian faith and its canonical Scriptures? If it is the latter, it represents not just an optional 'resource' for a theologically oriented biblical interpretation, but a task and an obligation. The obligation is of course not to become a 'Barthian', but rather to learn from Barth (together with other teachers of the catholic church) whatever there is to be learned about biblical interpretation and hermeneutics, in order then to reread the Bible with a little more discernment than before. If the *Church Dogmatics* does not persuade its readers to reread the Bible, then – by its own standards – it is a pretentious and presumptuous failure. If it succeeds in its aim, which is to train its own readers to read the Bible *differently*, then the fruits of this success would have to become evident, not least in the ongoing practice of 'academic' biblical interpretation. (There is in Barth no playing off the church against the academy, as though the church could safely abandon the academy to the forces of secularity and devote itself to ecclesial introspection. A theologically oriented biblical interpretation need not become irresponsible in relation to the academy as it strives to be responsible to the Christian community.) Yet a biblical interpretation informed by Barth's concerns would have a hard struggle on its hands as it sought to create space for itself in an academic discourse dominated by quite different concerns; there are few signs in contemporary biblical studies that anyone finds Barth worth attending to. His indirect influence on mid-twentieth-century biblical scholarship is acknowledged, but – it is said – the discussion has moved on since then. To attempt to reinsert Barth's concerns into this discourse would be a massive disruption of scholarly business-as-usual. Everything would have to be rethought.

Contemporary biblical scholarship is happy to talk about the biblical texts as texts, but much less happy to talk of them as articulating and communicating the truth about God's way with the world. Texts are relatively straightforward and manageable entities. Once one has mastered a few basic ground rules, it is not difficult to enter the ongoing debates about, say, the origins of the Pentateuch or the authorship of Ephesians. Truth, however, is infinitely mysterious and elusive. The discipline therefore enjoins silence at this point, not least for the sake of non-Christian or ex-Christian biblical scholars who do not want to be preached at. The question of truth is therefore left to a neighbouring discipline, that of 'systematic theology'; and what that discipline does with it is its own concern. So text and truth are shared out between two separate disciplines – an arrangement as unnatural as King Solomon's proposal that each of the two putative mothers should be awarded half a baby (1 Kgs. 3). In contrast to this, Barth's theology never abandons its roots in biblical interpretation and makes the disjunction of text and truth inconceivable.

Contemporary New Testament scholarship continues to pursue a 'quest of the historical Jesus' which sees the Gospels as historical sources that preserve a lesser or greater amount of 'authentic' historical data in among the 'inauthentic' material deriving from the early church. From Barth's perspective, this entire enterprise would appear to be more than questionable. On what basis do we assume that the 'real' Jesus is qualitatively different from the Jesus acknowledged by the early church as Lord and Christ? Are the criteria used in making this distinction really reliable? May we not and should we not read the Gospels (legendary elements and all) as *testimony* and not as 'historical sources'? What is the theological or anti-theological agenda served by the various current images of a so-called 'historical Jesus'?

Contemporary Old Testament scholarship is unsure of the identity of its object of study. Would it perhaps be preferable to rechristen this 'the Hebrew Bible' in order to assert its autonomy in relation to the New Testament and to the Christian faith? In opposition to this, Barth's emphasis on the convergent testimony of the prophets and apostles restates in a modern idiom the classical Christian emphasis on the *interdependence* of the two major divisions of the Christian canon, each of which stands or falls with the other. Might there not be an authentically Christian Old Testament scholarship on this basis? Does the failure to grasp this possibility stem from ignorance of the comprehensive scope of the event that constitutes and discloses the deity of the triune God?

Contemporary hermeneutics rightly raises the question whether the canonical or classical text is adequately understood when attention is focused merely on its historical circumstances of origin. The liberation of the text from an excessively narrow construal of its historical reality also has the effect of liberating the reader to determine the interpretative agenda. But, again from Barth's perspective, is this negative definition of readerly freedom as absence of constraint adequate to these texts? How is this purely human possibility related to the freedom of which the texts themselves speak, which is a divine gift? Is any consideration given to the question of how the texts themselves might wish to be interpreted, and what kind of readers they intend?

Contemporary biblical interpretation may also adopt a 'hermeneutic of suspicion' which seeks to identify and analyse biblical material that appears to legitimate social relations of oppression: the oppression of the poor by the rich, of women by men, of Jews by Christians. This work should not be too readily dismissed with a disparaging reference to 'political correctness'. But the question is whether the critical principle that this hermeneutic brings to bear on the texts is derived from the gospel, and thus from the very texts subjected to criticism, or whether it has been imposed on them from the outside, on the basis perhaps of an appeal to 'experience'. To subject the texts to an alien interpretative norm is to subvert their function of bearing witness to the truth.

These issues are briefly raised here to indicate that Barth's hermeneutics and biblical interpretation do not require one to bury one's head in the sand and to ignore the various scholarly activities that currently pass muster as 'biblical interpretation'. There will instead be a critical dialogue with these alternative approaches to biblical interpretation: 'critical', because the texts themselves seek to instil a methodological vigilance in their readers in that they do not speak lightly of God; and 'dialogue', because that is the way of charity, openness, and insight. Restated in new idioms, corrected where necessary, and set in a properly catholic context in which no one theological voice is allowed to dominate, Barth's distinctive approach to biblical interpretation and hermeneutics represents not just the past but also a possible present and future.

Appendix

The Bible in the *Church Dogmatics*

Although there is some secondary literature on Barth's biblical interpretation (see 'Further reading' below), it is initially more important to study Barth's own texts. However, the scale and the format of the *Church Dogmatics* make it hard to know where to start, and the following annotated suggestions for further reading may be helpful. Barth's small-print exegetical excursuses should not be read in isolation from the material that always precedes them in which he attempts to state the subject-matter in question in his own words. On the other hand, individual paragraphs (designated with the symbol §) and subsections can be read as relatively self-contained theological arguments.

CD I/1, pp. 88–124, §4, 'The Word of God in its Threefold Form'. The subsections of this paragraph discuss the Word of God as preached, written, and revealed, and as an interdependent whole. This is Barth's initial attempt to articulate a 'doctrine of scripture', which he does by setting it within a comprehensive theology of divine communicative action.

CD I/2, pp. 45–121, §14, 'The Time of Revelation'. The first subsection includes an important analysis of the inaccessibility of revelation to historical study. The following subsections are basic to Barth's understanding of the Old and New Testaments in their distinctiveness and interdependence.

CD I/2, pp. 457–740, §§19–21. These paragraphs constitute Barth's 'Chapter III: Holy Scripture'. (In Barth's two-part *Doctrine of the Word of God*, chapters II–IV elaborate on a massive scale and in reverse order the introductory account of the threefold form of the Word of God in §4.) The two subsections of §19 are important for Barth's witness/word dialectic, summarized above; the second includes a critique of the notion of verbal inspiration. §21.2, 'Freedom under the Word' (pp. 695–740) contains Barth's most extensive and systematic account of the practice of biblical interpretation.

CD II/1, pp. 257–321, §28, 'The Being of God as the One Who Loves in Freedom'. Barth argues here that a properly biblical doctrine of God entails the closest correlation between divine being and divine action.

CD II/2, pp. 195–305, §34, 'The Election of the Community'; pp. 306–508, §35, 'The Election of the Individual'. Barth's reworking of the doctrine of election in the context of the doctrine of God includes extensive exegetical reflections on Romans 9–11 (§34) and on the figures of the sacrificial animals of Leviticus 14, 16; Saul and David; the true and false prophets of 1 Kings 13; and Judas among the disciples (§35). The intention is to explore the convergence of the themes of 'election' and 'rejection', which become identical in the figure of Jesus Christ.

CD III/1, pp. 42–329, §41, 'Creation and Covenant'. In the first subsection (pp. 42–94), Barth argues against the tendency to isolate the creation stories from the rest of the Bible and reflects on the relation between history, 'saga' (legend), and myth. The rest of this paragraph is devoted to a verse-by-verse exposition of the two Genesis creation stories, emphasizing their relation to the event at the 'centre' of Christian Scripture.

CD III/2, pp. 437–511, §47.1, 'Jesus Lord of Time'. This subsection reflects on the 'historicity' of the resurrection in dialogue with Bultmann's programme of 'demythologizing', and applies the history/saga distinction to the Gospel resurrection narratives. In Jesus' bodily resurrection, the time of his earthly life is revealed in its eternal dimension; that is, it is made present to all previous and subsequent times, although without losing its own particular temporal location.

CD III/3, pp. 369–418, §51.1, 'The Limits of Angelology'. This subsection opens with further discussion of the significance for biblical history of saga or legend as the product of the imagination.

CD III/4, pp. 116–240, §54.1, 'Man and Woman'. In the course of this subsection, Barth discusses a number of biblical passages relating to gender. His earlier affirmation of biblical subordination language (*CD* III/1, §41.3 and especially *CD* III/2, §45.3), which many readers find troubling, is here noticeably muted. It should also be noted that there is a great deal of insightful exegetical material even in the problematic earlier discussions of the male/female relation.

CD IV/1, pp. 211–357, §59.2, 'The Judge Judged in Our Place', and §59.3, 'The Verdict of the Father'. Barth's treatment of Jesus Christ as embodying the divine grace and condescension to humankind ('The Lord as Servant') is here centred on the Gospels, in which the identity of Jesus is rendered in the form of his narrated history. In the third subsection, there is further extensive discussion of the resurrection narratives (building on §47.1).

CD IV/1, pp. 358–513, §60, 'The Pride and Fall of Man'. The first subsection argues that in the Bible the Law (through which we know our sin) should not be seen as prior to and independent of the gospel. The second and third subsections include extensive discussions of the Fall story of Genesis 3 (following on from the exegesis of Genesis 1–2 in *CD* III/1).

CD IV/2, pp. 154–264, §64.3, 'The Royal Man'. Throughout the chapter on 'The Servant as Lord', Barth reflects on the exaltation of humankind that is entailed in the condescension of God, and in this subsection he rereads the gospel narrative from this standpoint. There is extensive discussion here of Jesus' teaching, his miracles, and his way to the cross.

CD IV/2, pp. 403–83, §65.2, 'The Sloth of Man'. Four exegetical excursuses – on the Old Testament 'fool' (embodied in the figure of Nabal), on Amos, on David and Bathsheba, and on the wilderness generation's unbelief (Num. 13–14) – illustrate Barth's discussion of inaction towards God, inhumanity towards the fellow human, 'dissipation' in relation to the body, and 'care' in relation to time.

CD IV/3, pp. 38–165, §69.2, 'The Light of Life'. The structure of *CD* IV/1–3 is loosely based on the traditional view of Jesus' threefold office as prophet, priest, and king (in the order: priest, king, prophet). In the first half of this subsection, Barth sets Jesus' prophetic office in the context of a discussion of Old Testament prophecy.

CD IV/3, pp. 368–461, §70.1, 'The True Witness', and §70.2, 'The Falsehood of Man'. The opposition between Jesus as the true witness and the human falsehood that rejects this witness is illustrated from the book of Job – understood, like all the Old Testament writings, as a prophetic text. The two central roles are played by Job and his comforters respectively.

CD IV/4, pp. 3–40, §75.1, 'Baptism with the Holy Spirit'. A final statement of Barth's thesis that the history of Jesus as narrated in the Gospels is not only a past history but present and future as well.

Further reading

Ford, D., 'Barth's Interpretation of Scripture', in S. W. Sykes, ed., *Karl Barth. Studies of his Theological Method* (Oxford: Clarendon Press, 1979), pp. 55–87.

Ford, D., *Barth and God's Story* (New York: Peter Lang, 1981).

Hunsinger, G., 'Beyond Literalism and Expressivism', *Modern Theology* 3 (1987), pp. 209–23.

Jeanrond, W., 'Karl Barth's Hermeneutics', in N. Biggar, ed., *Reckoning with Barth* (London and Oxford: Mowbray, 1988), pp. 80–97.

Kelsey, D. *The Uses of Scripture in Recent Theology* (Philadelphia: Fortress, 1975), pp. 39–50.

McCormack, B., 'Historical Criticism and Dogmatic Interest in Karl Barth's Theological Exegesis of the New Testament', in M. Burrows and P. Rorem, eds., *Biblical Hermeneutics in Historical Perspective* (Grand Rapids: Eerdmans, 1991), pp. 322–38.

McGlasson, P., *Jesus and Judas: Biblical Exegesis in Barth* (Atlanta: Scholars Press, 1991).

Runia, K., *Karl Barth's Doctrine of Holy Scripture* (Grand Rapids: Eerdmans, 1962).

Torrance, T. F., *Karl Barth: Biblical and Evangelical Theologian* (Edinburgh: T & T Clark, 1990), pp. 82–120.

5 The Trinity

ALAN TORRANCE

> The doctrine of the Trinity is what basically distinguishes the
> Christian doctrine of God as Christian, and therefore what already
> distinguishes the Christian concept of revelation as Christian, in
> contrast to all other possible doctrines of God or concepts of revelation
> (*CD* I/1, p. 301).

Karl Barth's approach to the doctrine of God is manifest materially in his
discussion of the doctrine of the Trinity, as also in the way in which he
relates this doctrine to those of revelation, election, creation and reconciliation. To get to the heart of Barth's understanding of God, however, one is
required to recognize its *formal* significance and, more specifically, the fact
that his theology takes place within a *church* dogmatics. In contrast to so
many major theological expositions in the history of thought, Barth refuses
to treat the doctrine as if it had a self-contained locus within a 'systematic
theology' or exposition of Christian doctrine. How Barth treats the doctrine
of God and how he conceives the whole task of dogmatics are irreducibly
interrelated. It is this interrelationship which constitutes perhaps the most
distinctive facet of his whole approach and with which one must begin.

The task of articulating the nature of God (in the light of which every
other domain is to be conceived and reconceived) takes place within the
ecclesial domain, that is, within the context of God's giving himself to be
known, experienced, recognized and acknowledged as such. God is not
simply 'another object' to be interpreted or described by the human subject,
but the most concrete Reality in the light of which every facet of our
understanding requires to be reconceived. It is theologically invalid, therefore, for the human creature to approach this unique 'subject-matter' as if
we were its lord. No account of the nature of God can predetermine in any
respect, therefore, the way God must be – God is not a 'given' for thought. As
David Ford and Rowan Williams both emphasize, for Barth theology takes
the form of a *Nachdenken* which considers God's being in the light of God's

actual (and thus 'successful') Self-giving to be thought or understood – the dynamic Self-presentation and Address of the divine Thou.[1] In expounding the doctrine of the Trinity, therefore, Barth sets out to articulate the One who requires first to be perceived as Subject – the supreme Subject and Lord, who is only 'Object' for us to the extent that God actively constitutes us as subjects and then, in this light, himself as Object. This takes place as an otherwise unanticipatable and, indeed, inconceivable miracle of grace whereby the human being is reconciled and reconstituted for a form of perception that is nothing less than participation – a form of existence characterized by an event of recognition and acknowledgment which is identical with participation within the church. It is unthinkable for the person of faith, therefore, that she could 'break loose and be an autonomous knower of the Word',[2] since the person of faith can only conceive of herself as one who 'exists as a believer wholly and utterly by this object' (*CD* I/1, p. 244). We are 'subjects of faith' to the extent that we are bracketed as a predicate of the Subject God, bracketed in the way that the Creator encloses the creature and the merciful God sinful man, i.e. in such a way that man remains subject, and yet man's 'I' as such derives only from the 'Thou' of the Subject God (*CD* I/1, p. 245).

In short, the triune God becomes knowable through the triune event of God's Self-disclosure and our participation within this. The actuality (and what can only thus be perceived to be a possibility) of such knowledge is due, therefore, not to any congruity between God and humanity which is demonstrable *a priori*, or to the success of some speculative, philosophical project, or indeed to some strenuous act of spiritual self-transcendence. Rather, it is due solely to the one Word who stands outside, and to the risen Christ who passes through closed doors.[3] Recognizing and articulating the nature of the triune God is itself an event of grace conceived as the 'mutual indwelling or union of the divine and human possibility, of man's knowing and his being known' (*CD* I/1, p. 246) – an event of free acknowledgment for which the creature requires to be liberated; that is, set free for what we might term 'epistemic participation' by the Spirit in what Barth will present as the incarnate Son's epistemic communion with the Father.

The immediate significance of Barth's trinitarian approach to articulating the doctrine of the Trinity itself is that he obviates the traditional dichotomies between approaches which begin with the nature of God and those which begin from the standpoint of human knowing. His approach cuts right across any dichotomization between the *ordo essendi* (the order of being) and the *ordo cognoscendi* (the order of knowing). We neither *do* nor *can* begin by expounding some progressive series of moves which takes us from the state of human knowing *per se* to the possibility of knowledge of God. Nor can we separate consideration of the epistemological issues from discussions of the Being of God – it is fundamentally incompatible with Barth's trinitarian/ecclesial approach to consider God's being in isolation from God's *being with* humanity as the incarnate Son/Word and the Holy Spirit. The Trinity simultaneously addresses questions of God's being as the God who is Immanuel and questions of human knowing of God conceived as a *function* of God's being with us. Contrary to the thrust of so much Western thinking, Barth is clear that to consider the one is to consider the other.

At the same time, Barth's trinitarian approach also precludes decisions to begin 'from above', that is, 'from an ontic beginning in God', as Bromiley puts it, or 'from below', that is, from history or Scripture. The two are inseparably combined. To articulate the Word of God, God's triune Self-disclosure, *is* to engage in theological ontology. It is to interpret the Being of God. Secondly, however, to interpret God's Being as a concrete Being-Word (a real and concrete Address which is thus heard, recognized and acknowledged) *is* to engage in epistemology – it is to articulate that epistemic participation which is constitutive of the life of the *ecclesia*. All of this, moreover, is to be conceived as taking place *a posteriori*, that is, from within the context of the recognition of God's presence with and for humanity in Christ.

It is important to appreciate this if we are to obviate the confusions underlying objections to the 'from above' nature of Barth's approach. As the recognition story of Matthew 16 makes clear, the perception and acknowledgment of God's being and purposes with and for humanity is invariably 'from above' – flesh and blood simply do not provide the relevant epistemic access. At the same time, this 'from above' element is *for the sake of* our perceiving the One who is concretely 'with us'. God's Self-revelation does not direct us 'above' or to some spiritual beyond, it directs us to the 'Thou' who comes to us as the suffering servant, the Son in the far country. The concrete presence of the Holy Spirit with humanity occurs in order that God might be recognized precisely there and in that context.

In short, therefore, the triune God requires to be affirmed not only as the essential Subject-matter of theological discourse, but as the essential condition of its actuality and possibility. The Trinity constitutes both the ontic and the noetic basis of the Word revealed and defines, therefore, the whole compass – the beginning and end – of the theological task. 'God will and can make Himself manifest in no other way than in the That and the

How of this revelation.' At the same time, however, 'He is completely Himself in this That and How' (*CD* I/1, p. 297).

THE TRIUNE GOD AS REVEALER, REVELATION AND REVEALEDNESS

The fundamental weakness of the 'liberal Protestant' and, more specifically, 'Culture Protestant' theological traditions has been the self-selecting and self-ratifying nature of the social, cultural, and anthropological criteria which characterize their means of access to the task of theological interpretation. The relevant criterion (be it some form of ethical, noumenal, cultural or even nationalistic experience or affiliation) is predetermined to become identified with divine revelation itself. Appealing to some prior hermeneutical principle means that the material selected as 'revelation' simply serves to endorse the formal principle in operation. The criterion by virtue of which the theological message is recognized becomes the message itself.

In vigorous reaction to this and the extreme dangers here of domesticating God and therefore of reducing the gospel to the predeterminations of one's own culturally conditioned dictates, Barth emphasizes categorically that the Word of God is and remains its own criterion; the event of revelation includes the condition for the recognition of that same revelation. More specifically, with the tragedies of the First World War still fresh in his mind, and witnessing the emergence of the German Christians and the demonic turn of events which characterized the Germany of the early 1930s, Barth vigorously repudiated every kind of argumentation which might serve to justify interpreting revelation on the basis of independent criteria. The perception of the potentially devastating social effects of such theological confusion opened his eyes to the dangers inherent in the categories of natural theology and general revelation and, indeed, to the theological weaknesses underlying them. Both risked warranting the utilization of foreign or independent criteria as the means of interpreting divine revelation and consequently, both ran the risk of attaching divine ratification to some predetermined 'idolatrous' human agenda. 'To the extent that another standard is really applied here and not the Word of God itself, only confusion and destruction can actually result, no matter how true or weighty the other standard may be in and for itself. For the decisive word about its proclamation the Church cannot listen to any other voice than the voice of its Lord' (*CD* I/1, p. 255).

For Barth, the essential problem concerned not methodological or epistemological considerations but the doctrine of God. It was the doctrine of the Trinity that, for Barth, provided an alternative form of approach.[4] It is the Nicene nature of his theology which informs his repudiation of ill-conceived forms of anthropocentrism. As Athanasius affirmed against Arianism, it is solely as one recognizes that the Son and also the Holy Spirit, the subjective condition for the perception of the Son, are 'of one being with the Father' that we can, as human beings, interpret God's being and purposes *out of God*. Alternatively, we are left vainly engaged in the mythological projection (*muthologein*) of our prior human affiliations on to the divine, and thereby committed to a self-endorsing identification of our prior suppositions and self-understandings with God's will and purposes.[5] In stark contrast to the forms of 'religion' (predetermined immanence) to which this leads, Barth reaffirms the *homoousion* and thus the Trinity. 'If we really want to understand revelation in terms of its subject, i.e., God, then the first thing we have to realize is that this subject, God, the Revealer, is identical with His act in revelation and also with its effect' (*CD* I/1, p. 296). 'It is God Himself, it is the same God in unimpaired unity, who, according to the biblical understanding of revelation, is the revealing God and the event of revelation and its effect on man' (*CD* I/1, p. 299). It is the Trinity which constitutes the essential grammar of God's engagement with humanity and the possibility of theological objectivity. This approach has given rise to two kinds of concern.

First, does it not run the risk of reducing the Trinity to the grammatical form of revelation? Clearly, if Barth were guilty of distilling the doctrine along these lines, that would suggest serious inconsistency – suggesting not an attempt to articulate God's being 'out of' revelation, but an attempt to project some supposedly necessary logical or grammatical (subject–object–predicate) structure of divine revelation on to the being of God – the very antithesis of the *Nachdenken* Barth advocated as the essence of theological discourse. It is precisely this kind of criticism we find Jürgen Moltmann making when he argues that in 1927, 'Barth developed the doctrine of the Trinity out of the logic of the concept of God's self-revelation.'[6] Barth, however, vehemently rejected precisely this accusation made, as he saw it, by less than 'attentive' or 'sympathetic' readers of the first edition of Volume I. He writes:

> The serious or mocking charge has been brought against me that here is a grammatical and rationalistic proof of the Trinity, so that I am doing the very thing I attack elsewhere, namely deriving the mysteries of revelation from the data of a generally discernible truth. Naturally,

it is not my thought then, nor is it now, that the truth of the dogma of the Trinity can be derived from the general truth of such a formula.

To criticize Barth for this kind of rationalistic enterprise, one would have to 'show that the use is not controlled by the question of dogma, i.e., by subordination to Scripture, but by something else, most probably by the principles of some philosophy' (*CD* I/1, p. 296; *KD* I/1, p. 312). Barth's argument is not that any divine self-revelation will possess a triadic structure and thus affirm the divine triunity. Rather, he is suggesting that the specific dynamic of revelation to which Scripture attests requires, as a matter of fact, to be interpreted in terms of a trinitarian logic. To the extent that it has taken place, revelation can be seen to hold forth the God whose being and whose presence require to be identified with all three dimensions of God's Self-disclosure. We find ourselves unable to say anything other than that here '*God* reveals Himself. He reveals Himself *through Himself*. He reveals *Himself*. God, the Revealer, is identical with His act in revelation and also identical with its effect' (*CD* I/1, p. 296).

A second potential source of criticism concerns Barth's decision to expound the doctrine of the Trinity in the context of an interpretation of revelation. This, it might appear, risks implying that the Trinity exists *for the sake of* revelation and thus *for the sake of* our knowledge of God. It is in the second volume of the *Church Dogmatics* that Barth addresses any potential for such a misconstrual most directly. There his systematic exposition of the knowledge of God is located squarely within the context of the doctrine of God and not the other way round. Far from giving priority to *our* knowledge of God, he stresses that knowledge of God is proper only to God himself and any knowledge possessed by humans is derivative. 'God is known by God and by God alone.' This is not to assume any necessary epistemic reflexivity on the part of the omniscient. Rather, again, the very recognition of this fact is intrinsic to the event of revelation itself.

> If it is true that God stands before man, that He gives Himself to be
> known and is known by man, it is true only because and in the fact
> that God is the triune God, God the Father, the Son and the Holy
> Spirit. First of all, and in the heart of the truth in which He stands
> before us, God stands before Himself; the Father before the Son, the
> Son before the Father. And first of all and in the heart of the truth in
> which we know God, God knows Himself; the Father knows the Son
> and the Son the Father in the unity of the Holy Spirit. This occurrence
> in God Himself is the essence and strength of our knowledge of God. It

is not an occurrence unknown to us; rather it is made known to us through His Word; but it is certainly a hidden occurrence. That is to say, it is an occurrence in which man as such is not a participant, but in which He becomes a participant through God's revelation and thus in a way inconceivable to Himself.[7]

All human knowledge of God is thus secondary, the participation by the divine initiative in a knowledge of the otherwise inconceivable, that which is concealed from human purview (*CD* II/1, p. 179). It is in precisely these terms that Barth articulates God's transcendent mystery. 'The hiddenness of God is the inconceivability of the Father, the Son and the Holy Spirit; of the one true God, our Creator, Reconciler and Redeemer, who as such is known only to Himself, and is therefore viewable and conceivable only to Himself, and alone capable of speaking of Himself aright, i.e., in truth.' Barth continues, 'But He has not omitted to do this – to speak of Himself aright, i.e., in truth. He has seen to it that He is to be found by those who seek Him where He Himself has given Himself to be found' (*CD* II/1, p. 197). When we are dealing with the doctrine of the knowledge of God, therefore, 'we are already within the doctrine of God itself and not in the sphere of mere prolegomena, where other considerations rule'. The implications of this are quite clear; therefore, 'we are already concerned with God Himself when we want to speak directly of the nature of God' (*CD* II/1, p. 233). It is now that the full force of Barth's strategy in the *Church Dogmatics* becomes clear – why, that is, he begins with the 'Word of God' (Volume I) before moving to the 'Doctrine of God' (Volume II) and, secondly, why the first volume is at least as fully engaged with the doctrine of God as the second.

Central to the doctrine of the Trinity, therefore, is the doctrine of the knowledge of God – not *our* knowledge of God, but rather that knowledge of God internal to the mutual indwelling of the Godhead. Thus, our articulation of the Trinity stems from the church's acknowledgment of the self-articulation which derives from the divine self-knowledge – a divine self-disclosure which constitutes its life, its ethics and, indeed, its having any warrant whatsoever for the dubious and dangerous activity of theological discourse.[8] It is not until they receive their full trinitarian contextuality that the meaning of Barth's opening statements in his *Church Dogmatics* becomes clear – that 'as a theological discipline dogmatics is the scientific self-examination of the Christian Church with respect to the content of its distinctive talk about God' (*CD* I/1, p. 3).

THE ROOT OF THE DOCTRINE OF THE TRINITY

It would be mistaken, however, to think that the root of trinitarian theology is defined in terms of the possibility of theological discourse – this would be inappropriately anthropocentric. The root of the doctrine of the Trinity resides with the Lordship of God, in the threefold Self-unveiling of the God who by nature cannot be unveiled. God is Lord in his inscrutability. (Negatively, this means that God is not part of the furniture of the cosmos which human beings can examine at will.) He is Lord a second time in his Self-manifestation. And he is Lord a third time in his coming to us. The recognition of God in his manifestation can never be demonstrated historically in the way that Jesus' humanity can be demonstrated historically. As we have argued above, it is by way of the Spirit's presence in and with us that we are given the 'eyes to see' what 'flesh and blood' does not perceive. It is the Lordship of God in each of these three dimensions of God's Self-disclosure that, for Barth, constitutes the root of the doctrine of the Trinity.

This poses the question, however, as to why it is the Lordship of God in *revelation* that is the root of the Trinity and not, for example, God's Lordship in worship which, as with a more general interpretation of participation, also demands unequivocally trinitarian description. If worship can be described as the gift of participating by the Spirit in the Son's communion with the Father and if it denotes the very *telos* of human existence and communion with God, might Barth not have framed his trinitarian discussion and the root of the doctrine of triunity in these terms? This is an issue with respect to which I have been critical of Barth elsewhere.[9] In his defence, however, one might reiterate the point made above, namely, that God's triune Self-disclosure, which constitutes the life of the church, requires to be described as human participation in the triune life, that is, nothing less than an event of God's taking humanity to participate in the communion between the Father and the Son. The participation, communion, recognition and acknowledgment which Barth articulates in his trinitarian analysis of revelation could well be regarded as defining the very essence of participation 'in Christ' and thus including *in embryo* the essential koinonial structure of the Christian life in all its other dimensions as well.

A plethora of recent writings on the Trinity have suggested that Barth, in his trinitarian discussion, might have made more of the category of persons in relation. For reasons which should now be clear, Barth's approach is necessarily in tension with theologies which move from prior concepts of sociality or community to interpretations of the Trinity, and emphatically not because he did not wish to conceive of either God or human persons in 'relational' terms.[10] He consistently refused to interpret God's triunity with recourse to prior analogies or triadic principles, that is, to *vestigia* or traces of sociality outside of that unique 'sociality' established in revelation itself. Christian faith recognizes no 'second root' which might explain or articulate the triunity of God and which can all too easily become the 'first root'. This means that both the threeness and the oneness of the triunity (a term he prefers to 'Trinity') are to be interpreted out of revelation itself. Revelation commandeers or reconciles the language we use here such that it acquires its specific and concrete meaning. The danger that attends all attempts to produce conceptual analogues from human experience is invariably that the pressure of interpretation is found to be directed *from* these analogues *to* revelation (such that they themselves risk becoming the root of the doctrine) rather than the other way round as revelation demands. To endorse thinking about God from some control on our thinking, other than the unique content and context of revelation itself, is to risk admitting into the theological Ilium a Trojan horse 'in whose belly – we can hear a threatening clank'! (*CD* I/1, p. 336). For Barth, the attempts of Western Christianity since Augustine to expound and articulate the Trinity with recourse to triadic analogies have not served but, rather, have undermined the task of trinitarian exposition and articulation. It might be added that recent attempts to counterbalance the Augustinian *vestigia* with communitarian *vestigia* risk bequeathing to future generations a whole new series of problems.

UNITY, THREENESS AND TRIUNITY

So how is the triunity to be conceived and how do we approach the task of conceptualization here? Barth is insistent that the doctrine of the Trinity neither does nor should call into question the affirmation that God is One. Baptism is in the One name of God, Father, Son, and Holy Spirit and not in three divine names. This reflects the fact that the faith of the church does not have three objects, which would mean three Gods, but one. The deity is not threefold and there is no plurality of God within the one Godhead. Far from being abrogated by the 'threeness' of the persons, Barth argues, the unity of the essence of God 'consists in the threeness of the "persons"' (*CD* I/1, p. 350). In no respect, therefore, should the unity be regarded as a generic or collective 'unity'. The concern to avoid this underlies, in part, Barth's exposition of the doctrine in terms of the metaphor of repetition (*Wiederholung*): 'The name of the Father, Son and Spirit means that God is the one God in threefold repetition' and 'He is the one God in each repetition.' This 'repetition' is what he terms an 'eternal repetition' that exists from all eternity; that is, it implies no alteration or change in the Godhead. It is a repetition which is such that God is the one God 'only in this repetition' (ibid.).

In the light of Barth's nervousness vis-à-vis modern, individualistic interpretations of persons conceived as 'personalities', Barth controversially opts for the term *Seinsweise* – 'way of being' or 'mode of being' – in place of the term 'person' to refer to the members of the Godhead. This has led Barth's critics to complain that he emphasizes the unity of the Trinity at the cost of the threeness, even suggesting that his interpretation is 'modalist' – a charge which Geoffrey Bromiley, one of Barth's most careful commentators, dismisses as simply 'absurd'.[11] Nevertheless, Catherine Mowry LaCugna believes Barth's suggestion that 'person' be replaced by 'modes of being' does indeed result from 'a form of modalism' – adding, however, that 'whether this modalism is Sabellian could be debated'.[12] Jürgen Moltmann, moreover, in criticizing Barth's 'trinitarian monarchianism' suggests that 'viewed theologically' the degrading of the three 'persons' to 'modes of being' of the one identical subject is a late triumph for Sabellian modalism – the result being the transfer of the subjectivity of action to a deity concealed 'behind the three Persons'.[13] E. P. Meijering also suggests that Barth edges the doctrine in the direction of modalism. However, distinguishing carefully between modalism and Sabellianism, he argues, in stark contrast to LaCugna and Moltmann, that Barth's rejection of the term *prosopon* is evidence of Barth's determination to obviate any Sabellian connotations which might result from the terminology traditionally used of the Trinity.[14]

So, is Barth opening the door to modalism or is Bromiley correct in his summary dismissal of any such suggestion? It is difficult to see how Barth's utilization of the reiteration metaphor – as also his interpretation of the Trinity in terms of his triadic Revealer, Revelation, and Revealedness – could lend themselves to modalistic interpretations. The whole thrust of Barth's account, as Rowan Williams suggests, is to obviate any possibility of dissolving the Trinity into a 'neutral fourth'.[15] As Eberhard Jüngel points out:

> While modalism seeks the actual God beyond the three moments of revelation in a higher being in which are no distinctions, and thus allows the Thou of God to disappear and an 'objectifying' of God to appear in its place, the doctrine of the Trinity, according to Barth, has the task of preventing the 'revelation of God and thus his being' – from becoming 'an economy which is foreign to his essence'.[16]

The function of Barth's doctrine of reiteration is to preserve the divine Thou in revelation while precisely not reducing it to a subject concealed behind those distinctions in which, for Barth, God is truly who he is. What God is towards us, he *is* eternally and antecedently in himself. And what God is antecedently and from all eternity, God *is* towards us. As Williams comments, 'Thus, God is not Father in virtue of being *our* father and creator; "He already is that which corresponds thereto antecedently and in Himself." He *can* reveal himself as Creator and Lord of our existence because he is "antecedently and in Himself" Father, Originator, One who is capable of setting himself in relation to what is other than Himself'[17] (*CD* I/1, pp. 391, 165). To the extent that this is indeed the whole thrust of Barth's argument, it would seem to be difficult to make the charge of modalism stick.

So what precisely informs the fears expressed by Barth's critics here? The concept of *Seinsweise* ('ways' or 'modes' of being) does not seem to suggest the category of relations implied by the conceptuality of personhood. Barth's trade-off in electing to use the term made him suspect in this regard. At the same time, however, Barth remains unambiguous that the threeness in God's oneness is indeed grounded in the relations of Father, Son, and Spirit (*CD* I/1, p. 364). Related to this, there is concern as to whether Barth gives sufficient place to the notion of an intratrinitarian communion or mutuality within the Godhead. Karl Rahner, whose exposition of the Trinity was profoundly influenced by Barth, would later insist that 'there is properly no mutual love between the Father and Son, for this would presuppose two acts'[18] and, indeed, that 'within the Trinity there is no reciprocal "Thou"'.[19] This is where any apparent similarity between Barth's and Rahner's views ceases. This is evidenced not only in Barth's discussion of the mutual knowing within the Godhead, to which we have referred already, but also in his exposition of the perichoretic 'fellowship' which he describes as the 'definite participation of each mode of being in the other modes of being' (*CD* I/1, p. 370) as this undergirds his more developed exposition of the intratrinitarian relations later in the *Church Dogmatics*. What would have bolstered Barth's arguments against the underlying nervousness of some of his critics here would have been a weightier discussion of the continuing priesthood of Christ interpreted, as it requires to be, in terms of the intratrinitarian life. The priesthood speaks of our being taken to participate in the Son's eternal communion with the Father. Barth's discussion of this great theme of the *Epistle to the Hebrews* remained underdeveloped. This is reflected in the fact that his exposition of the Sacraments and the 'wondrous exchange' which informs them never attains the depth of insight we find in Calvin's discussions, for example. Had Barth's theologies of election and reconciliation, to which Christ's vicarious humanity is central, been more effectively integrated with the theology of worship conceived in terms of Christ's continuing priesthood, a consequence of this would have been a more robust exposition of the intratrinitarian relations as the ground of the existence of the body of Christ.

This having been said, Barth remained admirably consistent in seeking to ground his interpretation of the trinitarian relations in their exegetical roots and thereby recognizing 'the unique divine trinity in the unique divine unity' (*CD* I/1, p. 366). At the same time, he never sought to disguise the problems of conceptualization: 'The great difficulties which have always beset the doctrine of the Trinity at this point apply to us too – we can state it only in interpretation of the revelation attested in the Bible and with reference to this object' (*CD* I/1, p. 367). To succumb to the temptation to rationalize, however, is 'neither theologically nor philosophically possible'. It is intrinsic to the very specific nature of trinitarian description, that 'the *mysterium trinitatis* remains a mystery' (*CD* I/1, p. 368).

This brings us to the diametrically opposite criticism that is made of Barth's doctrine of God, namely that, far from under-determining the intratrinitarian relations, he assumes too much access to the internal being of God, failing adequately to acknowledge the divine mystery, the 'apophatic' element in trinitarian discourse. Suffice it to say that, while emphasizing the inconceivability of God, he categorically refuses to fall into the all-toocommon trap here of extrapolating a doctrine of the divine mystery from human mystification. To speak of the divine mystery is to make a theological statement, one indeed which concerns the being of God. This is true of a theological approach to the divine mystery; it is also true of approaches grounded in agnosticism. Inherent in the latter is a whole series of suppositions about revelation, that is, its possibility, conceivability, and limits. And integral to these are a whole series of further suppositions as to what God is and is not capable of accomplishing, what is and is not appropriate to God, and what God may and may not freely determine to do for humanity. The irony of the charge of over-determination is that such a charge is itself generally the expression of supreme theological confidence with respect to epistemic access to the divine purpose.

Noteworthy in Barth's exposition of the mystery of God is his refusal to repose in any false humility. He interprets the mystery of God in the light of what God determines that we affirm in revelation. He does not simply assume preconceptions as to the mystery of the transcendent.

Mystery does not just denote the hiddenness of God but His revelation in a hidden, i.e., a non-apparent way which intimates indirectly rather than directly. Mystery is the concealment of God in which He meets us precisely when He unveils Himself to us, because He will not and cannot unveil Himself except by veiling Himself. Mystery thus denotes the divine givenness of the Word of God which also fixes our own limits and by which it distinguishes itself from everything that is given otherwise. (*CD* I/1, p. 165)

The distinction between reverence before the mystery which articulates God's Self-disclosure and the mystery which is a projection of human mystification parallels an observation made by Eberhard Jüngel's defence of Barth against the charge of speculation. 'Paradoxical as it may sound,' he writes,

the doctrine of the Trinity in Barth's theology (1932) has the same function as the programme of demythologizing in the theology of Rudolf Bultmann – If we understand Bultmann's programme as the concern for appropriate speech about God (and therewith about man) and if we view the fulfilment of this concern as a concern not to objectify God or let him be objectified as an It or He, but to bring him to speech as Thou and thus to speak of him appropriately, then we shall not fail to recognize a conspicuous parallelism to the significance which Barth attributes (and gives) to the doctrine of the Trinity.[20]

The point is that both are concerned to avoid those forms of 'objectification' which constitute the unwarranted projection of human categories on to the divine, the *muthologein* to which we referred above. The effect of the Trinity for Barth is that it enables warranted theological discourse without denying either God's transcendence and mystery on the one hand or human creatureliness on the other.

BEING AND BECOMING IN GOD

Perhaps the most fundamental and radical charge made against Barth is one that utilizes a rather oblique comment made by his friend and pupil, Dietrich Bonhoeffer. The charge of 'revelation positivism' has become the stock criticism of those who are nervous about interpreting God's being out of revelation.[21] In its most consistent form this is no mean criticism – one, indeed, which seeks to undermine Barth's whole approach, lock, stock, and barrel! The reason I raise it here is that it is not actually a criticism of Barth's approach to revelation *per se* but, rather, of his doctrine of God. So wherein lies the appeal of this criticism? The answer seems to lie in the propensity to assume a 'general doctrine of being' in advance of a consideration of God's Self-disclosure, the result of which is to circumscribe God's Self-disclosure, thereby generating a kind of *deus absconditus*, that is, a god behind or beside or beyond God in His revelation. This connects with what Jüngel describes as the failure 'to resist the threatened absorption of the doctrine of God into a doctrine of being' (*CD* II/1, p. 260). If a whole series of prior suppositions about the nature of reality is not to constitute a Procrustean bed for the Christian faith and delimit any claims it might make about the ultimate nature of reality, then our suppositions about 'being' will them-selves have to be redefined in and through the semantic commandeering intrinsic to God's Self-disclosure.[22]

Barth grasped this with clarity, perceiving that it is imperative that we resist any temptation to interpret the doctrine of God in the light of prior assumptions vis-à-vis the being of God. God's being is inseparable from God's relating to himself, and thus from that non-temporal 'becoming', namely, that begetting and issuing constitutive of the 'being' of God. God's being requires to be interpreted in the light of – and not in advance of – the relational structuring of God's being. We simply cannot dichotomize be-tween God's being and that 'becoming' articulated by trinitarian discourse. So central is this theme to Barth's whole approach that Eberhard Jüngel gave his classic treatise on Barth's doctrine of God the title, *Gottes Sein ist im Werden* – 'God's Being is in Becoming'. As Jüngel summarizes the essential structure of Barth's argument, 'God's being as the being of God the Father, Son and Holy Spirit is a being in becoming'.[23] God's being requires to be conceived *at the most fundamental level*, therefore, in terms of the doctrines of perichoresis and appropriation and thus as 'self-related being'. There is no concept of being or ontological necessity which transcends this – or, indeed, to which we have access behind the back of God. The triune God determines to be the way he is. It is simply confused to think that theo-logical articulation can seek to penetrate beyond this – there is no 'beyond'.[24] Creaturely talk about God begins therefore with God's free Self-determination to be who he is. God's gracious determination to be known by human beings is a free expression of this same God. The entire inner coherence of Barth's theological enterprise lies in the manner in which he holds together the articulation of the given interrelatedness of God's triune Being and the triune nature of God's being in relation to us. He writes:

> Therefore we are not speaking only of an event which takes place on high, in the mystery of the divine Trinity. We are indeed speaking of

this event, and the force of anything that is said about the knowledge of God consists in the fact that we speak also and first of this event. But we are now speaking of the revelation of this event on high and therefore of our participation in it. We are speaking of the human knowledge of God and the basis of this revelation and therefore of an event which formally and technically cannot be distinguished from what we call knowledge in other connexions, from human cognition.[25]

Deriving from God's eternal being in becoming and from the relations constitutive of God's being, is God's becoming for humanity: a becoming in which God truly is who he is; a becoming which, though a free becoming on God's part, cannot ultimately be excluded from a description of the Being of God. At the same time, it is not a dynamic necessity for God; it does not, in any way, complete God's being. God is eternally complete in and of himself in his own triune life and does not need humanity to be so.

Barth's approach here requires to be distinguished from process interpretations which subsume the eternal within an everlasting, temporal becoming,[26] as also from idealist conceptions of a necessary process of divine Self-realization. Undergirding such moves stands his rejection of all 'spiritualizing abstractions', indeed, any form of 'spiritualizing which makes itself systematically absolute'. If God is conceived as a 'chemically distilled spirit, He does nothing, and in fact He can do nothing' (*CD* II/1, p. 267). The divine 'must be allowed to transcend both spirit and nature, yet also to overlap and comprehend both' (*CD* II/1, p. 266). This underlies Barth's use of the language of 'event, act and life' in describing God while simultaneously affirming the unqualified Lordship of God, the eternal completeness of God in himself and the divine freedom intrinsic to this.[27] 'When on the basis of His revelation we always understand God as event, as act and as life, we have not in any way identified Him with a sum or content of event, act or life generally' (*CD* II/1, p. 264). The divine Thou remains Lord and free while also requiring to be identified with his Act, his Becoming, his Self-uttering and, indeed, His Self-eventuation, as this includes all that is involved in the Event of God's Self-disclosure. This whole conceptuality is recapitulated in Barth's affirmation that God is Person where God's personhood is interpreted in an infinitely more profound manner than we can imagine by extrapolating from the everyday usage of that term. 'The real person is not man but God. It is not God who is a person by extension, but we. God exists in His act. God is His own decision. God lives from and by Himself.'[28] At the same time, God 'does not will to be God for Himself nor as God to be alone with himself. He wills as God to be for us and with us, who are not God – He does not will to be himself in any other way than he is in this relationship' (*CD* II/1, p. 274).

This highlights why, when it comes to the doctrine of election, Barth obviated the restrictive categories which haunted his own Reformed tradition, whereby an unambiguous affirmation of God's freedom led to a dichotomization between the being and act of God, and thus between Who God is in himself and Who God is towards humanity. It was consistent, therefore, that not only should Barth treat the divine love and the divine freedom under the doctrine of God, but that his christological reinterpretation of the election of humanity should be included within that same volume.

THE DIVINE PERFECTIONS

Rather than addressing the attributes of God in metaphysical terms, Barth articulates them in the light of the way in which God determines himself to be in revelation. This directs him to begin with an exposition of the love of God as it is manifest concretely in the event of the incarnation. 'God is He who in His Son Jesus Christ loves all His children, in His children all men, and in men His whole creation. God's being is His loving. He is all that He is as the One who loves' (*CD* II/1, p. 351). This analysis of the love of God sets the scene for his further expositions of God's grace and holiness, mercy and righteousness, patience and wisdom. Barth's second main category is the freedom of God. As with the love of God, the divine freedom 'has its truth and reality in the inner Trinitarian life of the Father with the Son by the Holy Spirit' (*CD* II/1, p. 317). As such it is defined positively as the freedom in which God loves from all eternity and as this is concretely manifest in the One in whom alone we find the 'abundance and plenitude of divine immanence' (*CD* II/1, pp. 319f.). To speak of God's love without at the same time affirming God's freedom would be to collapse God's subjectivity into a universal immanence, thereby reducing God's love to a world-principle, an abstract 'idea' or 'universal'. 'The only reason we have to distinguish between the living and loving of God is because He is not merely the idea of love but the One who loves in the very act of His existence . . . God loves and in this act lives' (*CD* II/1, p. 321). Whereas Barth reiterates the traditional affirmation that the freedom of God denotes God's aseity and absoluteness, he interprets this aseity and absoluteness as meaning very much more than mere 'absence of limits, restrictions, or conditions' (*CD* II/1, p. 301). Rather, they are seen to articulate the ultimacy of the free act of loving in which God lives – God's concrete loving of himself in his Son as also God's loving the world in him: 'The freedom of God is the freedom which consists and fulfils itself in His Son Jesus Christ. In Him God has loved Himself from all eternity. In Him He has loved the world' (*CD* II/1, p. 321). The integrative nature of Barth's argumentation continues in his discussion of God's unity and omnipresence, constancy and omnipotence, and his eternity and glory, all of which further articulate facets of God's loving in freedom.

Barth's concrete outworking of this same theme is developed still further and with even greater depth in the second part of Volume II where he turns to the doctrine of election. There we find the Reformed doctrine of election awoken from its dogmatic or scholastic slumbers, not least through the influence on Karl Barth of Pierre Maury. The result is that Barth reiterates the Reformed insight that election be treated under the doctrine of God and that it affirm a ('supralapsarian') double predestination from all eternity. While Barth's approach holds to these principles, he interprets the whole doctrine in a radically christological manner. The result is a radical reconstruction of this doctrine in the light of God's eternal Self-determination held forth in the incarnation, and one of the most creative discussions to be found in Barth's writings. 'The election of grace is the eternal beginning of all the ways and works of God in Jesus Christ. In Jesus Christ God in His free grace determines Himself for sinful man and sinful man for Himself. He therefore takes upon Himself the rejection of man with all its consequences, and elects man to participation in His own glory' (*CD* II/2, p. 94). As such 'the election of Grace is the whole of the Gospel, the Gospel *in nuce*' (*CD* II/2, pp. 13f.). Its focus is Jesus Christ, in whom God elects himself for rejection and man for election. In the incarnate Lord we find 'the beginning of God before which there is no beginning apart from that of God within Himself' (*CD* II/2, p. 94) and 'the decree of God behind and above which there can be no earlier or higher decree and beside which there can be no other, since all others serve only the fulfilment of this decree' (ibid.).

The result is a reworking of the doctrine of election in the light of what Calvin referred to as the 'wondrous exchange', what amounts to a summary of the patristic interpretation of *katallage* (exchange/reconciliation): 'he took what was ours that we might have what is his'. The love in freedom which defines the eternal being of God and which is grounded in the internal relations of the Godhead, means not only that God shares that epistemic koinonia internal to the divine life with human creatures by sheer grace, but that God elects himself for rejection so that in Christ we might be elected for participation within the divine life.

THE TRIUNE GRAMMAR OF SALVATION

We began by arguing that Barth's exposition of the Trinity makes knowledge of God a form of participation within the divine life, within God's Self-knowledge into which we are taken as 'secondary, subsequent subjects' (*CD* II/1, p. 181). The taking up of humanity into the 'event' of God's being is more than simply knowledge, however, it is humanity's salvation – a salvation which is fulfilment, 'the supreme, sufficient, final and indestructible fulfilment of being'. He continues, 'Salvation is that perfect being which is not proper to created being but is still future – To that extent salvation is its *eschaton* – being which has a share in the being of God – not a divinized being, but an eternal being which is hidden in God.'[29]

The beginning and end of this fulfilment, therefore, is to be defined in terms of the Being of the One who 'does not will to be Himself in any other way than He is in this relationship' and of whom we can say that 'His life, that is, His life in Himself, which is originally and properly the one and only life, leans toward this unity with our life'. 'What God does in all this, He is: and He is no other than He who does all this' (*CD* II/1, p. 274).

Notes

1 Even the force of the 'must' in this sentence must be an *a posteriori* force. The perception of God from within the body of Christ includes the perception that all theology must be a *Nachdenken*.

2 G. W. Bromiley, *Introduction to the Theology of Karl Barth* (Edinburgh: T. & T. Clark, 1979), p. 11.

3 'Even the idea of a *sacrificium intellectus* is only a last desperate attempt to make the knowledge of God a work of man, to have a human possibility correspond to what is God's work alone' (*CD* I/1, p 247).

4 Perceiving Barth as a dialectical theologian has been misleading here.

5 Athanasius described this as a kind of *mania* (madness). Cf. T. F. Torrance's discussion of Athanasius in *Theology of Reconciliation* (London: Geoffrey Chapman, 1975), pp. 215–66.

6 *The Trinity and the Kingdom of God* (London: SCM, 1981), p. 140.

7 *CD* II/1, pp. 48f. It is important to note that Barth interprets God's self-knowledge in trinitarian terms, given Rowan Williams' comments that there is a similarity of pattern between Barth's concept of the Word and Hegel's pan-unity of 'Absolute Spirit, the one and universal self-thinking thought'. R. D. Williams, 'Barth on the Triune God', in S. W. Sykes, ed., *Karl Barth. Studies of his Theological Method* (Oxford: Clarendon, 1979), p. 188. Pöhlmann further suggests that there are strong parallels between Barth's actualism and the dynamic conception of Being that characterizes Hegelianism (Horst George Pöhlmann, *Analogia entis oder Analogia fidei? Die Frage der Analogie bei Karl Barth* [Göttingen: Vandenhoeck & Ruprecht, 1965], p. 117). For further discussion of this, see

my *Persons in Communion: An Essay on Trinitarian Description and Human Participation* (Edinburgh, T. & T. Clark, 1996), pp. 244ff.

8 'Our knowledge of God is derived and secondary' (*CD* II/1, p. 49).

9 Cf Torrance, *Persons in Communion*.

10 See, for example, Barth's theological anthropology in *CD* III/2.

11 Bromiley, *Introduction*, p 16.

12 C. Lacugna, *God for Us. The Trinity and the Christian Life* (San Francisco: Harper Collins, 1992), p. 252.

13 J. Moltmann, *The Trinity and the Kingdom of God* (London: SCM, 1981), p. 139.

14 Prior to his conclusion that Barth does push us closer to Sabellianism, Meijering comments, 'Der Begriff der "Seinsweise" könnte an sich der sabellianischen Interpretation der Trinität näherkommen', *Von den Kirchenvätern zu Karl Barth* (Amsterdam: Gieben, 1993), p. 54. However, he also refers us to Barth's own rejection of the term *prosopon* as evidence of Barth's own desire to obviate any latent Sabellianism in the terminology used of the Trinity.

15 Williams, 'Barth on the Triune God', p. 166.

16 E. Jüngel, *The Doctrine of the Trinity: God's Being is in Becoming*, trans. Horton Harris (Edinburgh: Scottish Academic Press, 1976), p. 23 (Jüngel is quoting here from *CD* I/1, p. 382).

17 Williams, 'Barth on the Triune God', p. 165.

18 K. Rahner, *The Trinity* (New York: Seabury Press, 1970), p. 106.

19 Ibid., p. 76.

20 Jüngel, *Doctrine of the Trinity*, p. 22.

21 This charge originated in a comment made by Dietrich Bonhoeffer.

22 Jüngel, *Doctrine of the Trinity*, p. 63.

23 Ibid.

24 The whole fallacy of modalism is its failure to appreciate this.

25 *CD* II/1, p. 8; cited in Jüngel, *Doctrine of the Trinity*, p. 61.

26 Barth's comments with respect to revelation apply *a fortiori* to the case of process interpretations of the divine becoming: 'God is not swallowed up in the relation and attitude of Himself to the world and us as actualised in His revelation' (*CD* II/1, p. 260).

27 Cf. *CD* II/1, ch. 6. Cf. Jüngel, *Doctrine of the Trinity*, ch. 3.

28 *CD* II/1, p. 272. The identification of being and act in God has led Barth to be described widely as a theological 'actualist' (to be distinguished from philosophical actualism). The case is not convincing, however, and does not sit easily with Barth's statement, 'God is who He is in His works. He is the same even in Himself, even before and after and over His works, and without them. They are bound to Him, but He is not bound to them. They are nothing without Him. But He is who He is without them. He is not, therefore, who He is only in His works' (*CD* II/1, p. 260).

29 *CD* II/1, p. 181; cited in Jüngel, *Doctrine of the Trinity*, p. 61.

Further reading

Gunton, C., *Becoming and Being* (Oxford: Oxford University Press, 1978).

Jüngel, E., *The Doctrine of the Trinity. God's Being is in Becoming*, trans. Horton Harris (Edinburgh: Scottish Academic Press, 1976).

Torrance, A., *Persons in Communion: An Essay on Trinitarian Description and Human Participation* (Edinburgh: T & T Clark, 1996).

Williams, R., 'Barth on the Triune God', in S.W. Sykes, ed., *Karl Barth. Studies of his Theological Method* (Oxford: Clarendon Press, 1979), pp. 147–93.

Willis, W. W., *Theism, Atheism and the Doctrine of the Trinity* (Decatur, Ga.: Scholars Press, 1987).

6 Grace and being

The role of God's gracious election in Karl Barth's
theological ontology

BRUCE MCCORMACK

INTRODUCTION: ON THE CHRISTOCENTRICITY OF BARTH'S DOCTRINE OF ELECTION

When the history of theology in the twentieth century is written from the vantage point of, let us say, one hundred years from now, I am confident that the greatest contribution of Karl Barth to the development of church doctrine will be located in his doctrine of election. It was here that he provided his most valuable corrective to classical teaching; here too his dogmatics found both its ontic ground and its capstone. Nothing in that claim will seem surprising to those who are acquainted with Barth's teaching on this theme. But a more penetrating analysis will also, I think, yield the observation that it was in Barth's doctrine of election that the historicizing tendencies of well over a century of theology prior to him found, at one and the same time, both their relative justification and their proper limit. What Barth accomplished with his doctrine of election was to establish a hermeneutical rule which would allow the church to speak authoritatively about what God was doing – and, indeed, who and what God was/is – 'before the foundation of the world', *without engaging in speculation.*

The latter point especially has rarely been appreciated. Emil Brunner, who was happy enough with Barth's attempt to locate the *noetic* ground of election in the revelation which took place in Jesus Christ and even more pleased with the corrective Barth offered to Calvin's teaching, blanched at the point at which Barth made Jesus Christ the eternal, *ontic* ground of election. According to Brunner, to speak as Barth did of 'Jesus Christ' as the Subject of election was to posit the eternal pre-existence of the God-human, with the consequence that the incarnation is no longer a historical event.[1] Brunner's criticism need not detain us long in this chapter, resting as it did on a fairly drastic misunderstanding, but it did perform the helpful service of pointing to the truly novel element in Barth's teaching: viz. that at the beginning of all the ways of God with the world stood not a *Logos asarkos* (i.e., a 'Logos outwith the flesh' in Brunner's abstract and absolute sense) but the God-human, Jesus Christ. Now that is Barthian 'historicizing'! Clearly, this version of 'historicizing' does not base everything that is said about God on a reconstruction of the so-called 'historical Jesus' (as much of nineteenth-century historicist theology did). But it does make a good faith effort to respect the proper limits the historicity of human knowing places upon theology. And that was the point of all previous historicizing. Whether it is ultimately judged to be speculation will depend on the success of Barth's Christology. For it is in his Christology that Barth grounds the whole of his dogmatic edifice noetically.

This chapter will seek to accomplish two goals: first, to introduce Barth's doctrine of election to those unacquainted with it; and, second, to offer a critical correction to the doctrine of the Trinity in its light. The exposition will unfold in two major sections, corresponding to the twofold thesis which governs Barth's doctrine of election, viz. that Jesus Christ is the electing God and the elect human. The chapter will conclude by drawing some implications from Barth's theological ontology for Protestant dialogue with Roman Catholic theology.

JESUS CHRIST: THE SUBJECT OF ELECTION

The *Logos asarkos* not to be identified with the Hidden God of the *Decretum Absolutum*

Taken on the most superficial level, the revolution which Barth effected in the Reformed understanding of predestination was to replace Calvin's version of double predestination with a universal election. Certainly, that is the most conspicuous consequence of Barth's teaching in this area and those who have been weaned on Reformed understandings of predestination will likely focus their attention on that aspect. But the question, 'To whom does election apply?' is, from Barth's point of view, a secondary question. What is primary is the question, 'Who is the God who elects and what does a knowledge of this God tell us about the nature of election?' Barth's revolution is finally a revolution in the doctrine of God – which means, among other things, that he is working with a very different divine ontology than did his forebears in the Reformed tradition.

Jesus Christ is both the Subject of election and its Object, the electing God and the elect human. That is the fundamental thesis which shapes the whole of Barth's doctrine of election. The latter half of the thesis occasions no great surprise. Through the centuries, Reformed theologians have frequently spoken of the election of Jesus Christ to be the Mediator between God and human beings as the 'foundation' of the election of others.[2] The scriptural basis for such a judgment may be found in Ephesians 1:3–4: 'Blessed be the God and Father of our Lord Jesus Christ, who has blessed us in Christ with every spiritual blessing in the heavenly places, just as He chose us in Christ before the foundation of the world to be holy and blameless before Him in love.' It is the first half of the thesis, however, which has proved startling to many readers of Barth.

That Jesus Christ, the God-human in His divine-human unity, should be conceived of as the Subject of election, is a claim which finds no *direct* confirmation in the New Testament. Barth defends it through a close exegesis of the prologue to John's Gospel; a passage which identifies the Logos who was 'in the beginning' with God and was in fact God as the One who 'became flesh' (John 1:14) so that His 'glory' might even be observable to human eyewitnesses.[3] Now taken on one level, the claim established through this exegesis is unimpeachable and its truth has been indirectly acknowledged by seventeenth-century Reformed theologians. The Logos 'became flesh'; it is one and the same Logos (a self-identical Subject) who was 'without the flesh' (*asarkos*) and who now, through the incarnation in time, is 'within the flesh' (*ensarkos*). Orthodox Reformed theologians expressed this thought through a distinction between the *Logos incarnandus* (the Logos 'to be incarnate') and the *Logos incarnatus* (the Logos 'incarnate'). The distinction for them was one between the Logos as he appears in the eternal plan of God (predestination) and the Logos as he appears in the actual execution of that plan in time.[4] So, if precedent means anything at all, seventeenth-century terminology would allow Barth to speak of the *Logos incarnandus* (prior to historical 'enfleshment') as One whose being was 'determined' by the eternal divine decision for incarnation in time. And yet, there remains an important difference between this traditional usage and Barth's claim. For seventeenth-century theologians, the Logos appeared in the eternal plan of God as *incarnandus* only insofar as he was the *object* of election. In this view, the Logos is determined to be *incarnandus* in the eternal plan of God as a consequence of a *prior* decision made by the triune God. To be sure, any decision made by the Trinity is also made by the Logos. So there is a sense in which the Logos is also the Subject of this prior decision. But the Logos appears in this prior decision as One whose identity is *not yet* determined by the decision for incarnation. He is *incarnandus* only as a result of the subsequent decision; prior to making it, His being and existence are *undetermined*. If now Barth wishes to speak of Jesus Christ (and not an abstractly conceived *Logos asarkos*) as the *Subject* of election, he must deny to the Logos a mode or state of being above and prior to the decision to be incarnate in time. He must, to employ the traditional terminology, say that there is no Logos in and for himself in distinction from God's act of turning toward the world and humanity in predestination; the Logos is *incarnandus* in and for himself, in eternity. For that move alone would make it clear that it is 'Jesus Christ' who is the Subject of election and not an indeterminate (or 'absolute') *Logos asarkos*.

In part, at least, Barth's claim that Jesus Christ is the Subject of election was motivated by worries over speculation. If we were to posit the existence of a *Logos asarkos* above and prior to the eternal decision to become incarnate in time, Barth feared that we would be inviting speculation about the being and existence of the Logos in such a state or mode of being. After all, any putative knowledge of the Logos under these conditions would have to look away from the incarnation and seek other sources, other epistemic grounds. And it is precisely this worry that comes to expression in his critique of John Calvin's treatment of the so-called *extra Calvinisticum*.

Excursus: Barth's critique of the *extra Calvinisticum*

In the history of theology, the technical term *extra Calvinisticum* was coined by Lutheran polemicists to refer to the claim made by Reformed theologians that, even *after* the hypostatic union of the Logos with a human nature in the womb of the Virgin Mary, the Logos continued to fill heaven and earth but – and this was the controverted point – did so as *Logos asarkos*; i.e., without requiring that the human nature he had assumed was also omnipresent. To put it another way, the second person of the Trinity was, at one and the same time, completely within the flesh of Jesus (spatially circumscribed) and completely without the flesh of Jesus (not limited by space). The Lutherans rejected this claim because they thought that they saw in it a fatal Nestorian separation of the two natures in Christ. In their view, if the hypostatic union meant anything at all, it meant that once the union of natures has occurred, the Logos cannot be anywhere in heaven and earth in the absence of the human nature which he assumed. It should be noted that what lay beyond dispute in these early Protestant debates was that there was a valid distinction to be made between the *Logos asarkos* and the *Logos ensarkos* prior to the event in which the second person of the Trinity became enfleshed. The dispute had to do strictly and solely with the state of affairs which pertained *after* the hypostatic union, *after* the entrance of the eternal Son of God into time.

As the defender of a Logos Christology, Karl Barth quite naturally took an interest in this old debate. Barth had no wish to deny the propriety of the distinction between the *Logos asarkos* and the *Logos ensarkos* altogether. After all, the human nature (body and soul) of Jesus only came into existence at a particular point in time, in history. It was not eternal; the Logos did not bring it with him, so to speak, in entering history. Hence, there could be no denying the reality of a *Logos asarkos* prior to the incarnation (and, Barth would add, in agreement with his Reformed fore-bears, after the incarnation as well). And yet, there was something about the Calvinist rendition of this doctrine which made Barth uneasy.

> [T]here is something regrettable about that theory insofar as it could lead, as it has to the present day, to disastrous speculation about a being and activity of a *Logos asarkos* and, therefore, about a God who could be known and whose divine essence could be defined on some other basis than in and from the perception of his presence and action as incarnate Word. And it cannot be denied that Calvin himself (with especially serious consequences in his doctrine of predestination) went a long way in falling prey to the temptation of reckoning with such an 'other God'.   (*CD* IV/1, p. 181)

Barth's concerns, however, cut much deeper than this passage might seem to suggest at first glance. His concern was not just epistemological; it was not just to exclude the attempt to know God on any other basis than that of the Word incarnate in history (though his desire to forestall any form of natural theology clearly played an important role). Barring the door to speculation was not an end in itself. What was really at stake – as the immediate context in which this passage appears in *CD* IV/1 clearly demon-strates – was divine ontology. How is it possible for God to *become*, to enter fully into time as One who is subjected to the limitations of human life in this world, without undergoing any *essential* (i.e., ontological) change? The answer to this question had already been provided for in Barth's doctrine of election (as we shall see later). Here, in the context of his doctrine of reconciliation, he merely set forth the implications of his earlier teaching. The incarnation of the Word, he says, does not give rise on the ontic level to a rift in God 'between His being and essence in Himself and His activity and work as Reconciler of the world created by Him' (*CD* IV/1, p. 184). Now the crucial interpretive question to be raised here is: how does Barth intend us to take this claim? Does he merely wish to say that the activity of God the Reconciler is the perfect expression of the divine essence (so that essence precedes act as the ground of the latter)? Or, is he suggesting that the activity of God the Reconciler is in some sense (yet to be specified) *constitut-*

ive of the divine essence (so that what God is essentially is itself constituted by an eternal act of Self-determination for becoming incarnate in time – in which case eternal divine action would ground divine essence)? Either reading would make sense of the claim that God undergoes no change on the ontic level in becoming incarnate in time. So which of them is correct? I will return to that question in concluding this subsection. It is sufficient here to observe that Barth's fundamental thesis – in accordance with which 'Jesus Christ' is made to be the Subject of election – would certainly seem to require the latter reading. But, however that turns out, what is clear is that Calvin's version of the *extra Calvinisticum* leaves Barth worried about the supposition of an indeterminate state of being in the life of the Logos above and prior to the determination to enter time and become human. As we shall now see, Barth's worries here were well founded and led to his departure from Calvin's doctrine of predestination.

Barth's claim that Jesus Christ is the Subject of election carried with it a massive correction of the classical Reformed doctrine of predestination. For classical Reformed theology, the decree to elect some human beings and to reject others (i.e., election and reprobation) *precedes* the decree to effect election through the provision of a Mediator (viz. Jesus Christ). But if this logic holds, then what it means is that who or what the Logos is in and for himself (as the Subject of election) is *not* controlled by the decision to become Mediator in time; that the identity of this Logos is, in fact, *already established* prior to that eternal act of Self-determination by means of which the Logos *became* the *Logos incarnandus*. And if all that were true, then the decision to assume flesh in time could only result in something being added to that already completed identity; an addition which has no effect upon what he is essentially. Being the Redeemer, in this view, tells us nothing about who or what the Logos is in and for himself. It is merely a role he plays, something he does; but what he does in time has no significance for his eternal being. The question which such a view raises in dramatic form is: how coherent can one's affirmation of the deity of Jesus Christ be if his being as Mediator is only accidentally related to what he is as Logos in and for himself? Is Jesus Christ 'fully God' or not?

Calvin's mistake was not simply that he understood predestination to entail a pre-temporal division of the human race into two camps. That is only his most conspicuous error. But the root of the difference between Calvin and Barth lies at a much deeper level – at the level of divine ontology. The electing God, Barth argues, is not an unknown 'x'. He is a God whose very being – already in eternity – is determined, defined, by what he reveals himself to be in Jesus Christ; viz. a God of love and mercy towards the whole human race. That is what Barth means for us to understand when he says that Jesus Christ is the Subject of election.

We are now in a position to grasp the significance of the material content of Barth's doctrine of election. The content of God's gracious election is the covenant of grace. The eternal act of establishing a covenant of grace is an act of Self-determination by means of which God determines to be God, from everlasting to everlasting, in a covenantal relationship with human beings and to be God in no other way. This is not a decision for mere role-play; it is a decision which has ontological significance. What Barth is suggesting is that election is the event in God's life in which he assigns to himself the being he will have for all eternity. It is an act of Self-determination by means of which God chooses in Jesus Christ love and mercy for the human race and judgment (reprobation) for himself. Choosing reprobation for himself in Jesus Christ means subjecting himself as the incarnate God to the human experience of death – and not just to any death, but to spiritual death in God-abandonment. 'The meaning of the incarnation is plainly revealed in the question of Jesus on the cross: "My God, my God, why hast thou forsaken me?"' (*CD* IV/1, p. 185). Thus, ultimately, the reason ontology is very much to the fore in Barth's thinking is that *the death of Jesus Christ in God-abandonment, precisely as a human experience, is understood by him to be an event in God's own life.* And yet, Barth also wants to insist that when God gives himself over in this way to our contradiction of him and the judgment which falls upon it, he does not give himself away. He does not cease to be God in becoming incarnate and dying in this way. He takes this human experience into his own life and extinguishes its power over us. But he is not changed on an ontological level by this experience for the simple reason that his being, from eternity, is determined as a being-for this event.

What we see in the collision between Calvin and Barth, then, is not simply a clash between two views of the *extent* of election. At the most fundamental level, it is a clash between a theologian working with what we might call an 'essentialist' ontology and a theologian working with an 'actualistic' ontology. Calvin knows of a mode of being or existence on the part of the *Logos asarkos* which is independent of his being/existence as Redeemer. Such a view presupposes an 'essentialist' ontology in accordance with which the 'essence' of the Logos (or, as we might prefer, the 'self-identical element' which makes the Logos to be the Subject that it is) is understood to be complete in itself apart from and prior to all actions and relations of that Subject. And divine 'essence', on this view, is something hidden to human perception and, finally, unknowable.

Barth, too, knows of an 'essence' (a self-identical element) in God, but for him 'essence' is given in the act of electing and is, in fact, constituted by that eternal act. It is not an independent 'something' that stands behind all God's acts and relations. God's being, for Barth, is a being-in-act; first, as a being-in-act in eternity and then, corresponding to that, as a being-in-act in time. Philosophically expressed, Barth's ontology is thus 'actualistic' (i.e., being is actualized in the decision for activity in time). It would be even more accurate, however, to express Barth's ontology *theologically* as a 'covenant ontology' since it is not in 'relationality' in general that God's being is constituted but in a most concrete, particular relation. Most importantly, if the eternal being of God is constituted by His eternal act of turning towards the human race – if that is what God is 'essentially' – then God's essence is not hidden to human perception. It is knowable because it is constituted by the act of turning towards us. God in himself *is* God 'for us'. Knowing God in this way, we can trust that the love and mercy toward the whole human race demonstrated in Jesus' subjection of himself to death on a cross is 'essential' to God and that election is therefore universal in scope.

Is it Barth's view, then, that the incarnation of the 'Son' (and, we should add, the outpouring of the Holy Spirit) are *constitutive* of the being of God in eternity? We must be cautious in giving an answer. What is beyond question is that if we employ the word 'constitutive' in interpreting Barth's position, we must take care not to confuse his position with Hegel's. Barth's critique of Hegel is well known.[5] First, the divine act of Self-differentiation, of positing an Other over against himself and then reconciling that Other to himself is, for Hegel, a necessary rather than a free act. This means that creation and reconciliation are both necessary for God, which completely undermines the graciousness of those activities. Second, ultimately, the process by means of which God comes to full consciousness of himself (becomes, that is, Absolute Spirit) is indistinguishable from the process by means of which human beings come to consciousness of God. God comes to consciousness of himself in and through human consciousness of him. And that can only mean that God's being *becomes* (develops, unfolds) in and through the historical process. It also means – to apply this thought to the doctrine of the Trinity – that the act of Self-differentiation which 'constitutes' the Trinity is a historical, 'economic' act. The 'immanent Trinity' would be, in Hegel's view, a purely eschatological reality; it is the consequence of the economy of God. Incarnation is constitutive of the divine being in a very bold sense indeed. The historicization of God here knows no limits.

Barth's view differs from Hegel's on all of these points. First, Barth holds that the incarnation (and with it, creation and reconciliation) is a free act of

God. Second (and as a consequence of the first decision), Barth maintains a very strict Creator/creature distinction. God does not need to 'become' conscious of himself through the historical process; he is, prior to the creation, a fully Self-conscious, perfectly fulfilled being. Third, and most importantly, the act of Self-differentiation, by means of which the triune being of God is constituted, is an eternal act which may not be collapsed into the historical act of incarnation. The immanent Trinity is complete, for Barth, before anything that has been made was made (including time itself). It is not the consequence of the historical process; and it is here that historicization finds its limit.

In what sense, then, is the incarnation of the 'Son' and the outpouring of the Holy Spirit 'constitutive' of the eternal being of God? In this sense only: as a consequence of the primal decision in which God assigned to himself the being he would have throughout eternity (a being-for the human race), God is already in pre-temporal eternity – *by way of anticipation* – that which he would become in time. This is not to say that the incarnation is an eternal rather than a historical event. It is not to evacuate the incarnation of its historicity. It is to say rather that the being of God in eternity, as a consequence of the primal decision of election, is a being which looks forward. It is a being in the mode of anticipation. Herein we find the relative justification for the historicization which the doctrine of God underwent in the nineteenth century. History is significant for the being of God in eternity; but it is significant only because God freely chooses that it should be so. The limits of historicizing are located finally by Barth in the divine freedom.

In sum: to say that 'Jesus Christ' is the Subject of election is to say that there is no *Logos asarkos* in the absolute sense of a mode of existence in the second 'person' of the Trinity which is independent of the determination for incarnation; no 'eternal Son' if that Son is seen in abstraction from the gracious election in which God determined and determines never to be God apart from the human race. The second 'person' of the Trinity has a name and His name is Jesus Christ. Perhaps the most significant consequence of this move is that the immanent Trinity is made to be wholly identical in content with the economic Trinity. As Barth puts it:

> We have consistently followed the rule, which we regard as basic, that
> statements about the divine modes of being antecedently in
> themselves cannot be different in content from those that are to be
> made about their reality in revelation . . . The reality of God in His
> revelation cannot be bracketed by an 'only', as though somewhere

behind His revelation there stood another reality of God; the reality of God which encounters us in His revelation is His reality in all the depths of eternity.   (*CD* I/1, p. 479)

And yet, the distinction between the immanent Trinity and the economic Trinity has also been shown to be a necessary one (it is the distinction between eternity and time which may not be eradicated).

Implications for the doctrine of the Trinity: a critical correction

Throughout the exposition provided above, an unarticulated question hovered in the immediate background. We may now bring it more clearly to the light of day. What is the *logical* relation of God's gracious election to the triunity of God? We are not asking here about a chronological relation. Election is an *eternal* decision and as such resists our attempts to temporalize it; i.e., to think of it in such a way that a 'before' and an 'after' are introduced into the being of God in pre-temporal eternity. If election is an eternal decision, then it has never not taken place. No, we ask here about the logical relation of election and triunity. Which comes first logically? Which precedes and which follows? To pose this question is not simply to ask about the necessary order of human thinking about these states of affairs since, for Barth, human thought must be conformed to the 'actual order of things' (*CD* IV/1, p. 45). It is to ask about the relation of act and being in God, of will and of 'essence'.

It should be noted that Barth never put the question to himself in this precise form; act and being, yes, but never with the specific content of election and trinity. He should have, but he did not. It is tempting to suggest that he did not do so because of the way in which his thought developed and changed. Barth's mature doctrine of election only began to emerge from 1936 on – which means *after* he had completed his doctrine of the Trinity.[6] Logically, his mature view of election would have required the retraction of certain of his earlier claims about the relation of revelation and triunity, finding in them a far too open door to the kind of speculation his mature doctrine of election sought to eliminate. As an example of such claims, consider the following: 'We are not saying . . . that revelation is the basis of the Trinity, as though God were the triune God only in His revelation and only for the sake of His revelation' (*CD* I/1, p. 312). Of course, it would always remain true for Barth that God is triune in himself (in pre-temporal eternity) and not just in his historical revelation. Were he triune *only* in his revelation, the immanent Trinity would collapse into the economic Trinity. But that God is triune *for the sake of* his revelation? How could Barth deny this without positing a mode of existence in God above and prior to God's gracious election – the very thing he accused Calvin of having done? How can he (or anyone else) *know* that God is triune in and for himself, independent of his eternal will to be revealed? But Barth never, so far as I have been able to discover, corrected such statements. No retractions were ever offered.

The greatest obstacle, however, to putting Barth's failure to reconsider his ordering of Trinity and election down to his own development is that, even after his mature doctrine of election was in place, he continued to make statements which created the space for an independent doctrine of the Trinity; a triune being of God which was seen as independent of the covenant of grace. For example, in the context of his treatment of the covenant of grace, Barth wrote:

> In this context we must not refer to the second 'person' of the Trinity as such, to the eternal Son or the eternal Word of God *in abstracto*, and therefore, to the so-called *Logos asarkos*. What is the point of a regress to Him as the supposed basis of the being and knowledge of all things? In any case, how can we make such a regress? The second 'person' of the Godhead in Himself and as such is not God the Reconciler. In Himself and as such He is not revealed to us. In Himself and as such He is not *Deus pro nobis*, either ontologically or epistemologically. (*CD* IV/1, p. 52)

Why is it 'in *this* context' that we must not refer to the second 'person' of the Trinity as such? What context could there possibly be which would justify speaking in this way? If Barth had stopped there, we might well think that the note of 'in this context' had just been the result of a lapse in concentration. But, unfortunately, the passage continues: 'He [the second 'person' of the Godhead in himself and as such] *is* the content of a necessary and important concept in trinitarian doctrine when we have to understand the revelation and dealings of God in the light of their free basis in the inner being and essence of God' (ibid., emphasis mine). The only conclusion I have been able to come to is that Barth either did not fully realize the profound implications of his doctrine of election for the doctrine of the Trinity, or he shied away from drawing them for reasons known only to himself. Either way, in what follows I am going to register a critical correction against Barth, the goal of which will be to remove what I view as an inconsistency in Barth's thought.

The denial of the existence of a *Logos asarkos* in any other sense than the concrete one of a being of the Logos as *incarnandus*, the affirmation that Jesus Christ is the second 'person' of the Trinity and the concomitant rejection of free-floating talk of the 'eternal Son' as a mythological abstraction – these commitments require that we see the triunity of God logically as a function of divine election. Expressed more exactly: the eternal act of Self-differentiation in which God is God 'a second time in a very different way' (*CD* I/1, pp. 316, 324) and a third time as well, is *given in* the eternal act in which God elects himself for the human race. The *decision* for the covenant of grace is the ground of God's triunity and, therefore, of the eternal generation of the Son and of the eternal procession of the Holy Spirit from Father and Son. In other words, the works of God *ad intra* (the trinitarian processions) find their ground in the *first* of the works of God *ad extra* (viz. election).[7] And that also means that eternal generation and eternal procession are willed by God; they are not natural to him if 'natural' is taken to mean a determination of being fixed in advance of all actions and relations.

Such a view of the relationship of God's election and his triunity is wholly compatible with Barth's understanding of the doctrine of the Trinity along the lines of a single Subject in three modes of being. God is God three times, in three different forms, in an eternal repetition of himself in eternity. But if I am right, then the doctrine of the Trinity might well have been subordinated in the order of treatment to the doctrine of election. Barth took up the Trinity as the first part of his doctrine of revelation, as an answer to the question: 'Who is the God who reveals himself?' But, as we have seen, the answer to this question must take election into consideration.[8] Election must not be postponed until after the Trinity and certainly not until God's existence, nature and attributes (*CD* II/1) have been treated. It may well be that the necessity of reordering his treatment was precisely what prevented Barth from raising the question in the form in which we are pushing it here. To acknowledge the question and its importance might well have forced upon him the necessity of 'beginning again at the beginning' in a quite literal sense – which by this point in time (early 1940s) was utterly unthinkable.

In stressing the material compatibility of Barth's doctrine of the Trinity with his mature view of election, we are faced with a final critical question, and in raising it we come full circle back to our starting point in this chapter. What sense does it make to speak of 'Jesus Christ' as the Subject of election if, in God, there are not three individuals but one personality (one self-consciousness, one knowledge, one will)? What is clearly ruled out of court by Barth's doctrine of the Trinity is the seventeenth-century idea of a 'covenant of redemption'.

> The conception of this inter-trinitarian pact as a contract between the persons of the Father and the Son is . . . open to criticism. Can we really think of the first and the second persons of the triune Godhead as two divine subjects and therefore as two legal subjects who can have dealings and enter into obligations with one another? This is mythology, for which there is no place in a right understanding of the doctrine of the Trinity as the doctrine of the three modes of being of the one God. (*CD* IV/1, p. 65)

The second 'person' of the Trinity is the 'one divine I' a second time, in a different form – a form which is constituted by the anticipation of union with the humanity of Christ. If, then, this second form of the 'divine I' is – again, logically – the function of God's gracious election of human beings, our problem might seem to be exacerbated all the more. How can the second 'person' of the Trinity, understood in this way, participate in the decision which gives him his own distinctive mode of origination with its own distinctive *telos* in the historical incarnation (life, death, and resurrection of Jesus)?

In part, the conceptual difficulty we encounter here is the consequence of our inability as humans to comprehend the meaning of an eternal decision. We think of decisions as involving deliberation and, therefore, as involving a before and an after. First, there must be a subject; without a subject there can be no act. But that is to think all too anthropomorphically. That is to understand 'decision' under the conditions of our own finite experience, which is structured by time as we know it. But God's gracious decision is an eternal one and that means that the triunity of God cannot follow this decision in some kind of temporal sequence of events. The two things belong together because God is a Subject insofar as he gives himself (by an eternal act) his own being. We are only underscoring this point when we add that the 'one divine I' is fully himself in this second form (or 'person') and that if he makes a decision in his first form, he (the One Subject) is necessarily making it in his second and third forms as well. Seen in this light, to speak of Jesus Christ as the Subject of election is simply to affirm the oneness of God in his three modes of being.

JESUS CHRIST: THE OBJECT OF ELECTION

Jesus Christ is not only the electing God, he is also the elect human. The covenantal relation established by God's eternal act of Self-determination is a relation with the man Jesus and with others only 'in Him'. Implied in this claim is the further thought that 'true humanity' is the humanity realized in the history of Jesus of Nazareth.

The realization of the covenant of grace in time has the character of a history of encounters between God and a people chosen by him; a history which culminates in the relation which Jesus of Nazareth, as the Representative of all women and men, has with God. And what is the nature of this human relation to God as it is disclosed in Jesus of Nazareth? 'Not My will, but Thine, be done.' Jesus' relation to his Father finds its most characteristic expression in prayer; and it consists in following, obeying (*CD* II/2, p. 177). That this basic posture or attitude finds its corollary in the Lordship of God is obvious. But God's rule as it is disclosed in Jesus Christ betrays no 'autocratic Self-seeking'. It is rather 'a Self-giving to the creature' (*CD* II/2, p. 178). The election of Jesus, as the election of the humanity which exists in union with the Logos, is an election to a sharing in the suffering of judgment and wrath which God has eternally appointed for himself for the sake of human redemption. We falsify the situation of judgment, however, if we regard God's judgment as having been executed on a mere human being. It is the *God*-human in his divine-human unity who is subjected to this suffering.

But if Self-giving is the chief characteristic of God's rule, then it is not surprising to find that the rule of God does not exclude a genuine autonomy on the part of the creature. To say that Jesus of Nazareth is subjected by God to the suffering of wrath and judgment is true, but it is not the whole truth. In *free* obedience to the will of His Father, Jesus subjects himself to this suffering. We falsify the situation of judgment if we think of it as an event between 'God and God'.[9] It is the God-*human* in his divine-human unity who is the Subject of this suffering.

The man Jesus is not a mere puppet moved this way and that by God. He is not a mere reed used by God as the instrument of His Word. The man Jesus prays. He speaks and acts. And as He does so He makes an unheard of claim, a claim which makes Him appear the victim of delusion and finally brings down upon Him the charge of blasphemy. He thinks of Himself as the Messiah, the Son of God. He allows Himself to be called *Kyrios*, and, in fact, conducts Himself as such. He

speaks of His suffering, not as a necessity laid upon Him from
without, but as something He Himself wills.   (*CD* II/2, pp. 178f.)

Seen in the light of God's Self-giving and the freedom of Jesus' obedience
unto death, Barth concludes that:

> The perfection of God's giving of Himself to man in the person of
> Jesus Christ consists in the fact that far from merely playing with
> man, far from merely moving or using him, far from dealing with him
> as an object, this Self-giving sets man up as a subject, awakens him to
> genuine individuality and autonomy, frees him, makes him a king, so
> that in his rule the kingly rule of God Himself attains form and
> revelation. How can there be any possible rivalry here, let alone
> usurpation? How can there be any conflict between theonomy and
> autonomy? How can God be jealous or man self-assertive?
> (*CD* II/2, p. 179)

Genuine freedom as it is realized in Jesus is not a freedom from God but
a freedom for God (and, with that, a freedom for other human beings). 'To
the creature God determined, therefore, to give an individuality and autonomy, not that these gifts should be possessed outside Him, let alone against
Him, but for Him and within His Kingdom; not in rivalry with His sovereignty but for its confirming and glorifying' (*CD* II/2, p. 178).

Parenthetically, we may observe that Barth's reflections here have enor-
mous consequences for the philosophical conundrum of how to relate
divine omnipotence and human freedom. That divine sovereignty and
human freedom are compatible realities, that they belong to such different
planes of reality that they cannot possibly compete, is not something that
can finally be demonstrated philosophically (by philosophical 'compatibilism'). The demonstration of the truth of 'compatibilism' is strictly theological. It is found in the history of Jesus' free obedience to the will of his Father.
'Omnipotence' may not be defined in abstraction from the event in which
God gives himself to rejection, judgment, and wrath. By the same token,
human 'freedom' may not be defined in abstraction from Jesus' freedom for
self-surrender to these realities for the sake of redeeming the whole of the
human race. The unity of the two is finally christological; it is the unity of
the one God-human in his divine-human unity.

If now we take a step back from this consideration of the historical
realization of the covenant of grace to inquire into its eternal ground, what
we find is that 'double predestination' is not eliminated by Barth. It is simply
reconfigured. 'There are two sides to the will of God in the election of Jesus

Christ. And since this will is identical with predestination, from the very first and in itself it is a double predestination' (*CD* II/2, p. 162). God's eternal will is for fellowship with fallen, sinful human beings. 'When God of His own will raised up man to be a covenant-member with Himself, when from all eternity He elected to be one with man in Jesus Christ, He did it with a being which was not merely affected by evil by actually mastered by it . . .' (*CD* II/2, p. 163). Predestination is 'double' because, in choosing himself for the sinful creature, God was choosing reprobation, perdition and death for himself and mercy, grace, and life for human beings. God, as Barth puts it, 'decreed His own abandonment' (*CD* II/2, p. 168). He 'declared Himself guilty of the contradiction against Him in which man was involved; . . . He took upon Himself the rejection which man deserved; . . . He tasted Himself the damnation, death and hell which ought to have been the portion of fallen man' (*CD* II/2, p. 164). That he ordained himself for this in pre-temporal eternity means that Jesus Christ 'is the Lamb slain from the foundation of the world. . . .[T]he *crucified* Jesus is the "image of the invisible God"' (*CD* II/2, p. 123).

Equally important, however, is what this form of 'double predestination' means for 'true humanity'. To *exist* in covenantal relationship to God means the exaltation of the human. 'The portion which God willed and chose for him [i.e., for humankind] was an ordination to blessedness' – blessedness which consists in the *free* attestation of the overflowing of God's glory in which humanity is given a share (*CD* II/2, pp. 168f.). Here again, this is a christologically grounded claim. *The* 'royal' human is Jesus Christ (see *CD* IV/2, pp. 154–264). In his human life, the realization of what God has ordained for all occurred.

The election of Jesus Christ to be the 'royal' human, to inaugurate a new humanity under the conditions of the old, carries with it an implied human ontology which corresponds to that which we saw before in relation to divine ontology. For Barth, human ontology too is 'covenantal ontology'. To the act of Self-determination in which God chose himself for us there corresponds an act of human self-determination in which Jesus chose himself for God and other humans and then, and on that basis, we too choose ourselves for God and others. True humanity is realized in us where and when we live in the posture of prayer. Where this occurs, that which we 'are' corresponds to that which we have been chosen to be. There, true humanity is actualized by faith and in obedience.

Of course, it should be added that the *freedom* which is proper to the act of human self-determination in and through which true humanity is actualized means that we may also choose against God's ordination and, thereby, against our true selves. We may, in fact, continue – even after having been granted a share in revelation – to live in disobedience, to live as those who are reprobate. But to the extent that we do this, we falsify the true meaning of our being and existence. We attempt to do that which is objectively impossible, to expose ourselves to a threat which has 'already been executed and consequently removed' (CD II/2, p. 346).

To conclude: insofar as true humanity is realized only in the *act* of faith and obedience, 'covenantal ontology' is actualistic on the human side as well. Here, too, a certain 'historicization' has occurred – a Barthian version to be sure, but 'historicization' nevertheless. Barth has employed historical categories (categories of lived existence) to overcome the essentialistic treatment of classical theological anthropology.

CONCLUSION

In his famous 1951 book on Barth's theology, Hans Urs von Balthasar concluded that Barth had not been able to eliminate the 'analogy of being' after all; indeed, the 'analogy of faith' as taught by him required an 'analogy of being' to complete it.

> [I]f revelation is centered in Jesus Christ, there must be by definition a
> periphery to this center. Thus, as we [Roman Catholics] say, the order
> of the Incarnation presupposes the order of creation, which is not
> identical with it. And, because the order of creation is oriented to the
> order of the Incarnation, it is structured in view of the Incarnation; it
> contains images, analogies, as it were, dispositions, which in a true
> sense are the presuppositions for the Incarnation. For example,
> interhuman relationships – between man and woman or between
> friends – are a true presupposition for the fact that Jesus can become
> our brother. It is *because* man is a social being that he is capable in the
> first place of entering into a covenant with God, as God intended. And
> *this* natural order is for its part only possible on the basis of God's
> interpersonal nature, his triune nature, of which the human being is a
> true image.[10]

Von Balthasar is right to find an 'analogy of being' in Barth, but he is right for all the wrong reasons. That the order of the incarnation presupposes the order of creation, that Jesus can become our brother because human being is by nature (i.e., as created) interpersonal, and that human beings are able to enter into a covenant with God only because of their (inherent?) sociality – all of these claims give expression to an 'analogy of being' which remained throughout Barth's life utterly foreign to his thinking. But there is a true 'analogy of being' in Barth's thought which was first adumbrated as the predicate of the divine *act* of relating to the human creature[11] and which was then given concreteness in the doctrine of election set forth in *CD* II/2. 'Analogy of being', understood in Barthian terms, is an analogy between an eternal divine act of Self-determination and a historical human act of self-determination and the 'being' (divine and human) which is constituted in each. Human being in the act of faith and obedience in response to the covenant of grace corresponds to the being of the gracious God; that is the shape of the analogy. Barth's conflict with the Roman Catholic version was and always remained a conflict between his own covenant ontology and the essentialist ontology presupposed by the Catholic tradition which von Balthasar's thought continued to embody. To that extent, it was also a conflict between a modern and, in its way, 'historicized' mode of reflection on the being-in-act of God on the one hand and traditional theism on the other. Were that basic difference to be grasped, ecumenical dialogue might well find a new ground for its future.

Notes

1 Emil Brunner, *The Christian Doctrine of God*, trans. O. Wyon (Philadelphia: Westminster Press, 1949), p. 347. For a similar criticism, see G. Gloege, 'Zur Prädestinationslehre Karl Barths', in *Kerygma und Dogma* 2 (1956), pp. 212f. For a more than adequate response to these criticisms, see Walter Kreck, *Grundentscheidungen in Karl Barths Dogmatik* (Neukirchen: Neukirchener Verlag, 1978), pp. 215–18, 222–9. It should be noted that the language of 'noetic' and 'ontic ground' is Kreck's. See p. 188.

2 See H. Heppe, *Reformed Dogmatics* (Grand Rapids: Baker Book House, 1978), pp. 168f.

3 See Kreck, *Grundentscheidungen*, pp. 222–9.

4 See Heppe, *Reformed Dogmatics*, p. 452.

5 See K. Barth, *Protestant Theology in the Nineteenth Century* (Valley Forge, Pa.: Judson Press, 1973), pp. 384–421; esp. p. 418.

6 For more on Barth's development in this area of doctrine, see my *Karl Barth's Critically Realistic Dialectical Theology. Its Genesis and Development, 1909–1936* (Oxford: Clarendon Press, 1995), pp. 371–4, 455–63.

7 Barth's position is the opposite: 'Ontologically . . . the covenant of grace is already included and grounded in Jesus Christ, in the human form and human content which God willed to give His Word from all eternity' (CD IV/1, p. 45). But what sense does it make to speak of the second 'person' of the Trinity as 'Jesus Christ' without respect to the covenant of grace? Has not Barth here opened wide the door to a *Logos asarkos* in the absolute sense?

8 Hans Theodore Goebel rightly speaks of a 'demand', arising out of Barth's claim that the doctrine of election addresses the question of who the Subject of

revelation is, that the doctrine of the Trinity be 'determined' by the doctrine of predestination. See Goebel, 'Trinitätslehre und Erwählungslehre bei Karl Barth: Eine Problemanzeige', in D. Korsch and H. Ruddies, eds., *Wahrheit und Versöhnung: theologische und philosophische Beiträge zur Gotteslehre* (Gütersloh: Gütersloher Verlagshaus Gerd Mohn, 1989), p. 154.

9 This is the position of Jürgen Moltmann in his *The Crucified God: The Cross of Christ as the Foundation and Criticism of Christian Theology* (New York: Harper and Row, 1974), pp. 241–9.

10 H. U. von Balthasar, *The Theology of Karl Barth*, trans. E. T. Oakes, S. J. (San Francisco: Ignatius Press, 1992), p. 163.

11 In Barth's 1929 essay, *The Holy Spirit and the Christian Life*, trans. R. Birch Hoyle with a foreword by R. W. Lovin (Louisville: Westminster/John Knox Press, 1993), p. 5: 'If creature is to be strictly understood as a reality willed and placed by God in distinction from God's own reality, that is to say, as the wonder of a reality which by the power of God's love, has a place and a persistence alongside God's own reality, then the continuity between God and it (the true *analogia entis*, by virtue of which he, the uncreated Spirit, can be revealed to the created spirit) – this continuity cannot belong to the creature itself but only to the Creator *in his relation* to the creature.'

Further reading

Goebel, H. T., 'Trinitätslehre und Erwählungslehre bei Karl Barth: Eine Problemanzeige', in D. Korsch and H. Ruddies, eds., *Wahrheit und Versöhnung: theologische und philosophische Beiträge zur Gotteslehre* (Gütersloh: Gütersloher Verlagshaus Gerd Mohn, 1989), pp. 147–66.

Goebel, H. T., *Vom freien Wählen Gottes und des Menschen: Interpretationsübungen zur 'Analogie' nach Karl Barths Lehre von der Erwählung und Bedenken ihrer Folgen für die Kirchlichen Dogmatik* (Frankfurt am Main: Peter Lang, 1990).

Gunton, C., 'Karl Barth's Doctrine of Election as Part of His Doctrine of God', *Journal of Theological Studies* n.s. 25 (1974), pp. 381–92.

Gunton, C., 'The Triune God and the Freedom of the Creature', in S. Sykes, ed., *Karl Barth: Centenary Essays* (Cambridge: Cambridge University Press, 1989), pp. 46–68.

Kojiro, M., 'God's Eternal Election in the Theology of Karl Barth' (Ph.D. diss., University of Aberdeen, 1996).

Kreck, W., *Grundentscheidungen in Karl Barths Dogmatik: Zur Diskussion seines Verständnisses von Offenbarung und Erwählung* (Neukirchen-Vluyn: Neukirchener Verlag, 1978).

Sparn, W., '"*Extra Internum*": Die christologische Revision der Prädestinationslehre in Karl Barths Erwählungslehre', in T. Rendtorff, ed., *Die Realisierung der Freiheit: Beiträge zur Kritik der Theologie Barths* (Gütersloh: Gütersloher Verlagshaus Gerd Mohn, 1975), pp. 44–75.

7 Creation and providence

KATHRYN TANNER

Barth's treatment of creation and providence in the *Church Dogmatics* is notable for its effort to make those doctrines distinctively Christian, meaning by that doctrines that reflect the centrality of Jesus Christ for understanding God and world. The methodological and substantive effects of such a project on the doctrines of creation and providence are the focus of this chapter.

First and most obviously, the attempt to make creation and providence Christian doctrines is part of Barth's attack on natural theology. One should turn to Jesus Christ for one's understanding of a world created and ruled by God rather than draw conclusions about such matters from more general observation of the world and its natural and historical processes. One should not, then, assume that the world exists and search for its cause; this way leads to the philosopher's God, the Creator as world-cause (*CD* III/1, pp. 6, 11). Nor should one form conclusions about the point or direction of God's rule over the universe – about the providential arrangement of things – by following the lines of observable trajectories of historical events (*CD* III/3, pp. 20–3). Both ways of proceeding subordinate understanding of God for us in Jesus Christ to what one supposedly knows on independent grounds about God's creation and rule of the world, rather than the other way round.

The direction in which one's theological inferences run – from or to Christ – has important consequences for one's understanding of the world as God's own. For example, starting from a knowledge of the triune God in Christ, the world's existence can no longer be taken for granted and used as a basis for discussion of what brought it about. Instead, the world's existence becomes questionable given the already constituted fullness of a triune God who has no need of it; the fact that it exists can only be the result of the pure grace of God's love for it displayed most fully in Christ. When beliefs about providence stem from Christ rather than move to him, providence becomes, not the immanent movement of created powers, but those arrangements of the world that reflect God's prior intentions for the world in

Christ, arrangements that reflect God's primary intention to draw the world towards him. As with the free mercy displayed to sinners in Christ, the world is moved by God from grace to grace towards Christ, rather than Christ's being the natural result of the world's own powers.

Considered as an attack on natural theology, Barth's point in trying to formulate distinctively Christian accounts of creation and providence seems primarily epistemological – his concern is how one comes to know what one knows. The theologian is counselled not to look farther afield in reliance on natural capacities of observation and reason, but to make biblical witness to Jesus the starting point for all discussion of creation and providence. Barth's underlying worry, however, concerns not so much *where* one got one's ideas, but whether *what* one says about creation and providence reflects the centrality of Jesus for understanding all God's ways and works. One might avoid natural theology and base one's ideas on the Bible, and still not produce a distinctively Christian understanding of creation and providence in that sense. The centrality of Christ at issue amounts to a more substantive concern about the extent to which the doctrines of creation and providence are oriented to doctrines about Christ. It also poses a more specific procedural concern about how the Bible is read – whether the readings of the Bible from which accounts of creation and providence are drawn are also oriented by Christ.

Most fundamentally for Barth, Christian beliefs about creation and providence are oriented to Christ when they are part of the effort to magnify and shore up the importance of what has happened in him. The Son of God's assumption of human flesh is not something alien to the world, something about which the world might therefore remain indifferent. No, the world to which the Son of God comes is the Son's own world. That is what the idea of creation for the sake of Christ and the claim that Christ is himself the one in and through whom the world is created are designed to make clear – there is no neutral place to stand with respect to the event of Jesus Christ (*CD* III/1, pp. 54, 67). Similarly, the universal force of what happened in Christ requires discussion of creation and providence, doctrines that extend the range of Christian purview to the whole world and not just some segment of it (*CD* III/1, pp. 62–3). Jesus Christ is not an isolated occurrence, with an influence restricted to a particular slice of world-history – that slice of history extending through the history of Israel and into the church. Discussion of creation and providence in the light of Christ is a way of pointing out the world-historical significance of Jesus: Christ's coming changes the situation of the whole world; nothing is the same. Everything that Jesus touches is altered completely, moreover. Creation and providence show the breadth and depth of God's concern for the world so that Christ's coming cannot be viewed as an event with partial effects – effects, say, on the spiritual and individual aspects of human existence solely, to the exclusion of material and social existence. Finally, the doctrines of creation and providence give theological support for confidence and trust in Jesus' victory over the forces in the world that resist it. If the whole world is always Jesus' own, Jesus calls that world to what it already is: we, for example, are not at home in a world threatened by forces of darkness and chaos, but are called seemingly irresistibly in Christ to be who we really are (*CD* IV/3, pp. 270–3).

In constructing an account of creation and providence retrospectively from Christ in this way, Barth follows the lead of what biblical scholars, such as Gerhard von Rad, say about those sections of the Hebrew Bible that concern creation and providence (see *CD* III/1, pp. 239–49). Even when, as in the book of Genesis, they come first in the order of the presentation, discussions of creation and providence in the Hebrew Bible are written late as ways of reflecting on the significance of particular events in Israel's history with God – for example, the Exodus from Egypt. Talk of God's creation and providence is a way of showing how what happens to Israel is written into the nature of things more generally (*CD* III/1, pp. 268–9); it thereby highlights the importance of and guarantees trust in those saving acts of God. God, as Creator and Lord of all and not just Israel, has the power to deliver Israel from threat: nothing that threatens it escapes God's sphere of operation, a sphere of operation whose very range proves its awesomeness. Who God shows Godself to be in dealing with Israel can be counted on because that same character is reflected in all God's dealings from the beginning of time. God parts the waters in the Exodus from Egypt for Israel's protection just as God in the beginning keeps the waters within bounds to create the dry land; the expulsion from Canaan is like the expulsion from Paradise, and so on.

Biblical passages that discuss God's creation and providence cannot, then, be understood independently of others that specifically concern God's history with Israel. Thus, Genesis 1 and 2 – the primary locus of Christian accounts of creation – cannot be understood apart from later passages in the same book; and the subsequent books of the Hebrew Bible are the best commentary on the book of Genesis. Barth thinks he is merely extending the same principle by affirming that the best commentary on the Hebrew Bible is the New Testament witness to Christ (despite the fact that these earlier books in the Christian canon were obviously not written after the events that the New Testament proclaims). The Bible's discussion of creation and providence reflects what God does in Jesus Christ as much as (indeed, Barth would say better than) it reflects the covenant history between Israel and God (*CD* III/1, pp. 276, 320f.). Christian accounts of creation that hope to be biblical therefore cannot give isolated attention, as they usually do, to the first two chapters of the book of Genesis, filling out their theological meaning from who knows where. Instead, the meaning of those chapters must be developed in the light of the Bible's treatment of the whole covenant history of God and Israel that culminates in Jesus, in such a way that what the New Testament proclaims about Jesus is the key to understanding all that comes before it in the Bible.

Barth's recommendations about Bible reading in this way follow his generally supralapsarian understanding of the priority of Christ (*CD* II/2, pp. 133–45). God's decision to be for us in Jesus is not a reaction to previous events in the history of God's relations with us, but has a reality in its own right preceding the whole of that history. What is first in God's intention and what spurs God's relation with us from the very beginning – to be the loving Father of us all in Jesus Christ – comes last in execution. Therefore the history of God's relations with us, like the Bible, has to be read from back to front and only on that basis from the front in anticipation of the end.

The centrality of Christ for accounts of creation and providence is not secured, then, by their derivation from the Bible. The centrality of Christ is demonstrated primarily by how theological topics are arranged – whether doctrines of creation and providence are based in very particular claims about just this one Jesus Christ and are therefore materially influenced by such claims. This primary importance of topical arrangement helps explain why – except for *CD* III/1 – Barth's treatment of doctrines does not follow the events of biblical narrative; biblical commentary is usually relegated to excursuses.

This substantive or topical centrality of Jesus Christ for the doctrines of creation and providence means avoiding abstract accounts of God and creatures – that is, accounts of God and creatures that do not reflect the fact that really and concretely God and creatures are who they are in relation to Christ. According to Barth's doctrine of election, God from all eternity is that one who determines to be for us in Christ; this is the fundamental act of divine Self-determination that establishes who God is and how God acts in all God's relations with a world outside God. There is only one God – the God of Jesus Christ – and God is *that* God in all God's dealings with creatures. If God is only God as God is for us in Christ, creatures are also only what they are insofar as they belong to Christ. They exist as objects of God's good pleasure (according to the doctrine of creation) and are preserved, accompanied, and ruled by God (the main topics treated under the rubric of providence in *CD* III/3) only insofar as they are so for the sake of Christ, in order to be the creatures who are for God in Christ.

How does avoiding abstract characterizations of God and creatures affect the doctrines of creation and providence? How are traditional Christian teachings changed thereby?

The most general effect on both doctrines is to unite them with all other theological topics under the rubric of the grace of God displayed in Christ. When one discusses creation and providence, one is not then discussing nature in contrast to grace. Creation and providence are themselves forms of grace – lesser and more general forms to be found included in the supreme and quite particular act of God's free and loving regard for us in Christ. The completely unmerited and incredibly beneficent act of God in Christ whereby God destroys sin and exalts us to fellowship with God by taking our place as faithful covenant partner is surrounded in time and space by a number of other acts of God that are similarly free and loving, acts of God which God's act in Christ presupposes or implies. Thus, although God might have remained alone without detriment to God's own fullness and splendour, God freely chooses to be with another who is not God, to exist alongside something not Godself, by creating the world. In a similar act of free love, God goes beyond mere coexistence with the world to show concern for it, an active engagement with it. God preserves the world from the threat of nothing, gives it room for its own active responses to God's initiatives to it, and directs it in service of the fellowship that God establishes in the beginning with a particular people, Israel. That fellowship with Israel is a still greater gift, which creation and providence do not themselves demand, since in it God does not merely show concern for creatures but enacts a real partnership with certain humans who are directed by God to make their whole lives a sign of God's unmerited singling out of them as God's own people. In Christ, finally, God is not merely the partner of a particular group of human beings, but actually becomes human in a free act of delivering God's human partners from the threat of sin and death. That act of becoming human is a greater gift too in that it communicates God's partnership to all humanity, and through humanity to the whole of creation, while elevating the character of the relation to God enjoyed by creatures: the church (and through the church, all of humanity and the world) becomes no mere partner, but indirectly united with God in and through Jesus Christ who is immediately in himself both God and a human being.

One can put the same account of grace after grace in more overtly trinitarian terms – terms more concrete in that they more fully reflect who

God really is. By creating the world in a free act of love, the unity in fellowship that God is as triune is reflected outward in God's being with another that is not God – the world. The Father's relation with the Son is reflected in the world's relation with the triune God. That relation starts to become a real fellowship in imitation of the fellowship that is the intra-trinitarian life of God when God initiates a covenant with Israel and becomes the God of this people and they the people of this God. Despite the active threat against creation that enters the world with sin, God patiently and mercifully upholds the world in expectation of Israel's eventual faithful commitment of itself to God. Providence is thereby a more indirect expression of the same active concern for fellowship that God displays in relation to Israel and that extends the fellowship of the triune God outward in relations with what is not God. Finally in Christ, not just Israel, but humanity in general and, through human beings, the whole world, enjoys not just a version of God's fellowship in Godself extended outward to what is not God, but incorporation into the very triune life of God. This man Jesus (in contradistinction to all other creatures) is one with the Son of God, thereby sharing in the divine triune life and participating in God's reconciling and redemptive work; united to Jesus through the work of the Holy Spirit (and only in that way), all creatures may hope to enjoy the same.

In sum, creation and providence together with all the events in God's history of relations with the world are bound together as acts of grace that find their centre in the supreme act of God's free love which is Jesus Christ. Though they are all grace, they are not the same grace. United, they are nevertheless distinct. God's act of bringing the world to be (creation) is not the same as God's gift of time and space to it and direction of its history in service of the covenant set up with Israel (providence). That covenant means a different calibre of relationship with God from the world-history that serves it. The covenant fulfilled in Christ takes a new shape in that God takes the place of faithless Israel (reconciliation). At the eschaton, or end of time, the whole world's response to what Christ has achieved will be itself a new thing through the power of the Holy Spirit, in that the grace of Christ will be revealed with utter clarity in and through everything in a way not obvious now (redemption).

All these acts of grace are united yet distinct in imitation of the unity and distinction of the triune God: creation and providence, the covenant fulfilled in Christ, the eschatological redemption of all things, are the acts of the self-same God, yet as distinct as the individual members of the Trinity to whom they are especially attributed – the Father, Son, and Spirit respectively (*CD* III/1, pp. 48–9). It is the distinctiveness of these acts of grace that ensures, indeed, that they *are* each graces, in the sense of being free and not required by what has come before. Most significantly, though graces, none is the grace of God found in Christ in a way that would enable who and what Christ is to be the necessary consequence of any other act of God. These distinct acts are yet one in that the character of God as the same one who ever loves in freedom remains a constant throughout and in that they all flow in or away from, or appear at closer or greater remove from, that extreme or ultimate expression of God's free love for us in Christ, which is the centre of all God's gracious acts.

The distinction of creation and providence from God's gracious act in Christ to which they are nevertheless united is expressed in the following general ways. Creation and providence are distinct from the fulfilled covenant of grace of Christ as the minimal and most general are to the maximal and most particular. In other words, creation and providence are the most minimal things one can say about everything given the fact of Jesus Christ. God must be *for* what is not God in at least these ways if God is so fully and concretely the way God is for us in Christ. One can at least make the very general claim that the world actually exists as the object of God's favour and concern if God has taken such extraordinary measures on its behalf in Christ (*CD* III/1, p. 332). At a minimum and in a rather unspecified sense, one must say that the world is under the direction of God if it has its centre in just this one Jesus Christ.

Or, one might say creation and providence come up as one widens one's purview from Christ. The distinction between creation and providence, on the one hand, and the covenant that culminates in Christ, on the other, is a difference between a wider and a narrower focus moving out from Christ. Creation and providence express what the world looks like as one looks away from the standpoint of Christ and the covenant that culminates in Him. That is, creation and providence are the minimal and most general things one can say about the *whole* world given the fact of Christ.

Moreover, the farther one moves out from the fulfilment of the covenant in Christ, the murkier its implications get; the distinction between creation and providence, on the one hand, and the covenant fulfilled in Christ, on the other, is a difference between hidden and revealed. What God's being for us in Christ means for the covenant is clear, as is its import for human beings. Given the fact that God is a human being in Christ and that God's becoming so alters the terms of the covenant with Israel to which Jesus as a Jew belongs in a way that brings it to completion, the significance of Christ for either covenant or human existence is directly apparent. Far more difficult is determining in any definite way the meaning of what happens in Christ for the world beyond the human and outside the human history that can be directly tied to Christ – Israel and the church. Proposals about creation and providence to that extent remain rather tentative and vague, despite the fact that something has to be said of them if Christ is of comprehensive, world-historical significance (see *CD* III/2, pp. 38–41).

Finally, creation and providence are distinct yet related to the grace of Christ as subordinate preconditions or presuppositions for a far more important given fact. They are the road or means to it. In this sense, creation and providence are the external bases for what God has always intended to do in Christ. God's being for us in Christ requires the existence of the world as a theatre or space for its occurrence and requires the existence of created subjects who are to be God's partners made over in that special way by him (*CD* III/1, p. 97). Similarly, providence provides the wider history, a continuum of ongoing existence among active created agents in their own right, a broader framework of historical space and time, in which the covenant history with God can appear and come to fulfilment in Christ as a unique, quite exceptional line of human history (*CD* III/3, pp. 6f.).

These relations are not, however, merely external ones: the goal that creation and providence serve intrinsically determines their character; creation and providence anticipate what is to come. Therefore, the distinction between them and the covenant fulfilled in Christ is a difference between prophecies or signs of promise and the hoped-for reality, which they intimate by what they are.

This last point brings us back to the fact that the distinction among graces is predicated upon their unity. That unity has major implications for the way Barth develops his accounts of creation and providence. The unity of creation and providence with the grace of God in Christ, the fact that creation and providence are in some strong sense the expression of the *same* grace of Christ, shows itself in the character of creation and providence. As Barth likes to put the point, the internal basis of creation and providence is the covenant fulfilled in Christ or, more fundamentally, that internal basis is the election of Jesus Christ as the be-all and end-all of God's ways and acts *ad extra*. Various aspects of traditional Christian accounts of creation and providence are altered by Barth accordingly.

To begin with creation, God's act here cannot be understood abstractly as one of simple unconditional and supreme power, as if God were not really and always the one whom God shows Godself to be in Jesus. If the Father who creates is the Father of Jesus, this act of creation must be seen as one of free loving beneficence, a Fatherly act of favour (*CD* III/2, p. 29). In other words, one may be sure that the world exists as a good gift if the God who creates is the God of Jesus Christ.

When seen in Christ, God's act in creation takes on, moreover, the specific characteristics of reconciliation. In short, creation becomes an act of separation or division like that found in the cross of Christ (*CD* III/1, pp. 122, 133). More fully stated, the unmerited acceptance of human beings and the rejection of chaos, sin, and death on the cross of Christ – the Yes and No of God's act in Christ – are mirrored by God's acceptance of only some things for creation and the rejection of others. Creation, then, displays the character of justification as unmerited acceptance; Barth accordingly applies to it the language of free mercy most obviously suitable to God's acts for a world of sin in Jesus. Moreover, the subordination of God's No to God's Yes that is clear in Christ – the destruction of sin on the cross for the sake of righteousness – finds a correspondence in the way darkness or nothingness forms around what God creates as a quite secondary consequence of God's creative affirmation – the divine Yes – that brings the world to be. The way Jesus' coming is a light in the darkness of a world of sin and death is then matched by the way light shines out of the darkness when God speaks God's Word in creation. And like the antagonism displayed on the cross by the forces of chaos, sin and death, this darkness from the beginning carries a threat against creation, a threat that breaks in with sin. What God rejects in Christ is not a mere neutral non-being, and therefore creation too suggests deliverance.

What is created, the creatures themselves, also cannot be treated in abstraction from what is to come in Christ. For example, the destiny of humans for fellowship with God is reflected in the creation of men and women as partners. And the antitheses of God's Yes and No in Christ are repeated in antitheses within creation – most importantly in the Genesis story, water versus land, and light versus darkness; but also such antitheses as strength versus weakness, constancy versus change (antitheses which figure centrally in the history of God for us in which strength appears in weakness and God's faithfulness is expressed despite our falling away). Indeed, the whole world bodies forth Christ. Thus the simplest facts and the most mundane experiences of life in this world, from the rising of the sun that conquers darkness to the land that keeps back the sea, reflect God's victory in Christ over what threatens us through our own fault.

Because it is a free act of love like that found in Christ, accounts of God's creation of the world are protected from both monism and dualism (*CD* II/1, pp. 500–2). As a free act, creation is not a necessary emanation from God's own being. The world is genuinely distinct from the God who creates it. Because it is an act of divine love, what God creates does not exist independently of God. God binds Godself to the world in love and therefore creatures never exist without participating in a history of engagement with God. To put this christological opposition to both monism and dualism another way, the fellowship of love between creatures and God, as that exists through Christ and by the power of the Holy Spirit, requires God and creatures to be genuinely two, but it also requires their existence together.

The fact that the world is the creature of Christ – created *by* the Word or Son of God who is one with the man Jesus from all eternity, created *for* Christ as the goal for the sake of which creatures are all that they are – provides christological grounds for the idea of creation *ex nihilo*. Creation has its basis in the Word of God who is Jesus Christ and in that Word of God alone. Nothing else – say, the dark or formless nothingness – contributes to the existence of creatures as its preparation or underlying condition (*CD* III/1, pp. 102–16). Nor do creatures somehow give rise to themselves; creatures are not self-engendered. The unconditional grace found in Christ – the fact that God steps into our place as God's covenant partners to do and be that of which we are otherwise utterly incapable, the fact that in Christ we become faithful partners of God through God's own act alone – is matched by a creation without presuppositions, a creation that presupposes nothing but a free act of God's love.

Besides supporting these rather traditional Christian affirmations about creation, the christological turn to Barth's account of creation gives it a distinctive stress on God's creation of the world as an act in time (*CD* III/1, pp. 13–15). Here Barth opposes himself to accounts of creation that think of it primarily as a relation of dependence on God characteristic of all times and places. He also opposes accounts that, while thinking of creation as the first moment of the world, view it as an act of God that gives rise to time without itself being temporal. If, as Barth believes, God becomes a creature of time in Jesus Christ without jeopardizing God's divinity, there is no reason to deny that God's act of creation is a temporal act. Affirming that it is so makes clear that creation conforms with the character of all God's acts for us by being, like them, genuine occurrences or events. What happens in Jesus affects all times, but that does not stop it from being a particular event that one can date and place. Creation must then be an event like this too, something that happened once and for all, though an event that is unobserv-able – what Barth calls a pre-historical event of history which has as its closest analogue the equally unobservable but nonetheless real occurrence of Jesus' resurrection (*CD* III/1, pp. 80, 78). Creation is the first, pre-historical moment in the history of the world dedicated to Christ, the prehistory of the covenant in other words. It is that moment when the world comes to be through God with nothing preceding it but God. As such, it also, however, like the event of Jesus Christ, embraces all time (*CD* III/1, pp. 27, 60). Although it might be difficult to understand how, all history has this same immediate relation to God the Creator despite the fact that the rest of this history, unlike the first moment, has something coming before it, the preceding history of the world (*CD* III/1, pp. 60, 77, 80f.).

By stressing the event character of creation (and only on that basis, its universal import), Barth can make clear that here the creature begins the encounter with something that comes to it from without – God (*CD* III/1, pp. 85f.). Creation is no timeless truth that one might take for granted, something with the constancy of a law of nature that one might therefore confuse with the internal workings of the world – say, with a law of cause and effect. Indeed, no good analogue exists within the common workings of the world for the relation between creature and Creator. The real model for that relationship is the trinitarian one of the relation of Father to Son through the Holy Spirit (*CD* III/1, p. 14).

This understanding of creation has interesting implications for the genre of Christian description concerning creation. If creation is an unobservable event, the primary account of it, to which the theologian should always return in his or her ruminations, will take the form of an imaginative story – a tale or saga. The book of Genesis, Barth believes, is a story of that sort and therefore should not be read as the mythological clothing for eternal truths better expressed without it. If creation is an event of free grace like that found in Jesus Christ, what one needs to express about it can only be expressed by narrating unrepeatable events. Creation is not appropriately conveyed in generalizations about timeless principles or in stories that merely supply the colourful, and ultimately expendable, vehicles for them – what Barth calls myths (*CD* III/1, pp. 84f.).

In the case of providence, Barth establishes that this act cannot be understood independently of who God is in Jesus Christ by the unusual claim that providence is the execution of predestination (*CD* III/3, pp. 4–6). In other words, predestination – God's decision from all time that the world should be reconciled in Christ – is not a particular instance of some general way that God is with the world as a whole. Instead, the way God is with the world as a whole is a consequence of God's decision to be with us in Christ; it is part of the way God's eternal determination to be God in Jesus Christ is unrolled in time. Providence *is* simply that determination in its implications for the history of the world as a whole.

As such, providence can be understood only in the light of that history of the covenant that is the direct realization in time of God's intentions to be with us in Christ. Barth hereby reverses how general and special providence are often related in Christian theology (*CD* III/3, p. 185). The special history of God's acts that culminates in Christ – the salvation history which the Bible primarily relates – is not a particular case of the general way God works in the world. Providence does not, in other words, set the terms for God's working to which salvation history must conform. Instead, the whole meaning of providence generally is to be found in the covenant of grace: providence reflects what happens in the covenant, provides the place for its occurrence, serves it, and is thereby thoroughly conditioned and determined by it (*CD* III/3, pp. 26, 36–8, 40f.). 'There is no other meaning or purpose in history,' since 'the creation of all the reality distinct from God took place on the basis of this proposed covenant and with a view to its execution' (*CD* III/3, p. 36). The goal that God pursues on the special line of salvation history must also be what God pursues on all the other lines of history that surround that special history. In this way, God's special history with Israel, as it finds its fulfilment in God's becoming human in Jesus Christ, becomes the model for God's history with the world generally.

Providence makes clear how the world's relation with God reflects what is apparent about it in Christ: that God has a partnership with creatures that calls for their free and active responses, that this is a fellowship that includes conflict, and that, despite this conflict, God remains faithful to those loving intentions which God's fellowship with us primarily expresses. In contradistinction to creation, then, which is God's once and for all bringing of the world into existence, providence concerns God's upholding of the world against threats of chaos and destruction so that it continues over time; it concerns God's interactions with creatures who also act and the fact that, in this history with the world, God does not merely hold chaos and destruction at bay, but directs the world for a loving purpose. In providence, the world comes under God's use and is shown to be the sort of world that can be so used – a world with a history. God preserves, accompanies, and rules the world – the three rubrics under which Barth discusses providence – as these forms of God's providence reflect in a wider sphere God's action in Christ to save creatures threatened by sin and death.

Preservation, in particular, expresses the patient faithfulness of God's loving intentions, which are so clear in Christ. Through human sin, forces of chaos and destruction actively threaten the world, but God does not leave the world to its own devices; God does not let the world destroy itself, but actively works to keep these forces at bay. By such means, the world remains so that Christ may come into it (*CD* III/1, p. 380). Preservation is not a continual creation, a stepping in and out of existence by God's hands; the world has, instead, a constancy to match the constancy of God's eternal intentions for it (*CD* III/3, pp. 68f.). Because threatened, its preservation is, moreover, a kind of deliverance that imitates the deliverance to come in Christ (*CD* III/3, p. 78).

The structure of God's accompaniment of creatures who act also mirrors God's action in Christ. That structure is formally quite similar to Thomas Aquinas' account of divine concursus – divine action with creatures who also act. God's action for creatures always precedes the creature's own action: the creature's action is always only a response to what God has already done for it. This sequence, or order of call and response, is irreversible, and in that sense one must say that God's action is never conditioned by the creature's action. The creature is, moreover, most itself and properly free only when its actions so follow God's primary action for it.

Barth makes this abstract structure reflect fellowship in Christ through his use of language of personal relationship: God's initiative and the creature's response assume the form of direction and obedient acknowledgment or the call and response of love (*CD* III/3, p. 107). Barth also uses God's incarnation in Jesus Christ to develop and explain the structure of divine accompaniment. Although what happens in Christ happens nowhere else – in the sense that no other creature is God – something like it happens everywhere. The precedence of divine action in the account of accompaniment reflects the precedence of the Son of God as agent in Barth's understanding of the way God becomes human for our salvation, for our exaltation in fellowship with God. There is nothing to the man Jesus Christ – the man Jesus has no existence at all – before the Son of God actively assumes his human nature. Existing only in the Son of God, all that Jesus Christ does as a human being reflects that prior fact. What happens on the human side of Jesus Christ – his exaltation as a man, meaning by that his service in God's reconciling work, his participation in God's Lordship – always happens only as a consequence of what the Son of God already does in him – become human. If one must affirm that Jesus, insofar as he is genuinely and truly human, is perfectly himself as a human being and therefore perfectly free in this sort of following after God's initiative, why deny the same sort of being themselves and freedom in obedience to creatures of the world generally with whom God also engages (though without becoming them)?

Finally, on the topic of God's rule over the world, like what happens in Christ, the creatures' correspondence to God's operations takes the form of service: the response of creatures follows God's call so that creatures serve God's plans. God's accompaniment of creatures who act is therefore not without character or direction – no more here than in Jesus. Rather, the God of Jesus 'bends their activity to the execution of His own will of grace, subordinating their operations to the specific operations which constitute the history of the covenant of grace' (*CD* III/3, p. 105). Just as the man Jesus executes God's reconciling intentions for the world, the world as a whole serves in its way the history of the covenant. In that fashion, the whole world exists under God's Lordship: the history of the world is arranged for the sake of the covenant fulfilled in Christ, in order to support or reflect it (on the sides of both its Yes and its No).

God directs or controls the effects of creaturely action for such ends through a form of divine precedence that neither takes the place of the creature's action, nor mechanically compels it, nor works with it as one act among others. By means of such precedence, God makes the acts of creatures God's own without jeopardizing their integrity. The model again is Christ in his divinity and humanity. The hypostatic union means that one should see the Son of God as the agent of everything that happens in Christ. This is a precedence of divine agency on a different plane from the mutual determinations of Christ's divine and human natures, in which God has God's being for us as the one who comes into our circumstances of sin and death to reconcile us, and humanity has its being for God as the one exalted to participation in God's reconciling work. The Son of God, in short, controls these mutual determinations and in that way their irreversible relationship is made clear: the man Jesus is exalted in relation to God only because the Son of God humiliates himself in his relation to us. The Son of God does not become less than God by taking such action; such action, indeed, proves divinity in the sense of demonstrating a genuine lordship over the usual disjunction between strength and power within the world. Nor is the humanity of Christ altered in that some God-like or exceptional human capacities are added on to it. The exceptional character of Jesus' humanity is simply a product of the exceptional fact that the Son of God gives his own existence to it. Since there is nothing to Jesus apart from it, that exceptional fact has as its consequence a perfect correspondence between the action of this man Jesus and the Son of God's obedience to the Father: this man's dying on the cross, in other words, serves God's purpose of reconciling us to him. Indeed, in the events of Jesus' life the two operations are one: this man's dying on the cross *is* God's reconciling of us. One is talking about the same events, and not different ones, when one says that God entered into our situation of sin and death, and the human was exalted in Christ. If God is who God is in Jesus, God should be at work everywhere in much the same way: directing, in an irresistible but non-coercive fashion, a history between God and creatures whereby the two are one in act yet remain completely themselves. In short: no synergism (as if God and creatures were agents on the same plane); no monism (as if God were the only actor); no determinism (as if God pulled creatures away from their own best inclinations).

Barth thinks his account of providence renders traditional versions of it more concrete and sure. This is the Father of the Son we are talking about here, the King of Israel who shows Lordship in patient mercy and in wrath only for the sake of love, the God who conquers sin and death by graciously taking on himself the world's miserable circumstances. With that God in mind, the doctrines begin to make sense and become existentially meaningful. Barth suggests this is especially true for ideas of divine accompaniment and rule. Hindering their acceptance is the abstract thought of some other God at work here and not the God of love – and some other creature besides the one that God loves in Christ. Without a christological treatment of these doctrines, fear breaks out over God's precedence. One fears God is a tyrant suppressing the creature's own initiatives and freedom. One either rejects such a God, or submits hopelessly to a blind fate, or tries desperately to find room for action of the creature that is not a reaction to God's prior movement towards it and which therefore conditions God's own initiatives (*CD* III/3, pp. 115–17).

Dispelling such fears is what the doctrine of providence is all about (*CD* III/3, pp. 240f.). Understanding both God and creatures in Christ, one can be assured that the world is a place where God's mercy, wisdom, and goodness finally reign. Only in Christ is it sure that the world will be preserved, that God works in it for the creatures' good, and that forces of chaos and destruction will not triumph within it.

In conclusion, it might be fitting to ask about the significance of creation and providence for eschatology, for the way things will finally be in Christ. Because Barth reads everything in the light of Christ, his treatment of the world has an anthropocentric cast – it centres on human beings because, after all, Jesus Christ is human. It is important to remember, however, that Christ is to have a worldwide effect – not only on all people, but on the whole world. The consummation of the world will be as extensive as its beginnings in creation and providence. The world is for the glorification of God, the self-manifestation of God in what is not God. That process begins with creation, continues in a historical fellowship of God with a particular people, Israel, and ends with Jesus as the one through whom the whole world will show forth God in unity with God. Human beings have a special role to play in that only they can explicitly witness to Christ through their whole being as creatures of self-determined response; they are God's only partners as beings who knowingly and freely respond. But this privilege of human beings does not exclude other creatures from having their end in Christ; it merely specifies the manner of their inclusion (see *CD* III/1, p. 187). As Israel mediated participation in fellowship with God to the nations, so humanity has its hope in Christ in indissoluble connection with the hope of the whole cosmos (*CD* III/1, p. 238). Through Christ's church that forms in the manner of explicit witness, the whole world that (as we have seen) is full of signs and intimations of Him will become a kind of witness of the triune God in its own right. 'We have always to remember that God's glory really consists in His self-giving, and that this has its centre and meaning in God's Son, Jesus Christ, and that the name of Jesus Christ stands for the event in which man, and in man the whole of creation, is awakened and called and enabled to participate in the being of God' (*CD* II/1, p. 670). 'It is from this point of view that all His creatures are to be viewed ... [F]ar from having their existence of themselves and their meaning in themselves, they have their being and existence in the movement of the divine self-glorification, in the transition to them of His immanent joyfulness' (*CD* II/1, p. 648). The signs of Christ in creation and providence are even now transformed by Christ's coming so that, no longer hidden in their function as signs, they fully participate in the revelation or self-manifestation of God, God's communication of what God is to what is not God. As the light of Jesus Christ 'rises and shines, it is reflected in the being and existence of the cosmos which is not created accidentally, but with a view to this action and therefore to this revelation. As it shines in the cosmos, it kindles the lights with which the latter is furnished, giving them the power to shine in its service' (*CD* IV/3, p. 153; see also pp. 159, 163f.; and *CD* III/3, p. 159).

Further reading

Hunsinger, G., 'Double Agency as a Test Case', in *How to Read Karl Barth* (Oxford: Oxford University Press, 1991), pp. 185–224.

Moltmann, J., 'Creation, Covenant and Glory', in *History and the Triune God* (New York: Crossroads, 1992), pp. 125–42.

Santmire, H. P., *The Travail of Nature* (Philadelphia: Fortress Press, 1985), pp. 145–55.

Webster, J., 'Creation and Reconciliation', in *Barth's Ethics of Reconciliation* (Cambridge: Cambridge University Press, 1995), pp. 59–98.

Whitehouse, W. A., *Creation, Science and Theology: Essays in Response to Karl Barth* (Grand Rapids: Eerdmans, 1981).

8 Karl Barth's Christology

Its basic Chalcedonian character

GEORGE HUNSINGER

'*In Christ two natures met to be thy cure.*'[1] When George Herbert wrote these words, he captured the essence of Chalcedonian Christology, with all its strange complexity and simplicity, in a single elegant line. It is sometimes overlooked that the interest behind Chalcedonian Christology has always been largely soteriological. Herbert's line, however, makes the point very well. It is the saving work of Christ – *to be thy cure* – which serves as the guiding intention behind the Chalcedonian definition of Christ's person, just as the definition of his person (following Herbert) – *in Christ two natures met* – serves as the crucial premise of Christ's saving work. Change the definition of Christ's person – make him less than fully God and fully human at the same time – and the saving cure Christ offers changes drastically as well. In other words, just as it makes no sense to have a high view of Christ's person without an equally high view of his work, so a high view of Christ's work – in particular, of his saving death – cannot be sustained without a suitably high view of his person. The work presupposes the person just as the person conditions the work.[2]

Much in this saving work depends, furthermore, on how *in Christ two natures met*; in other words, on how his natures are defined and related. It has not always been appreciated just how minimalist the historic Chalcedonian definition really is in this respect. Chalcedonian Christology does not isolate a point on a line that one either occupies or not. It demarcates a region in which there is more than one place to take up residence. The region is defined by certain distinct boundaries. Jesus Christ is understood as 'one person in two natures'. The two natures – his deity and his humanity – are seen as internal to his person. He is not merely a human being with a special relationship to God, nor is he merely a divine being in the guise of a phantom humanity. He is, in the language of Chalcedon, a single person who is at once 'complete in deity' and 'complete in humanity'. The restraint in these predications, astonishing as they are, is significant. No definition is given of either Christ's deity or his humanity except that, whatever else they might entail, they are present in him in a way that is unabridged, perfect, and complete. Further specifications of his 'deity' and his 'humanity' are not ruled out, but neither are they supplied.[3]

Two observations are in order here. First, from a Chalcedonian point of view, any definition of Christ's two natures that does not meet this minimal standard will fail, because it will not be sufficient for understanding Christ's saving work. Other features of his humanity and his deity will no doubt prove also to be greatly important, but unless both of the natures in Christ's person are seen as complete in themselves, no adequate account can be given of his saving significance. Second, this minimalism suggests that the Chalcedonian definition is not determined exclusively by soteriological interests. It is also largely a hermeneutical construct. It attempts to articulate the deep structure of the New Testament in its witness to the person of Christ. It arises from an ecclesial reading of the New Testament, taken as a whole, and then leads back to it again. It offers a framework for reading to guide the church as it interprets the multifaceted depiction of Jesus Christ contained in the New Testament.

The minimalism of Chalcedon, in other words, is not only constitutive but also regulative. It is constitutive with respect to salvation, and regulative with respect to interpretation. More precisely, it is constitutive regarding Christ's person in the work of salvation, and regulative for the church in its interpretation of Scripture. As a hermeneutical construct in particular, Chalcedon offers no more and no less than a set of spectacles for bringing the central witness of the New Testament into focus. It suggests that just because Jesus was fully God, that does not mean he was not also fully human; and that just because he was fully human, that does not mean he was not also fully God. When the New Testament depicts Jesus in his divine power, status, and authority, it presupposes his humanity; and when it depicts him in his human finitude, weakness, and mortality, it presupposes his deity. No interpretation will be adequate which asserts the one at the expense of the other.

A Chalcedonian reading is guided not only by a minimalist definition of Christ's two natures in themselves, to be fleshed out more thoroughly by attending to the New Testament itself, but also by a certain conception of how these two natures are related in one and the same person. Chalcedon proposes that when Christ's two natures met, they did so 'without separation or division' and 'without confusion or change'. Neither his deity nor his humanity surrendered their defining characteristics, and yet they converged to form an indissoluble unity. Again the Chalcedonian formulations are notable for their open-textured reticence. Note that they are negatively rather than positively phrased. Neither separation nor confusion is tolerable. No more is said about how Christ's two natures are related than to rule out these unacceptable extremes. Each nature retained its integrity while engaging the other in the closest of communions. The relation of Christ's two natures, as stated by Chalcedon, suggests an abiding mystery of their unity-in-distinction and distinction-in-unity.

In short, any Chalcedonian Christology that is true to type will display certain basic features. It will see Jesus Christ as 'one person in two natures'. It will regard him as at once 'complete in deity' and 'complete in humanity'. And it will hold that when these two natures met in Christ, they did so 'without separation or division' and yet also 'without confusion or change'.

Although Karl Barth offers one of the most fully elaborated Chalcedonian Christologies ever to have appeared in Christian doctrine, his Christology has been regularly classified otherwise, and indeed in diametrically opposite ways. The two basic alternatives to Chalcedonian Christology are, of course, the Alexandrian and the Antiochian types. At this point matters become tricky, because there are in fact relatively Alexandrian ways to be Chalcedonian as there are also relatively Antiochian ways. The categorical boundaries, in other words, are fluid and can shade off into matters of degree. The centrifugal force involved in Chalcedon's key affirmations makes a certain grey area seem inevitable. 'Complete in deity' and 'complete in humanity', after all, repel one another like two identical magnetic poles. Even the most conscientious Chalcedonian effort is likely to veer off at some point in an Alexandrian or an Antiochian direction. Nevertheless, there are Alexandrian and Antiochian extremes that Chalcedon was designed to avoid. It is often thought, however, that these extremes represent in a blatant form certain tendencies endemic to the types as a whole. When Barth's Christology has been classified as other than Chalcedonian, it is alleged that he succumbs to one or another of these tendencies or extremes.

Chalcedon, as has been shown, basically sets forth two terms and a relationship. The terms are 'deity' and 'humanity', and their relationship is one of 'unity-in-distinction' within one and the same person. Extreme versions of Alexandrian and Antiochian Christology (at least when seen from a Chalcedonian point of view) define at least one of the terms deficiently, or their relationship deficiently, or both. For our purposes, it will not be necessary to explore every single area and degree of possible deficiency. Only two are relevant for understanding the existing allegations that what we have is a non-Chalcedonian Barth.

'Docetism' is the extreme or subtle Alexandrian tendency that stresses Jesus' deity at the expense of his humanity. His humanity is in effect no longer real but merely apparent. It is so overpowered by its union with his deity that it ends up being less than 'complete'. The union between the two natures finally obliterates their distinction. Jesus becomes the kind of divine being with a phantom humanity that Chalcedon wanted to rule out. When Barth's Christology is classified as 'Alexandrian', or when it is criticized for being 'docetic', the allegation is that Barth's conception of Christ's humanity is deficient.

'Nestorianism', on the other hand, is the extreme or subtle Antiochian tendency that has much the opposite result. It stresses Jesus' humanity at the expense of his deity. Although it thinks of Jesus as in some sense 'divine', it does not think of him as 'complete in deity'. It does not see the union of his two 'natures' as being internal to his 'person'. Rather it sees the 'divinity' of Jesus as arising from the special character of his union as a human person with God. His 'divinity' is more nearly adjectival than substantive, not intrinsic but participatory. His union with God is fundamentally extrinsic to the constitution of his person, for his person is that of a human being. No matter how elevated by virtue of this union he may be, no matter how 'divine', he is in himself never more than 'fully human', and thus never also 'fully God'. When Barth's Christology is classified as 'Antiochian', or when it is criticized for being 'Nestorian', the allegation is that Barth's conception of Jesus' union with God, and thus of Jesus' complete and intrinsic 'deity', is deficient.

No brief essay such as this could possibly sort through all the relevant texts and all the relevant issues, which are often finally quite technical, in order to demonstrate that the charges against Barth for being non-Chalcedonian do not stand up. Only some fairly general points of clarification and orientation can be offered. One point, however, has been almost universally overlooked. Barth is probably the first theologian in the history of Christian doctrine who alternates back and forth, deliberately, between an 'Alexandrian' and an 'Antiochian' idiom. The proper way to be Chalcedonian in Christology, Barth believed, was to follow the lead of the New Testament itself by employing a definite diversity of idioms. Any other strategy for articulating the Chalcedonian mystery would inevitably have unbalanced or one-sided results. Because Barth wanted to do justice to the whole mystery of Christ's person, as complete no less in deity than in humanity, he boldly set out to construct a large-scale collage, so to speak, out of seemingly incompatible materials.

The point of Christology, Barth believed, is to comprehend the incomprehensibility of the incarnation precisely in its incomprehensibility. The New Testament, he suggested, directs us to this incomprehensibility by the very way that it juxtaposes two different modes of depiction. On the one hand, Jesus of Nazareth is depicted as the Son of God; and on the other, the Son of God is depicted as Jesus of Nazareth. The one mode is illustrated by the synoptic tradition; the other, by the Johannine tradition. The conclusion Barth drew is significant: 'It is impossible to listen at one and the same time to the two statements that Jesus of Nazareth is the Son of God, and that the Son of God is Jesus of Nazareth. One hears either the one or the other or one hears nothing. When one is heard, the other can be heard only indirectly, in faith' (*CD* I/1, p. 180). No harmonization of these different statements would be either possible or desirable. Although both, it is important to note, speak of the humanity and deity of Jesus Christ, they do so 'with such varying interests and emphases' that we can only 'misunderstand both' if we try to select merely the one while discarding the other, or else to smooth away the unresolved tensions between them (ibid.). The alternative that Barth proposed was actually to retain and uphold the tensions through a strategy of juxtaposition (thus emulating the strategy of the New Testament itself).

Adopting a strategy of juxtaposition meant surrendering the deeply ingrained expectation that the mystery of the incarnation could be contained by a conceptual scheme. The name of Jesus Christ, Barth commented, 'is not a system representing a unified experience or a unified thought; it is the Word of God itself' (*CD* I/1, p. 181). It points to a *Novum* in human experience and human history which cannot be understood on the basis of what is generally the case, but only on the basis of itself. The *Novum* of the incarnation is so unique that (contrary to someone like Kierkegaard) it cannot even be explained as an absurdity, for that would imply not only that the limits of our minds can circumscribe God's rationality, but also that we are in a position to know in advance what is possible or impossible for God. 'The Incarnation is inconceivable', Barth wrote, 'but it is not absurd, and it must not be explained as an absurdity' (*CD* I/2, p. 160). It is rather to be understood as something that, for all its inconceivability, actually took place in and by the freedom of God.

What makes Barth's Christology different from Alexandrian and Antiochian Christologies is mainly that these two alternatives, each in its own way, tend to resolve the incarnational mystery into something more nearly conceivable on the basis of ordinary experience and history. They opt for the unified thought at the expense of the ineffable actuality. Yet once the project of constructing a fully cohesive system is abandoned, the relative value of each can be appreciated and retained. 'The christologies of Alexandria and Antioch', Barth stated, '. . . mutually supplement and explain each other and to that extent remain on peaceful terms.' 'We are dealing with testimonies to one reality, which though contrary to one another, do not dispute or negate one another.' In their original New Testament forms, 'their relations are so interlocked, that if we are to understand one we must first do justice to the other and *vice versa*'. Certainly no 'systematic unity or principle' can be found that will eliminate the antithesis at stake in saying that Jesus was 'complete in deity' and 'complete in humanity' at the same time (*CD* I/2, p. 24). But by speaking now in an 'Alexandrian' idiom, and now again in an 'Antiochian' idiom, by switching back and forth between them dialectically, Barth hoped to provide as descriptively adequate an account as might be possible of an event that was, by definition, inherently ineffable.

The reason why a non-Chalcedonian Christology has been imputed to Barth, one way or the other, would seem to be rooted mainly in a failure to appreciate that he employs a dialectical strategy of juxtaposition.[4] The discussion is always jinxed when one or the other prong in Barth's two-sided dialectic is seized upon in isolation as if it could stand for his Christology as a whole.[5] However, it might still be wondered whether Barth did not finally leave us with the worst of both worlds. When speaking in an Alexandrian idiom, did he not offer a deficient view of Christ's humanity; and when speaking in an Antiochian idiom, did he not in turn offer a deficient view of Christ's deity? Although at some point these become questions with complex ramifications, at least something can be said in response without foreclosing the need for a fuller and more technical discussion.

The charge that Barth's Alexandrian idiom offers a deficient view of Christ's humanity does not, at first, seem to rest on especially technical considerations. It seems to rest mainly on an intuition that Jesus' humanity cannot really be 'complete' if Jesus is also 'complete in deity'. Jesus' humanity, it is said, cannot be 'complete' unless his will is 'independent' of God's will. If the relation of Jesus' will to God's will is seen as one of 'absolute dependence', and if this relation is seen as internal to Jesus' constitution as a 'person', then Jesus cannot possibly be 'complete in humanity'.[6] There are at least two questions here. One is how to conceive of the relation between divine and human agency in general, and of their relation in the incarnation in particular; the other is how we can know what really constitutes 'complete' humanity.

Barth's answer involves the rejection of a hidden premise. If 'two natures' Christology is valid, as Barth assumes, on the basis of the New Testament as interpreted by the Fourth Ecumenical Council (Chalcedon), then it does not seem unreasonable to give up the expectation that the 'person' of Christ can be grasped by a 'unified thought'. Yet the objection seems to cling to such an improper expectation, for in effect it demands a 'principle' that will 'explain' just how Jesus can be the kind of person that Chalcedon describes. By definition, Barth holds, no such principle is either possible or necessary, except for the freedom of God, which makes the Incarnation possible in such a way that Jesus' full humanity is in fact upheld rather than compromised (as the New Testament narratives themselves plausibly attest). Moreover, on the same grounds (Chalcedon), it does not seem unreasonable to suppose that we do not know in the abstract what 'deity' and 'humanity' really mean, but that we must learn to understand them in the light of the incarnation itself, which first shows us what true deity and true humanity really are in their fullness, rather than the reverse (i.e., understanding the incarnation in the light of prior definitions of 'deity' and 'humanity'). While much more could be said, these are the main lines of response. 'Complete in humanity', Barth contends, needs to be defined on the basis of the incarnation itself, and no conception of divine and human agency will be adequate which rejects seeing their relation (with the integrity of each term) as a fully ineffable actuality, grounded in the freedom of God.[7]

The diametrically opposite charge – that Barth is 'Nestorian' in Christology – has also been alleged. Barth is said to be 'Nestorian' on the grounds that he offers a deficient view of Christ's deity in which the union of Christ's humanity with God is seen as external to the constitution of Christ's person. This charge, too, seems to rest mainly on a failure to appreciate Barth's dialectical strategy of juxtaposition.[8] Barth ventures that, from one perspective, Jesus of Nazareth, who is in himself no less 'complete' in deity than in humanity, can nonetheless be described in his humanity as the perfect covenant partner of God. Although Barth never deploys this perspective without careful qualification and supplementation, he does expound it by speaking of Jesus in his humanity as 'attesting', 'corresponding to', 'representing', or otherwise standing in 'analogy' to God. When all Barth's dialectical and substantive countermoves are disregarded, his discourse in this idiom can be flattened into 'Nestorianism'. Taken in isolation, this way of foregrounding Christ's humanity can be construed (or better, misconstrued) as though his humanity stood for a 'person' who was separate from and other than God.

When everything is taken into account, however, it is hard to see how Barth could reasonably be charged with teaching that the relation of Jesus Christ to God, and thus of Christ's two natures, is 'exclusively analogical'.[9] Such a criticism would be something like wresting a postcard from a stereoscope and declaiming, 'See! It's not really three-dimensional after all!' In a way that seems compatible with the Sixth Ecumenical Council (which affirmed that Christ's having two 'natures' entailed his also having two 'wills'),[10] Barth teaches: 'In the work of the one Jesus Christ everything is at one and the same time, but distinctly, both divine and human' (*CD* IV/2, p. 117). The relation of double agency, of divine and human willing, in the person of Christ is thus not only one of 'coordination in difference' (*CD* IV/2, p. 116), but also one of 'mutual participation' for the sake of a common and single work (*communicatio operationum*) (*CD* IV/2, p. 117). When in Christ's person two natures, and thus also two wills or operations, met, they did so not merely analogically or externally, but in a relation of mutual participation, indwelling or *koinonia*, and thus in a Chalcedonian unity-in-distinction and distinction-in-unity (*CD* IV/1, p. 126).

Barth counts on it that his readers will understand him only if they read dialectically. Fair-minded readers will grant his premise, at least for the sake of argument, that a 'systematic conspectus' of the incarnation is impossible. They will not discount him when he posits that although two different statements are equally necessary (that 'Jesus of Nazareth is the Son of God' and that 'the Son of God is Jesus of Nazareth'), we are simply incapable of listening 'to both at the same time', but can only listen 'either to the one or the other at the one time' (*CD* I/1, p. 180). Whether agreeing with him or not, they will at least take seriously the special nuance that he finds in the New Testament understanding of faith. Faith, he remarks, means seeing 'the validity of each [statement] in the other'. Faith means 'the perception either way of what is not said' (ibid.). 'We can listen only to the one [statement] or the other', he reasons, 'registering what is said by the one or the other, and then, in and in spite of the concealment, we can in faith hear the other in the one' (*CD* I/1, p. 181 rev.). Judicious readers will at least appreciate that Barth has made a fresh, thoughtful, and distinguished attempt to be Chalcedonian in Christology precisely by speaking now in an Alexandrian, and now again in an Antiochian, voice.[11]

In conclusion, at least something might be said, however sketchily, about certain other far-reaching innovations that Barth made in constructing Christology within the premises of Chalcedon. First, he actualized the traditional conception of the incarnation. Second, he personalized the saving significance of Christ's death. Finally, he contemporized the consequences of Christ's resurrection.

The incarnation, Barth argued, is best understood as a concrete history, not as an abstract state of being. The person of Jesus Christ, who is at once truly God and yet also truly human, does not exist apart from his work, nor his work apart from his person. Rather, his unique person is *in* his work even as his saving work is *in* his person. 'His being as this One is his history, and his history is this being' (*CD* IV/1, p. 128). The incarnation is the event which occurs in the 'identity' of his truly human action with his truly divine action (*CD* IV/2, p. 99). 'He acts as God when he acts as a human being, and as a human being when he acts as God' (*CD* IV/2, p. 115 rev.). The incarnation, the meeting of two natures in Christ, is what occurred as he enacted his saving history. Although his deity and his humanity were actual from the very outset (*conceptus de Spiritu Sancto!*), their union was never essentially static. It was a state of being in the process of becoming.

This apparently simple thesis illustrates how Barth's Chalcedonian Christology managed to be resoundingly traditional and brilliantly innovative at the same time. The divine and human identity of Jesus Christ in its historical enactment had to be taken seriously, Barth urged, as a qualitative and indivisible whole. It would not do to understand the significance of Christ's singular identity by dividing it up into parts. The humiliation of Jesus Christ, to take a key example, was not to be separated, whether chronologically or ontologically, from his exaltation. Rather, both were to be conceived as occurring together simultaneously in the course of their enactment. The humiliation of the Son of God took place in and with the exaltation of the Son of Man.[12] Humiliation and exaltation were regarded as two ways of looking at the incarnation as a whole, not as two different stages in sequence. 'It was God who went into the far country, and it is the human creature who returns home. Both took place in the one Jesus Christ' (*CD* IV/2, p. 21 rev.). God was in Christ, humbling himself for the good of the creature, even as the human creature was exalted on the basis of that self-humiliation. 'It is not . . . a matter of two different and successive actions, but of a single action in . . . the being and history of the one Jesus Christ' (*CD* IV/2, p. 21). But since this simultaneity could not be grasped by a 'unified thought', Barth again resorted to his dialectical strategy of juxtaposition.[13] The received tradition of Christ's two 'states' (humiliation and exaltation) was thereby subjected to a powerful and ingenious restatement whose strengths and weaknesses have yet to be adequately assessed.[14]

The history of Christ's humiliation and exaltation culminates in his death. 'His death on the cross was and is the fulfilment of . . . the humiliation of the Son of God and exaltation of the Son of man' (*CD* IV/2, pp. 140f.). It is the moment of their supreme simultaneity. 'It is only then – not before – that there did and does take place the realization of the final depth of humiliation, the descent into hell of Jesus Christ the Son of God, but also his supreme exaltation, the triumphant coronation of Jesus Christ the Son of man' (*CD* IV/2, p. 141). As he died the death of the sinner, the Son of God entered the nadir of his humiliation for our sakes, even as his exaltation as the Son of man attained its zenith in that sinless obedience which, having freely embraced the cross, would be crowned by eternal life. His humiliation was always the basis of his exaltation, even as his exaltation was always the goal of his humiliation, and both were supremely one in his death on our behalf. 'It was in this way that the reconciliation of the world with God was accomplished in the unity of his being' (CD IV/2, p. 141 rev.).

The saving significance of Christ's death cannot be adequately understood, Barth proposes, if legal or juridical considerations are allowed to take precedence over those that are more merciful or compassionate. Although God's grace never occurs without judgment, nor God's judgment without grace, in Jesus Christ it is always God's grace, Barth believes, that is decisive. Therefore, although the traditional themes of punishment and penalty are not eliminated from Barth's account of Christ's death, they are displaced from being central or predominant.

> The decisive thing is not that he has suffered what we ought to have suffered so that we do not have to suffer it, the destruction to which we have fallen victim by our guilt, and therefore the punishment which we deserve. This is true, of course. But it is true only as it derives from the decisive thing that in the suffering and death of Jesus Christ it has come to pass that in his own person he has made an end of us as sinners and therefore of sin itself by going to death as the one who took our place as sinners. In his person he has delivered up us sinners and sin itself to destruction. (CD IV/1, p. 253)

The uncompromising judgment of God is seen in the suffering love of the cross. Because this judgment is uncompromising, the sinner is delivered up to the death and destruction which sin inevitably deserves. Yet because this judgment is carried out in the person of Jesus Christ, very God and very man, it is borne only to be removed and borne away. 'In the deliverance of sinful man and sin itself to destruction, which he accomplished when he suffered our punishment, he has on the other side blocked the source of our destruction' (CD IV/1, p. 254). By taking our place as sinners before God, 'he has seen to it that we do not have to suffer what we ought to suffer; he has removed the accusation and condemnation and perdition which had passed upon us; he has cancelled their relevance to us; he has saved us from destruction and rescued us from eternal death' (ibid.). The cross reveals an abyss of sin swallowed up by the depths of suffering divine love.

By virtue of his unique person, Christ was in a position to take our place in both a positive and a negative sense. As the Son of Man, he effected our reconciliation with God by living as the true covenant partner whom God had always sought but never found. He thus fulfilled the meaning of human existence as intended in the election of Israel. As the Son of God, on the other hand, he gave a universal significance and depth to his reconciling work that would not have obtained had he been no more than a human being. As the Son of God incarnate, 'he has the omnipotence in the power of this work to bear our sins, to bear them away from us, to suffer the consequences of our sins, to be the just One for us sinners, to forgive us our sins' (*CD* IV/1, p. 235). Barth thus retains the tradition of Christ's 'active' and 'passive' obedience. They, too, occur simultaneously and pertain to Christ's history as a whole. As the Son of Man, Christ did right at the very place where we had done wrong (active obedience). As the Son of God, he suffered our punishment in order to remove it once and for all (passive obedience) (*CD* IV/1, p. 237). The righteousness fulfilled in his death, through his active and passive obedience, secured the triumph of grace.

The reconciling work of Christ is thus presented from two perspectives, both of which are rooted in the unique constitution of his enacted person as complete in deity and complete in humanity. He is the priestly Son of God who ventured into the far country of sin and death that he might suffer their desolation in our place and bear it away. He is also, at the same time, the royal Son of Man who is exalted to homecoming with God by virtue of his covenant faithfulness, his unbroken obedience, even to the point of embracing a shameful and violent death. Although the righteousness of the Law is fulfilled in his person, both actively and passively, it is essentially his person and not the Law, his compassion, not his vicarious punishment, that determines his saving significance. He completely embraces our destruction, carrying us to death in his death, that we might be raised in and with him to newness of life.

This dual, dialectical perspective extends, finally, into Barth's discussion of Christ's resurrection. Just as the cross represents the fulfilment of Jesus Christ's life history as the history of reconciliation, so his resurrection represents the fulfilment of that same life history as the history of God's Self-revelation. Reconciliation and revelation (and therefore love and knowledge) are always deeply interconnected in Barth's theology, never dissociated.[15] 'Revelation takes place in and with reconciliation. Indeed, the latter is also revelation. As God acts in it he also speaks . . . Yet the relationship is indissoluble from the other side as well. Revelation takes place as the revelation of reconciliation' (*CD* IV/3, p. 8). In other words, revelation culminates in Christ's resurrection much as reconciliation culminates in his cross. The reconciliation fulfilled by Christ's death is the very substance manifested in the revelation at once fulfilled and yet inaugurated by his resurrection.

Because reconciliation can only be described dialectically as divine humiliation for the sake of human exaltation, revelation as the heart of the resurrection requires an equally dialectical mode of explication. From one perspective, Christ's resurrection reveals reconciliation as the humiliation of God's Son in human flesh. From this standpoint, the resurrection is 'the great verdict of God'. It fulfils and proclaims 'God's decision concerning the cross'. It shows that God accepts the cross as the self-abasing act of compassion in which God's Son, for the sake of the world, 'fulfilled the divine wrath . . . in the service of divine grace' (*CD* IV/1, p. 309). From the other perspective, however, Christ's resurrection reveals that reconciliation must also be seen as the exaltation of the Son of Man. 'What is revealed is that in his identity with the Son of God this man was the Lord' (*CD* IV/2, p. 151). Faithful to God even unto the cross, this man is raised again, exalted and revealed as 'the reconciliation of the world with God, and therefore the new humanity, the dawning of the new creation, the beginning of the new world' (*CD* IV/2, p. 145 rev.). In his resurrection, this man is revealed as the Lord and Saviour of the world.

While Barth accepts the full 'historicity' of Christ's resurrection,[16] he puts the accent in another place. He does not allow the question of historicity (a peculiarly modern obsession) to obscure the resurrection's chief theological significance. Christ's resurrection means, above all, that the reconciliation Christ accomplished enjoys eternal reality and significance. That reconciliation itself, Barth holds, is 'intrinsically perfect' and complete (*CD* IV/3, pp. 7, 327). 'It does not need to be transcended or augmented by new qualities or further developments. The humiliation of God and the exaltation of humankind as they took place in him are the completed fulfilment of the covenant, the completed reconciliation of the world with God' (*CD* IV/2, p. 132 rev.). Reconciliation is eternally valid as a living, indivisible whole, because Christ is risen from the dead.

What needs to happen – and in Christ's resurrection and ascension what does happen – is for this reconciliation to be made contemporaneous with the rest of history. Easter involves Christ's 'transition to a presence which is eternal and therefore embraces all times' (*CD* IV/1, p. 318). 'His history did not become dead history. It was history in his time to become as such eternal history – the history of God with the human beings of all times, and therefore taking place here and now as it did then' (*CD* IV/1, pp. 313f. rev.). 'He is present here and now for us in the full efficacy of what . . . he was and did then and there' (*CD* IV/1, p. 291). The resurrection means Christ's 'real presence' to us now, and 'our contemporaneity to him' in what he so perfectly accomplished then in our stead (*CD* IV/1, p. 348). It means 'the contemporaneity of Jesus Christ with us and of us with him' (*CD* IV/2, p. 291). It makes him 'the Contemporary of all human beings' (*CD* III/2, p. 440 rev.). Because Christ is risen from the dead, no time or place, no human life, is bereft of the presence (whether manifest or hidden, incognito for the time being or openly known) of the only Mediator and true Advocate between heaven and earth.

In closing, one last point should be noted about the Christology Barth constructed within the premises of Chalcedon. The saving work of Christ, as Barth explicated it, could not possibly have occurred unless in his person he had been both complete in deity and complete in humanity. His incarnational history could not otherwise have been at once the history of our reconciliation with God and of God's Self-revelation to us. Unless two natures had met in Christ 'without separation or division' yet also 'without confusion or change', neither reconciliation nor revelation, as Barth explained them, could have taken place.

Yet Barth discerned one further element in Chalcedon. No symmetry between the two natures that met in Christ was possible. Christ's deity after all was deity, whereas his humanity was merely humanity. The precedence, initiative, and impartation were always necessarily with his deity even as the subsequence, absolute dependence, and pure if active reception were always necessarily with his humanity (*CD* IV/2, p. 116). In this light, from a Chalcedonian viewpoint, the relative superiority of Alexandrian over Antiochian Christologies emerges. For whereas Alexandrian Christology is typically correct on at least two out of three essentials, Antiochian Christology is typically correct on only one. Chalcedon, it will be recalled, sets forth two terms and a relationship. Alexandria is typically correct on one of the terms ('complete in deity') and also about the relationship (deity intrinsic to Christ's person with asymmetrical precedence over his humanity), but Antioch is typically correct about only one of the terms ('complete in humanity'), though its participatory notion of divinity can also allow for a kind of extrinsic asymmetry. That Barth's Christology of dialectical juxtaposition makes this kind of discrimination possible even as it attempts so ingeniously to do justice to all three of the essentials is yet another tribute to its basic Chalcedonian character.

Notes

1 George Herbert, 'An Offering', in *The Life and Works of George Herbert*, vol. II, ed. G. H. Palmer (Boston: Houghton Mifflin, 1905), p. 393 (italics added).

2 This latter sentence, by the way, states a basic rule of all Christology, although as applied here it sheds light on a particular type, namely, the Chalcedonian. In any Christology (at least when internally coherent), the person (*p*) and the work (*w*) of Christ mutually imply each other: If *w*, then *p*; and if *p*, then *w*. Insofar as modern Christology has typically abandoned a high view of Christ's person, it has also abandoned the correspondingly high conception of Christ's saving work that Chalcedonian Christology is meant to sustain. Only a high Christology can state without equivocation, for example, that Jesus Christ is 'the Lamb of God who takes away the sin of the world' (John 1:29). If Christ's saving work consists in no more than his functioning as a spiritual teacher, a moral example, a symbol of religious experience, or even a revered bearer and transmitter of the Holy Spirit, a high or Chalcedonian view of Christ's person is *logically* unnecessary. As modernist Christologies typically evidence (though not always forthrightly), such a saving figure need only be 'fully human' without also being 'fully God'.

3 The wording of the Chalcedonian definition, of course, includes certain elaborations that analytically unpack what it means to say that Christ's deity and his humanity are each 'true' (*alethos*) and 'complete' (*telios*) in themselves. His deity is said to be 'consubstantial' (*homoousios*) with the Father, just as his humanity is said to be 'consubstantial' (*homoousios*) with us. His deity is properly eternal, since he was 'begotten before all ages of the Father', whereas his humanity is properly temporal, since he was 'born of the Virgin Mary' (who is 'the Mother of God' in his humanity). Since his humanity is complete, it consists in 'a reasonable soul and a body' (not in a body alone), and he is 'in all things like us, except without sin'. For the full text of 'The Symbol of Chalcedon' in Greek, Latin, and English, and with notes, see Philip Schaff, *The Creeds of Christendom*, vol. II (New York: Harper and Row, 1931), pp. 62–5.

4 Whereas most of the massive christological discussion in *CD* IV/1 speaks in an 'Alexandrian' idiom offset by the occasional 'Antiochian' counterpoint, the proportions in the equally massive *CD* IV/2 are more or less reversed, while the proportions in *CD* IV/3 are perhaps about equal. In this way Barth attempted to carry out his announced procedure for using the two 'idioms': 'Our task is to hear the second in the first, and the first in the second, and, therefore, in a process of thinking and not in a system, to hear the one [Jesus Christ] in both' (*CD* I/2, p. 25). Note that the ground on which Christology takes shape here is much closer to 'narratology', or the study of narrative structures and strategies, than it is to metaphysics.

5 Although Charles T. Waldrop pays close attention to both strands in Barth's Christology, he thinks that only one of them (the Alexandrian) is basically characteristic. He remains at a loss to account for the other massive strand (the Antiochian) that he cannot deny is also there. Significantly, he never once takes Chalcedon seriously as a christological type. He simply contents himself with a forced option between Alexandria and Antioch. Being essentially a systematizer of the Antiochian type (like so many other modernists), he not only ignores

Barth's repeated, explicit avowals of Chalcedon, but also the dialectical strategy that Barth uses for implementing it. See Waldrop, *Karl Barth's Christology: Its Basic Alexandrian Character* (Berlin: de Gruyter, 1984).

6 Waldrop uses the terms 'complete' and 'independent' interchangeably in this respect. He assumes that no 'person' can be 'complete in deity' and 'complete in humanity' at the same time, on the (question-begging) grounds that no humanity can be complete unless it is constituted as a 'person' that is other than God. See ibid., *passim*, but esp. pp. 172–5.

7 For Barth's principled refusal of 'explanation' in favour of 'description', and for his programmatic allowance for God's freedom by way of dialectical juxtaposition (as opposed to a unified explanatory 'system'), see *CD* I/1, pp. 8f. For some indications of how 'deity' is defined in the light of the incarnation, see *CD* IV/1, pp. 129, 159, 177. For a corresponding way of defining 'humanity', see *CD* IV/1, p. 131 and *CD* III/2, pp. 203–22. For a summary of how Barth views divine and human agency, see G. Hunsinger, *How to Read Karl Barth: The Shape of His Theology* (New York: Oxford University Press, 1991), pp. 185–224.

8 Although Regin Prenter sees that Barth's strategy is dialectical, he lacks the kind of sympathy and imagination that would be required for understanding it. He discerns neither its underlying rationale nor its actual function. There is perhaps something tone-deaf about the way he typically notices and yet misreads Barth's dialectic. He insists on seeing divisions where Barth posits unities, and on seeing fusions where Barth posits distinctions. His argument that the Antiochian strand in Barth's Christology is 'Nestorian' may be found in 'Karl Barths Umbildung der traditionellen Zweinaturlehre in lutherischer Beleuchtung', *Studia Theologia* 11 (1958), pp. 1–88, on pp. 10–43.

9 Prenter repeatedly makes this charge. See, for example, ibid., p. 41.

10 See P. T. R. Gray, *The Defense of Chalcedon in the East* (Leiden: Brill, 1979), pp. 451–553; K. J. von Hefele, *A History of the Christian Councils*, vol. V (Edinburgh: T & T Clark, 1896).

11 For a recent technical assessment of Barth's Christology as 'Chalcedonian', see G. Taxacher, *Trinität und Sprache* (Wurzburg: Echter, 1994), pp. 349–71.

12 In Barth's parlance, the term 'Son of God' is a kind of shorthand for 'the Son of God was Jesus of Nazareth' while the term 'Son of Man' stands for the reverse statement that 'Jesus of Nazareth is the Son of God'.

13 The humiliation of the Son of God is the theme of *CD* IV/1, and the exaltation of the Son of Man is the theme of *CD* IV/2. Note that Barth made a similar move regarding the tradition of Christ's threefold office as prophet, priest, and king. Although the human mind is only capable of considering them *seriatim*, each is always included in the others in such a way that they each pertain simultaneously to Christ's person and work as a whole. Barth took them up one by one, devoting a massive discussion to each: the priestly office in *CD* IV/1, the royal office in *CD* IV/2, and the prophetic office in *CD* IV/3.

14 Barth's moves here would need to be compared carefully to Reformed and Lutheran orthodoxy as well as to Luther and Calvin and to Patristic theologians like Athanasius and Cyril. Although Prenter makes an interesting start in this direction, he is not careful enough to be useful.

15 The discussion and evaluation of Barth in A. E. McGrath's *Iustitia Dei: A History*

of the Christian Doctrine of Justification From 1500 to the Present Day (Cambridge: Cambridge University Press, 1986) is impaired (among other reasons) by the unfortunate assumption that they are indeed dissociated (pp. 170–84). Barth establishes their interconnection unmistakably in *CD* I/1 and constantly reiterates it thereafter all the way through to the end of the *Church Dogmatics*. How could it be otherwise when both reconciliation and revelation find their identity in Jesus Christ, who is himself both of them in one? A similar flaw mars the more recent analysis of Alan Torrance, who fails to appreciate the inseparability Barth establishes between 'knowledge' (*Erkenntnis*) and 'communion' (*Gemeinschaft*) throughout his theology, not only centrally in *CD* II/1 but as early as *CD* I/1. See Torrance, *Persons in Communion: An Essay on Trinitarian Description and Human Participation* (Edinburgh: T & T Clark, 1996). Knowledge of God and love for God, it might be noted, are as inseparable for Barth as they are for Calvin.

16 'The statement that Christ is risen necessarily implies that a dead man is alive again and that his grave is empty' (*CD* IV/2, p. 149). 'The Resurrected is the man Jesus, who now came and went among them as such, whom they saw and touched and heard, who ate and drank with them' (*CD* III/2, p. 448). Like the creation of the world *ex nihilo*, however, this event transcends and exceeds the 'historical' even as it includes it, for it has neither an ordinary historical cause nor an ordinary historical effect. Barth resorts to the term *Geschichte* rather than the term *Historie*, not because he denies the resurrection's historicity, but because in this event 'history' in the modern, Troeltschean sense reaches its categorical limit (*CD* III/2, pp. 446f.).

Further reading

Hunsinger, G., *How to Read Karl Barth. The Shape of his Theology* (Oxford: Oxford University Press, 1991).

Marshall, B., *Christology in Conflict. The Idea of a Saviour in Rahner and Barth* (Oxford: Blackwell, 1987).

Thompson, J., *Christ in Perspective. Christological Perspectives in the Theology of Karl Barth* (Edinburgh: Saint Andrew Press, 1978).

Waldrop, C. T., *Karl Barth's Christology: Its Basic Alexandrian Character* (Berlin: Mouton, 1984).

9 Salvation

COLIN GUNTON

INTRODUCTION

Karl Barth is a systematic theologian in the respect that nothing written in one place is said without implicit or explicit reference to other theological themes. We shall therefore not understand him when he speaks of salvation if we fail to bear in mind something of what he has said about revelation and the Trinity, and above all the doctrine of election. While there may not be a single dogmatic 'centre', in the sense of a single organizing idea, to Barth's theology, there is an overall unity to his conception of God's action. It is that focus on action which supplies both the possibilities for, and the impassable limits of, any systematic theological construction. The realities of and limits to our knowledge of God's action provide the parameters for all human theological speech.

It is further the case that Barth fought a lifelong battle against what he called abstraction: the treatment of any topic out of relation to the fact that the divine action which provides the basis and possibility of theology is action in relation to the world. In Christ, God moves into free and loving relation with the world, particularly the human world, so that any theology that does not bear on ethics broadly conceived – that is to say, any theology without bearing on a life lived before God – is not Christian theology. This second feature in particular has a broad bearing on our topic. First, because Barth is an evangelical theologian – a theologian rooted in the gospel of Jesus Christ – everything that he wrote, certainly in the *Church Dogmatics*, is concerned with salvation: with the end to which human life is directed. As we shall see, the character of that divine action which gives theology its possibilities and limits is primarily saving, rather than, say, creating, action, so that in one sense the whole of Barth's theology is, if not a theology of salvation, at least one directed to the articulation of God's purposes for and realizing of salvation. All the other things that God does – creation, reconciliation, redemption – are, he says, 'grounded and determined in the fact that

God is the God of the eternal election of His grace' (*CD* II/2, p. 14). A second bearing is that because earlier treatments of the relation of Christology to soteriology smacked to Barth of abstraction, in the volume dedicated to reconciliation he attempted a new, non-abstract integration of topics often treated separately as the person and work of Christ. The person of Christ *is* his saving work, so that an adequately articulated Christology will also be a theology of salvation.

What then is meant by salvation? Once one has moved beyond its etymological connotations of health and safety – those two modern substitutes for religion – it is evident that 'salvation' is in central respects an eschatological concept, involving safe and final arrival at one's intended destination. (Intended by whom or what we need not at this stage inquire.) Theologically, it involves some form of relation to God, however differently it is conceived in the various religions and in the different forms of Christian belief. So far as the Christian faith is concerned, there is a range of views, involving at one end ontological views of salvation, in which in some ways the whole being of the person is transformed or completed; and, at the other, more moralizing views in which the relation of the human being to God is reoriented rather than some personal transformation achieved. In this light it is clear that Barth's is not a ' merely' moral view of the matter, for there are clear echoes of the Patristic teaching that in salvation the believer is in some way taken up into the life of the triune God, although it is certainly not right to speak of deification.[1] In any case, because for Barth relation is an ontological category, a change in relation is likely to involve ontology, the being of the saved. It follows, then, that it is more than the merely epistemic conception – of salvation merely in terms of knowledge – sometimes charged. As we have already seen, a concern with ethics in the broadest sense so determines Barth's thought that such accusations can be rejected *a limine* (at the outset), to use an expression much loved by the master himself. We shall look later at why such charges are levelled, but first we must examine something of what he actually says.

EXPOSITION

For Barth, salvation is the fulfilment of a covenant, an eternal covenant, according to which God purposes to bring the human race into reconciled relation with himself. Salvation is reconciliation between God and the human creation whom he loves in Christ:

> 'Reconciliation' in the Christian sense of the word . . . is the history in
> which God concludes and confirms His covenant with man,

maintaining and carrying it to its goal in spite of every threat. It is the history in which God in His own person and act takes to Himself the disobedient creature accursed in its disobedience . . . 'Reconciliation' thus means and signifies Emmanuel, God with us, namely God in the peace which He has made between Himself and us but also between us and Himself.   (*CD* IV/3, pp. 3f.)

The covenant is eternal in that it is written into the heart of God's relations with that which is not God. It is a covenant of election as the heart of the gospel, the gospel quintessentially: 'The election of grace (*die Gnaden-wahl*) is the sum of the Gospel – we must put it as pointedly as that. But more, the election of grace is the whole of the Gospel, the Gospel *in nuce*. It is the very essence of all good news' (*CD* II/2, pp. 13–14). And what is the content of that gospel? That 'God is for man too the One who loves in freedom' (*CD* II/2, p. 3). It is here that we must take account of the universal aspects of Barth's teaching. In the face of his Augustinian and Calvinist heritage, which taught that God's gracious purposes are limited to a few and they chosen for salvation before the creation of the world, he sought to take with full seriousness the biblical teaching which affirmed that election is 'in Christ'. And that 'in Christ' takes us to the heart of the being of God, which is saving being: 'in Himself, in the primal and basic decision (*Ur- und Grundentscheidung*) in which He wills to be and actually is God . . . God is none other than the One who in His Son or Word elects Himself, and in and with Himself elects His people' (*CD* II/2, p. 76). Jesus Christ is the beginning, middle and end of God's electing and saving action, so that any account of Barth's theology of salvation must either begin here or, in some other way, bring this into the centre. Salvation, eschatologically considered, means the completion of the purpose of election which takes its origin in the very eternal being of God.

One prominent theme takes us to the heart of our topic. The cross is a substitutionary bearing by God in Christ of God's rejection of human sin. Barth can speak of the one rejected, because through Jesus' rejection the rejection that the human race has merited is taken away. 'The rejection which all men incurred, the wrath of God under which all men lie, the death which all men must die, God in his love for men transfers from all eternity to him in whom he loves and elects them, and whom he elects at their head and in their place' (*CD* II/2, p. 123). '[T]he rejected man, who alone and truly takes and bears and bears away the wrath of God is called Jesus Christ' (*CD* II/2, p. 349). The purpose of this action is human salvation: he bears our rejection, so that we may be elect, by which is meant brought into reconciled relation with God. However, although the substitutionary bearing of rejection is at the heart of the matter, salvation is achieved by more than merely the cross, which is for Barth the crux of a broader story having its beginnings in eternity and taking shape in the whole history of Jesus Christ.

We shall begin with the latter and move later into a treatment of eternity. Consistent with his universalistic leanings, it is the resurrection on which Barth leans the chief weight: it is there that God the Father gives his 'verdict': 'The resurrection of Jesus Christ is the great verdict of God, the fulfilment and proclamation of God's decision concerning the event of the cross . . . It is its acceptance as the act of His obedience which judges the world, but judges it with the aim of saving it' (*CD* IV/1, p. 309; cf. p. 305). We could go further and say that Barth is above all a theologian of the resurrection, rather than of the incarnation or cross – a feature of his thought which gives it a strongly realized eschatology. Whatever may still be to come is chiefly the outworking of that eschatological salvation which is realized here. Although, however, the resurrection may bear the chief weight, it must not be forgotten that in one respect Barth shares with Irenaeus a concern to see the whole of the events that form the life, death, and resurrection of Jesus as the way by which salvation is achieved. There is a *recapitulatio* (recapitulation) here, a strong conception of the second Adam fulfilling the promise of and to the first.[2]

The saving history that is Jesus Christ is spelled out in *CD* IV/1–3. According to them salvation is achieved by the self-same historical happening characterized as, respectively, a divine act, a human act and a divine-human act. Thus does Barth weave into the doctrine of salvation the three dogmatic focuses of orthodox Christology, the divinity, humanity and divine-humanity of Jesus. Given the fallen human situation, this threefold act takes place in face of, in overcoming and in revealing the true character of the human enmity to God that is sin in its various forms. Barth also integrates other themes treated differently in the tradition, notably for our purposes the three offices of Christ as priest (divine), king (human), and prophet (divine-human). The order – altering the traditional prophet, priest and king – is significant, as we shall see. To complicate the matter further, the theology of the two states of Christ according to the Reformation tradition – his humiliation and glorification – are also woven into the fabric in altered form.

Salvation as divine act is the topic of *CD* IV/1, undoubtedly the finest of the part-volumes, which shows Barth to be a great theologian of the sheer grace of God in the best traditions of the Reformation. There are at least two focuses to his exposition of the achievement of the human priestly act of the eternal Son of God. The first elaborates the outcome of the substitutionary bearing by God the Son of the human rejection of and by God. According to the logic of the treatment, this divine Self-giving to death, this substitution, is universal in its bearing and scope. Probably wrongly taking Paul's teaching in 2 Corinthians 5:14 that 'one died for all, and therefore all died' to refer to the whole human race, Barth understands the cross to be both the historical outworking of the universal divine will to elect and the effective slaying of the 'old Adam'. The almost platonic realism of Barth's conception of the effect of Jesus' death on the whole human race is evident in the following passage:

> We died: the totality of all sinful men, those living, those long dead, and those still to be born, Christians who necessarily know and proclaim it, but also Jews and heathen, whether they hear and receive the news or whether they tried and still try to escape it. His death was the death of all, quite independently of their attitude or response to this event ... (*CD* IV/1, p. 295)

What then happens? There is both action and revelation, not – we must be careful to note – simply revelation, which has to be distinguished from it. 'This fact that God has here come amongst us in the person of His Son, and that as a man with us He exercises judgement, reveals the full seriousness of the human situation' (*CD* IV/1, p. 219). The action is that of a divine judge who exercises real judgment by at once revealing one state of affairs and bringing about another. Because it is the historical act of the eternal God, rooted in his eternity, it has eternal significance.

In what respect is salvation achieved? This leads us to the second focus, where Barth already begins to treat of the human appropriation of that which is achieved on the cross. What is held to happen is that God's self-giving humility gives rise to a judgment on human pride which overcomes this pride by rendering it redundant. The situation is roughly as follows. The essence of sin is to stand in a position of superiority to one's neighbour, taking the superior stance of the divine judge over against him. 'All sin has its being and origin in the fact that man wants to be his own judge' (*CD* IV/1, p. 220). In other words, sin is that human stance in which we seek to play God over against the other, and in that very act of pretension displace God in an act of hostility to grace, effectively becoming what we are not. God saves us by refusing to be the judge that we affect to be, by going into the dock himself, and becoming, in that very self-humiliation which is the history of Jesus Christ, 'the judge judged in our place'. By submitting to his own judgment, he removes the necessity for ours and so liberates us from the terrible burden of seeking to be what we are not. This is the way of the Son of God into the far country, the act of condescension by which God himself bears the consequences of our sin and frees us from it.

Is this a 'psychologizing' account? Certainly, insofar as judgment is construed metaphorically as equivalent to sitting in judgment, the plight from which we are freed is a false orientation to God, ourselves and our neighbour. But, despite the shape of the metaphor, this is also an ontological conception. By changing the relationship, God reshapes human being. In a recent study of the theology of Philip Melanchthon, Christoph Schwöbel has argued that this Reformer enables us to broaden our conception of the Reformation's theology: *sola gratia, sola fidei, sola scriptura* – and *solo corde* (by grace alone, by faith alone, by Scripture alone – and by the heart alone). Pride is a sin centred on the *heart*; and it is by changing this that a reorientation of the whole person is effected.[3] In this respect, it is clear that Barth's is a version of the classic Reformation theology of the gracious reorientation of the person to God by the death of Christ.

Has Barth, by this metaphorical construing of judgment, conflated atonement – the definitive divine act by which the human relation to God is changed for ever – with justification, about which he appears now to be speaking? Not necessarily, for Barth is concerned with identifying sin – the first of the three characterizations as pride, sloth and falsehood – in the light of its removal. Salvation is, in the midst of time, whatever it may mean eschatologically, the way by which a new *status* is given to the human being. The doctrine of justification must therefore be understood as first of all a movement brought about by divine pardon and judgment, from one status to another. 'I was and still am the former man: man as a wrongdoer . . . But I am already and will be the latter man: the man whom God has elected and created for himself . . . the man who is . . . righteous before God' (*CD* IV/1, p. 544). The status is one of acceptance by God through pardon. Is this merely 'imputation', legal fiction? That depends upon what status we give to the declarative act through which we are pardoned, and to the eschatological promise under which pardon is declared. '[T]he reality of his future already in the present, is no less than this: *totus justus*' (*CD* IV/1, p. 596). Eschatological reality is realized in the pardon spoken in the present. What happens here changes the status or standing of the human race as a whole before God. It is certainly more than a psychologizing account, just as a human declarative act of marriage or adoption concerns the creation of new realities. This one, because it is declared by God, concerns – perhaps better, determines – the being of the whole of the human race.

The complicating factor – and what makes it appear that Barth is saying the same thing in two places – is that he appears to attribute universality to both atonement and justification. Is, then, justification as well as atonement already of universal bearing? We approach an answer to the question of how Barth distinguishes universal divine act and – possibly particular – human appropriation through aspects of the second part-volume, to which we now turn. Barth himself describes the move as one from God acting as reconciler (*Versöhner*) to the one who is reconciled in him (*CD* IV/2, p. 3), a different perspective from which the one reconciling work is articulated. While the former part-volume spoke of salvation as a divine work, albeit one performed by the 'Lord as Servant', here we have the same thing happening through human action: 'The Servant as Lord'. Corresponding to the self-humbling of God, and indeed the other side of that same action, is the elevation of 'the new and true and royal man who participates in the being and life and lordship and act of God', and is 'as such the Head and Representative and Saviour of all other men' (ibid.). In him, the one who was once the object of the work of God now becomes an active subject (*CD* IV/2, p. 19).

'The unassumed is the unhealed': that patristic slogan is essential to the doctrine of salvation, which, because it is concerned with salvation through the life, death, resurrection and ascension of a human being, must be understood in its human implications. In Barth's words, in a conception surely owing something to the parallelism of divine and human action in Philippians 2: 'His human work runs parallel to the work of God. In His speech and action, in His person, there is actualized the Kingdom of God drawn near' (*CD* IV/2, p. 292). The word 'actualized' indicates the fact that, again in parallel with Paul, Barth is operating with a dynamic conception of the sometimes static-sounding 'human nature'. And part of the point is that this human story, completed as it is by the resurrection and ascension which are real, this-worldly, *events* (*CD* IV/2, pp. 142f.), is like the atoning cruci-fixion, universal in its bearing, so that we encounter again the realistic, apparently platonizing side of Barth's christological anthropology. Early in the volume, the reference to election is repeated: 'The exaltation of the Son of man' is in some sense the exaltation of us all: 'The decision and action in which God in his Son elected and determined himself for man, and . . . man for himself' (*CD* IV/2, p. 31). This is, in Barth's words, an exaltation of human essence: 'He raised up human essence [*Wesen*] to essence in Himself and therefore as true God became and was also true man' (*CD* IV/2, p. 44). (How it can be said that Barth is a theologian who diminishes the human race confounds belief.) That is then the second moment of the divine act that achieves human salvation: the judgment that brings acquittal is *also* the achievement of genuine and, it would seem, universal humanity.

But, it would also seem, it is an eschatological universality, and it is here that we must attend to the elusiveness of Barth's concepts. He is rightly aware that when one is dealing with the relations of the eternal with the temporal, there is no simple matter of 'before' and 'after'. His concern with God as *event* would appear to complicate the matter still further. '[W]e are forced to understand what has to be said about the connexion between the man Jesus and all other men in ontological and *for this very reason* in dynamic terms' (*CD* IV/2, p. 282, my italics). This may be like platonic realism, but it is only so eschatologically and as action. What happens to Jesus, especially in the resurrection, is his coronation (*CD* IV/2, p. 292), but it is one that involves us all, in a movement that corresponds to it. 'In him, in virtue of his death, we who in ourselves are not holy are the saints of God' (*CD* IV/2, p. 294). But it is partly by anticipation. 'In Jesus Christ a Christian has already come into being, but in himself and his time he is always in the process of becoming' (*CD* IV/2, p. 307). (Notice that Barth is now speaking of the Christian, not of the human race as a whole.) Thus the historical salvation achieved by the Son of Man is sanctification – a making holy – and it is to Barth's explicit treatment of this that we now turn.

Like justification, sanctification is treated ontologically by Barth and represents a move from the transcendent declaration of pardon to a more immanent conception of participation. Sanctification is participation in Jesus' holiness. That is not to say that we have here a second divine act; it is, rather, a second 'moment' of the one divine act, one with a different bearing (*CD* IV/2, p. 501). Salvation is a unified divine act with various aspects. What is the difference?

> It is one thing that God turns in free grace to sinful man, and quite another that in the same free grace He converts man to Himself. It is one thing that God as the Judge establishes that He is in the right over against this man, thus creating a new right for this man before Him, and quite another that by His mighty direction He claims this man and makes him ready and willing for His service. (*CD* IV/2, p. 503)

It is at this place that Barth faces up to the question of universality. He appears to have claimed that all are justified; surely not all sanctified? Even there, Barth will go as far as he can to establish the sheer gracious generosity of his God:

> The sanctification of man, his conversion to God, is, like his justification, a transformation, a new determination, which has taken

place *de jure* for the world and therefore for all men. *De facto*, however, it is not known by all men, just as justification has not *de facto* been grasped and acknowledged and known and confessed by all men, only by those who are awakened to faith. (*CD* IV/2, p. 511)

There, to be sure, is to be found the basis for the charge that Barth conceives salvation 'merely epistemically'. But he does not. This is a matter of confession, being awakened to faith, in what has been done by the prevenient gracious act of the electing God before anyone came to it. We now move to examine something of how this takes place.

Of the third part-volume it must be said that, although it is of greater length than its predecessors, leading the publishers of the translation to distribute it between two tomes, it cannot be said to add much to Barth's understanding of salvation, except perhaps to reinforce his contention that it is a finished act. It is the part-volume devoted to what can be called the 'mediatorship of Christ', to that focus of his one saving action that sees him as both God and man mediating between loving God and lost humankind. In what does this mediatorship consist? It is largely a matter of revelation: 'Jesus Christ is not only the High-priest and King but also the Prophet, Herald and Proclaimer of this accomplishment' (*CD* IV/3, p. 165). The prophetic war against evil is to be waged by revelation of the salvation achieved by the atonement. As Barth points out, this does not mean information:

> We cannot impress upon ourselves too strongly that in the language of the Bible knowledge . . . does not mean the acquisition of neutral information, which can be expressed in statements, principles and systems, concerning a being which confronts man, nor does it mean entry into passive contemplation of a being which exists beyond the phenomenal world. What it really means is the process or history in which man, certainly observing and hearing, using his senses, intelligence and imagination, but also his will, action and 'heart', and therefore as a whole man, becomes aware of another history which in the first instance encounters him as an alien history from without . . . and in such a compelling way that he cannot be neutral towards it, but finds himself summoned to disclose and give himself to it in return . . . (*CD* IV/3, p. 184)

The model is the conversion and transition of Saul to Paul, of his move from ignorance to knowledge, a revelation with life- and ultimately world-changing consequences (*CD* IV/3, p. 209). Moreover, because these are words spoken in a hostile environment (*CD* IV/3, pp. 166f.), we are here confronted with a real drama (*CD* IV/3, p. 168). 'A war is waged against sin, death, and the devil' (*CD* IV/3, p. 179).

Two features of this are of a piece. First is the rather non-participatory conception of knowledge there given. Is it enough to say that this is a matter of becoming 'aware of another history which encounters us', or should we not speak here much more in terms of a participation in the body of Christ? It is here that we become particularly aware of the relative underweighting of the pneumatological and ecclesial dimensions of Barth's way of speaking of the appropriation of salvation. This is certainly not to suggest that they are not there. The structure of Volume IV incorporates two sections on the Holy Spirit in each of the part-volumes, relating the salvation achieved in the threefold activity of Jesus Christ to both the Christian community and the believer. There is no doubt that Barth has a doctrine of the Spirit and is far too fine a dogmatician not to see its place. But in dogmatics, a proper distribution of weight between the various topics is important, so that the underweighting of the place of the Spirit in relation to the humanity and ministry of Jesus in Barth's thought carries implications for pneumatology elsewhere. It simply cannot say all that a doctrine of the Spirit ought to say.

The reason is this. Crucial to any understanding of salvation is the relation of the Holy Spirit first to Jesus and then, *and consequently*, to those who are incorporate in Christ by the act of that same Spirit. If the relation of the Spirit to Jesus is underplayed; if, that is to say, his humanity is made too much a function of his direct relation to the Father rather than of that mediated by the Spirit, thus far is the link between his humanity and ours weakened, because more weight is placed upon the miraculous transference of what happened *then* to ourselves *now*, less on that relation mediated in the present by the Spirit of Christ through his body, the church. That it is indeed a miracle need not be denied; what is needed is an account of mediation, of what is transmitted from then to now, and by what means.

Let us in this light review Barth's treatment of the humanity of Christ in the second part-volume. There is no doubt that here we have a real humanity, whose course in time is expanded in 64.2. Here is one who 'is ignored and forgotten and despised . . .' (*CD* IV/2, p. 167); who also 'ignored those who are high and mighty and wealthy . . .' ; who represented revolutionary values, though not any particular political programme (*CD* IV/2, pp. 171f.), and who 'like God Himself, is not against men but for men . . . ' (*CD* IV/2, p. 180). In all this, Jesus' humanity, in its very Godlikeness (*CD* IV/2, p. 248), is a real temporal happening (*CD* IV/2, pp. 142f.). Yet conspicuous by its almost total absence is reference to Jesus' temptation and his relation to the Spirit – or to God the Father through the Spirit – which shaped *this* human life as distinctly what it was. Significant also is the fact that the ascension, where is centred a doctrine of Jesus' continuing human priesthood, is given no distinct treatment, always being linked with the resurrection, as if the two form a single event (*CD* IV/2, pp. 132ff.). The tendency is to reduce the human life to a series of illuminating episodes, which might equally well characterize another human life, rather than the working out of this particular human life in its particular historical and theological context.

The second feature is related, and is the fact that Jesus is the one who mediates knowledge of himself: 'He Himself is the reconciliation of the world to God which He declares. As he declares this and therefore Himself ... as in the discharge of His prophetic office He mediates and establishes knowledge of Himself, He encounters man ...' (*CD* IV/3, p. 183). Although Barth does here refer to the 'I am' sayings of the Fourth Gospel, according to which the incarnate Jesus does indeed reveal something about himself, we must ask whether Barth's use of this does not represent something of a distortion. That Gospel's account of revelation after Jesus' historical glorification does it in a somewhat more trinitarian way, according to which the Paraclete mediates knowledge of God the Father through the Son. We can, to be sure, sympathize with Barth's motives here. From early in the *Church Dogmatics*, he had fought against the nineteenth-century tendency, involving an appeal to a much repeated saying of Melanchthon – later recanted, as Barth, rarely among commentators, observes[4] – that knowledge of Christ's *being* is not to be sought, only his effects ('benefits'). The latest exponent of this, Rudolf Bultmann, may be in Barth's sights. Yet, once again, we cannot be content with Barth's formulation if we are to give the Spirit a weighty enough role for this to be seen as a genuinely triune act, albeit in inseparable relation to both God the Father and Jesus Christ. Are we not concerned more concretely with the mediation of a form of personal relation as much as with the revelation of a once-for-all act, though undoubtedly with the latter prominent in an account of the relation?

The two features combine to give the whole the rather abstract air that it has, suggesting that Barth's schematism has done rather more than bring about the metamorphosis of the traditional 'two natures' doctrine that Regin Prenter charged, claiming that Barth is doing with the doctrine roughly the opposite of that for which it was devised.[5] The real weight of what Barth has to say about the mediatorship of Christ has already been said in the previous part-volumes, so that this third form of the one divine reconciling action sometimes appears to be little more than the risen Jesus Christ's bringing home to the believer his own past work. T. F. Torrance makes a similar point in saying that in *CD* IV/3, 'Christ seemed to be swallowed up in the transcendent Light and Spirit of God, so that the humanity of the risen Jesus appeared to be displaced by what he called "the humanity of God" in his turning toward us.'[6]

That is not to say that there are not important and interesting themes developed on the way; that goes without saying about any of Barth's writing. Three of them are worth mentioning here. The first is the association of the notion of the telling of truth with the overcoming of evil. There is much to be said on biblical grounds for the linking of the demonic with the lie: with the blindness, amounting to slavery, which, by calling evil good, witnesses only to the sin against the Holy Spirit. Barth's prophetical construing of the notion of victory by the Word is, we might say, a non-violent construing of the military language of victory: 'A word shall quickly slay him.' Barth's centring his treatment of this Christology and soteriology on the remarkable story of Gottliebin Dittus also has the function of linking together his earliest and his latest writing days (*CD* IV/3, pp. 168–71). Jesus *is* victor. This theme illustrates the second great strength of this theology, that whatever may be the systematic weaknesses of his treatment of salvation, Barth's theology, with its insistence on a living Christ, is infinitely preferable to Schleiermacher's conception of salvation as influence mediated from a historical past and his accompanying assertion that the resurrection and ascension have no determinative place in Christian dogmatics.[7] Similarly, in response to one of the first criticisms of Barth's universalism, Berkouwer's claim that he has reduced the gospel to 'the triumph of grace',[8] Barth objects: 'We are concerned with the living person of Jesus Christ. Strictly, it is not grace, but He Himself as its Bearer, Bringer and Revealer, who is the Victory, the light which is not overwhelmed by darkness, but before which darkness must yield as it is itself overwhelmed' (*CD* IV/3, p. 173).

We shall return to this matter. The third point of value is Barth's construing of the third dimension of the working out of salvation – after justification and sanctification – in terms of vocation. This again shows a concern to avoid abstraction and to link eternity with life in time. It also looks forward to his obviously long-pondered way in which to couch an ethic of reconciliation, with his decision to centre on invocation characteristically at once idiosyncratic, illuminating, and systematically coherent. Vocation (God's calling to discipleship) gives rise to invocation as the right human response, and so the way of being both before God and in the world. The reference to invocation takes us to the posthumously published ethics of reconciliation, part of *CD* IV/4. It is characteristic of Barth that he follows none of the traditional ways of developing an ethic, but links the Christian life to the petitions of the Lord's Prayer.

QUESTIONS

Already some of the strengths and weaknesses of Barth's doctrine of salvation have been set out. We have reserved treatment of the central question to be asked of it to the last, and it is a version of that to be asked of any theology. How does it relate eternal God to temporal creation, and does it do it in such a way as to preserve at once the sovereignty and priority of divine action and the proper *Selbständigkeit* – relative independence – of the world? On an answer to this question hangs, if not all the law and the prophets, at least the proper weighting of the different elements of a dogmatic theology of salvation.

There should be no objection to a claim that salvation begins in and has its centre and end in the sovereign action of the eternal God; in that sense, it is rooted in eternity. Barth's way of doing this is through his doctrine of election, as we have seen. We repeat: for Barth, reconciliation is 'the historical event in which there took place in time that which was the purpose and resolve and will of God from all eternity . . . ' (*CD* IV/2, p. 31). Moreover, because this is not simply historical action but the outcome of the priestly divine Self-giving which is the way of the Son of God into the far country of human sin, the *action* both reveals and in a sense *realizes* the very eternal being of God, and does it in relation to the world. This is because the eternal being of God is a primal decision to be a certain kind of God – an electing God – an eternal being which involves an orientation to human salvation. The cross is therefore the taking place, under the conditions of human sin, of the orientation to reconciliation which is the very being of God.

Allusion has already been made to what has been called Platonism in Barth's treatment of salvation. The most marked tendency, perhaps, is to see Jesus Christ as a kind of platonic form of humanity, so that salvation is universally achieved *already*, and its appropriation only a matter of knowing that we are saved. Criticisms of this kind have been made at least as early as Robert Jenson's first study of Barth in 1963.[9] In two respects, this seems to me not to be as much of a problem as is sometimes made out, even conceding that it is a justified charge. First, if it is the case that we are saved by free grace, prior to any worthiness or act of ours, in fact in the face of a form of being which is hostile to God, what else is salvation but the acknowledgment of that which has been done for us already? (It is the acknowledgment of this which is part of the point of baptism, infant baptism indeed.) What else do Barth's critics want? Second, it is not necessarily a problem that all this is rooted in eternity. The charges of Platonism must not obscure the fact that this universal salvation is not established by Barth in any way philosophically, but in God's personally active eternity. God's eternity means here his contemporaneity to all times, and the application of a simple 'before' and 'after' is therefore impossible.

Rather, more subtle questions should be asked, and they concern eschatology and ecclesiology. Clearly, Barth takes account of the eschatological dimensions of salvation. 'Ahead of us lies salvation, and – since, having shared His death, we must now share His life with Him as well – we can do nothing but glory in it.'[10] What seems to be lacking, rather, is a proper grounding of these points in pneumatology and ecclesiology. There can be no doubt that both of these do play a role; the question is whether they are given sufficient weight in the development of the themes, and it seems clear from what we have already reviewed that they are not.

In the background are two dogmatic decisions which determine the shape of things. The first is the giving of election priority over creation and eschatology. 'It is because of this that we put the doctrine of election . . . at the very beginning, and indeed before the beginning, of what we have to say concerning God's dealings with His creation' (CD II/2, p. 89). The outcome is that 'under the concept of predestination . . . we say that in freedom (its affirmation and not its loss) God tied Himself to the universe' (CD II/2, p. 155). 'In this primal decision God did not remain satisfied with His own being in Himself. He reached out to something beyond . . .' (CD II/2, p. 168). Because the commitment to human salvation is in some way written into the heart of God in a way that commitment to creation is not, the created order as a whole is given a rather instrumental place in the works of God, as but the outer basis of the covenant. This brings the human creation into undue prominence. God's 'self-determination is *identical* with the decree of His movement towards man' (CD II/2, p. 91, italics added). That salvation is primarily focused on the human race is not a problem, whatever the New Age movement may say; that it is only focused on it is. If the material context in which the saints live their lives is treated merely or largely instrumentally, as happens in Origen and in the long succession of those who have followed him, then a number of other matters are underweighted, especially the humanity of our Lord Jesus Christ. In our context, it means that the overturning of the 'two natures' doctrine has a distinctive effect on the treatment of the three offices of Christ. We have seen that the prophetic office is linked to the victory over evil by the word. Similarly, the kingly office is ordered to a fine celebration of the triumphal homecoming of Christ the Son of Man and the elevated calling and dignity of the human race which are consequent upon it. But the fact, already noted, that the doctrines of the Holy Spirit and the ascension play so little structural part in this is a symptom that something somewhere has gone astray.

To what disorder does the symptom point? This brings us to the second questionable dogmatic decision underlying Barth's treatment of salvation. It is to be found in the fact that the priesthood of Christ is ordered to the divinity of Christ. What is lost is the priesthood exercised by Christ in his humanity. Now, it may be objected, is that not there in the treatment of the fact that it is as human that the Son of God exercised his priestly ministry? A decision on that depends upon whether it is the case, as I believe it to be, that it is one thing to speak of the humanity of God and another to speak of the humanity of Jesus Christ. A return to the more traditional Reformed way of speaking of the priesthood of Christ in terms of his divine-human – or even human-divine – mediatorship, exercised during Jesus' ministry in the power of the Holy Spirit and eternally by virtue of his ascension, as human, to the right hand of God, might mitigate some of the more problematic aspects of Barth's universalism.

That is not to deny the immense and positive benefit Barth has brought by moving away from the objectionable aspects of the decree of election in the direction of a universal love of God become incarnate for the whole of the human race. Published during some of the worst days of recent history, the affirmation that all are elect, Jew and Gentile, Nazi and victim alike, all are at once elect and determined to obedience to the command of the one triune God, this has been one of the great modern works of theology, actually achieving reconciliation between divided human beings by its short- and long-term effects. Even in its dogmatic deficiencies, it remains a source of perennial devotional and intellectual power, and, at the very least, a challenge to succeeding generations to begin to approach its comprehensiveness and depth.

Notes

1 In *CD* IV/1, p. 15, Barth speaks of 'our salvation, i.e., our participation in His being'.
2 K. Barth, *Christ and Adam. Man and Humanity in Romans 5* (Edinburgh: Oliver and Boyd, 1956).
3 In the Fall, the heart was turned away from God and so has to be conquered by a stronger *affectus* than that which holds it in thrall. C. Schwöbel, 'Melanchthon's

Loci Communes von 1521: Die erste evangelische Dogmatik', *Melanchthons bleibende Bedeutung. Eine Ringvorlesung der Theologischen Fakultät*, ed. J. Schilling (Kiel: Christian-Albrechts-Universität zu Kiel, 1998), pp. 57–82.

4 This was, says Barth, 'an act of rashness of which he later repented', knowing as he did that there can be no treatment of *beneficia Christi* without considerations of the *mysteria divinitatis* (*CD* II/1, p. 259).

5 R. Prenter, 'Karl Barth's Umbildung der traditionellen Zweinaturlehre in lutherischer Beleuchtung', *Studia Theologica* 11 (1957), pp. 1–88. The charge of christological Platonism recurs.

6 T. F. Torrance, *Karl Barth. Biblical and Evangelical Theologian* (Edinburgh: T & T Clark, 1990), p. 134.

7 F. Schleiermacher, *The Christian Faith*, trans. H. R. Mackintosh and J. S. Stewart (Edinburgh: T & T Clark, 1928), §. 99.

8 G. C. Berkouwer, *The Triumph of Grace in the Theology of Karl Barth*, trans. H. R. Boer (London: Paternoster Press, 1956).

9 R. W. Jenson, *Alpha and Omega: A Study in the Theology of Karl Barth* (New York: Thomas Nelson, 1963).

10 Barth, *Christ and Adam*, pp. 1f.

Further reading

Bloesch, D. G., *Jesus is Victor! Karl Barth's Doctrine of Salvation* (Nashville, Tenn.: Abingdon Press, 1976).

Ford, D. *Barth and God's Story* (Frankfurt and Bern: Peter Lang, 1981).

H. Kung, *Justification: The Doctrine of Karl Barth and a Catholic Reflection* (Philadelphia: Westminster Press, 1981).

Thompson, J. *Christ in Perspective. Christological Perspectives in the Theology of Karl Barth* (Edinburgh: Saint Andrew Press, 1978).

Webster, J. *Karl Barth's Ethics of Reconciliation* (Cambridge: Cambridge University Press, 1995).

10 The humanity of the human person in Karl Barth's anthropology

WOLF KRÖTKE

(Translated by Philip G. Ziegler)

ANTHROPOLOGY AS THE DOCTRINE OF THE 'REAL MAN'

'The ontological determination of humanity is grounded in the fact that one man among all others is the man Jesus' (*CD* III/2, p. 132). Within the framework of a general human effort at understanding humanity, this principle of Karl Barth's theological anthropology is at first glance very provocative. For Barth, in fact, means that if we want to know who and what the human being is, we are not in the first place to look to ourselves. Nor are we to begin with what the empirical sciences say about the human being; nor are we to orient ourselves to the phenomena of human existence past and present in an attempt to interpret the experiences which are there expressed. All this, according to Barth, can and must be thoroughly considered, acknowledged, and brought to light. It is, however, unsuited for *establishing theologically* what it is that constitutes the essential character of the human. We are not to learn who and what the human is by observing human beings and their history in general, but rather to do so in the concrete human person to whom, according to Christian faith, God bound himself and entered into human history.

This principle of theological anthropology is particularly provocative today because it does not at first appear to show how it can be connected with what we already know generally about the human being. And without such a connection, all statements of theological anthropology are in danger of hanging isolated in space, simply incomprehensible outside of theological discourse. If this were to be the case then in the opinion of many, theological anthropology would gamble away a significant opportunity with which it is faced in a time shaped by secularism and atheism. This is the opportunity of being able to explain, even in our time, that precisely when human existence is at issue at least *the question of God* is unavoidable. Elaborating this question holds the promise that human beings are able to recognize and understand that their lives are always already concerned with God.

In following this line of thought, appeal is made above all to the fact that, as a creature endowed with consciousness, the human being is capable of transcending everything to be found in him- or herself and in the world. According to the broad consensus of contemporary theological anthropology, this structural *openness* of the human person to a 'free ground' that is not at our disposal, or to the mystery of being, which manifests itself in, for example, the question of the meaning of life, is to be interpreted as proof that the human being is essentially related to God.[1] Against the atheistic claim that the human being can only be truly human when he or she sees through faith in God as an illusion, this theological anthropology purports to show that human beings forfeit their humanity if they are not able to affirm God as their proper ground. In this way, anthropology becomes a *function of the question of God*. The universal need to develop an idea of God and to reckon with God as an unavoidable reality is supposed to be expounded beginning from the human person's self-manifestation in enacting his or her existence.

Karl Barth's theology took shape in dealing with this anthropological grounding of the whole of theology as he met it in the so-called liberal theology of Germany around the turn of the century, and as it encountered him in the existential interpretation of Christian faith in the work of Rudolf Bultmann as he understood it. As is seen in the development of his theology in the *Church Dogmatics* in particular, Barth's concern was not to call into question or contest the structural openness of the human as God's creature to God. On the contrary, this is also one of the fundamental assertions of his own anthropology. To be human means to stand in relation to God ontologically and structurally: the human is 'a being which from the very outset stands in some kind of relation to God' (*CD* III/3, p. 72). The human being is 'opened and related to God Himself' (*CD* III/2, p. 72). This affirmation is retained. But what Barth contested is that this is an insight that human beings as they actually exist are able to attain in and of themselves.

In contesting this, the argument that can be and is in fact marshalled from an atheistic perspective against the claim of a structural God-relation in the human being was not decisive for him. This argument contends that the capacity for transcendence as such leads into nothingness and is in itself a meaningless escapade of the evolution of life, to which human beings in their freedom must in fact assign a meaning in the course of their lives. But although Barth could have availed himself of this argument, the problem that drove him was not the debate with atheism which so worries the churches and theologies of Europe at the present time. For the most part, Barth did not regard atheism or a-religiosity as something Christian faith really has to fear (cf. *CD* IV/3.2, p. 621). Thus, dissociating himself from Dietrich Bonhoeffer's theological evaluation of religionlessness as maturity,[2] he also contested the claim that 'in this century ... we have to do with a world which is alienated from God in a distinctively radical and refined way, having become totally secular, autonomous, adult and profane' (*ChrL*, p. 126). For Barth, atheism was only a rash variant of *religion*, in which human beings 'blurt out' what religion tends to conceal; that is, that when approached on the basis of human efforts at achieving transcendence, God as he truly is remains unknown (cf. *ChrL*, pp. 128ff.). Moreover, Barth did not understand atheism as something fundamentally opposed to religion, 'as its few fortunate and countless unfortunate devotees tend to asseverate' (*CD* I/2, p. 324). In the adoration of 'authorities and powers ... to which the atheist usually subscribes with the happiest and most naive credulity' (*CD* I/2, p. 321), atheism shares a fundamental characteristic of religion which in fact we find in every person. This is the desire of the human being to have God at his or her disposal, filling transcendence with an image of God which is 'arbitrarily and wilfully evolved by man' (*CD* I/2, p. 302). It is in this sense that Barth's famous definition holds good: 'Religion is unbelief. It is a concern, indeed, we must say it is the one great concern, of godless man' (*CD* I/2, pp. 299–300). Because this is the case, there can be no possibility of seeking a basis for theological anthropology in the actual religious constitution of the human being in which we reach beyond ourselves to the mystery of reality – a mystery which can then subsequently be called 'God'.

There has been much debate as to whether Barth's understanding of religion adequately comprehends the phenomenon of religion and human religiosity.[3] What is most often pointed out is that, explicitly or not, people do conduct themselves religiously by orienting themselves to a transcendent reality or power beyond their control which they certainly do not understand as their own work, but rather by which they see themselves passively affected.[4] And so when Barth sets the experience of God's revelation, which also implies the encounter with the true humanity of Jesus, in opposition to religion, he appears to overlook the fact that all religion is somehow involved with a revelation, and that Christian faith is thus also a religion in this sense. Yet this objection misses the point of Barth's way of thinking theologically, without which his anthropology also cannot be understood. For in his anthropology he proceeds from the presupposition that every human being stands in relation to God; because God stands in relation to him or her, no human person can become 'ontologically godless' (*CD* IV/1,

p. 480). Thus, with Augustine it holds true that the human 'heart is restless until it rests in Him' (*ChrL*, p. 118). Human beings can have 'impressions' of the reality of God in the world which 'lay hold of us with serious force' (*ChrL*, p. 122), so that 'we may not speak of an absolute, independent, and exclusive ignorance of God in the world' (*ChrL*, p. 127). This is indicated by the religions, and it is also similarly reflected in atheism's concern for a true humanity that is not alienated from itself.

But Barth did not see himself in a position to 'generalize and to systematize' such phenomena 'along the lines of a natural theology' (*ChrL*, p. 122), as happens when the concept of religion is made the basis for Christian theology and thereby also for theological anthropology. In his view, what results from such a move is not only an abstract picture of God, but also an abstract and erroneous picture of the human being. For Barth, an obvious historical lesson concerning such abstractions was given both in German 'Culture Protestantism' with its understanding of Christians as bourgeoisie, and in the criminal reduction of the human to 'racial essence' in the religious ideology of the 'German Christians' in the 1930s. Wherever the human being is supposed to be understood theologically in relation to God on a purely human basis, the danger looms of replacing real humanity with a short-sighted and constricting image of the human, thereby suppressing and impeding possibilities for the free development of real human being.

In contrast, Barth's anthropology desires to be a doctrine of the 'real man' (cf. *CD* III/2, pp. 132ff.), as encountered in unity with God in the history of the life and death of Jesus Christ. In this one, whose reality is not distorted and obstructed by human images and ideologies, we are able to perceive our own human reality in the richness of our possibilities, and thence to begin to lead a truly human life. Naturally, proceeding theologically in this way presupposes that those who do not have faith in God in Jesus Christ or have already constructed a religious image of the human always need first of all to be made familiar with the concrete, real human person who discloses their humanity as well. But in Barth's view, this was not a deficiency of theological anthropology. For it is human to encounter a new reality and to allow one's long-standing fixed convictions about reality to be interrupted so that the old can be set in a new light. Those who are no longer able to allow a new reality to encounter them have sightless eyes. On the other hand, God's honouring of the human being is expressed in the fact that he deals with us as creatures fit for 'encounter' (cf. *CD* III/2, p. 163). Through the historically concrete interruption of the old coherence of their lives, people are able not only to encounter God in a new way, but also to encounter themselves anew once again, and thereby to overcome all despair and resignation over the way we fail to be human. According to Barth, the Christian church would gamble away the richness of the event of true, human reality from which it arises if it were to forget this or push it into the background in favour of a general image of the human. In order that this should not occur in the 'exposition of the doctrine of man', Barth looks 'in the first instance at the nature of the human . . . as it confronts us in the person of Jesus, and only secondarily – asking and answering from this place of light – at the nature of man as that of every man and all other men' (*CD* III/2, p. 46).

THE HUMAN BEING AS GOD'S 'PARTNER'

As the Christian faith understands him, the man Jesus, whom God bound to himself, is not an 'accidental' man. Barth shares with the old doctrine of the *en-* and *anhypostasis* of the human nature of Jesus Christ the view that this man only existed at all because God united himself with him (cf. *CD* IV/1, pp. 50f.). Thus, in the history of the life and death of Jesus Christ a *divine action* takes place which is already grounded in God's eternity and so does not represent some kind of divine 'escape from th[e] dilemma' (*CD* II/2, p. 90) of the problems which humanity causes for God. If we take seriously the fact that the eternal God has here bound himself with a man, then the history which here takes place is to be understood as a history really grounded in the eternity of God. Barth set this out in an interpretation of the doctrine of election, one of the most genuine accomplishments of his theological thinking, and at the same time a place at which essential decisions about the structure of theological anthropology are taken. In the man Jesus, the eternal triune God has elected all human beings as his covenant partners in a free act of the overflowing of his love (*CD* II/2, pp. 9f.). In the context of the present discussion, this statement contains three important implications for the question of the basis of anthropology.

The God with whom human beings are involved is capable of partnership in the freedom of his love. He is not a deity ruling abstractly over humanity. As Father, Son, and Spirit, he is a God who is able to relate to another reality and this means able to have a history. 'God was always a Partner. The Father was the Partner of the Son, and the Son of the Father. And what was and is and will be primarily in God Himself is history in this partnership' (*CD* IV/2, p. 344). Therefore, when this God determines that he will be the God of the human creature, this can never mean that the creature is thereby 'engulfed and covered as by a divine landslide' or 'swept away' as by a divine flood (*CD* IV/4, p. 163). Those elected by this God are for their part set 'on [their] own feet' as God's partners (CD IV/3.2, p. 941). As a reality distinct from God, they can be independent and free in relation to God. To this extent, there is no room for the objection raised against Barth that in his theological thinking the human is simply 'eliminated'.[5] This objection has been raised because Barth's emphasis on the divine freedom in which God elects the human has been understood as an axiom of God's authoritarian lordship over the human. This is not correct. Of course, Barth rightly emphasizes that it is totally meaningless to speak of God if in his eternity he is not understood as the God who precedes the human and acts freely. Yet, at the same time, through the history of Christ – which is itself grounded in God's eternity – we learn that in this 'precedence', God constantly acts as a partner who wills the election of human beings such that they themselves are able to correspond to this election in free human partnership. Thus, the *free correspondence* to God in which the human being is allowed to be plays a dominant role in Barth's anthropology.

The eternal election of all human beings in the man Jesus gives their human existence an indelible determination which through God always precedes the enactment of their own lives. The human person has 'no abstract being', *coram deo* (CD III/4, p. 663). The human person is not a neutral, undefined 'essence' that can become conscious of itself only in radical questionability. Rather, the person is summoned by God really to enact his or her existence as God's partner. This means that the human person ought to 'allow himself to be loved by God' (CD II/2, p. 410), ought to give thanks to God for his love, and 'for his part, may be joyful in time and eternity' (CD II/2, p. 412). The human creature ought to answer with its own human 'yes' the 'Yes' that God has spoken and speaks again to it. For this reason Barth cannot understand the freedom that God grants the human person in the covenant with himself as an abstract freedom to choose between affirming and denying God. Freedom is 'not the freedom to sin' (CD III/2, p. 197). Certainly, God has not taken away the human decision to choose rightly, for then the human would simply be God's marionette. A person can and must really decide for him- or herself. God has given time and space in this world for this to take place. But a person can and must decide rightly in face of the fact that he or she must also say 'no' to disobedience. If, however, the human chooses what is false – that is, the negation of the electing God – then in so doing he or she simultaneously destroys the freedom which God has granted. The freedom to affirm God and to give thanks to God is forfeit in the decision to deny God. If this freedom is to be preserved for us in the future as well, then denying God can only be understood as an 'impossible possibility' for the human creature.

In the *Church Dogmatics*, sin – and indeed evil itself, which Barth understood as 'nothingness' – is denoted by the terms 'impossible possibility' or 'ontological impossibility'.[6] This unusual conceptuality has led to many misunderstandings in the discussion of Barth's understanding of human sin. The meaning of these statements can, however, be made clear by reference to the doctrine of election. When God elects the human person to be his partner, he intends that the human person should grasp the possibility of this partnership. But where the human person does not in fact do so, God from the very beginning has decided to step in and realize this possibility with his own divine life in the life and death of the man Jesus Christ. In this sense, God's electing decision is to be understood as a twofold predestination. 'In the election of Jesus Christ God has ascribed to man . . . election, salvation and life; and to Himself . . . reprobation, perdition and death' (*CD* II/2, p. 163). 'There is sure and certain salvation for man, and a sure and certain risk for God' (*CD* II/2, p. 162); thus begins God's history with humanity and thus it is enacted in the life and death of Jesus Christ. Over against this, everything sinful in human being is without meaning or ground. It cannot be derived either from God's determination of the human or from God's conduct toward the human. It has no ground whatsoever (cf. *CD* III/3, pp. 353f.). It is absurd. That is why it does not belong in an anthropology that deals with God's elected, ontologically good creature. Sin is only an actual, ontic human pattern of action that can be justified neither by appeal to God nor to a 'predisposition' of the human. In the enactment of sin, the human person does not give place to being but rather gives place to annihilation. And so, according to Barth, there exists no account of things in a position to make what is sinful 'fit' somewhere and thereby render it understandable in some genuine sense. Of course, theology can and ought to identify every good reason in relation to God's being and that of the human. But for sin with its sheerly destructive character, there is absolutely no reason. Sin is something unreal that can only cling to the being of the human person by destroying it and exhausting it like a parasite. Once it has done this work of destruction, then it is what it is – nothing. God's election sets itself against any such meaninglessness in the lives of human beings. Accordingly, God's determination of human freedom is such that it only gives room to the possibility of life with God, and not to the devastating impossibility of life without and against God. Theology and theological anthropology take account of this when they handle sin as the 'nothingness' that continues to fight and which has to be fought against in the structure of thought as well.

This understanding of sin – itself a consequence of the election of all human beings to be free partners in the covenant with God – has decisive significance for anthropology. God does not constrain anyone into actually becoming 'impossible . . . as [His] covenant partner' (*CD* IV/1, p. 528) through leading life in such a way as to allow the destruction of the relation with God by one's acts and omissions. Of course, there is the terrible, destructive denial of God by the human person, yet 'God does not deny the human' (*CD* IV/3.1, p. 119). Therefore Barth says:

> In the absurd way which is all that is possible in this connection, man is [not] able [to be] . . . absolutely and ontologically godless. It is terrible enough that he can and does actually become relatively godless.[7] But he cannot really escape God. His godlessness . . . cannot make God a 'manless' God . . . Man has not fallen lower than the depth to which God humbled himself for him in Jesus Christ. But God in Jesus Christ did not become a devil or nothingness. (*CD* IV/1, pp. 480f.)

These remarks are thus something like the *Magna Carta* of the humanity grounded in Christian faith. When this faith looks at human beings as it were with God's eyes, there is no one among them who has to be regarded as a hopeless case. Even in the face of the most terrible, indeed criminal, human acts, this faith cannot hold the human in contempt (*Menschenverachtung*). From the very beginning, God in his history with humanity differentiates between human existence as an existence in partnership with him and the perpetration of sin in human life. Thus the great possibilities of human existence always remain the wider horizon that characterizes every human person and to which every person is to respond. For in every human being we encounter God's honoured partner, one who is 'always of value and interesting . . . because God is his Friend, Guarantor and Brother' (*CD* IV/3.1, p. 800). Hence, 'human rights and human dignity' are 'not a chimera' (*ChrL*, p. 270) for the Christian understanding of the human, but rather a reality which is fundamental when the human person is seen in the light of Jesus Christ. Therefore, it is no accident that Barth's anthropology presses into an ethics concerned with a life of human dignity and affirmation for all persons. It cannot be an ethics merely for the Christian community, but must seek a life for all people which truly deserves to be called 'human'.

THE HUMAN AS THE IMAGE OF GOD

The anthropology that Barth sets out is part of the doctrine of creation (*CD* III/2). In accord with what has been said so far, creation cannot be understood as an independent sphere alongside God's decision to elect and to save. Rather, as Barth sees it, it is the first work of the realization of this decision. Creation was called into existence by God as a space for the realization of this decision. Hence, it cannot be understood without reference to the covenant with humanity which God wills to realize within the creation in history. Barth set out the relationship of covenant and creation in the well-known formula that 'covenant is the internal basis of creation', and creation is the 'external basis of the covenant' (*CD* III/1, pp. 94ff.). Correspondingly, creation is structured by God in such a way that it is suitable for the accomplishment of the covenant.

In relation to the human creature, this means that God created this creature as one 'which in all its non-deity and therefore its differentiation can be a real partner; which is capable of action and responsibility in relation to Him' (*CD* III/1, pp. 184–5). Thus, the earthly being of the human creature manifests a similarity or analogy to God's own being. We have to recognize this similarity or analogy in the concrete man Jesus in whom God has elected the whole of humanity and in whom the true human existence intended by God is realized. For the 'humanity of Jesus is . . . the repetition and reflection of God Himself, no more and no less. It is the image of God, the *imago dei*' (*CD* II/2, p. 219). What is true of this man subsequently is also true for humanity in general: it 'is created in the image of God' (*CD* II/2, p. 324).

The decisive thing for understanding what is, in the framework of the theological tradition, a novel grounding of the doctrine of the image of God in humanity, is the precise way in which we are to conceive of the 'analogy' or 'similarity' between human existence and God's own existence. Barth himself emphasizes that it is not a matter of an *analogia entis* (cf. *CD* II/2, p. 220), which he characterized bluntly as an 'invention of the Antichrist' in the foreword to the first volume of the *Church Dogmatics* (*CD* I/1, p. xiii). For by *analogia entis*, he understood the attempt of Roman Catholic theology to construe, on the basis of the human, a creaturely affiliation to God whose measure is human being itself. It is an open question whether this gets to the heart of the classical doctrine of the *analogia entis*.[8] In any event, Barth himself wants to understand the analogy in the sense of an *analogia fidei*, which is to say that he understands the correspondence between the existence of God and the existence of the human person as something that only discloses itself in faith in the God who affirms all human beings in the man Jesus. With this understanding of the *analogia fidei*, three fundamental and constitutive aspects of the human creature in its correspondence to God come into view.

Humanity as co-humanity

In Barth's understanding, in the light of faith in Jesus Christ, it is evident that it is no accident that the human creature exists structurally in relations. Rather, this relationality must be understood as an external expression of the fact that the triune God himself exists as Father, Son, and Spirit in relations, namely in the relation of love (*CD* II/2, pp. 220f.). In the man Jesus, God turns this love of his *ad extra* in such a way that, in the first instance, the relation of God and Jesus corresponds to God's own inner self-relation. As God is for him, so Jesus is the man for God. But he is the man for God in a definite form of humanity, namely in his being for other human beings. 'The humanity of Jesus, His fellow-humanity, His being for man as the direct correlative of His being for God, indicates, attests and reveals this correspondence and similarity' between him and God (*CD* III/2, p. 220). But humanity in general participates in this correspondence and similarity in such a way that the human person is human only in relation to fellow human beings. Human 'existence with fellow humans' is the 'basic form of humanity' in which a person is the 'parable of the existence of his Creator' (*CD* III/2, pp. 203ff.). Therefore, relatedness to others marks out the human creature as belonging to God. It reminds the human person that he or she is determined to be God's covenant partner. It makes the enactment of a life of co-humanity into the task of a lifetime which does not take place at some distance from God, but which, on the contrary, is itself intrinsic to our relation to God. And so, a 'humanity without the fellow-man' (*CD* III/2, p. 229) is a possibility ruled out by the knowledge of God.

According to Barth's interpretation, this is particularly underlined by the *locus classicus* for the idea of humanity in the image of God, namely Genesis 1:26f. (cf. *CD* III/1, pp. 288ff.). Barth interprets this text in such a way that God is said to create the human as man and woman, 'because He is not solitary in Himself, and therefore does not will to be so *ad extra*' (*CD* III/2, p. 324). Thus, 'woman is to man and man is to woman supremely the other, the fellow-man' (*CD* III/2, p. 288). This is so because what is manifest in the irrevocable differentiation and relatedness of man and woman is that in order 'to be God's partner in this covenant, man himself requires a partner' (*CD* III/1, p. 290), and cannot be understood as God's creature without this partner. The exegetical legitimacy of this interpretation of Genesis 1:26f. will have to be debated. Nevertheless, it is in fact very significant that Barth conceived co-humanity in this kind of concrete way, in which the existence of human beings – over and above all other individual relations – is understood as a summons to understand all human relations as relations based on partnership. Such relations are not those in which one lords it over the other, but rather those in which people ought to be for one another 'companions, associates, comrades, fellows and helpmates' (*CD* III/2, p. 288). Everything that is to be said about humanity has its 'proper locus' (ibid.) in the relation of man and woman, and can acquire the power to illumine and invigorate the realization of humanity as a whole from there. If we were to excise this 'primal form' of co-humanity from thinking about humanity, we would 'know nothing of the I and the Thou and their encounter, and therefore [know nothing] of the human' (*CD* III/2, p. 289).

Unfortunately, in his ethics Barth spoiled the gain of this emphasis on the significance of sexual differentiation – one which has not been taken for granted in theological anthropology to this day – by interpreting the relation of man and woman as an ordered relation in which the man takes precedence and the woman is subordinate (cf. *CD* III/4, pp. 169–72). Not unjustly, this has brought the accusation of 'patriarchy' against him.[9] Yet, it is not evident exactly why the 'existence in the encounter with other humans' (*CD* III/4, p. 116) to which the differentiation of human being as male and female points must be understood in such stratification. If 'the female is to the male, and the male to the female . . . the fellow-man' (*CD* III/4, p. 118), then it is much more reasonable to conceive the mutual communication of equally human human beings in their otherness as the 'basic form of humanity'.

The human person as the soul of the body

Barth's idea that the human person exists in a definite order that implies precedence and subsequence, as we have just described it, becomes more appropriate, however, in my view, when fruitful use of it is made in the course of describing the being of the individual human person. The person is 'the soul of his body', that is, the 'subject, form and life of a substantial organism' (*CD* III/2, p. 325), in that in its unity with the body the soul is accorded priority in the structuring of an individual life. Once again, Barth grounds this in the man Jesus as the 'whole man'. 'The interconnection of the soul and body and Word and act of Jesus' is 'of lasting significance . . . from within' because it is 'not a chaos but a cosmos, a formed and ordered totality' (*CD* III/2, p. 332). Christologically, this relation is also to be understood as a creaturely 'depiction' of and 'correspondence' to the relation between God and humanity, a relation that is an event in Jesus Christ. The true man Jesus is a whole man because he wills and fulfils himself. 'He lives in sovereignty. His life of soul and body is really His life. He has full authority over it' (*CD* III/2, p. 332). On this basis, it is true for human beings in general that they also have to fashion, to take responsibility for, and to risk their own lives in the life-giving presence of God's Spirit. In this, Barth sets himself against both an abstract materialism which wants to understand the human person merely on the basis of corporeality, and equally against an abstract spiritualism of the kind he believed could be found in the tradition of the Greek doctrine of the immortality of the soul (cf. *CD* III/2, pp. 382ff.). The human person only lives in the relation of the soul to the body (*Körper*) which, precisely by being ensouled, becomes the body (*Leib*) in the biblical sense of the word. 'The organic body [*Leib*] is distinguished from the purely material body [*Körper*] by the fact that . . . it is besouled and filled and controlled by independent life' (*CD* III/2, p. 378). Without this ensouling the human person would be 'subjectless', just as conversely a human being would be 'objectless' should the significance of the body be denied (*CD* III/2, p. 392). 'I cannot be myself without at the same time being my body.[10] I cannot answer for myself without at the same time answering for my body' (*CD* III/2, p. 378). But I can only do this because the soul is the formative 'centre' which makes human life into an 'independent life' over against God and other human beings (*CD* III/2, p. 397).

Barth greatly emphasized this element of the independence of the human being, an independence that finds expression in an individual's own perceiving, thinking, willing, desiring, and active existence. For this reason, every human being must be regarded as distinctive and unsubstitutable in the eyes of God and other people. A human being is never merely one number among many and may never be degraded into a mere object that others can treat like a thing. In just this way, the man Jesus himself has his 'own mystery' that befits him (see *CD* III/2, p. 328), a mystery which is not abolished even by God. And so also for the human generally, partnership with God means that a person can and must be the 'subject of his own decision' (*CD* III/2, p. 396), and that this is not taken away by God. It is also in this context that Barth's strong statements about the capacity of the human person to encounter God, to hear him, and to answer him are made. As the soul of the body, the human creature is 'qualified, prepared and equipped for this activity' (*CD* III/2, p. 396). This is an ontologically grounded creaturely capacity which is neither founded nor abolished by actual religiosity or a-religiosity. It is subject neither to debate nor to human disposition. It must be presupposed in theological anthropology as something self-evident.

The theological ethic associated with this anthropology is therefore also relieved of the need to justify itself at length in the secular world for asserting that the human person is claimed by God in the freedom of ethical responsibility. Moreover, inasmuch as the human person is an indelible image of God, this capacity to hear God must be constantly exercised so that it does not atrophy and actually wither away in sin. Thus, it is no accident that the theologically explicit character of Barth's ethical and political discourse made him one of the most listened to and seriously received theologians of his day, at least in the German-speaking world.[11] Where what is at issue is our own responsibility for taking decisions in the area of ethics and politics, it must be made clear that in relation to all the ambiguous human decision-making, God is a constant advocate of decisions that are to be called 'truly human'.

The human person in limited time

As Barth understands them, decisions in favour of the human creature and humanity are *per se* subject to a definite limit. There can be no absolute decisions, but only relative ones. Given the determinative context of anthropology described above, this is not only the case because every decision which affects the common life of human beings must be set in relation to the dignity and rights of other people, and mediated thereby. Beyond this, the embodied character of human existence impresses upon us the fact that every human being is limited in space. The humanness of the human person would be lost if he or she were to be regarded – as is possible by means of modern technology – as a creature without limits, whose threatened and vulnerable character need not be taken into account in a fundamental way. Something similar is also true for the temporal limitation of the human person, a limitation which Barth treated alongside co-humanity and the soul-body structure as the third constitutive reality of creaturely existence (cf. *CD* III/2, pp. 437ff.). The uniqueness of the human existence of Jesus in time corresponds to the uniqueness of the event of salvation and makes our living a 'unique opportunity' (cf. *CD* III/2, pp. 535ff.). It is limited by the past and it is limited by the future. Once we were not and once we will no longer be. The time given to us is delimited time and therefore finite. So, in distinction from God, we are mortal.

Barth did not understand this to be an evil or negative fate which the Creator imposed upon us as a result of our sin. Every human being once was not. But this does not mean that he or she comes from nothing or arises 'out of an abyss that has spewed us out only to swallow us up again' (*CD* III/2, p. 576). Rather, our life is preserved and borne by the summons of the Creator, so that we are able to place full confidence in the path which has been affirmed by God (cf. *CD* III/2, pp. 576f.). What is more problematic, however, seems to be the fact that we must die. For between our birth and our death lies our life in sin by which we make death into the 'radical negation of life': 'Death means that our existence as human beings is really and finally a negation' (*CD* III/2, p. 625). For us death becomes 'the final evil [*malum*]', the 'sign of God's judgment' (*CD* III/2, p. 626) because it finally confirms that by our actions and omissions we have made space for the destruction of the earthly relationships in which we exist.

Yet according to Barth, death as the natural creaturely limit of temporally finite human existence must be differentiated from this actual form of death which, for Jesus, is the form of death on the cross. Jesus also could only suffer death because he was mortal. With this thesis of the mortality of Jesus' humanity, indeed of all humanity, Barth contradicted a significant christological and anthropological tradition. According to this tradition, human death is the result of sin, and since Jesus was understood to be without sin, his death could only be conceived in such a way that he took it upon himself freely.[12] For Barth, on the other hand, the assertion of the mortality of Jesus and thereby the natural mortality of all human beings is an 'anthropological necessity' (*CD* III/2, p. 630) because otherwise Jesus himself, as a human being, would have been incapable of dying even if he had freely willed it.

For this reason, Barth could also not agree with the argument made from eschatology which favours an understanding of the 'human being without death', an argument being put forward once again in our day.[13] Such an argument says that Christian hope orients itself to an eternal life in which the finitude sublated in God does not include death. Yet, in Barth's understanding 'eternal life' did not mean the negation of the mortality of the human, but rather the 'redemption of his this-sided, finite and mortal being' by the eternal, gracious God (*CD* III/2, p. 633). The human 'as such . . . has no beyond. Nor does he need one, for God is his beyond . . . His divinely given promise and hope and confidence . . . is that even as this one who has been he will participate, not in nothingness, but rather in the eternal life of God Himself'(*CD* III/2, pp. 632f. (ET amended)). Under this promise, it is possible for human beings to affirm that they must die because in hope in Jesus Christ they learn to differentiate the death which they bring upon themselves from the end of life which belongs to their constitution as creatures.

This does not mean that by virtue of this differentiation, this end simply becomes something unproblematic. Rather, Barth ascribes it to what he calls the 'darker side' of the good creation which is not to be confused with evil (cf. *CD* III/1, pp. 372ff.). Good, creaturely existence is not a paradisal existence free from suffering. It is vulnerable and imperilled. To it belong sorrow, pain, and the experience of meaninglessness. Of course, humans can and should do everything they are capable of doing so that the 'brighter side' of their creatureliness can be the first word time and again (*CD* III/1,

pp. 370ff.). Above all, they can and should be concerned to resist aggres-
sively the real evil which, in Barth's view, tends to attach itself with relish to
the 'shadow side'. But the goal of human action can never be to negate the
boundaries of human existence and to lead human beings to believe in the
illusion of a life without inescapable limitations, without old age, sickness,
and death. Only idols, and not God, make such promises. For this reason,
human life is to be a matter of singing the praise of the creatureliness of the
human being precisely in the face of this 'shadow side'.[14]

Barth's anthropology is therefore marked by great realism in relation to
the actual existence of human beings. Undoubtedly, it wants to be understood as encouragement to enact the true humanity for which God created
the human. Hence, it shows the wealth of possibilities which are available to
the human as the partner and image of God in his or her creaturely relations,
and which can be made use of with great freedom. But in this freedom,
human beings ought – with modesty, humility, and not least with cheerful
composure – to remain aware of the fact that their actions will never be
divine and absolute, but always earthly and relative. For this reason, Barth
himself was an outspoken opponent of all human ideologies that bring
actual human life under the control of some sort of ideal, concept, or system,
and precisely in so doing lose sight of the real human being.[15] For this
reason above all, he regarded it as the task of the Christian community, in a
society controlled time and again by ideologies, to stand up in defiance
against 'the clerics . . . , the pharisees and scribes . . . , the tyrants . . . , the
spirit of the age in politics, society and science'[16] – for the sake of discerning
the human person as he or she really is before God.

LIVED ANTHROPOLOGY

We began from the assumption that in contemporary theology Barth's
anthropology is suspected of being too specifically theological, that is, of
giving too little room to the experiences which people have today. However,
upon careful examination of Barth's exposition of his anthropology, this
suspicion cannot be sustained. Rather, close examination indicates that it is
precisely the concentration on the centre of the Christian faith that opens up
a perspective on every human being which encourages us to see the human
creature soberly, both in its great possibilities and in its actual failures; but
even more, this concentration encourages us to view the human creature
with hope. Theology and church therefore need not concern themselves
over whether they capture the human creature in its structural constitution
and in the problems that affect its life directly, when they think from the

'bright place' which God created in the world in the true man, Jesus Christ. Neither do church and theology need to crawl off into a religious corner where sullenness and resignation about humanity reign in relation to the many and difficult problems which confront the human today on small and large scales. Rather, on the basis of faith's experience of true human existence in the midst of the world of disorder and injustice, the Christian community and individual Christians are always in the process of setting out anew in order to stand up concretely for true human existence in the midst of a world of injustice.

In the ethics of the doctrine of reconciliation, one of the published fragments of Barth's literary estate, with which his work on the *Church Dogmatics* broke off, the summons to just such a Christian life becomes the last word of Barth's theology. For when, on the basis of the Kingdom of God that has come, Christians petition for the universal coming of this Kingdom, 'only man can be at issue in their . . . thinking and speech and action' (*ChrL*, p. 269). '[A]ccording to the measure of what is possible for them, their action must in all circumstances take place with a view to people, in address to people, and with the aim of helping people' (*ChrL*, p. 266). For they are indeed witnesses of the God 'who seeks and magnifies his honour by thinking of men, by taking them to Himself, by establishing their right as their Creator, Father, Judge and Deliverer, by creating and giving to them perfect life, freedom, peace and joy' (*ChrL*, p. 266).

Anthropology, as Barth understood it, can and must be lived out as a practical anthropology in the Christian community and in the lives of individual Christians in the midst of society and in opposition to all the inhumanity that reigns there; it must be lived out in active service of a better human righteousness. The Christian community may never allow itself to be surpassed by anyone in its solidarity with real people. But rather – and this is not the least of its tasks – this community will represent to all people the world of human beings reconciled in Christ when, in freedom, it offers them 'the image of a strangely human person' (*ChrL*, p. 204).

Notes

1 For a characteristic recent example, see W. Pannenberg, *Anthropology in Theo-logical Perspective* (Edinburgh: T & T Clark, 1985).
2 D. Bonhoeffer, *Letters and Papers from Prison* (London: SCM Press, 1971), pp. 278–82.
3 See here W. Krötke, *Der Mensch und die Religion nach Karl Barth* (Zurich: TVZ, 1981).
4 On recent critical discussion of Barth's understanding of religion, see J. Ring-

leben, 'Religion und Offenbarung. Überlegungen im kritischen Anschluß an Barth und Tillich', in U. Barth and W. Gräb, eds., *Gott im Selbstbewußtsein der Moderne. Zum neuzeitlichen Begriff der Religion* (Gütersloh: Mohn, 1993), pp. 111–28.

5 Cf. F. W. Graf, 'Die Freiheit der Entsprechung zu Gott. Bemerkungen zum theozentrischen Ansatz der Anthropologie Karl Barths', in T. Rendtorff, ed., *Die Realisierung der Freiheit. Beiträge zur Kritik Karl Barths* (Gütersloh: Mohn, 1975), pp. 115ff.

6 For a detailed account of this, see my study, *Sünde und Nichtiges bei Karl Barth* (Neukirchen: Neukirchener Verlag, 1983).

7 This sentence, present in the *KD*, is absent from the English translation–TR.

8 On this, see E. Jüngel, 'Die Möglichkeit theologischer Anthropologie auf dem Grunde der Analogie', in *Barth-Studien* (Gütersloh: Mohn, 1982), pp. 210ff.

9 For this criticism, see C. Janowski, 'Zur paradigmatischen Bedeutung der Geschlechterdifferenz in K. Barths "Kirchlicher Dogmatik"', in H. Kuhlmann, ed., *Und drinnen waltet die züchtige Hausfrau. Zur Ethik der Geschlechterdifferenz* (Gütersloh: Mohn, 1995), pp. 140ff.

10 This sentence, present in the *KD*, is absent from the English translation – TR.

11 There is a characteristic story from 1946, told by Barth of his meeting with Wilhelm Pieck, later to be the first president of the DDR: 'On that occasion the elderly Pieck made the curious comment: What Germany needs now is a new enforcement of the Ten Commandments. To which I, brave theologian replied: Yes, especially the first!', in J. Fangmeier and H. Stoevesandt, eds., *Karl Barth. Briefe 1961–1968* (Zurich: TVZ, 1975), p. 553.

12 For a contemporary debate with Barth on this problem, see H. Vogel, 'Ecce homo. Die Anthropologie Karl Barths', in *Verkündigung und Forschung* (1949–50), pp. 102ff.

13 Cf. W. Pannenberg, *Systematic Theology*, vol. II (Edinburgh: T & T Clark, 1994), pp. 265–75.

14 According to Barth, the music of Mozart can stand as an outstanding example of how the praise of the creation can be sung in the face of the creation's shadow side: see *CD* III/3, pp. 297–9.

15 In the ethics of the doctrine of reconciliation, ideologies are related to the lordship of demons (*ChrL*, pp. 224–7).

16 K. Barth, 'Die Botschaft von der freien Gnade Gottes' in M. Rohkrämer, ed., *Karl Barth. Texte zur Barmer Theologischen Erklärung* (Zurich: TVZ, 1984), p. 156.

Further reading

Gunton, C., 'The Triune God and the Freedom of the Creature', in S. W. Sykes, ed., *Karl Barth. Centenary Essays* (Cambridge: Cambridge University Press, 1989), pp. 46–68.

Hunsinger, G., *How to Read Karl Barth. The Shape of his Theology* (Oxford: Oxford University Press, 1991), pp. 185–224.

Jüngel, E., *Karl Barth. A Theological Legacy* (Philadelphia: Westminster Press, 1986), pp. 104–38.

McLean, S. D., *Humanity in the Thought of Karl Barth* (Edinburgh: T & T Clark, 1981).

Webster, J., *Barth's Ethics of Reconciliation* (Cambridge: Cambridge University Press, 1995).

Webster, J., *Barth's Moral Theology. Human Action in Barth's Thought* (Edinburgh: T & T Clark, 1998).

11 The mediator of communion

Karl Barth's doctrine of the Holy Spirit

GEORGE HUNSINGER

The doctrine of the Holy Spirit is, as Adolf von Harnack once observed, the 'orphan doctrine' of Christian theology. Unlike the doctrine of the Trinity or the doctrine of Christ's person, it has never been stabilized by a conciliar decision of the church, although it is as vexing, contested and uncertain as any doctrine the church has ever known. An omen of things to come emerged as early as the Council of Nicaea (AD 325). Diverted by dissension over other questions, the council produced a creditable statement of the church's belief in God the Father, and especially of its belief in the deity of God the Son (which was, of course, the chief point at issue), but then closed rather weakly by stating its belief, 'and in the Holy Spirit' – with no further elaboration at all.

The deficiency was partly remedied by the ensuing Council of Constantinople (AD 381). Words were added to the Nicene Creed which have remained normative for the church ever since. The Holy Spirit in whom the church believes, the Creed now stated, is 'the Lord and Giver of life, who proceeds from the Father; who with the Father and the Son together is worshipped and glorified; who spoke by the prophets'. This statement, however slight, acknowledged the Holy Spirit's full and unabridged deity, indicated something of the Spirit's place within the Holy Trinity, and affirmed that the Spirit communicates God's Word to us through select human intermediaries. Unaddressed, however, were many matters that would divide Christendom throughout its history right down to the present day. To speak only very generally, these were matters having to do with revelation and salvation, with ecclesiology, ministry and sacraments, with eschatology and society, with justification, sanctification and glorification, and above all, as perhaps the overarching issue, with the unity and distinction between the saving work of the Spirit and the saving work of Christ.

Although Karl Barth's views on these unresolved matters have been vigorously disputed, the discussion has not been very fruitful so far for the simple reason that the scope and intricacy of his thought have yet to be sufficiently grasped. One point, for example, that has been widely over-looked is that Barth saw 'revelation', 'reconciliation', and 'redemption'[1] as standing in a set of relationships that were subtle, flexible, and complex. Revelation and reconciliation, for example, were regarded as inseparable. Just as revelation without reconciliation could only have been empty, so reconciliation without revelation could only have been mute. Revelation in fact imparted the reality of reconciliation, even as reconciliation formed the vital truth that revelation made known. Neither could be had without the other since both were identical with Jesus Christ. Above all, they embraced a complex temporality. Revelation and reconciliation each centred in-alienably on what had taken place in the life history of Jesus Christ there and then, while yet involving receptive, eucharistic, and participatory mo-ments, continually, here and now. The relationship between what had already taken place 'there and then' and what continues to take place 'here and now' was, in effect, the decisive issue at stake in Barth's doctrine of the Spirit's saving work, as seen from the standpoints of both revelation and reconciliation.

'Redemption', on the other hand, which Barth defined as the future of reconciliation, was his category for the saving work of the Holy Spirit in its own right. Everything about the Spirit as seen less directly from the stand-points of revelation and reconciliation was, from the standpoint of redemp-tion, to have been placed centre stage, redescribed teleologically as a whole, and thereby amplified and enriched. A twofold perspective would result. Whereas reconciliation was redemption's abiding ground and content, redemption was reconciliation's dynamic consequence and goal. Redemp-tion as the peculiar and proper work of the Spirit represented the consum-mation of all things, the resurrection of the dead, and eternal life in communion with God. It was the absolute future which would at once reveal and impart Jesus Christ in his inexhaustible significance for the whole creation. Whereas from the standpoint of reconciliation, the work of the Spirit served the work of Christ; from the standpoint of redemption, the work of Christ served the work of the Spirit.[2]

Since Barth thought that reconciliation never occurred without revel-ation, nor revelation without reconciliation, no critique which presupposes their separation or fails to see their connection could possibly be of much interest, yet such critiques are commonplace. Similarly, since he thought that reconciliation was to be fulfilled by redemption, no critique can be very illuminating which presupposes that he saw reconciliation as the whole story in and of itself. Very ambitiously, Barth intended to develop a doctrine of the Holy Spirit's saving work that would be rigorously Christocentric, yet without becoming deficient in its grasp of essential trinitarian relations. No subordinationism, whether implicit or explicit, could be tolerated. Christ's reconciling work was not to be devalued but rather upheld as 'intrinsically perfect' (*CD* IV/3, p. 327), yet no 'subordinationist' displacement could be allowed of the Spirit's own special work of redemption. While the Christocentric aspect dominated Barth's discussion of the Spirit as seen from the standpoint of reconciliation, the anti-subordinationist aspect, for which programmatic hints are dropped regularly along the way (e.g., *CD* IV/2, pp. 507–11), was to have been established most fully from the standpoint of redemption. Not until such large-scale structural moves as these are more carefully pondered in Barth's dogmatics will the discussion of his views on the Holy Spirit begin to be more satisfying and worthwhile.[3]

An overview of Barth on the Holy Spirit can be gained by seeing that he regards the Spirit as 'the mediator of communion'. The 'communion of the Holy Spirit' (2 Cor. 13:14), in which believers become 'individually members of one another' (Rom. 12:5), is established as the Holy Spirit unites them with Christ by faith. Furthermore, through their definitive union and communion with Christ, as mediated by the Spirit, they are also at the same time given an indirect share in the primordial communion that obtains between the Father and the Son to all eternity. It is finally because the mediation of the Spirit obtains at this primordial level, as the eternal bond of love within the Holy Trinity, that the Spirit can also serve as the mediator of communion in other ways. The Spirit thus plays a role in originating and maintaining the incarnation, or the communion between Christ's deity and his humanity (*communio naturarum*), as well as a role in sustaining through time the primordial communion between the incarnate Son and his heavenly Father. The loving bond between Christ and believers by which they are incorporated into him as a community, as the body of which he himself is the head, takes place by the Spirit on this trinitarian and incarnational basis. The mediation of the Spirit thus moves in two directions at once: from the eternal Trinity through Jesus Christ to humankind, and from humankind through Jesus Christ to the eternal Trinity. It is a mediation of communion – of love in knowledge, and of knowledge in love – as the origin and goal of all things, made possible by the saving work of Christ.

A comprehensive discussion would show that, in Barth's theology, the saving work of the Spirit is trinitarian in ground, Christocentric in focus, miraculous in operation, communal in content, eschatological in form, diversified in application, and universal in scope. Not all of these themes can be developed here. After a very short introduction to the trinitarian and Christocentric aspects of Barth's pneumatology, only the themes of miraculous operation and communal content are presented more fully. Even so, what follows is no more than a sketch.

TRINITARIAN IN GROUND

Following Augustine, Barth views the Spirit as the eternal act of love, of communion and of peace obtaining within the immanent Trinity. 'He is', writes Barth, 'the common element, or, better, the fellowship, the act of communion, of the Father and the Son' (*CD* I/1, p. 470). He is the act in which the Father and the Son mutually love one another – their ineffable communion, their inseparable unity, their unbroken peace – to all eternity. The Holy Spirit is the love in which God dwells eternally in and for himself. As such, the Spirit is not only consubstantial with the Father and the Son, but also hypostatic in the same sense as they are. 'He is what is common to them', writes Barth, 'not insofar as they are the one God, but insofar as they are the Father and the Son' (*CD* I/1, p. 469). It is 'the essence of the Holy Spirit' to exist hypostatically in no other way than as 'the full consubstantial fellowship' between the Father and the Son (*CD* I/1, p. 482). As the blessed bond of peace in whom and by whom the two share their common unity, the Holy Spirit thus occupies a 'mediating position between the Father and the Son' (ibid.). Through the person or *hypostasis* of the Spirit, their ineffable communion in love and knowledge is conveyed, confirmed, and fulfilled to all eternity.

Barth's Augustinian way of speaking about the Spirit's role in this primordial trinitarian communion is textured and complex. Agential and non-agential language are both seen as necessary. A kind of mysterious conceptual iridescence results. Following Barth's pattern of usage, we might say that the Spirit 'mediates' the communion between the Father and the Son. We could then say that the Spirit is the 'mediator' of this communion, but we might also want to say that the Spirit is equally its 'mediation', or even that the Spirit just *is* this communion itself. The Spirit is the *koinonia* between the Father and the Son, being at once both its mediator (agential) and yet also its mediation (non-agential), but in any case a primordial, concrete form or *hypostasis* of the one being or *ousia* of God. The Spirit is thus fully God, equal in glory and excellency to the other two *hypostases*, even though very different from them in the order and manner of his subsistence within the dynamics of the eternal Trinity. The main point, however, is clear. The Holy Spirit is God insofar as God is eternally communion (*koinonia*).[4]

CHRISTOCENTRIC IN FOCUS

The Holy Spirit's saving work is also conceived as Christocentric in focus. Far from the Spirit-oriented Christology that some have suggested he presented, what Barth actually develops is a Christ-centred pneumatology. Indeed, this distinction points to an important difference between Barth and the modernist or liberal theologies he opposed. For in Barth's theology, it is Jesus Christ who constitutes the saving significance of the Holy Spirit in a way that is not true in reverse. That is, the saving significance of Jesus Christ is not to impart and bear witness to the Holy Spirit so much as it is the saving significance of the Holy Spirit to impart and bear witness to Jesus Christ. 'There is no special or second revelation of the Spirit', writes Barth, 'alongside that of the Son' (*CD* I/1, p. 475). The Holy Spirit brings no 'independent content' of his own, but instead a content which is determined 'wholly and entirely' by Jesus Christ (*CD* I/1, p. 452).

The significance of the Holy Spirit is not found directly or independently in himself. The Spirit does not signify, as in so many Spirit-oriented Christologies, that salvation consists exclusively or chiefly in effecting something *in nobis*, whether religious experiences, renewed dispositions, or a new mode of being in the world. On the contrary, the presence and power of the Spirit are understood to attest what the incarnate Word of God has done for our salvation apart from us (*extra nos*) (cf. *CD* IV/1, pp. 211–83) and to mediate our participation in it by faith (*participatio Christi*) (cf. *CD* IV/2, pp. 518, 526–33, 581–4). The Spirit who enabled Christ alone to accomplish our salvation as a finished work there and then is the very Spirit who enables us to participate in it and attest to it here and now. Because the person of Jesus Christ has not only enacted but is and remains our salvation, he is and remains the enduring focus of the Spirit's work.

The Spirit mediates the *Christus Praesens*

Barth argues that the operation of the Holy Spirit and the presence of Christ coincide.[5] The Holy Spirit, he writes, 'is no other than the presence and action of Jesus Christ himself: his outstretched arm; he himself in the power of his resurrection, i.e., the power of his revelation as it begins in and with the power of his resurrection and continues its work from this point' (*CD* IV/2, pp. 322–3). It is by the power of the Holy Spirit that Jesus enables human beings to see, hear and accept him for who he is – 'the Son of Man who in obedience to God went to death for the reconciliation of the world and was exalted in his humiliation as the Son of God' (*CD* IV/2, p. 323). The Holy Spirit is the power whereby Jesus as such attests and imparts himself as crucified and risen. 'Thus the only content of the Holy Spirit is Jesus; his only work is his provisional revelation; his only effect the human knowledge which has [Jesus] as its object' (*CD* IV/2, p. 654). The Spirit establishes and mediates a communion of love and knowledge between Christ and faith.

As disclosed by the Spirit, in other words, the knowledge of Jesus is not something merely cognitive, for it claims those who are addressed by the gospel as whole persons. In the power of the Spirit through the proclamation of the gospel, Jesus is present to believers and believers to him. 'Where the human Jesus attests himself in the power of the Spirit of God, he makes himself present; and those whom he approaches in his self-attestation are able also to approach him and to be near him.' Mutual self-presence becomes the basis for mutual self-impartation. 'More than that, where he makes himself present in this power, he imparts himself; and those to whom he wills to belong in virtue of this self-presentation are able to belong to him' (ibid.). Just as Jesus gives himself by the Spirit to those who receive him, so also are those who receive him enabled to belong to him by the Spirit in return. The Spirit mediates the self-impartation of Jesus himself, through which believers are drawn into union with him in order to receive and return his love.

In short, the saving activity of the Holy Spirit, as understood by Barth, is always Christ-centred in focus. In various Christocentric ways the Spirit functions as the mediator of communion. In the incarnation (*conceptus de Spiritu sancto*), he effects the union of Christ's deity and humanity (*communio naturarum*). In Christ's obedience as fulfilled in his death, he operates as the bond of peace between the Father and the Son. In the risen Christ's ongoing self-revelation and self-impartation, he creates communion between Christ and faith. In no sense that would be independent, supplemental, or superior does the Spirit's activity ever focus on itself, for in the one economy of salvation the Spirit serves the reconciliation accomplished by Christ from beginning to end.[6]

MIRACULOUS IN OPERATION

The work of the Holy Spirit, as Barth saw it, is miraculous in operation. The Holy Spirit is seen as the sole effective agent (*solus actor efficiens*) by which communion with God is made humanly possible. In their fallen condition (*status corruptionis*), human beings cannot recover a vital connection with God. Their minds are darkened, their wills are enslaved, and the desires of their hearts are debased. Through the proclamation of the gospel, however, the impossible is made possible, but only in the form of an ongoing miracle. This miracle is the operation of the Holy Spirit, not only to initiate conversion (*operatio initialis*), but also to continue it throughout the believer's life (*operatio perpetua*). The only condition (necessary and sufficient) for new life in communion with God is the Spirit's miraculous operation in the human heart (*operatio mirabilis*). Faith in Christ, hope for the world, and consequent works of love have no other basis *in nobis* than this unceasing miracle of grace. Faith, hope, and love, in other words, do not depend on regenerated capacities, infused virtues, acquired habits, or strengthened dispositions in the soul. Those who are awakened to lifelong conversion by the Spirit never cease to be sinners in themselves. Yet despite their continuing sinfulness, the miracle of grace never ceases in their hearts.[7]

Against emanationism

What Barth is asserting can be explained against the foil of what he rules out. The familiar alternatives of either divine 'determinism' or human 'free will' are both categorically rejected. Only some of their subtler forms can be considered here.[8] One of these would be the kind of 'emanationism' that emphasizes divine grace at the expense of human freedom. As being used here, 'emanationism' would be the belief that God and only God is the acting subject in works of Christian love. Christian love would be the prolongation of divine love, and Christians would be the channel through which it flows. They would function merely as passive instruments that are used by God, possessing no relevant agency of their own. By contrast, Barth affirms that 'it is not the work of the Holy Spirit to take from us our own proper capacity as human beings, or to make our capacity simply a function of his own overpowering control. Where he is present, there is no servitude but freedom' (*CD* IV/2, p. 785). No view of Christian love would be acceptable to Barth which did not allow for genuine human agency and freedom.[9]

Against synergism

When human freedom is stressed at the expense of divine grace, on the other hand, the opposite error occurs. The belief, known as 'synergism', that human freedom 'cooperates' with divine grace in effecting salvation would be an example. Roman Catholic and modern Protestant theologies, as Barth sees them, both exhibit this failing. In his pointed and famous essay *No!*, for example, Barth rejects several options that he thinks resemble Brunner's unfortunate 'point of contact'. These include the 'Augustinian' position in which divine and human activity are 'indirectly identical', and the 'Thomistic' position in which 'the divine *causa materialis* and the human *causa instrumentalis*' cooperate in effecting salvation.[10] What is common to all such views, Barth objects, is 'the systematic coordination of nature and grace' (*No!*, p. 96). Coordinations are properly 'systematic' when the formal relations between their terms can be stated without resort to paradox, anomaly, or disjunction in describing the radically new. Systematic coordinations offer familiar, intelligible pictures based on such schemes as 'causality' (superior and inferior), 'growth' (gradual and partial), or some other form of 'commensurability' (mutually limiting and complementary aspects of a larger unified whole).

No 'synthesis' which systematically coordinates God and humankind (grace and nature), whether with respect to reason or volition, can, Barth argues, be valid (*No!*, p. 99). Grace is not a matter of repairing this or that human capacity, but of contradicting fallen human nature as a whole, with all its capacities or incapacities, so that it actually transcends itself despite its fallenness. The 'formal relation' between grace and nature is that of 'miracle', not superior and inferior 'causality', or gradual and partial 'restoration' (*No!*, p. 101). Grace and nature are not partial, mutually limiting components of a single reality. Not even dialectically can they be identified as one. Although coexisting together in a certain common history and moving towards a common goal, they do not coexist in any 'natural' or 'commensurable' way. Grace is rather that miracle by which human reason in its radical fallenness is so contradicted, disrupted, and liberated that it provisionally grasps revelation. At the same time, human volition in its radical fallenness is likewise so contradicted, disrupted, and liberated that it provisionally fulfils the divine will (*No!*, p. 97). Barth writes:

> The doctrine of the point of contact . . . is incompatible with the third article of the creed. The Holy Spirit, who proceeds from the Father and the Son and is therefore revealed and believed to be God, does not stand in need of any point of contact but that which he himself creates. Only retrospectively is it possible to reflect on the way in which he 'makes contact' with human beings, and this retrospect will ever be a retrospect upon a *miracle*.   (*No!*, p. 121 rev.)

The root metaphor for this strange operation *in nobis* is not something analogous to ordinary processes but something unheard of, something that is not organic but disruptive, not gradual or cumulative but instantaneous and continual, not something partial but total. What the miraculous operation of the Holy Spirit brings about, that is, is not essentially restoration or healing but resurrection from the dead.

Human cooperation does not effect salvation

Barth does not deny that human freedom 'cooperates' with divine grace. He denies that this cooperation in any way effects salvation. Although grace makes human freedom possible as a mode of acting (*modus agendi*), that freedom is always a gift. It is always imparted to faith in the mode of receiving salvation (*modus recipiendi*), partaking of it (*modus participandi*), and bearing witness to it (*modus testificandi*), never in the mode of effecting it (*modus efficiendi*). As imparted by the Spirit's miraculous operation, human freedom is always the consequence of salvation, never its cause, and therefore in its correspondence to grace always eucharistic (*modus gratandi et laudandi*).[11] These distinctions apply both objectively and subjectively, that is, not only to salvation as it has taken place *extra nos*, but also as it occurs *in nobis*. Since to be a sinner means to be incapacitated, grace means capacitating the incapacitated despite their incapacitation. Sinners capacitated by grace remain helpless in themselves. Grace does not perfect and exceed human nature in its sorry plight so much as it contradicts and overrules it.

> What happens is this: *in nobis*, in our heart, in the very centre of our existence, a contradiction is lodged against our unfaithfulness. It is a contradiction that we cannot dodge, but have to validate. In confronting it we cannot cling to our unfaithfulness, for through it our unfaithfulness is not only forbidden but cancelled and rendered impossible. Because Jesus Christ intervenes *pro nobis* and thus *in nobis*, unfaithfulness to God has been rendered basically an impossible possibility. It is a possibility disallowed and thus no longer to be realized . . . one we recognize as eliminated and taken away by the omnipotent contradiction God lodges within us.[12]

In this miraculous and mysterious way, by grace alone – that is, through a continual contradiction of nature by grace that results in a provisional 'conjunction of opposites' (*coniunctio oppositorum*) – the blind see, the lame walk, and the dead are raised to new life (cf. Matt. 11:4).[13]

Descriptive adequacy defies systematic coordination

When this miraculous operation is described without resort to 'synthesis', 'system', or relativizing conceptual 'coordination' – that unholy triumvirate against which Barth railed in theological construction – the results can only be counter-intuitive. His account of the 'awakening to conversion', which, he says, 'has its analogy only in the resurrection of Jesus Christ from the dead' (*CD* IV/2, p. 556), is a good example. Conversion happens to and in the human person. 'It involves the total and most intensive conscription and cooperation of all one's inner and outer forces, of one's whole heart and mind' (*CD* IV/2, p. 556 rev.). Not merely something inward, it includes the physical and social dimensions of one's life as well. Nevertheless, while showing that divine action 'does not exclude but includes human action' (*CD* IV/2, p. 556), conversion belongs to 'that order of action which is specifically divine' (*CD* IV/2, p. 557 rev.). Therefore, 'on this aspect – its true and proper aspect – it is a miracle and a mystery'. It is 'not the work of one of the creaturely factors, coefficients and agencies which are also operating and perceptible' (ibid.). Any awakening to conversion is rather solely the work of God, 'who uses these factors and himself makes them coefficients and agencies for this purpose' (*CD* IV/2, p. 557).

In a pithy conclusion that typifies his anti-systematic thought, Barth remarks:

> We are thus forced to say that this awakening is both wholly creaturely and wholly divine. Yet the initial shock comes from God. Thus there can be no question of coordination between two comparable elements, but only of the absolute primacy of the divine over the creaturely. The creaturely is made serviceable to the divine and does actually serve it. It is used by God as his organ or instrument. Its creatureliness is not impaired, but given by God a special function or character. Being qualified and claimed by God for cooperation, it cooperates in such a way that the whole is still an action which is specifically divine.   (ibid.)

Note that this awakening is seen from two different standpoints which are merely juxtaposed, not synthesized. For the occurrence is not said to be partially divine and partially creaturely, but 'wholly divine' and 'wholly creaturely'. Emphasis falls strongly on the asymmetry that Barth posits between divine and human agency. The two factors repel all systematic coordination as 'comparable elements', for divine agency as such retains 'absolute primacy' as the sole effective factor in conversion. The human person is an 'organ or instrument' of this divine work, yet not passively (as in 'emanationism'). Rather, the human will actually 'cooperates' with the divine work, and in its own way actually enacts it ('wholly human'), yet without becoming its secondary cause (as in 'synergism'). Human freedom is not coerced, yet neither does it operate by its own strength. Divine grace is not conditioned by human freedom, yet uses it to achieve the divine ends. Human freedom depends on nothing but divine grace, yet ordinary human capacities are strangely actuated ('given a special function or character') despite their manifest inutility. Freedom is given only as it is actually received, and the gift is not intermittent but continual.

No familiar 'system' of causality or growth, no unified conceptual scheme, can accommodate this set of anomalies or adequately describe it. As a miraculous operation, conversion conforms only to something like the 'Chalcedonian pattern'. Divine and human agency thus cooperate 'without separation or division', 'without confusion or change', and 'without symmetry or systematic coordination' regarding efficacy.[14] This drastic alternative to conceptual closure expresses Barth's core belief that the saving work of the Holy Spirit is miraculous in operation.[15]

COMMUNAL IN CONTENT

The work of the Holy Spirit, as Barth saw it, is communal in content. Communion in three distinct forms – with Christ, with the Trinity, and with one another – all take place by the Holy Spirit. As the mediator of communion, the Spirit unites believers with Christ, through whom they participate in the eternal communion of the Holy Trinity, while at the same time they also find communion with one another. 'Communion' means love in knowledge, and knowledge in love, thus fellowship and mutual self-giving. It means sharing and participating in the being of another, without the loss of identity by either partner; for in true fellowship the identity of each is not effaced but enhanced; indeed, the identity of each is constituted not in isolation but only in encounter with another. The deepest form of communion, as depicted in the New Testament, is mutual indwelling, an I–Thou relation of ineffable spiritual intimacy (*koinonia*). The Spirit who proceeds from the Father and the Son, the Spirit of the Lord Jesus Christ, is at once the mediator of this indwelling and yet also the indwelling itself, the mediator, the mediation, and the very essence of what is mediated. The Holy Spirit is the Spirit of *koinonia*.

Koinonia with Christ: uniting the disparate

The mutual indwelling of Christ's two natures, established by the Spirit in the incarnation, serves as the backdrop for his uniting of Christ with the church. In both cases, Barth suggests, 'the work of the Holy Spirit is to bring and to hold together that which is different' (*CD* IV/3, p. 761). If an analogy may be permitted, the Holy Spirit operates something like the 'strong force' in modern physics, which holds disparate entities together within an atom's nucleus; for the Spirit serves as the incarnation's ultimate unifying ground, holding together the otherwise disparate realities of deity and humanity in

Christ's person (*CD* IV/1, p. 148). Unlike the strong force, however, the unity effected by the Spirit can be described only as 'a history', not as 'a datum or a state' (*CD* IV/3, p. 761). In that sense, the Spirit's unifying work is paradigmatic. It applies not only to the incarnation, but also to 'that which would seem necessarily and inexorably disparate in the relationship of Jesus Christ to his community' (*CD* IV/3, p. 761 rev.; cf. *CD* IV/2, pp. 652f.). The miraculous operation of the Spirit joins disparate realities for the sake of communion.

By mediating Christ to the community and the community to Christ, the Spirit establishes 'the unity of Jesus Christ in the heights and in the depths, in his transcendence and in his immanence'. He grounds 'the unity in which Jesus Christ is at one and the same time the heavenly head with God and the earthly body with his community' (*CD* IV/3, p. 760). As in the incarnation, what happens is a linking of the divine and the human: 'the divine working, being and action on the one side and the human on the other'. Two freedoms are mysteriously conjoined: 'the creative freedom and act on the one side and the creaturely on the other'. Disparate realities unite across the divine/human ontological divide: 'the eternal reality and possibility on the one side and the temporal on the other' (*CD* IV/3, p. 761). The Spirit 'brings and holds together Christ and his community, not to identify, intermingle or confound them, not to change the one into the other, or to merge the one into the other, but to coordinate them, to make them parallel, to bring them into harmony and therefore to bind them into a true unity' (*CD* IV/3, p. 761 rev.). The Holy Spirit 'constitutes and guarantees the unity of the *totus Christus*' (*CD* IV/3, p. 760) through a mediation of *koinonia* in union, correspondence, and love.

Participating through Christ in the *koinonia* of the Trinity

Communion with Christ in the Spirit involves participation in the communion of the Holy Trinity. Those joined to Christ by faith are granted a share through him in that communion where God is eternally God: the primordial communion of love and knowledge between the Father and the Son in the Holy Spirit. When he seeks and creates fellowship (*koinonia*) for its own sake (*CD* II/1, p. 276), God has no other end than this participation in view. 'He receives us through his Son into his fellowship with himself' (*CD* II/1, p. 275). 'He takes us up into his fellowship, i.e., the fellowship which he has and is in himself' (*CD* II/1, p. 276). 'In his unique being with and for and in another', the triune God 'does not exist in solitude but in fellowship' (*CD* II/1, p. 275). 'His innermost self is his self-communication; and loving the world, he gives it a share in his completeness' (*CD* II/1, p. 277). Love means 'not to wish any longer to be and have oneself without the beloved' (*CD* II/1, p. 33 rev.). In seeking and creating this communion, God 'wills to be ours, and he wills that we should be his. He wills to belong to us and he wills that we should belong to him. He does not will to be without us, and he does not will that we should be without him' (*CD* II/1, p. 274). The very God who does not will to be and have himself without us, the God of love, is the God who through the Son in the Spirit takes us up into his communion with himself. 'God brings us to participate in the love in which as the Father he loves the Son, and as the Son the Father' (*CD* IV/2, pp. 778f.). Through this participation God makes our action 'a reflection of his eternal love', and makes us 'into those who may and will love' in return (*CD* IV/2, p. 779).

Our participation in the love of the Holy Trinity is grounded, it may again be noted, solely in the freedom of God. God is free to be present with the creature, despite the indissoluble divine/human ontological divide, in order to establish this participation. Divine freedom for *koinonia* with the other is what Barth means by 'the absoluteness of God'. 'The absoluteness of God . . . means that God has the freedom to be present with that which is not God, to communicate himself and unite himself with the other, and the other with himself'. This divine/human union and self-communication 'utterly surpasses all that can be effected in regard to reciprocal presence, communion and fellowship between other beings' (*CD* II/1, p. 313). Divine freedom for *koinonia* is another name for the Holy Spirit, who unites us with Christ, and through him with the eternal Trinity, in unsurpassable communion.

We do not participate in God's eternal love without participating in the truth of God's self-knowledge. 'Revelation' is the effecting of this participation.[16] No knowledge of God occurs apart from fellowship with God (*CD* II/1, p. 182), so that knowing and loving God are inseparable (*CD* II/1, pp. 32f.). Knowledge of God, in Barth's theology, is essentially a form of *koinonia*.[17] The key word is again 'participation'. Our knowledge of God through the gospel is true, Barth urges, because it participates in the truth of God's self-knowledge. 'God knows himself: the Father knows the Son and the Son the Father in the unity of the Holy Spirit. This occurrence in God himself is the essence and strength of our knowledge of God.' 'Through God's revelation' we become 'participants' in this occurrence (*CD* II/1, p. 49), receiving and having a part in God's eternal self-knowledge (*CD* II/1, p. 68). For as 'God gives himself to us to be known in the truth of his self-knowledge' (*CD* II/1, p. 53), 'we receive a share in the truth of his knowledge of himself' (*CD* II/1, p. 51).

While our participation in God's self-knowledge is 'true and real', it is always an 'indirect participation' (*CD* II/1, p. 59). It is indirect because it is mediated in and through Jesus Christ. Through the true humanity of Jesus (with whom we are united in *koinonia* by faith) we come to share, indirectly, in God's own trinitarian self-knowledge. In the humanity of Jesus Christ, God has lowered himself to us in order to raise us to himself (*CD* II/1, p. 55). As God's one true covenant partner, Jesus is 'the first and proper [human] subject of the knowledge of God'. Through our union with Christ effected by the Spirit, God gives us 'a part in the truth of his knowing' and, through his knowing, in the divine self-knowledge. 'The eternal Father knows the eternal Son, and the eternal Son knows the eternal Father. But the eternal Son is not only the eternal God. In the unity fulfilled by the grace of the incarnation, he is also this man Jesus of Nazareth.' Everything depends on the particular 'knowledge that is and will be present in this man, Jesus', for his human knowing of God is, by its coinherence with the eternal Son, the appointed vehicle of mediation through which we come to take part in the truth of God's self-knowledge (*CD* II/1, p. 252). As we are 'taken up into fellowship with the life of the Son of God' (*CD* II/1, p. 162), we are given 'fellowship in his knowledge of God' (*CD* II/1, p. 252).

Koinonia with one another in Christ

As the Spirit incorporates us into Christ, and so into communion with the Holy Trinity, we also become members one of another. Between the first and second comings of Christ, the principal work of the Spirit is to form the community of Christ. The Spirit gathers the community in faith (*CD* IV/1, pp. 643–739), builds it up in love (*CD* IV/2, pp. 614–726), and sends it out into the world in hope (*CD* IV/3, pp. 681–901). 'The Holy Spirit', writes Barth, 'is not a private spirit'; the community that he gathers is not 'a pile of grains of sand or an aggregate of cells'. In Christ the individual presupposes the community, even as the community comes to fruition in each member. 'There cannot be one without the other.' Scripture ascribes salvation to the individual, Barth observes, only 'in the existence of the community', and salvation is appropriated by the community only 'in the existence of the individuals of which it is composed' (*CD* IV/1, p. 149). In principle, therefore, 'there can be no possible tension between the "individual" and the "community"' (*CD* II/2, p. 313). No compromise needs to be made between them, and 'no continual reacting' needs to occur 'on the one side or the other' – i.e., no individualism at the expense of the community, no collectivism at the expense of the individual. Nevertheless, the Holy Spirit works 'first in the community of God and only then . . . in individual Christians' (*CD* IV/1, p. 154). While 'we must not cease to stress the individual' (*CD* IV/1, p. 150), we must not fail to see that 'the being of the Christian . . . is a being in relation' (*CD* IV/1, p. 153). It is primarily in the *koinonia* of the community, therefore, not in the individual as such, that the work of the Holy Spirit is fulfilled (*CD* IV/1, pp. 150f.).

The precedence of the community in Barth's pneumatology is distinguished from an abstract collectivism. The community 'does not lead to any independent life in relation to its members. It lives in them' (*CD* II/2, p. 311). The community gathered by the Spirit is a true fellowship, not 'a collective in whose existence . . . the individual is not required as such', and for which the individual's 'particularity is a *pudendum*'. The union of believers is firm, 'but it is a union in freedom, in which the individual does not cease to be this particular individual', so that each member is united to the others in all his or her particularity (*CD* IV/2, p. 635). The individual, Barth writes, 'does not stand merely in or under the whole, but in his own place he is himself the whole. And whatever proceeds from the whole proceeds from himself. As each is for all, so all are for each' (*CD* II/2, p. 312). The community as a whole thus 'reaches its consummation' as the Holy Spirit works in the lives of its individual members (*CD* II/2, p. 314). 'The *particula veri* of "individualism"' (*CD* II/2, p. 311) is not lost, namely, that the Spirit actually exercises authority and operates 'in their hearts and in their free personal responses' (*CD* II/2, p. 314). The primacy of the community, therefore, does not exclude but includes the significance of the individual as a locus of the Spirit's communal work.

What makes this community distinctive is that its members uphold one another in fellowship instead of causing one another to fall (*CD* IV/2, pp. 816f.). It is a community that lives by the forgiveness of sins, where one sinner may love another, because the sins of each and all have been taken away. It is also a community whose members bear faithful and joyful witness to Christ for the sake of each other and the world. 'Only by the Holy Spirit do they become free for this action. But by the Holy Spirit they do become free for it. By the Holy Spirit the individual becomes free for existence in an active relationship with the other in which he is loved and finds that he may love in return' (*CD* IV/2, p. 818). Finally, it may be mentioned that the *koinonia* established by the Spirit also equips the community in freedom for solidarity (though not conformity) with the world (*CD* IV/3, pp. 762–95).

The saving activity of the Holy Spirit, as understood by Barth, is therefore communal in content. The Spirit is the presence and power of *koinonia* joining believers to Christ and through him to God and one another. 'In the Holy Spirit', writes Barth, 'they thus know themselves in and with him [Christ]; themselves in their union with him, and also with one another, in the fellowship of faith and hope and love in which they express themselves as his and find self-awareness as this people which has a common descent' (*CD* IV/2, p. 651). *Koinonia* with Christ in the Spirit means *koinonia* with the Trinity and with one another, including solidarity with the world.

Notes

1 Although these terms obviously need to be defined, only a rudimentary orientation can be offered here. For more on the interconnection between 'revelation' and 'reconciliation', see my 'Karl Barth's Christology', chapter 8 of this volume.

2 The volume on 'redemption' in Barth's projected dogmatics was unfortunately never written, and the volume on 'reconciliation', though massive, remained incomplete.

3 For representative criticisms, see P. J. Rosato, *The Spirit as Lord: The Pneumatology of Karl Barth* (Edinburgh: T & T Clark, 1981); T. Smail, 'The Doctrine of the Holy Spirit', in J. Thompson, ed. *Theology Beyond Christendom* (Allison Park, Pa.: Pickwick, 1986); C. Gunton, *The Promise of Trinitarian Theology* (Edinburgh: T & T Clark, 1991); R. Jenson, 'You Wonder Where the Spirit Went', *Pro Ecclesia* 28 (1993), pp. 296–304; W. Pannenberg, *Systematic Theology*, 3 vols. (Grand Rapids: Eerdmans, 1988–98).

4 Although Barth would say that God's being (*ousia*) is in communion (*koinonia*), he would not speak of God's being as communion. He would instead see God's *ousia* as a readiness for *koinonia*. *Koinonia*, he would say, logically presupposes the three divine 'modes of being' (*hypostases*). Although there is no *ousia* without the *hypostases* and no *hypostases* without the *ousia*, the divine *ousia* is logically prior. Barth identifies the *ousia* itself as a single, self-identical divine subject, who is free and sovereign in trinitarian self-differentiation. The one divine *ousia* exists in and only in the three divine *hypostases*. *Koinonia* presupposes the three divine *hypostases*, just as the *hypostases* presuppose the one divine *ousia*. It is therefore in the Holy Spirit, and not directly in the divine *ousia* as such, that the eternal *koinonia* of the three *hypostases* is to be found. The relation between the one *ousia* and the three *hypostases* cannot be captured by a single, unified thought (*CD* I/1, pp. 368f.; cf. pp. 359, 382).

5 In this respect, Barth follows Calvin closely. See W. Krusche, *Das Wirken des Heiligen Geistes nach Calvin* (Göttingen: Vandenhoeck & Ruprecht, 1957), pp. 146–51. 'What is distinctive about the Holy Spirit is not that he becomes present in and for himself, but rather that he makes Christ present. Calvin can speak of this in two ways. He can say that *the Spirit* makes Christ and the salvation he effected present, or that *Christ* makes himself and the salvation he effected present *through the Spirit*' (p. 151). Although Barth employs the second of these idioms throughout volume IV of his dogmatics, that should not be taken to imply that he holds a merely non-agential view of the Spirit. Barth's chosen idiom is appropriate to the doctrine of reconciliation, where he understands the accomplishment of reconciliation in a thoroughly Christocentric way. One would

expect the other, more agential idiom (which recurs throughout the dogmatics) to have re-emerged prominently in the doctrine of redemption.

6 A good example of a contrary view can be found in R. W. Jenson, *Systematic Theology*, vol. I (New York: Oxford, 1997), pp. 146–61. Jenson requires a supplemental saving work of the Spirit, since he explicitly denies what Barth takes to be the very heart of the New Testament, namely, that 'Christ fully accomplished our salvation at Golgotha' (p. 179). Most of Jenson's censure of Barth's pneumatology can be traced back to this fundamental disagreement.

7 The commendable effort by Eugene F. Rogers, Jr. to bring Barth and Aquinas into convergence founders at this very point, for Rogers does not take Barth's conception of the Spirit's miraculous operation adequately into account. Stated in terms of Thomistic vocabulary, supernatural operations in the soul, as Barth understands them, do not require the actuation of habits, nor do they tend toward such actuation. Barth believes that Thomistic views to the contrary cannot (logically cannot) escape the problems of synergism. When Barth states that human freedom is *entirely* dependent on grace, he means without the subvention of infused habits, virtues or principles in the soul. See Rogers, *Thomas Aquinas and Karl Barth: Sacred Doctrine and the Natural Knowledge of God* (Notre Dame Press: University of Notre Dame, 1995), pp. 188–92; cf. 76–79.

8 For more on Barth's rejection of determinism, see G. Hunsinger, *How to Read Karl Barth: The Shape of his Theology* (New York: Oxford, 1991), pp. 207–15; for his rejection of 'Pelagian' and 'Semipelagian' forms of autonomy, see pp. 215–18; cf. pp. 223f.

9 Barth sees 'emanationism' reflected in some statements of Nygren, who in turn draws upon Luther (*CD* IV/2, p. 752).

10 K. Barth, *No! Answer to Emil Brunner in Natural Theology* (London: Geoffrey Bles, 1946), pp. 65–128; on p. 85. (Further citations are given directly in the text.)

11 This way of formulating Barth's position brings out its implicit resolution of the sixteenth-century 'synergist' controversy between Philippist- and Gnesio-Lutherans. Barth in effect takes something from both sides of the dispute while transcending each. Although he agrees with the Philippists in insisting on something like a *modus agendi*, he sides with Gnesio-Lutherans like Flacius on the question of human incapacity. (See his favourable and perceptive comments on Flacius and the surrounding controversy in *CD* III/2, pp. 27–29.) Barth transcends the overly restrictive 'active/passive' polarity, around which the dispute bogged down, by allowing for a 'mode of acting' that without being causal is at once receptive, participatory, witnessing, and eucharistic. His resolution differs from that taken by *The Formula of Concord* (and perhaps keeps him closer to Flacius and even Luther) in that it assimilates *renovatio, regeneratio,* and *conversio* into the paradigm of 'resurrection' rather than into that of a gradual process like 'healing'. On the historical controversy, see C. E. Luthardt, *Die Lehre vom freien Willen und seinem Verhältnis zur Gnade* (Leipzig: Dörffling und Franke, 1863), pp. 191–278.

12 K. Barth, 'Extra Nos–Pro Nobis–In Nobis', *The Thomist* 50 (1986), pp. 497–511, on p. 510. (Cf. *CD* IV/4, pp. 13–23, on p. 22.)

13 Note that Barth speaks of sanctification 'in direct analogy to the doctrine of justification' (*CD* IV/2, p. 515) as involving a provisional state of '*simul peccator et sanctus*' (*CD* IV/2, p. 575; cf. 572f.).

14 On the Chalcedonian pattern in Barth's thought, see Hunsinger, *How to Read Karl Barth*, pp. 185–8, 201–18.

15 A fuller discussion would need to explore the place Barth might still allow for gradual or cumulative regeneration within the spiritual life of the believer. Although such a place cannot be completely ruled out (e.g., *CD* IV/2, pp. 566, 794), it seems undeniable that in Barth's soteriology this aspect is underdeveloped and excessively diminished. A Barthian solution after Barth might try to move in a dialectical rather than a synthetic direction, alternating back and forth between a holistic scheme informed by 'resurrection' ('again and again') and a gradualistic scheme informed by 'regeneration' ('more and more').

16 The Holy Spirit, as Barth develops at great length, is both the subjective reality and the subjective possibility of revelation (*CD* I/2, pp. 203–79). The Spirit, in other words, is the means by which we come to enjoy 'the communion with God which is realized in the revelation of God' (*CD* I/2, p. 257). God's revelation in Jesus Christ cannot be known apart from our reception of it and participation in it through the miraculous operation of the Holy Spirit.

17 The important work by A. J. Torrance, *Persons in Communion: Trinitarian Description and Human Participation* (Edinburgh: T & T Clark, 1996) curiously overlooks this point. Only by driving a wedge between 'revelation' and 'communion' in Barth, as though they were not mutually coinherent, can Torrance reproach Barth for focusing on revelation at the expense of communion.

Further reading

Hunsinger, G., *Disruptive Grace* (Grand Rapids: Eerdmans, 2000).

Rosato, P. J., *The Spirit as Lord. The Pneumatology of Karl Barth* (Edinburgh: T & T Clark, 1981).

Smail, T. A., 'The Doctrine of the Holy Spirit', in J. Thompson, ed., *Theology Beyond Christendom* (Allison Park, Pa.: Pickwick, 1986), pp. 87–110.

Thompson, J., *The Holy Spirit in the Theology of Karl Barth* (Allison Park, Pa.: Pickwick, 1991).

12 Christian community, baptism, and Lord's Supper

JAMES J. BUCKLEY

FOR AND AGAINST CHURCH AND SACRAMENT

Barth has a curious ambivalence towards the topic of this chapter. On the one hand, he called his great work <u>Church</u> Dogmatics (emphasis added). Each of its volumes (not to mention Barth's many other essays and books) speak within and about the church – or, as Barth came to put it, the body of Christ and thus provisional representative of all the world. In this sense, Barth was a key participant in a peculiarly modern debate over church and the rise of 'ecclesiology'. On the other hand, Barth was always a sharp critic of the church, whether in his early commentaries on Paul's letter to the Romans, his many essays on the German 'Church struggle' in the 1930s, or his smiles over triumphalistic claims that the nineteenth and twentieth centuries are 'the century of the Church'.[1] Indeed, he preferred to speak of 'the Christian community' rather than 'the Church'. What are we to make of this ambivalence? Barth's theology *from the midst of this Christian community* could all but guarantee that he would be marginal to those sections of the modern world for which the church is decreasingly a foothold for personal and professional fame and fortune. Yet his *deep criticisms of the church* could seemingly guarantee that Barth would also be marginal to the very community from which and to which he spoke. Barth forces us to ask how, if at all, we can speak with one voice for and about as well as against the church.

This seeming ambiguity over the church in Barth is duplicated and heightened in his treatment of what many Christian churches call 'sacraments'. On this score, too, Barth spoke in and about a community centred on Jesus Christ, '*the* sacrament',[2] in the community's prayer and preaching, baptism and the Lord's Supper, and life amidst the nations. On the other hand, Barth came to hold what he called a 'neo-Zwinglian' position on the sacraments (*CD* IV/4, p. 130) – affirming that baptism and the Lord's Supper are human actions, denying that they are sacraments. Barth ended his

Church Dogmatics before he could treat the Lord's Supper extensively – and there will be correspondingly little treatment of this practice here. The point is that in one breath Barth could align himself with liturgical reform, while in the next breath he could distance himself from most of the theology that was used to justify that renewal in the twentieth century. Again, how, if at all, is it possible to speak *from within and about* as well as *against* the church's life of communal prayer, worship, and 'sacraments'?

How, then, are we to interpret Barth? Was and is Barth ahead of his time, seeing unsettling issues where others saw easy consensus, calling the church to a new consensus even beyond the dialectic of No and Yes to the church? Or shall we say that, while Barth remains a doctor of the church on any number of issues, he offers fewer lessons on the subject of this chapter?

Companions, let us say, are those who eat bread (*panis*) together. Each listens as well as speaks. This essay will begin by listening to Barth, from the historical background to his theology of church and sacraments in the *Church Dogmatics*; only then will I permit some others at the table to speak up. However, veteran theologians will know, and theological novices ought to learn, that the effort to listen is always filtered through what we would like to be said. I hope to lay before the reader (especially novices in Barth's theology) some representative samples of Barth's theology of the Christian community. But, by the end of the chapter, I hope to use these texts in a way that sheds light on Barth's critics – and Barth's possible responses to those critics as he addresses the question of how Christians are called to exist within as well as against the church. Listening risks merely summarizing Barth; speaking risks merely using Barth for ends extrinsic to his theology. Both risks are necessary as one way to resist confusing guests and Host.

BARTH AND THE HISTORY OF CHURCH AND SACRAMENTS

Barth knew that his dogmatic theology of 'Church and sacraments' depended not only on a multiplicity of issues in biblical interpretation as well as pastoral practice but also on a history of controversies in the Christian community over church, baptism, and Lord's Supper. Indeed, Barth presumes readers who know something about the scenes of church history when 'Church and sacraments' have been at stake – the church and churches of the biblical canon, the Donatist debates in North Africa, the schism between Greek and Latin Christians in the Middle Ages, and the sixteenth-century creation of Christian confessions – Catholic and Protestant, Lutheran and Reformed, Magisterial and Radical. Even more important, Barth's theology of the Christian community, baptism, and the Lord's Supper presumes a narrative of the historical circumstances of the church in our own time – historical circumstances that Barth read differently in different periods of his life.

Barth's history of Protestant theology (written during the totalitarian threats of the 1930s, but not published until the more democratic late 1940s) begins with a characterization of the eighteenth century as the Age of Absolutism – i.e., the age when a human being is taken to be 'primarily the discoverer, the believer, and the exploiter of the miracle of human power' in cosmology, geography, science, technology, and especially politics. It is this absolutism that is also applied to theology. Barth calls the eighteenth century 'the classical century of the state Church', surprising those who identify *pre*-modern Christendom with 'established religion'. Modern man '"nationalizes" the Church and the Church allows this nationalization', elevating 'the idea of the relativity of all confessions to the status of a universally valid truth with the full weight of political power' long before theologians thought to do so. Modernity, from this point of view, is the birth of the question of what the normative human community and its rituals are – or (in other words) the birth of 'ecclesiology' as the study of normative *human* community, of 'Church sacramentology' as the study of normative *human* rituals and symbols. The result of this theology of church and sacraments was that 'the Church was led and claimed by the state in such a way that the state was primarily concerned for itself and for the Church only to the degree that this concern matched its own interests, put, with the utmost naivety, in the foreground'. Christianity thus becomes 'a more *individual*, more *inward* matter'. The church then becomes 'a free and voluntary religious assembly'. The church is there for pietists and rationalists – but 'not to disquiet me, but to strengthen me'. Similarly, there are sacraments, but they are relatively dispensable – relative to the discovery of a μυστηριον (*musterion*, the Greek word translated into the Latin *sacramentum*) 'within himself: he himself becomes the visible sign of the invisible grace'. Thus, in Barth's view, the church and its sacraments are enveloped on the one end by a totalitarian political community and on the other end by the individual in all his or her mysterious (sacramental) inwardness.[3]

A quarter-century later Barth would offer a narrative that, although not denying the truth of the earlier story, was more focused on the church's dispersal throughout democratic nations than its captivity by totalitarianisms of the right or left.[4] At the beginning of the last fully completed volume of the *Church Dogmatics* (1959), Barth noted that 'the Church in the modern period has slowly but recently lost its position in the world in the form in which it could previously enjoy it'. Barth rehearsed various proposed causes (the fragmentation of Christendom, the attractions of alien religions, the fashioning of autonomous individuals and nations) as well as the major Christian responses (reaction and restoration, self-satisfying religiosity, accommodation to secularism). Barth did not wish to overlook this shadow, although he is weary of each generation noticing the shadow as if it were the first to do so (CD IV/1, p. 19).

Nonetheless, Barth points out the 'remarkable coincidence'

> that at the very time and in the very situation when the secular world began to free itself from the Church, the Church began, not to free itself from, but to be unmistakenly free for the secular world, namely, free for the service to its own cause within the secular world which for so long it had for the most part neglected in pursuit of its own fantasies.

Barth is thinking of the increased focus on 'the form of a Church of the Word'; Christian missions unparalleled since the Christianization of Europe; the reform of the church's 'internal paganism'; a 'serious wrestling with the question of the knowledge of God'; a questioning of classical distinctions between clergy and laity, theologians and non-theologians; and the ecumenical striving for 'the unity of the Churches in the one Church of Jesus Christ'. In each case, Barth goes out of his way to point out the limits of each of these accomplishments. But in all of them he finds a 'turning of the Church to the world which has so remarkably accompanied the turning of the world from the Church' (CD IV/3, IV/1, pp. 21, 26, 33, 35, 37).

These narratives are important for two reasons. First, as I have already suggested, Barth's theology of church and sacrament must be read in the context of the history of modern theology – if not Barth's own narratives, then some other. Barth's theology of church and sacrament is as far from aiming to repristinate the Christian past as it is from imitating modernity's journey away from the church (even when the journey is undertaken in the name of comforting or criticizing the church). In fact, the two narratives above reflect two different circumstances in the twentieth century – the challenges of the church to and by totalitarian and democratic cultures.

Second, as a result, Barth's own theology of the Christian community changed as he wrote against and with the grain of modernity thus narrated. The genesis of Barth's theology of the Christian community is as real and controverted as the genesis of his theology more generally. I will not here focus on this genesis and growth for the same reasons that I did not dwell on Barth's historical context (i.e., like Barth, I wish to focus on his dogmatics of

Christian community, baptism, and Lord's Supper). However, it is essential to have some markers of Barth's development on the table.

GENESES

Barth's early theology was indebted to what he would later regard as the most powerful brand of Protestant liberalism. This was not the brand of neo-Protestant theology represented by those who capitulated to modernity's absolutism (e.g., the early Schleiermacher or Troeltsch). Barth's early theology was part of a more ecclesial or churchly movement, appealing to the later Schleiermacher and climaxing in Wilhelm Hermann. For example, in an early essay, Barth chided 'modern theology' for a religious individualism and historical relativism which made it impossible to 'work for the kingdom of God' in the pastorate – except by abandoning theology for a conservative authoritarianism that Barth also rejected. Barth's way out of this dilemma was the theology of Wilhelm Hermann, with its focus on 'the communion of the Christian with God' – and, more importantly, the discovery of 'Religious Socialism' as the social movement most pertinent to the gospel.[5]

In the first edition of his commentary on Paul's epistle to the Romans, Barth insists on the importance of the body of Christ in the organic growth of the Kingdom – and contrasts that body with the church. The body of Christ is the community that comprehends all (and not, like the church, just some) as well as the organism created by Christ (not, like the church, created by human beings).[6] The second edition of Barth's commentary on Romans yields a full-fledged dialectical critique of the church. 'Circumcision, Religion, the Church, do not possess positive content: they are tokens and signs which must be understood negatively, and they are established only in so far as their independent significance diminishes and finally dies' (*R*, p. 130).

Barth included sacraments here also. They are not fellowship with God but 'only *significant* of fellowship with God' – 'here, surely, under the wrath of God, Zwingli and the liberals are right'. In Barth's exegesis of Romans 9–11, Paul's pain over Israel becomes Barth's pain over the church – a church that negates the gospel but is all the more essential to it. 'The more the Church is the Church, he [who hears the gospel] stands within it, miserable, hesitating, questioning, terrified. But he [who hears the gospel] does stand within the Church, and not outside as a spectator.' How to do this is 'the KRISIS of the twofold nature of the Church' (*R*, pp. 74, 335, 343). This is one answer to the question of how Christians can be critics of the church from within the church.

Barth would later criticize this theology for its 'powerful onesidedness', including the 'almost catastrophic opposition of God and the world, God and humanity, God and the Church'.[7] However, to claim that the church is the locus of judgment 'is also to say that it is the *locus* of revelation', i.e., God's judgment.[8] We might call the theology of church and sacraments at this point an apophatic or negative ecclesiology and sacramentology in contrast to the kataphatic or positive ecclesiology and sacramentology Barth would later develop.

In any case, as Bruce McCormack puts it, it was during his first semesters in Göttingen (1921–2) that 'the Church came to be seen by [Barth] as the *locus* of authority in theology (rather than simply the *locus* of judgment as in the commentary on Romans)'. In his *Göttingen Dogmatics*, 'Barth advocated for the first time an ecclesial hermeneutic'. Further, as he moved from Göttingen to Münster (1925), 'Barth was increasingly coming to regard Catholicism as his major opponent, rather than liberal Protestantism'[9] – not least because Catholic reviewers of *Romans* 'displayed a genuine understanding of the point at issue' (*R*, p. 21).[10]

But the debates with Catholics in the late 1920s were eclipsed by what came to be called 'the German Church struggle' – the political and theological argument between Christians who supported and who opposed Hitler. Barth was the theological leader of the opposition; among other things, he almost single-handedly authored the 1934 Barmen Declaration. For the purposes of this chapter, the most important paragraph is the repudiation of the 'German Christians' in the Barmen Declaration's commentary on Ephesians 4:15–16.

> The Christian church is the community of brethren in which Jesus Christ presently works in the word and sacraments through the Holy Spirit. With her faith as well as her obedience, with her message as well as her ordinances, she has to witness in the midst of the world of sin as the church of forgiven sinners that she is his alone, that she lives and wishes to live only by his comfort and his counsel in expectation of his appearance.[11]

There follows a repudiation of the false teaching that the church can turn itself over 'at will or according to some dominant ideological and political convictions'. But the story of the Confessing Church was not, Barth thought, a 'heroic or saintly story'. The church spoke out too late and, when it spoke, it was too silent on the Jews, on the treatment of political prisoners, 'and so much else against which the Old Testament prophets would certainly have spoken out'. The Confessing Church was the church, as always, despairing of herself, setting her hope in God alone.[12] And so, even as participant in the Confessing Church, Barth was among its best critics.

THE DOGMATICS OF CHRISTIAN COMMUNITY, BAPTISM AND LORD'S SUPPER

The project of most importance for Barth's theology of church and sacraments from the 1930s until his death was the *Church Dogmatics*. A survey can scarcely hope to do justice to the movement of Barth's theology of these issues, not least because the work of placing the individual volumes in Barth's intellectual and social circumstances has barely begun. Here I simply identify the sections of the *Church Dogmatics* most pertinent to our topic, knowing that readers can turn to other chapters of this book for more complete elaboration. Whether and how these sections amount to an adequate theology of church and sacraments will be discussed in the final section.

The first volume of Barth's *Church Dogmatics* is a doctrine of the Word of God in its threefold form – revealed, written, and preached – as the criterion of dogmatics. Church and sacraments are located as the product of God's triune revelation (*CD* I/1, §8–*CD* I/2, §18), as authority under the Scriptures and so also freedom (*CD* I/2, §§19–21), and most extensively as the Word of God proclaimed in the church (*CD* I/2, §§22–4). Barth insists that this church proclamation includes preaching and sacraments – word and action, neither alone nor separate but 'preaching with the sacrament, with the visible act that confirms human speech as God's act' (*CD* I/1, pp. 56–71). This proclamation, like the bread and wine of communion, *is* the very Word of God only as it *becomes* this Word of God (*CD* I/1, pp. 88f.). Proclamation is proclamation insofar as it is the proclamation of a hearing church as well as the teaching church (*CD* I/2, §§23–4).

In these volumes, Barth is a critic of pietistic-modernist, as well as Roman Catholic, theologies of the church, primarily for lacking a theology of the Word – modernists collapsing the Word into silence and Roman Catholics giving sacraments a priority over the Word (*CD* I/1, §3). But the Evangelical church has its own problems, not least that 'the administration of the sacrament does not constitute the rule, but has become a solemn exception to the rule' (*CD* I/2, pp. 762f.).[13]

Such self-criticisms are surely part of the reason why the next volume of the *Church Dogmatics* is Barth's most extensive experiment in conceiving of revelation as sacrament. 'Revelation means the giving of signs. We can say quite simply that revelation means *sacrament*, i.e., the self-witness of God, the representation of His truth, and therefore of the truth in which He knows Himself, in the form of creaturely objectivity and therefore in a form which is adapted to our creaturely knowledge' (*CD* II/1, p. 52).

Further, 'the first sacrament' is the humanity of Jesus Christ and there is 'a sacramental continuity' stretching backward into the existence of Israel and forward into the existence of the church. However, Barth also insists that 'we must not overlook the fact that in revealing Himself in this way, He also conceals Himself . . . God exposes Himself, so to speak, to the danger that man will know the work and sign but not Himself through the medium of the work and sign' (*CD* II/1, pp. 54f.).

How, then, can Christians attend to God's *revelation* in work and sign that *conceal*? Barth's doctrine of the election of Jesus Christ elaborates this sacramental continuity in dramatic form. The election of Jesus Christ is also the eternal and ongoing election of the community. This community, Barth says, is a 'mediate and mediating' community, one yet differentiated as Israel and the church. Israel's specific service is to reflect the judgment of God in the promise heard, the passing of the old man. God wants (though he does not need) this service – as does the church. But Israel as a whole was disobedient – even if this cannot obscure God's promises to them. The church's service is to reflect the mercy in divine judgment, faith in the promise heard, and the coming of the new humanity. In this way the church is a confirmation – both positively and negatively – of God's election of Israel (*CD* II/2, §34).[14]

But the church is also a creaturely community and thus subject to the claims Barth makes about being a creature in God's cosmos. For example, the church can be one of creation's 'permanent objective reminders' of God's rule. Barth says that one need only think of the 'remarkable claim', the capacity for 'resistance' and for 'renewal' of the church, to see this (*CD* III/3, pp. 200, 204–10). Or, in his volume on the ethics of creation, 'the basic form of the active life of obedience understood and affirmed as service of the cause of God is man's direct or indirect co-operation in the fulfilment of the task of the Christian community' (*CD* III/3, p. 483; see also pp. 483–516). And this means, first, the action of presenting oneself for baptism, and 'allowing himself to be accepted by the community, as one who had behind him the death of Jesus Christ as the end of the old aeon and therefore of his own old life, and before him the resurrection and return of Jesus Christ as the revelation of the new heaven and the new earth and therefore of his own new life' (*CD* III/4, p. 490).

Thus, even as Barth thought that 'the community must accept the fact that it will always be a small minority' (*CD* III/4, pp. 484, 504), ethics becomes increasingly central – an ethics centred on God's action in Jesus Christ and human correspondence to this action. Baptism here is crucial, but is not (or is no longer) described as a 'sacrament'; the Lord's Supper remains in the background.

In *CD* IV, Barth gathers his treatment of the church under the rubrics of the Holy Spirit and the gathering, upbuilding, and sending of the Christian community. The community is gathered as a being-in-act whose 'special visibility' is to be the earthly-historical form of the existence of Jesus Christ as one, holy, catholic, and apostolic. This community is thus gathered between the time of the first and second *parousia* of Jesus Christ – a fact which is both its weakness and its strength (*CD* IV/1, §§62.2–62.3). The community is 'built up' as the 'real Church' by being (-in-history) the provisional representation of the whole world, constructed and eschatologically completed by God – especially in its worship. It is thus that the community is the *communio sanctorum* – a community which can grow inwardly in that the community lives and Jesus lives, which is indestructibly upheld in the face of dangers from within and without, and which is ordered on a basic 'Christologico-ecclesiological law' that is specified in a church law of service, liturgy, life, and example (*CD* IV/2, §§67.1–67.4). Finally, this community is sent as a people of God in world-occurrence who see 'the providence of God and the confusion of people' in Jesus Christ, who understand their freedom and dependence in this situation, and who thus exist totally on the basis of the 'two names' of Jesus Christ and the Holy Spirit. This community can thus exist in knowledge of, solidarity with, and obligation to the world since it is empowered to confess Jesus Christ in response to and correspondence with God's existence for the world. The task of witness has its content in Jesus Christ and all humanity, its addressee in a humanity joyfully addressed as saved, and its purity in seeing its task as living and constant while neither neglecting nor patronizing the addressee. On this basis and with this task, the sending of the community is accomplished in a ministry which is definite and limited and full of promise, whose nature is that of witness in proclamation and explication and application of the gospel, and whose forms are a unity in plurality of speech and of action (*CD* IV/3, IV/2, §§72.1–72.4).

The final fragments of Barth's *Church Dogmatics* are an 'ethics' of reconciliation, corresponding to his treatment of ethics in the second and third volumes of the *Church Dogmatics*.[15] The command of God here, Barth says, is the invocation of God enunciated in Psalm 50:15: 'Call upon me!' Specifically, the central prayer is 'the so-called our Father' – a centre that has a circumference or framework, for calling upon God has a beginning and a continuation, a 'foundation' and 'renewal': baptism and the Lord's Supper (*ChrL*, pp. 43–5, 50, 85, 212, 234).

One result – not, Barth insists, the 'motif and goal' (*CD* IV/4, p. xi) – of locating baptism and the Lord's Supper as this *lex agendi* (law of acting) and *lex orandi* (law of praying) is a negative thesis.

> Baptism and the Lord's Supper are not events, institutions, mediations, or revelations of salvation. They are not representations and actualizations, emanations, repetitions, or extensions, nor indeed guarantees and seals of the work and word of God; nor are they instruments, vehicles, channels, or means of God's reconciling grace. They are not what they have been called since the second century, namely mysteries or sacraments. (*ChrL*, p. 46)

What, then, are baptism and Lord's Supper? *CD* IV/4 depicts baptism as the differentiated unity between divine action (baptism in the Holy Spirit) and human action (baptism in water). The divine action is united to the human action insofar as the life and death of Jesus, which took place on our behalf, become a 'pledge and promise' for everyone in the resurrection and for the community in the work of the Spirit; the human action is united to the divine action insofar as the human action has its basis in Jesus' baptism and its goal in baptism with the Holy Spirit. In sum, the differentiated unity of divine and human action in baptism comes from and heads toward Jesus Christ; it is only in the movement from its origin to its goal that the divine action (baptism with the Holy Spirit) and human action (baptism with water) form a differentiated unity. Although Barth has a number of objections to infant baptism, his central objection is that it does not reflect this movement (*CD* IV/4, pp. 102ff.).

Barth tells us that the Lord's Supper was to be regarded as the 'crown' of his ethical section (*CD* IV/4, p. ix; cf. *CD* IV/2, p. 658). The Lord's Supper would have been 'the thanksgiving which responds to the presence of Jesus Christ in his self-sacrifice and which looks forward to His future' (*CD* IV/4, p. ix). Elsewhere the Lord's Supper is called the 'action of actions' and it is hinted that the Lord's Supper typifies the *unio cum Christo* of the community (*CD* II/2, pp. 640f.; *CD* IV/3, p. 761). But Barth could also worry that Vatican II Catholics make more of the Lord's Supper than the New Testament requires.[16] Barth also thought that his critique of infant baptism was less important than his constructive alternative – as well as his insistence that the Lord's Supper weekly be the church's norm.[17]

CRITICS AND COUNTER-ARGUMENTS

Making sense of both what Barth affirms and denies about baptism and the Lord's Supper depends on understanding them as churchly events. One way to bring out the debates on Barth's own terms is to consider Barth's warning against 'the Church in excess' as well as 'the Church in defect'. The former is 'the presumptuous church which exalts itself and puffs itself up' – the latter 'the church which does not take itself seriously enough because it is only half sure of its cause' – the one church a complementary reaction to the other (*ChrL*, pp. 136–40). On one level, Barth's critics can be divided into those who think Barth commits his own mistakes – some critics thinking he has a church in defect, some a church in excess. Can there be genuine theological inquiry on this issue, or must we be satisfied (on Barth's own terms) with dialectical point and counterpoint?

Most critics of Barth's theology of Christian community, baptism, and Lord's Supper have proceeded by ignoring it – not always out of ignorance of Barth's theology, but often because they think Barth himself ignores the important issues in this regard. For example, I earlier sketched Barth's hint that the topic of 'Church and sacraments' became a separate topic in modernity precisely as the world turned from this church and its sacraments; church and sacraments acquired, we might say, a new visibility for some precisely when they became invisible to most. And we saw that, at least early in his life, Barth read modern theology as a futile effort to conceive church and sacraments as primarily *human* community and rituals. On a practical level, this meant that the nation-state (*the* modern visible community) subsumed the church, while spirituality became the central outward sign signalling and, for all practical purposes, causing grace. On a theoretical level, ecclesiology and sacramentology, we might say, became subdivisions of sociology and ritual studies. A theologically liberal critique of Barth – Protestant or Catholic – would accuse him of ignoring or marginalizing the humanity of the church and its founding rituals. Barth offers a church in excess – not (the irenic liberal might admit) an institutionally excessive church but the excess of a church which must be divine event, or nothing at all.[18]

But, Barth might counter-argue, in acquiring a social theory's practical and theoretical visibility for most, church and sacraments lost or marginalized their particular visibility. To the liberal substitution of a social theory for church (or 'community in general' for 'Christian community', or ritual theories for the particular actions of baptism and Lord's Supper),

Barth could only say 'No'. The church must be embodied, visible for all to see – but embodied as the special visibility of the body of Christ.

Ironically, the most powerful response to such liberal social theories and ritual studies since Barth has come from an Anglo-Catholic whose common ground with Barth on this issue itself remains invisible. John Milbank argues that the variety of modern 'social theories' (including 'ritual studies') – liberal, positivistic, dialectical, and postmodern – are not innocent, neutral, objective tools that Christians can use to study the true visibility and humanity of the church, baptism, and Lord's Supper; instead, they bring with them their own (largely pagan) theologies that replace rather than redescribe or illumine church and sacraments. Milbank proposes a counter-history, counter-ontology, and counter-ethics centred on the church as eucharistic sacrament.[19]

One irony of Milbank's critique of liberal Catholic and Protestant ecclesiologies and sacramentologies is that he (like many of the liberal Catholics and Protestants he opposes) barely mentions Barth. His discussion is largely (although not exclusively) intra-Catholic. This is not because his 'postmodern' ecclesiology has not done its homework, but because Barth is read as part of a tradition that has only been able to assemble the church's counter-witness in *ad hoc* ways (e.g., the Confessing Church).[20] The implicit charge of such Catholics (here I include Greek Orthodox, Roman Catholic, and Anglo-Catholics like Milbank) is that Barth has a church in defect – a church profoundly focused on the Head, ever suspicious of the Body in an *ad hoc* and therefore only occasionally obedient way.

But this hardly does justice to Barth's willingness to rethink his position in the light of (among other things) Catholic theology. Indeed, by the end of his life, Barth was reassessing his relationship to Roman Catholic theology in ways he had not done since his conversations in the 1930s. He had 'critical' questions for Vatican II – but more often 'questions of clarification'.[21] He warned Protestants that their criticisms of Catholics may well have become not so much wrong as simply uninteresting in the light of Vatican II. He applauded Hans Küng's *The Church* (if not always Küng's other writings) as well as strands of Balthasar's theology (e.g., *CD* IV/4, p. xi). However, the Catholic debate with Barth was rapidly eclipsed by the argument between post-Vatican II reformers on the basis of *aggiornamento* (bringing the church up to date) and on the basis of *ressourcement* (returning to sources in Scripture and tradition) – Küng taking the first route, Balthasar the second. Thus, on the one hand, conservative and liberal Catholics seemed to conclude that Barth would either lead one out of the Catholic church (like Küng?) or back to its pre-modern past (like Balthasar?).

On the other hand, it came to seem to many students of Barth (Evangelical or, like this author, Catholic) that such Catholics were reliving liberal–conservative battles that Barth was well beyond.

Is there a way beyond this point-counterpoint between Barth's supposed church in excess and defect, and Barth's hypothetical responses? One crucial development has come from those who have taken seriously Barth's use of biblical narratives as the moving centre of a theology of 'Church and sacraments' that could aptly locate the church in its mission to the world before God. Hans Frei, in particular, emphasized how the *Church Dogmatics* came to dwell increasingly on the biblical narratives of Israel and Jesus – of individual Israelites like David, the disciples called and sent by Jesus, of non-Christians like Job and the vast secular world that forms the background or foreground of these biblical narratives. If so, then 'Church and sacraments' are identified narratively. The church is not trapped in a dialectic of defect and excess but is a pilgrim people, called and sent to visibly attest the coming One on behalf of the nations, to call this community to judgment and to mercy from the centre of world history.[22] One debate today is whether Barth is a dialectical theologian who uses biblical narrative or a narrative theologian who subsumes dialectic in the more layered movements of biblical narrative – or, somehow, both.

Another challenge to Barth's theology of church and sacrament comes from those who might well concede his narrative theology of Christian community (along with baptism and the Lord's Supper), but argue that Barth did not and perhaps could not follow the ecumenical debates to their next level of convergence among the churches. For example, although there are undoubtedly agreements between Barth's theology and the World Council of Church's *Baptism, Eucharist, and Ministry*, there are many more questions and clear oppositions. It will be recalled that, for all his criticisms of the movement toward church unity, Barth thought it was one of a handful of the most important movements of our time. One wonders what Barth would have made of the proposal that churches mutually accept both infant and adult baptism as 'equivalent alternatives' in view of 'the continuing character of Christian nurture'. Is this sheer compromise, or does it signal an emerging consensus on baptism less as an 'event' than as a continuum of catechumenal practices?[23]

On the other hand, it is hard to imagine that Barth would not dissent from the 'sacramental' readings of baptism and the Lord's Supper in the World Council of Churches' text. The issues on this score, I suggest, are twofold. One issue has to do with our practice of baptism and the Lord's Supper. For example, can churches that only baptize adults find reason regularly to celebrate the Lord's Supper – or will the Supper continue to be an exception rather than a rule? Or can churches that ordinarily baptize infants do more than reproduce Christendom? A second and more theoretical (dogmatic) issue is whether Barth's denial of sacramentality denies what churches for whom sacraments are 'signs' and 'causes' of God's free grace are concerned to affirm. Thomas Aquinas' treatment of the sacraments, I think, presents the largest challenge. To oversimplify, sacraments are signs in that baptism and eucharist signify or relate to the Jesus Christ whom they remember, foretell, and display; sacraments are causes insofar as they are effected by 'God alone' through the instrumental power of his creatures in the words and deeds (form and matter) of the sacraments.[24] But why not argue (we can imagine Barth saying) that this delicate balance of signs and causes is really an incoherent set of claims – an incoherence exacerbated by its inseparability from classic metaphysics (*CD* IV/4, p. 124)? Better to cut the Gordian knot of 'sacrament' (we can hear Barth argue) and focus on baptism and Lord's Supper as human actions that found and sustain the Christian life in response to the Spirit's command.[25] Is Barth's a-theology of sacraments inconsistent with the rest of his theology, or is it pointing the way to a more radically reformed dogmatics of worship?[26]

But more is at stake than these arguments over the practice and theory of baptism and the Lord's Supper. Barth's apparent marginality to recent agreements among Christians on church and sacraments could be read as the fault of an ecumenical movement that has yielded increasing agreement, but rarely full agreement, on the crucial controversies among Christians over the church and its offices (priestly, episcopal, and Petrine), and over the nature and practice of sacraments. But Robert Jenson has suggested that Barth's theology is part of the reason for the current stall in ecumenical movement. Barth's theology of time (Jenson suggests) comes down firmly on the side of Protestant discontinuity rather than Catholic continuity; his Christology only too often yields a church with something like two natures, only occasionally united (ecclesiological 'occasionalism' or 'Nestorianism'); his theology of the Spirit identifies the Spirit too closely with the Son, leaving too little room for the Spirit's new and distinctive future work.[27] These issues of the church's and our sacraments' existence in time, in Christ, and in the Spirit are formidable. For example, Barth was not unsympathetic towards pneumatological critiques of his theology. But he also wondered whether pneumatology can do the synthetic job some hope for without falling back into Hegel's or at least Schleiermacher's Spirit. This, I think, remains to be seen. But it is no accident that debates over Barth on the

Christian community, baptism, and the eucharistic Supper lead back to crucial matters of trinitarian theology and Christology handled in other chapters of this volume.

Notes

My thanks to Frederick Bauerschmidt, Steven Fowl and Charles Marsh for comments on an earlier draft of this chapter.

1 K. Barth, *Protestant Theology in the Nineteenth Century. Its Background and History* (Valley Forge: Judson Press, 1973), pp. 26f.

2 For examples, see 'Die Lehre von den Sakramentum', *Zwischen den Zeiten* 7 (1929), pp. 427–60 (here p. 439) and *CD* IV/4, p. 102.

3 Barth, *Protestant Theology*, pp. 36f., 41, 85, 87f., 91, 105, 113, 116f., 121.

4 See E. Busch, *Karl Barth. His Life from Letters and Autobiographical Texts*, trans. J. Bowden (Philadelphia: Fortress Press, 1976), pp. 169, 197, 220–2.

5 Karl Barth, 'Jesus Christ and the Movement for Social Justice' (1911), in G. Hunsinger, ed. and trans., *Karl Barth and Radical Politics* (Philadelphia: Westminster Press, 1976), pp. 19–45; Busch, *Karl Barth*, chs. 2–3; B. L. McCormack, *Karl Barth's Critically Realistic Dialectical Theology. Its Genesis and Development 1909–1936* (Oxford: Clarendon Press, 1995), pp. 69, 91.

6 McCormack, *Dialectical Theology*, pp. 153f.

7 Ibid., p. 244 (quoting Barth).

8 Ibid., p. 285.

9 Ibid., pp. 318, 323, 336, 347, 376.

10 See also the collected essays from this period in *Theology and Church. Shorter Writings 1920–1928*, trans. L. Pettibone Smith (New York: Harper and Row, 1962), perhaps esp. 'Luther's Doctrine of the Eucharist: Its Basis and Purpose' (1923), as well as McCormack, *Dialectical Theology*, pp. 376–91.

11 J. H. Leith, ed., *Creeds of the Churches*, rev. edn. (Atlanta: John Knox Press, 1973), pp. 520f. See also K. Barth, *Texte zur Barmer Theologischen Erklärung* (Zürich: Theologischer Verlag, 1984).

12 K. Barth, *The German Church Conflict*, essays from 1933–9, trans. P. T. A. Parker (Richmond, Va.: John Knox Press, 1956), pp. 45f.

13 For a theology of worship during this time outside the *Church Dogmatics*, see *The Knowledge of God and the Service of God*, trans. J. L. M. Haire and I. Henderson (London: Hodder and Stoughton, 1938 (German 1938)).

14 An important text outside the *Church Dogmatics* published around this time is *The Teaching of the Church regarding Baptism*, trans. E. A. Payne (London: SCM, 1948 (German 1943)).

15 I speak of fragments because Barth intended the fourth and final part of Volume IV of the *Dogmatics* to include more than the current *CD* IV/4 on baptism. Barth's *The Christian Life. Church Dogmatics IV/4. Lecture Fragments*, trans. G. W. Bromiley (Grand Rapids: Eerdmans, 1981) includes drafts of materials not included in *CD* IV/4. For the context, analysis, criticism, and bibliography on Barth on baptism, see J. Webster, *Barth's Ethics of Reconciliation* (Cambridge: Cambridge University Press, 1995).

16 For unpublished sources of Barth's incomplete theology of the Lord's Supper, see M. Barth, *Das Mahl des Herrn* (Neukirchen-Vluyn: Neukirchener Verlag, 1987), p. 4 (partially translated as *Rediscovering the Lord's Supper* (Atlanta: John Knox, 1988)). See also E. Busch, 'Das Abendmahl als Eucharistie. Gedanken zur Einführung einer regelmässigen Abendmahlsfeier', in *Wort und Gemeinde. Problem und Aufgaben der Praktischen Theologie. Eduard Thurneysen zum 80. Geburtstag* (Zürich: EVZ-Verlag, 1968), pp. 482–501; P. D. Molnar, *Karl Barth and the Theology of the Lord's Supper. A Systematic Investigation* (New York: Peter Lang, 1996).

17 *Letters 1961–1968*, eds. J. Fangmeier and H. Stoevesandt, trans. G. W. Bromiley (Grand Rapids: Eerdmans, 1981), p. 307.

18 See, for example, H. R. Niebuhr, *Social Sources of Denominationalism* (New York: World Publishing, 1957 (original 1929)); J. M. Gustafson, *Treasure in Earthen Vessels. The Church as a Human Community* (New York: Harper and Brothers, 1961).

19 J. Milbank, *Theology and Social Theory. Beyond Secular Reason* (Oxford: Basil Blackwell, 1990).

20 The most massive (although neither the first nor the last) Roman Catholic critique of Barth's ecclesiology of 'event' remains C. O'Grady, *The Church in the Theology of Karl Barth* (Washington: Corpus, 1968), which (to oversimplify) argues that Barth's theology of the church as 'event' renders the church an occasional appearance, uncommitted to habitual worship, office, and institutions.

21 K. Barth, *Ad Limina Apostolorum. An Appraisal of Vatican II*, trans. K. R. Crim (Richmond, Va.: John Knox Press, 1968 (German 1967)), pp. 22, 24, 26, 34. For the reading of Catholic theology behind the following remarks, see J. J. Buckley, 'Postliberal Theology: A Catholic Reading', in R. Badham, ed., *Introduction to Theology* (Nashville: Abingdon Press, 1998).

22 See H. Frei, *The Identity of Jesus Christ. The Hermeneutical Bases of Dogmatic Theology* (Philadelphia: Fortress Press, 1975), esp. Part V; and G. Lindbeck, 'The Church', in Geoffrey Wainwright, ed., *Keeping the Faith. Essays to Mark the Centenary of Lux Mundi* (Philadelphia: Fortress Press, 1988 and Allison Park, Pa.: Pickwick Publications, 1988), ch. 8.

23 *Baptism, Eucharist and Ministry*, Faith and Order Paper No. 111 (World Council of Churches, 1982). See also M. Barth, *Rediscovering the Lord's Supper*, pp. 103–13.

24 See T. Aquinas, *Summa Theologiae* 3a.60–5; B. Leeming, S. J., *Principles of Sacramental Theology* (Westminster, Md.: Newman Press, 1956).

25 It should not be taken for granted that Barth denies what Thomas affirms. For one thing, students of Thomas would have to show that the sacraments are only apparently 'a "missing" topic in Aquinas' treatment of prayer', including contemplation (rather than Barth's petitionary prayer) as Aquinas' 'prayer *par excellence*'; see C. Valeck, O. P., 'Appendix 6. The Sacraments in Thomas Aquinas' *Summa Theologiae*', *Summa Theologiae*, vol. 39 (2a2ae, pp. 8of.), trans. K. D. O'Rourke, O. P. (London: Blackfriars and Eyre & Spottiswoode, 1964), p. 267.

26 For an argument to inconsistency, see Webster, *Barth's Ethics of Reconciliation*; for a more radically reformed theology of worship, see J. H. Yoder, *Body Politics*.

Five Practices of the Christian Community Before the Watching World (Nashville, Tenn.: Discipleship Resources, 1992).

27 See R. Jenson, *Unbaptized God* (Philadelphia: Fortress Press, 1992); 'You Wonder Where the Spirit Went', *Pro Ecclesia* 2 (1993), pp. 296–304.

Further reading

Cochrane, A. C., *Eating and Drinking with Jesus. An Ethical and Biblical Inquiry* (Philadelphia: Westminster Press, 1974).

Buckley, J. J., 'A Field of Living Fire. Karl Barth on the Spirit and the Church', *Modern Theology* 10 (1994), pp. 81–102.

Healy, N., 'The Logic of Karl Barth's Ecclesiology', *Modern Theology* 10 (1994), pp. 253–70.

Jenson, R., *Unbaptized God* (Minneapolis: Fortress Press, 1992).

Jüngel, E., 'Invocation of God as the ethical ground of Christian action', in *Theological Essays*, trans. J. B. Webster (Edinburgh: T & T Clark, 1989), pp. 154–72.

Molnar, P. D., *Karl Barth and the Theology of the Lord's Supper. A Systematic Investigation* (New York: Peter Lang, 1996).

O'Grady, C., *The Church in the Theology of Karl Barth* (Washington DC: Corpus Books, 1968).

Webster, J., *Barth's Ethics of Reconciliation* (Cambridge: Cambridge University Press, 1995).

13 Barth's trinitarian ethic

NIGEL BIGGAR

THE PROPHETIC FEEBLENESS OF NEO-KANTIAN CHRISTIANITY

The best way to grasp the driving convictions of someone's thought is often to identify what he is thinking against. When understood as a response, assertions that initially appeared abstract and anaemic now acquire vital significance. So it is with Karl Barth's theology and ethics.

The liberal Protestant heritage into which Barth was inducted had been decisively and variously shaped by Immanuel Kant (1724–1804). One of Kant's legacies was the tenet that specifically religious acts – that is, of prayer and worship – are idle distractions from the true, moral content of Christianity; and by 'moral' here is meant the fair treatment of other rational human beings. All that is valid in religion is reducible to morality; and morality is reducible to the performance of one's duties to one's fellows.

In the intellectual hands of Albrecht Ritschl (1822–89), the social dimension of Kantian morality – the kingdom of 'rational ends' or intrinsically valuable individuals – was combined with the Gospels' notion of the Kingdom of God to produce a Christian ethic with an emphasis on community. What made this ethic Christian was Jesus' moral teaching about the brotherhood of man (to use a phrase characteristic of one of Ritschl's disciples, Adolph von Harnack (1851–1930)), not his religious teaching about the redemptive activity of God the Father. What was valid in Christianity was its affirmation of human duty and community, not the actions of divine grace. This is one reason why Ritschl and his followers may be fairly described as 'neo-Kantian'.

Among the theologians who most impressed Barth as a young theological student in the early 1900s were two of Ritschl's disciples, Harnack and Wilhelm Herrmann (1846–1922); and their influence helped to incline him, as the pastor of an industrial parish in the years immediately preceding the outbreak of the First World War, towards the identification of Christianity and socialism that was being espoused by Leonhard Ragaz (1868–1945) in his Religious Socialism. Barth, however, never entirely lost a sense of the transcendence of God, and so did not ally himself completely with Ragaz. Nevertheless, his politics were sufficiently socialist (and therefore internationalist) that, when on the very day that war broke out in August 1914, Herrmann and Harnack and almost all of Barth's German theological mentors publicly aligned themselves with the Kaiser's war policy, Barth was stunned. He read their failure to resist the ideology of war as symptomatic of a disastrous flaw in their ethics and, more deeply, in their theology.

THE PRIORITY OF THE TRANSCENDENT GOD

The ethical failure of his liberal Protestant heritage was not responsible for introducing Barth to the notions of God's priority and transcendence, but it did clear the way for them to come to the fore of his thinking. It began in his mind a process of radical revision that was to culminate in the completion of the second edition of his commentary *The Epistle to the Romans* in 1921. During this period he was struck by the discovery that Christianity is not in the first place about human being and religion and morality at all, but about God;[1] and about God, not just as the symbolic epitome of human achievement but as an active, living, transcendent reality whose nature is unsettlingly strange to humans. Barth made this discovery, partly through reading the Bible (see his 1916 lecture, 'The Strange New World within the Bible'); and partly through reading Kierkegaard (1813–55), whose famous 'infinite qualitative distinction' between time and eternity, human beings and God, he quotes in the preface to the second edition of *Romans*.[2] According to this point of view, God is a stranger to humans and he stands in judgment or *krisis* upon them, and especially upon all their religious and moral pretensions. Foremost among these pretensions is that of being able to comprehend God's will unambiguously and so to achieve a secure foundation for ethics. Against this, in *Romans* (especially the section entitled 'The Problem of Ethics', pp. 424–38) and in his 1922 address, 'The Problem of Ethics Today', Barth stressed: the moral complexity and ambiguity of the human situation; the broken or fragmentary nature of human thought, which requires it to move dialectically from part-truth to part-truth, and sets absolute comprehension forever beyond its grasp; the naturally self-justifying inclination of the sinful human spirit; the eschatological status of God's Kingdom; and humanity's radical dependence upon God's grace both for forgiveness and for the possibility of human behaviour and thought ever becoming transparent to 'the light of the coming Day' (*R*, pp. 434f.).

There are a number of respects in which this 'Dialectical Theology' or 'Theology of *Krisis*' of the early 1920s contributed to the ethical thought that Barth later developed in his *Church Dogmatics*: the suspicion of ethical system or method as pretending to absolute comprehension and spiritual self-sufficiency; the eschatological relativization of all human goodness and ethical understanding; and the need to integrate into the very heart of ethics an earnest acknowledgment of humankind's radical dependence upon God in all his sovereignty, freedom, and mystery.

In *CD* II/2 (first published in 1942), as in the earlier lectures on ethics that Barth delivered at the universities of Münster and Bonn in 1928–9 and 1930–1 respectively, this acknowledgment finds expression in the concept of discovering what one should do by hearing a command of God. Such a moral epistemology presents the right as something obligatory and not merely convenient; as a claim that bears down upon us and to which we are subject. In this respect, the conception is Kantian: we are accountable to a transcendent moral authority; and insofar as our sinful wills are not entirely consonant with that authority, we experience its claims as alien and coercive – that is, as imperatives. However, it is distinctly unKantian in that we do not discover what is right simply by means of a process of autonomous reasoning; that is, by deducing from the universal moral law of reason what is required in particular situations. Rather, we discover it in a unique event of encounter with the living God and his special command to us here and now. At this point in Barth's thinking, Kierkegaard's 'religious' dimension clearly displaces the Kantian 'ethical' dimension; and moral life is accordingly understood as a response of the human individual to a unique command of God, and not as the conformity of human instances of rationality to the moral requirements of universal practical reason. The focus here is also very strongly on the interpersonal relationship between the human individual and God, a focus which never allows us to treat God merely as a useful concept, but always presents him as a reality at least as free, spontaneous, and living as human persons.

There are two obvious problems with conceiving how we come to know what is right in these terms. One is that it is difficult to locate an event of hearing a command of God in ordinary human experience. Even if one does regard God as a real, living super-Person, one is not aware of being constantly confronted by divine commands to do this or that. Sometimes we know what we should do without thinking about it. At other times, when we are not sure what is right, we have to think and not merely 'listen'. The other problem attending Barth's moral epistemology has been a common ground for objection to divine command theories throughout the history of Christian ethics, and one of the main reasons why Barth's own ethic has had only limited influence on contemporary Christian thought; namely, its apparent irrationalism. On first impression, and especially if one gets no further than *CD* II/2 (chapter VIII, 'The Command of God') in exploring the ethic of the *Church Dogmatics*, it would appear that a divine command comes like a thunderbolt out of heaven, brooking no questioning, displacing all thinking. It alone *decides* what is right. It is utterly concrete, requiring no further human reflection to give it specific form, but only human consent to realize it. Here, the infinite qualitative distinction opens up between the mysterious divine will and sinful human reason.

However, not all is quite as it first seems. For one thing, in *CD* III/4 (first published in 1951), Barth himself expressly denies that he is proposing that we 'be governed from moment to moment and situation to situation by a kind of direct and particular inspiration and guidance'. 'This', he asserts, 'is not what is meant' (*CD* III/4, p. 15). For another thing, Barth's exposition of God's command in *CD* II/2 needs to be read, and qualified, in the light of what follows in the subsequent ethical sections.

THE CHRISTOLOGICAL QUALIFICATION

If the 'Theology of *Krisis*' bequeathed to Barth's later thought a pronounced voluntarist[3] and irrationalist strand, there was nevertheless one crucial respect in which the ethic of the *Dogmatics* differed from it: its concentration upon God's self-revelation in Jesus Christ. In the latter half of the 1920s, Barth had realized that a theology that takes seriously the idea of the Word of God – as he believed it should – must move beyond speaking of humanity's relationship with God simply in terms of *diastasis* (separation or breach); and by the time he started work on the first volume of the *Church Dogmatics* in 1931, his thinking had acquired a strong focus upon the *grace* of God's mysterious, sovereign freedom that was manifested in Christ.

This focus had two important effects upon Barth's divine command ethic. First, it established that the purpose of any command of *this* God – God *in Christ* – is gracious; it intends the salvation of the one it bears down upon. In the light of Christ it becomes clear that the ultimate point of the Law is the gospel.[4] At this point the Kantian character of Barth's ethic recedes even further, and reveals something basically eudaimonist:[5] we should obey God's command, not out of spineless deference to the capricious wishes of an almighty despot, but out of regard for our own best good, which this gracious God alone truly understands and which he intends with all his heart.

The christological focus of Barth's theology from the late 1920s onwards not only reveals the benevolent form of God's commanding, but also informs its content. Barth's Christology is an orthodox incarnational one that takes Jesus to be the second person of the Trinity. God's command, then, is at once the command of the Father, the Son, and the Holy Spirit – or, to give the three persons functional or 'economic' titles: the Creator, the Reconciler, and the Redeemer. Barth's christological focus develops into a trinitarian structure for his theology, and so for his theological ethic as this is developed first in the Münster-Bonn lectures and then in the *Church Dogmatics*.

THE TRINITARIAN STRUCTURE

In giving a trinitarian structure to his ethic, Barth proposes that what human beings ought to do is basically determined by what sort of being they are and by the conditions of their existence. The nature of human being and existence is fundamentally theological: the very first thing to be said about humans is that they stand in relation to God. Or, rather, that they stand in three distinct relations, because their relationship to God is complex and has three dimensions: that of creature to Creator; that of sinner to Reconciler; and that of heir of eternal life to Redeemer. These dimensions are not ontologically discrete; they interact and qualify each other. But we must consider them each in turn.

Epistemologically, the command of God the Reconciler comes first. For, according to Barth, it is only (or primarily) through the Word of God that we can truly know the nature of human being and existence; and by 'the Word of God' he means primarily Jesus Christ, the incarnate Son of God, and not the Bible. Logically, however, the command of God the Creator takes precedence, since the reconciliation of sinners to God (and their final redemption) presupposes that those reconciled sinners (awaiting final redemption) are already creatures.

The initial thing to be said about human being, then, is that it is creaturely; and, for Barth, to be creaturely is to have a being with a given nature that is characterized by a fourfold structure: responsibility to God the Creator; responsibility to fellow humans; responsibility for life; and responsibility within the limits of a certain time. This is the complex structure with which God has created human nature. Human freedom, therefore, is not absolute: we cannot simply reinvent ourselves. Our freedom is finite: insofar as we make ourselves, we do so only under certain given conditions. These conditions specify God's command; they entail certain specific claims or obligations or duties. Responsibility to God involves keeping Sunday as a day of worship, bearing express witness to God, and turning to him in prayer (*CD* III/4, pp. 47–115). Responsibility to fellow humans involves: a voluntary interdependence between the two sexes, in which it is nevertheless given to the male to 'lead' and the female to 'follow'; a mutual honouring between parents and children, in which parents should guide and children should obey; and a reciprocity between neighbours, whether near or distant, in which national loyalties are held to be radically provisional (*CD* III/4, pp.116–323). Responsibility for life involves respecting and protecting one's own life and that of one's fellows as a loan made by God to be used through the Christian community in the service of the sanctification of the world (*CD* III/4, pp. 324–564). Responsibility within the limits of a certain time involves cooperating in this task by heeding one's own special vocation to exploit a few unique opportunities (*CD* III/4, pp. 565–685).

Barth's specification of God's command in terms of the fourfold created structure of human being might well seem odd. It might seem odd because it has been common to classify Barth's ethic simply as a version of divine command theory, and to assume that it therefore has no place for constant, natural orders that give rise to moral rules: since right and wrong are decided by God's commanding, and since God is free to command as he pleases, there can be no constant features of the nature of created reality from which we can rationally derive reliable ethical principles. The mistake here is to assume that all divine command ethics are of the same kind. It may be true for some of them that God's will has no discernible constancy – no 'character' – and that his commanding is therefore entirely arbitrary and unpredictable. It certainly is true that Barth's treatise on God's command in *CD* II/2, in its determination to impress upon us that the origin of what is good and right is *God*, tends to beat the voluntarist drum so loudly as to suggest that moral knowledge is the result simply of an *ad hoc* apprehension of God's will for here and now that excludes all possibility of rational generalization into reliable ethical constants. Nevertheless, in *CD* III/4 it becomes quite clear that, for Barth, God's will has a certain character that is expressed in the permanent structures with which he has created human nature, and that his commands, therefore, do have certain constant features.

This has often been overlooked, partly because Barth generally preferred to avoid speaking of 'orders of creation' in the *Church Dogmatics*,[6] in order to distance himself from certain aspects of the Lutheran ethical tradition, namely, marriage as a universal obligation, and the family and the nation as divine institutions deserving of primary loyalty.[7] The main reason for Barth's rejection of these as orders of creation is that (a christologically centred reading of) Scripture does not support their candidature; but he was also aware that the family and the nation are historically fluid phenomena (*CD* III/4, pp. 22, 141, 148, 241f., 299–305).

Another reason why Barth's affirmation of the constant character of God's commanding, and its expression in the created structure of human nature, has often been overlooked is his explicit and quite uncompromising repudiation of the ethical tradition of natural law.[8] But this was not at all a repudiation of the ontological notion that moral law is based, proximately and in part, on human nature. It was rather a repudiation of the claim that we can know this law sufficiently well by reflection on experience and without recourse to the Word of God in Jesus Christ.

This epistemological point should remind us, in case we had forgotten, that the command of God the Creator to his human creatures is only one dimension of a complex and fully integrated command, and that it is already informed by the other, logically subsequent, dimensions. Therefore the command of the Creator is not the legalistic command to conform to natural orders; it is rather the liberating command of God the Reconciler, addressed to sinful and oppressed creatures, to live freely and gladly within the given structures of their nature. The law of the orders of creation exists to enable *life* – and, in the face of sin, the command to observe these orders is issued to enable *new* life.

Since Barth does not hold that marriage or the family are orders of creation, he does not have to justify celibacy or orphanhood in the service of God's Kingdom in terms of the command of God the Reconciler trumping the command of God the Creator, thereby introducing conflict into the Trinity. Instead, he is able to represent vocational celibacy and orphanhood as *unusual forms* of the natural structures of voluntary interdependence between the sexes and the mutual honouring of parents and children, which have been called into being by the reconciling activity of God (*CD* III/4, p. 261). Therefore, the command of God the Reconciler is not to be seen as suspending the orders of creation, but rather as developing them in response to new circumstances.

It would be misleading, however, to speak of the command of the Reconciler merely as modifying the command of the Creator; for this could easily be misunderstood to imply that the orders of creation furnish the substance of a Christian ethic, to which the ethical import of God's act of reconciliation in his Son makes only marginal adjustments. This is certainly to underestimate the contribution of reconciliation, even if Barth was inclined to underestimate the contribution of creation by talking of it as mere 'prologue' to 'the main statement' (*ChrL*, pp. 9–11). The doctrine of reconciliation both informs the ethical dimension of creation from the beginning and supplies its (teleological) end. The God whom we are to worship, then, is not simply Creator but a gracious Father who has acted in his Son to reconcile sinners to himself; and our disposition towards him should accordingly move beyond a creaturely awareness of absolute dependence (*pace* the Stoics and Schleiermacher) to a filial engagement in absolute trust (*ChrL*, pp. 49–109). This trust should express itself, first of all, in confident prayer for the completion of the process of the coming of God's Kingdom, and with it the secure establishment of just relations between human beings (*ChrL*, pp. 111–204). Subsequently, it should also find expression in correspondent engagement through the Christian community in the struggle for human justice; which struggle will take the basically negative form of revolt against 'the lordless powers' (*ChrL*, pp. 205–71). These powers are human potentialities which, in rebellion against the primary order of creation (the worship of God), have become oppressive idols. Of these Barth names four species: political absolutism, materialism, ideological dogmatism, and what he calls 'chthonic' ('earthy') powers, such as technology, fashion, sport, pleasure, and transportation (*ChrL*, pp. 213–33).

In the light of the command of God the Reconciler, then, living within the given structure of our creaturely nature amounts to this: that, worshipping God as Creator and as gracious Reconciler, we should use our lives in the service of his Kingdom and so in revolt against the lordless powers, within the moral terms set by the natural structure of relationships between man and woman, parents and children, and all human neighbours, and within the limits of our individual vocations to seize the unique opportunities afforded us by our time and place.

It is notable that one cannot expound the content of the command of God the Reconciler without already referring to the command of God as Redeemer. The epilogue is anticipated in the main statement, as the prologue is presupposed by it. In God's act of reconciliation in Jesus Christ, the advent of God's Kingdom has begun; but it is not yet complete. Redemption (or sanctification) as a completed state, then, lies in the future. We, accordingly, stand 'between the times' in an ambiguous mixture of light and darkness, encouraged by the manifestation of God's reconciling grace in the past, but still radically dependent upon the final manifestation of his redemptive grace yet to come. Therefore, we hasten towards the consummation of God's Kingdom, but not imagining (*pace* the Religious Socialists) that this is something simply within our own power to realize. We cannot identify our own activity straightforwardly with the activity of God. At best, it is analogous or 'correspondent', never identical. Therefore, our engagement in the service of God's Kingdom, within the structure of our nature, is subject to a radical eschatological qualification. If we hasten as we should, we do so towards a future that is finally God's gift, not our own achievement. Our hastening, then, should always be one that is also a prayerful waiting upon God's gracious initiative.[9]

THE SUSPICION OF CASUISTRY

It is clear from our account of its trinitarian structure that Barth's ethic is systematic in the sense that it comprises a number of conceptual elements that are combined into a coherent, complex whole. Barth, however, was wont to repudiate any notion of ethical 'system'; for by this he understood a structure of principles founded on a basic view of things, and capable of comprehending particular cases through the methodical specification of rules and their application. Such a foundationalist, deductive casuistry[10] seemed, in its pretended self-sufficiency, to encapsulate the sinful human aspiration to be independent of God (*CD*, III/4, pp. 7f.). Hence his tendency in *CD* II/2 to conceive of hearing God's command in terms that either exclude or radically subvert moral reasoning.

Barth, however, misunderstood casuistry. In common with most of his Protestant peers – including Emil Brunner (1889–1966), Dietrich Bonhoeffer (1906–45), and Helmut Thielicke (1908–86) – he thought of it as a quasi-mechanical process of logical deduction from first principles to concrete cases. It seemed to him to be the epitome of ethical rationalism.

However, although it is true that the Roman Catholic casuistry that was dominant in the nineteenth and early twentieth centuries did have this closed, absolutist character, there is nothing about casuistry as such that necessarily makes it so. An alternative model may be found in the work of the Anglican moral theologian, Kenneth Kirk (1886–1954), the Methodist ethicist, Paul Ramsey (1913–88), and the moral philosopher, J. M. Brennan.[11] Here, casuistry proceeds by analogy rather than deductive logic. The meaning of a moral rule is grasped through paradigmatic cases; we know what is prohibited by the rule against murder, for example, through certain typical instances of it. The application of a rule, therefore, is not a matter of logical deduction, but one of comparing the case in hand with the paradigms, in order to determine whether it is analogous (that is, of the same moral kind). If it is analogous, then the rule applies in this case, too. But if it is disanalogous in some morally significant respect, then there are two possibilities. Either another rule can be found whose paradigms it does fit; or it requires the formulation of a new rule and the correlative revision of adjacent old ones. The point to be noted here is that this kind of casuistry involves a dialectical movement back and forth between rule and case, a process in which a given system of principles and rules is open to learning from novel moral experience, and to reforming itself accordingly.

Because Barth was unaware of this open, dialectical species of casuistry, he repudiated casuistry as such. As a result he was inclined, especially in *CD* II/2, to propose the hearing of a divine command as a substitute for moral reasoning about cases, as if depending on God and making rational judgments were mutually exclusive. And even later on, in *CD* III/4 and IV/4, when he was willing to admit that God's commanding can be described in terms of certain constant features (for example, that human life should be respected), he remained reluctant to describe these characteristics as 'principles' that could be specified into rules (for example, that human life should be protected) and used to judge moral cases (for example, of homicide). Indeed, sometimes he implies that God may decide at any time simply to trump the rule (and command, for example, that life should not be protected). At other times, he implies that God would not trump the rule, but that since only he knows what it really means (that is, what 'protection' really involves), his command may nevertheless require kinds of conduct that do not look to us at all like protection (*CD* III/4, pp. 397f., 401, 411–13). Either way the result is the same for us: what God commands at least *appears* to require the suspension of a moral norm.

The problem with this voluntarist, Kierkegaardian concept of God's commanding (as, incidentally, with Joseph Fletcher's 'situation ethics') is that it does not so much open up a received body of moral wisdom to gaining new insights and revising itself accordingly, as it puts it on notice that it can be rendered redundant at any moment and without reasons given. In which case, it becomes difficult to see what kind of authority such a moral tradition could claim to have.

Much to his credit, however, Barth was not consistent on this matter; for in addition to his explicit, radical, voluntarist account, he pursued lines of ethical thinking that are far less radical and considerably more rational (though not rationalist), although largely unannounced. According to this alternative account, there is a discernible constancy in God's will as expressed in his historic acts and commands. This will can be specified in terms of rules prescribing or enjoining kinds of human behaviour; and these rules can be applied to cases in order to make moral judgments about them. For example, the rule that life should be protected always applies to cases of homicide; and, according to Barth's judgment, it rules out as altogether impermissible at least one kind of killing (euthanasia), but permits other kinds (suicide, self-defence, abortion, capital punishment, and war) in exceptional cases (*CD* III/4, pp. 397–470). Barth does attempt to justify such casuistic discrimination by identifying the morally significant features of these exceptional cases, but because of his suspicion of casuistry his explicit justifications are usually haphazard. Sometimes, however, if one digs beneath the surface (for example, of his occasional wartime writings on the moral status of Allied belligerency against Nazi Germany), one can discover a much more thorough casuistical analysis than Barth would have been happy to own up to.[12]

In this alternative account, then, Barth concedes much more in practice to casuistry than his theory allows. But what happens to the nature of hearing God's command? Certainly, it is tamed; but it is not rendered toothless. No longer does it threaten to subvert the enterprise of moral reasoning; but within the realm of the permissible, defined by rationally derived moral rules, it retains room for decisive action. What Barth has in mind here is that the application of a rule to a particular case might not determine that only one course of action is permissible, but that two or more are equally so. In such a case one should decide between the options, not according to individual whim, but according to God's command. The example that Barth himself gives concerns a case where an inevitable choice must be made between the life of a mother and that of her unborn child (*CD* III/4, pp. 421f.). Barth does not believe that there is any valid rule (such as: that mothers' lives are preferable to those of foetuses) to decide this case. It might be that the mother is being called to complete her life with a faithful and generous act of self-sacrifice so that her child will be able to fulfil his destiny. Or it might be that she is being called to save her life, and the child to surrender his, so that she can perform some further service required of her. There is no rule to be applied here; but there is a command to be heard – or, to use a concept that Barth developed later in *CD* III/4, there is a personal vocation to be heeded.

ETHICAL METHOD: FROM THE BIBLE VIA DOGMATICS

According to this alternative account, then, the hearing of a personal vocation occurs within the terms stipulated by an ethical system built upon the foundation of a set of first principles. That this system is structurally open does not (*pace* Barth) make it any less of a system.

But where does this system come from? Where does Barth find his first principles? Immediately, they derive from his systematic theology. The ethic of the *Church Dogmatics* is presented in the final part of each of the three substantive volumes that were either completed or begun before the end of Barth's life.[13] The structure of *Church Dogmatics* makes its method clear: to move *from* dogmatics *to* ethics. Such movement is generated by Barth's thoroughly Christian concept of God, who demonstrably and consistently wills to bring his human creatures into a state of proper freedom and gladness, and so to elicit from them acts that conduce thereto (and are therefore 'right'). At the same time, this movement aims to ensure that consideration of right human action is thoroughly governed by a Christian concept of God. So: dogmatics must be the root of ethics, and ethics must be the flower of dogmatics.

The dogmatic ground on which Barth's ethic is built is radically orthodox. It is orthodox in the sense that it assumes an incarnational Christology (that is, that Jesus was the incarnate Son of God) and therefore a trinitarian theology (that is, that God is at once Father, Son, and Spirit). It is radically orthodox in the sense that it traces with extraordinary relentlessness the reciprocal qualifications that each person of the Trinity makes of the activity and nature of the others – and especially the Reconciler of the Creator, and the Redeemer of the Reconciler.

Barth's orthodoxy might be described as 'postmodern' in that he makes no attempt to justify his dogmatic assumptions in terms of logical possibility, common experience, or historical evidence. But this is not because he has abandoned all claim to truth for the Christian 'story', and wishes merely to assert its democratic right to a voice alongside all the other voices clamouring for attention in the ideological marketplace. Barth believes passionately in the truth of the orthodox Christian story. He believes that God is a living Reality and that the incarnation happened. But he does not believe that the reality of God or of the incarnation can be philosophically proven or historically demonstrated; in part because apprehension of such things requires, not only enlightenment of the mind, but first and foremost conversion of the depths of the will; and in part because it is not the business of dogmatics to presume to demonstrate God, but rather, through both what it says and how it says it, to clear the way for God to manifest himself.

Barth's ethical method begins with the theological tenets of orthodox dogmatics. It begins, above all, with Jesus Christ as the Word of God incarnate. But does it not therefore actually begin with the Word of God written, the Bible? The answer to this is both Yes and No. It is Yes, insofar as the Bible is the original and primary witness to God's self-revelation in Jesus. But it is No, because the Reality to which the Bible points transcends it;

because therefore there remains scope for dogmatic theology at least to develop, if not to improve upon, the biblical witness; and because the Bible does not furnish us with a single ethical system.

The Bible's contribution to Barth's ethic is indirect, through dogmatics; and in particular, through its history of God's relationship of grace with humankind, which finds its focus in the history of Jesus Christ. Only within the context of this fundamental theological narrative does Barth turn to consider the significance of the Bible's directly ethical material. This comes in two forms: story and rule. Predictably, Barth prefers particular moral stories, which he sees as providing 'instances' of human 'correspondence' to God's activity. Primary among these, of course, is the story of Jesus himself. This he summarizes in *The Christian Life*,[14] not in terms of self-sacrificial suffering (in contrast to the Roman Catholic tradition of *imitatio Christi*) or of pacifism (in contrast to the Anabaptist tradition of 'following after' Jesus), but in the more directly religious and morally broader terms of the filial invocation of God for the coming of his Kingdom, and of the corresponding revolt against the lordless powers for the sake of human justice.

Although, for reasons that should now be clear, Barth was (rightly) adamant that the Bible should not be approached primarily as a sourcebook of moral rules (*CD* II/2, p. 675), and although he denied (again, rightly) that either the Decalogue or the Sermon on the Mount should be taken as fundamental moral codes (*CD* II/2, pp. 679–700), he was nevertheless concerned that morally prescriptive material in the Bible should be incorporated into his own more comprehensive ethical scheme; and he was usually careful to engage in broad-ranging exegetical argument in order to support his chosen ethical principles.

Barth's ethical method, then, is to proceed from the Bible through its notion of salvation history to incarnational Christology, out into a systematic trinitarian theology and then on to ethics; and only at this last point does the Bible's specifically ethical material come into play.

So far, the sources of Barth's ethic that we have considered have been restricted to the Bible and to Christian dogmatics. But what about philosophy and the empirical sciences? Have they no role?

Yes, they do; but a strictly subordinate one. Barth is not so naive as to suppose that the only sources of moral wisdom are the Bible and subsequent Christian theology; or that these are free from philosophical suppositions and the appeal to empirical observations. He is perfectly happy to see aspects of moral philosophy (for example, Kant's) or of the social and behavioural sciences borrowed by a theological ethic. But he insists that such borrowing always be discriminating. It must always be subject to the criterion of compatibility with the Christian theological presuppositions of the ethical system into which it is incorporated. The word that Barth chose to denote the approach of theological ethics to philosophical or scientific material leaves no doubt about the locus of control: 'annexation' (*CD* II/2, p. 524).

However, although Barth was willing in principle to incorporate the consideration of empirical data into his ethic, his practice tended to fall a long way short; and he has been widely (and fairly) criticized for the superficiality of his empirical analysis when treating moral issues such as homosexuality, war, and work. One of the reasons for this weakness is that Barth undoubtedly took as his own priority the task of explicating the ethical implications of Christian dogmatics; and another is his persistent suspicion of casuistry.

CONCLUSION

It follows that if one wants a close ethical analysis of particular forms of human conduct – say, euthanasia or homosexual practice – then Barth's ethic is generally not the place to look. Careful moral deliberation about, and discrimination between, different sets of empirical data – between different cases – was not his forte. However, if what is wanted is an ethic that is deeply rooted in an extraordinarily integrated system of trinitarian theology, traces the ethical implications of an incarnational Christology with unequalled tenacity, is rigorously oriented toward the practice of prayerful acknowledgment of the living reality of God, and is also susceptible of extension into the business of fine casuistry, then one could do nothing better than to turn to Barth.

Notes

1 Note: 'in the first place'. In Barth's thinking, the theological priority of the transcendent God should not eclipse secondary concern for secular human activity and relations. In his 1922 lectures on Calvin, he affirmed the propriety of attention to the 'horizontal' (ethical) dimension as well as to the 'vertical' (religious) dimension.

2 *The Epistle to the Romans*, trans. E. C. Hoskyns (Oxford: Oxford University Press, 1933), p. 10.

3 'Voluntarism' refers here to the ethical theory according to which what is right or wrong is determined simply by God's will (*voluntas* in Latin), and that God may alter his determinations arbitrarily. God's will is free, then, in the sense that it is not constrained by any 'external' canons of reason.

4 Thus Barth reverses the Pauline and Lutheran sequence of Law and gospel; but

he does not reverse the sense. He is not denying that an immediate function of the Law is to expose moral feebleness and to make manifest the need for God's grace. Rather, he is asserting that the ultimate rationale of the Law is to indicate (at least part of) the route to the actualization of the human good.

This assertion is not made nearly so clearly in the Münster-Bonn *Ethics* as in the *Church Dogmatics*. In the latter, the treatise on the command of God the Reconciler explicitly enjoys material primacy and is governed by the filial concept of 'invocation'; whereas in the former the equivalent treatise is not accorded the same primacy and is dominated by the concept of 'law'.

5 'Eudaimonism' refers to that ethical theory which defines the right in terms of the good, and claims that the reason why what is right obliges us is that it conduces to our proper good or well-being (or, to use Aristotle's word, *eudaimonia*). Eudaimonism stands in stark opposition to Kant, who argued that the genuinely good will does what is right, not because it hopes to gain anything thereby (e.g., human fulfilment or salvation), but simply out of sheer 'respect' for the moral law.

6 A rare exception may be found at the foot of page 301 of *CD* III/4.

7 This marks an important point of difference between the *Church Dogmatics* and the earlier Münster-Bonn *Ethics*, where the concept of 'orders of creation' is used without embarrassment and where both marriage and the family are identified as instances (*Ethics*, pp. 225–46).

8 See N. Biggar, *The Hastening that Waits: Karl Barth's Ethics* (Oxford: Clarendon Press, 1995), pp. 55f.

9 See Biggar, *Hastening*, pp. 81–8.

10 'Casuistry' refers to the methodical process of bringing moral rules to bear upon particular cases.

11 K. Kirk, *Conscience and its Problems: an Introduction to Casuistry* (London: Longman, Green, and Co., 1927); P. Ramsey, 'The Case of the Curious Exception', in *Norm and Context in Christian Ethics*, eds. G. Outka and P. Ramsey (London: SCM, 1968), pp. 67–135; J. M. Brennan, *The Open Texture of Moral Judgements* (London: Macmillan, 1977).

12 See Biggar, *Hastening*, pp. 39f. and Appendix 1.

13 *CD* II/2, ch. VIII, 'The Command of God', and *CD* III/4, 'The Command of God the Creator' were both completed. *CD* IV/4, 'The Command of God the Reconciler', was begun but remained incomplete upon Barth's death in 1968. The projected Volume V, on the doctrine of Redemption (and the command of God the Redeemer) was never begun; although some of its probable content can be surmised from Barth's existing writings – especially the Münster/Bonn *Ethics* and the published volumes of the *Church Dogmatics*.

14 *The Christian Life* is the title under which Barth's 1959–60 lectures on the 'Command of God the Reconciler' were published. Intended to complete *CD* IV/4, these remained unfinished upon Barth's death.

Further reading

Biggar, N., *The Hastening that Waits: Karl Barth's Ethics* (Oxford: Clarendon, 1995).

Hunsinger, G., ed. and trans., *Karl Barth and Radical Politics* (Philadelphia: Westminster Press, 1976).

Matheny, P. D., *Dogmatics and Ethics: The Theological Realism and Ethics of Karl Barth's "Church Dogmatics"* (Frankfurt: Lang, 1990).

Webster, J., *Barth's Ethics of Reconciliation* (Cambridge: Cambridge University Press, 1995).

Willis, R. E., *The Ethics of Karl Barth* (Leiden: E. J. Brill, 1971).

Yoder, J. H., *Karl Barth and the Problem of War* (Nashville: Abingdon Press, 1970).

14 Karl Barth and politics

In a letter written to Eberhard Bethge in 1968, Karl Barth reflected on how his political commitments did and did not emerge in his theological work. Noting that attention to these was not always prominent, Barth still referred to 'the direction I silently presupposed or only incidentally stressed: ethics – co-humanity – servant church – discipleship – socialism – peace movement – and, hand in hand with all that, politics'.[1] In this chapter, I describe and develop some of the themes Barth mentioned. I will not make a case for the full coherence of these themes in Barth's mature theology because I am not sure that there is an account of this sort, i.e., of Barth's full-fledged and finished 'political ethics'. But my discussion will include a portrayal and an alignment of Barth's political ideas that display both how they might make sense together, and how they might yet exist in conflict or tension. Maybe that is enough to introduce and make clearer the 'direction' of which Barth speaks.

My study points out how Barth (1) affirmed both Christian political responsibility and its theologically required independence from political ideologies and 'natural law' approaches as such. Responsibility without independence leaves Christians captive to the ideologies and approaches, and hence unable politically to witness in freedom to God's sovereign grace. In his understanding of the political order, Barth (2) often focused on the divinely ordained role of the state in protecting citizens from one another and guaranteeing the freedom of the church to preach the gospel. These safeguards are founded on the rule of law backed by threat of coercion. Nevertheless, he denied that political systems were either post-lapsarian arrangements untethered to redemption in Jesus Christ, or orders of preservation that witness to redemption *only* by *simply* 'clearing a space' for evangelization. He rather argued that (3) the political community may itself be a positive parable or analogue to the Kingdom of God. (4) Since Barth envisioned political community as establishing in its proper activities an external, provisional, and relative *humanization* of existence for human creatures, one may profitably look to his account of creaturely fellow humanity to specify the direction of the state's parabolic witness to the Kingdom. (5) An example of this specification includes Barth's examination of human work and its accompanying indication of how the church ought to stand with the poor. Distinct but not wholly separate from this interpretive line, (6) Barth's reflections on the morality of warfare in the *Church Dogmatics* gesture towards a 'practical pacifism' for Christian political witness, which offers a moral context for faithful discernment about the meaning of peace and the possible legitimacy of war. They also, however, raise difficult questions about the adequacy of his stand on the proper use of force in political relations. In any case, (7) Barth's suggestion that Christian witness transcend the orders and powers of the world in service to the neighbour illuminates Barth's political ethics, while confirming the aforementioned stance of practical, non-violent witness to the state. Christian commitments to 'peace movements' or to 'socialism' ought to preserve a moment of recognition that God remains free from us in God's freedom for us, and that there is an 'indissoluble antithesis' of God's Kingdom to all human kingdoms. Here as before but in a different key, Christian political responsibility is affirmed coincident with its independence before God.

FREE RESPONSIBILITY

Christians, 'for whom it is not hidden that in the history of Jesus Christ their own history has taken place', may live in the freedom made possible by that history. It is a history of the grace of the sovereign God who reveals that human guilt and need are taken away by Christ, and that all humanity is called in him to the glory of God.[2] Jesus Christ is the one Word of God, and Christian communities live by the fact that they hear and witness to this Word as it is attested in Holy Scripture.

For reasons noted in the next section, Barth believes that a non-political Christianity is impossible. Here, another denial has to be stressed: Christian political responsibility can acknowledge no source of Christian proclamation separate from the one Word of God. The point is grounded in the identification of revelation with the history of Jesus Christ, and is stated explicitly in the First Article of the Barmen Declaration, a document drafted by Barth in May 1934. The declaration states the faith of the German Confessing Church in opposition to the 'Evangelical Church of the German Nation':

Jesus Christ, as he is attested to us in Holy Scripture, is the one Word of God whom we have to hear, and whom we have to trust and obey in life and death. We condemn the false doctrine that the church can and must recognize as God's revelation other events and powers, forms and truths, apart from and alongside this one Word of God. (*CD* II/1, p. 172)

As a tool of Hitler's Third Reich, the 'Evangelical Church' held among its guiding principles that 'race, folk, and nation' were 'orders of existence granted and entrusted to us by God. God's law for us is that we look to the preservation of these orders.' It was led by a 'Reichsbischof', condemned the 'mission of the Jews' as a 'grave danger to our nationality', and professed 'faith in our national mission that God had committed to us'.[3] Barth saw behind this accommodation to Nazism the error of 'natural theology', in which God's knowability in nature, reason, or history is proclaimed as divine revelation beyond the claim of Jesus Christ.

So Christian responsibility is free in its independence from any and every ideology standing untested by the one Word of God. There is no presumed 'eternal covenant' or systematic correlation between Christian faith and cultural-political viewpoints that a natural theology might underwrite. The church 'trusts and obeys no political system or reality but the power of the Word, by which God upholds all things, including all political things'.[4]

Consider two related features of this freedom. First, it directs witnesses fundamentally and concretely to the good of human beings. 'Christians can look only where they see God looking and try to live with no other purpose than that which God acts in Jesus Christ.'

Their concern is with man. From the very start they are 'humanists'. They are not interested in any cause as such. In regard to every cause, they simply look and ask whether and how far it will relatively and provisionally serve or hurt the cause of man and his right and worth. No idea, no principle, no traditional or newly established institution or organization, no old or new form of economy, state, or culture, no so-called patrimony, no prevailing habit, custom, or moral system, no ideal of education and upbringing, no form of the church, can be for them the a priori of what they think and speak and will, nor can any negation or contesting of certain other ideas and the social constructs corresponding to them. Their a priori is not a cause . . . It is the righteousness of God in Jesus Christ and therefore, in correspondence with this, the man who is loved by God, his right and worth – solely and simply man. (*CD* IV/4, pp. 266, 267–8)

On this matter, Barth's vision fits with the American Catholic Bishops' recent reminder that 'the church is not bound to any particular economic, political, or social system'; the important questions are, 'What is the impact of the system on people? Does it support or threaten human dignity?'[5]

Theological freedom not only makes for this kind of moral independence; it follows that it fosters strategic independence as well. This is the second feature. It emerges in Barth's answer to criticisms that he did not oppose Soviet communist totalitarianism with the same vigour as he did National Socialism. Barth distinguished the latter's 'madness and crime' which 'tried to represent and recommend itself in the guise of a falsified Christianity', and that actually tempted and bewitched many Christians.[6] He reiterates the church's 'freedom to judge each new event afresh' in the light of the Word of God. But he also warned Christians in the West against too readily identifying 'Western judgment' with 'Christian judgment', observing that the attempt to enlist Christians for battle in the Cold War remained 'not quite honest' because of its uncritical stance towards the injustice of Western capitalist 'democracies'. Strategically, it is better to renounce partisanship that exacerbates a dangerous power struggle only for the purpose of 'expressing badly certain completely unclarified and imperfectly grounded Western feelings'.[7] Christian political witness must beware of responding to inhumanity in culturally self-serving ways that, more generally, reflect this or that current array of seemingly feasible political options on the scene.

PROTECTION

In a 1948 essay, Barth defined political systems as: '[T]he attempts undertaken and carried out by men in order to secure the common political life of man by certain coordinations of individual freedom and the claims of the community, by the establishing of laws with power to apply and preserve them'.[8]

The order of law within a particular region or country is guaranteed by the threat of coercion which operates as a last resort in securing the common political life. At the same time, the political order 'must be supported by the free responsibility of its members'. Barth often declared that political systems exist to preserve the common life from chaos, and to that extent they 'create and preserve a space for that which must happen in the time between the beginning and the end . . . a space for the fulfilment of the purpose of world history, a space for faith, repentance and knowledge. They create a space for the life and mission of the Christian Church and therefore a space for something the whole world needs.'[9]

As a divine ordinance expressing God's patience and wisdom, the political order gives the church time for the proclamation of the gospel. And since the state in this way 'renders a definite service to the divine providence and plan of salvation', a non-political Christianity is not possible. 'The church can in no case be indifferent or neutral towards this manifestation of an order so clearly related to its own mission.'[10]

The state's purpose, then, has a christological foundation in its mission to protect freedom for the proclamation of the gospel through laws which are backed by threat of force, and which protect the innocent and bring evildoers to justice. The state ought not, moreover, to make any inward claim upon its subjects in terms of some particular philosophy of life. Barth sought in this manner to display an inward and vital connection between the political order and the order of redemption. He wanted to move away from an abstract and autonomous conception of God as Creator and Preserver as a basis for Christian political ethics, because such a basis invariably interposes the dangerous distraction of natural theology. Note however that this *internal* connection between the political and the redemptive remains a *negative* connection that seems more involved with removal of impediment than it is with a positive witness to redemption. The link depends on the idea that the state must use coercion against (illegitimate) coercion to clear a space for the gospel to be preached in freedom.[11] Now, does Barth go further and say in his political ethics that the state's internal connection to the work of redemption may also be in some way a *positive witness* to the character of God's fellowship with us in Jesus Christ? Yes, he does.

PARABLE

A 1946 study of 'The Christian Community and the Civil Community' presented both an internal and a positive connection between political life and the work of redemption. Barth carried forward the theme that, through the order of law defended by force, the state is 'to protect man from the invasion of chaos and therefore to give him time: time for the preaching of the gospel; time for repentance; time for faith'. Yet, Barth adds that the meaning and purpose of the civil community is 'the safeguarding of both the external, relative, and provisional freedom of individuals and the external and relative peace of the community, *and to that extent the safeguarding of the external, relative, and provisional humanity in their life both as individuals and as a community*'. Safeguarding this humanity may yield 'an external, relative, and provisional embodiment' of the Kingdom of God. The state as 'allegory, correspondence, and analogue' to the Kingdom 'may reflect indirectly the truth and reality which constitute the Christian community'. This is possible even though the state does not know of the Kingdom as the work of Jesus Christ and even though no appeal is or can be made to the Word of God in the running of its affairs. The state nonetheless needs the Christian community to remind it, on the level of humanization, of its origins, limits, and goals. The Christian community stands as an 'inner circle' within the 'outer circle', which is the state, and both communities have their common centre in Jesus Christ. The Kingdom of God will *surpass* both of these communities, while Jesus Christ is taken *already* to be their source and Lord.[12]

The Christian community sets out a 'direction and a line' in its political witness that reminds people of God's Kingdom. This is neither a defensive repetition of church organization nor an anticipatory realization of the Kingdom of God. But the state may still be a 'parable' whose shape and reality 'in this fleeting world should point towards the Kingdom of God, not away from it'. Note these four examples of how the Christian community could enact its appropriate, 'implicit, indirect, but none the less real witness to the gospel'.[13]

(1) Since the church is faithful to the God who in becoming a human neighbour stands for humanity, its political interests ought always to be directed towards real human beings and not in abstract causes such as 'capital' or the 'state' or the 'honour of the nation or the progress of civilization or culture or the idea . . . of the historical development of the human race'.

(2) Since the Christian community witnesses to the divine justification that would protect all and exempt no one, it must support a state constituted by an order of law affording equal protection of all citizens.

(3) Inasmuch as the church responds in gratitude to God's costly action in Christ on behalf of the lost, it 'will always insist on the state's special responsibility for these weaker members of society': 'the poor, the socially and economically weak and threatened'. Practically this requirement perfects the call to political equality, since this must never become 'a cloak under which strong and weak, independent and dependent, rich and poor, employers and employees, in fact receive different treatment at its hands: the weak being unduly restricted, the strong unduly protected. The church must stand for social justice in the political sphere.'

(4) The church is called to be children of God in freedom as persons bound to their Lord. Thus the church will affirm, on the one hand, political rights of self-determination and 'the freedom to live in certain spheres (culture, art, science, faith), safeguarded but not regulated by the state'; on

the other hand, these freedoms are qualified by the responsibilities of citizens to preserve the conditions of peace, freedom, and humanity for themselves and their fellows.[14]

FELLOW HUMANITY

Barth was careful to say that his 'parables' were just examples that needed to be 'extended, deepened, and particularized'. He cautioned that 'translations and transitions' from the Christian gospel to political life will always be open to discussion regarding details, and that the approach of drawing correspondences will not apply to every problem. He continued to maintain that 'the clarity of the message of the Bible will guarantee that all the explications and applications of the Christian approach will move in one unswerving direction and one continuous line'.[15]

One way to explicate this last claim is to reflect on Barth's idea that humanity is always fellow humanity; a human creature is defined by divine promise to be the covenant partner of God. Creaturely freedom is freedom for the good of a history of relationship with God. But the human creature in his or her own sphere of activity with other humans should reflect and correspond to this destiny as covenant partner by living with others in fellowship. The normative human life is never expressed in lonely isolation, where one would seek to find fulfilment in neutrality or hostility towards one's fellows. It is rather a being-in-encounter in which one's distinctive life is qualified by and fulfilled in connection with the life of the other.

Barth describes 'creaturely covenant' in terms of mutual seeing, mutual speaking and hearing, and mutual assistance. Each fellow must first be open to the other with a view to his or her benefit. He or she is not merely an embodiment of this or that role or cause or group; rather, he or she must be *seen* realistically as bearing particular needs and a particular point of view. Mutuality of speech and hearing requires that each party try to interpret him- or herself to the other, in order for both to discover in particular a common sphere of life and interest. The discovery of this intersubjective space is directed towards assistance – each party helps and is helped by the other from within the shared space. Human creatures ought to bear responsibility for their lives, but they are also essentially dependent. Self-responsibility and dependence are acknowledged and coordinated through patterns of mutual help, and the 'secret' of humanity is that this qualification of the action of humans manifestly fulfils them. The relationship is enacted on both sides with gladness (*CD* III/2, pp. 250–72).

What is called for, in short, is a differentiated freedom realized in fellowship, a 'freedom to be oneself with the other, and oneself to be with the other'. Since all act within the grace of creation, this is a possibility for Christians and non-Christians alike.

Humanity is fellow humanity on account of the triune God's decision to enact with humanity a covenant of reconciliation. The creation of human beings in the relation of I and Thou, biblically narrated in the creation of male and female, has the covenant as its internal basis, and is accordingly a sign and prefiguration of the bond between Christ and his community. Fellow humanity is a 'real witness . . . to this first and final element in the will and decree of God' (*CD* III/2, p. 318). It is, by an analogy of relationship, the *image of God*, who is I and Thou, the Father of the Son and the Son of the Father, in relation and yet one and the same in the Spirit.[16]

Suppose we contend that the parables of the Kingdom of God realized in political life emerge in the provisional and relative humanization that is fellow humanity: the unswerving direction and continuous line of the church's political responsibility appears in its work for a civil community that enables and encourages coequal fellowship for its citizen members in various spheres of social life, including political activity itself. I propose one example from Barth that supports this interpretation below.

HUMAN WORK

'Work' refers to a person's active affirmation of his or her existence as a human creature. It is required by and corresponds to God's providential rule. An incidental but necessary presupposition of service and acceptance of God's Kingdom within the community of disciples, work embodies 'the desire of men to "prolong" their own lives and those of their relatives, i.e., to maintain, continue, develop and mould them, to secure and hold at the common table of life a place in closest keeping with their desires and requirements, or, in less grandiose terms, to earn their daily bread and a little more' (*CD* III/4, p. 525). 'Working to live' establishes an external basis of service, a measure of independence in caring for one's life (which does not exclude being assisted by others).

Barth offers five criteria for discerning whether our work is 'commanded and right'. It must be 'objective', or competently and diligently aligned with the ends of the activity in question. Workers ought not to be 'dilettantes or bunglers'. Work also should authentically benefit the cause of humankind. It ought to express 'reflectivity' or 'disciplined self-concentration', as well as the absence of tension that marks work's internal limit in rest and freedom for God (*CD* III/4, pp. 545f.). Finally, Barth argues that work ought to be human, 'in the special sense of fellow human'.

Since *in fact* work conforms so little to normative humanity, Christian praise of it can only be 'muffled' and 'modest'. What ought to take place in cooperation appears primarily as an isolated or hostile struggle for existence. What should be governed by mutual coordination of human needs is perverted by the lust for security that super-abundance brings, or for possessions, or for power over others. 'The genuine and vital claims of man are not empty and inordinate desires of this kind' (*CD* III/4, p. 538). When, however, the organization of work involves concentrated private ownership of the means of production, the opportunity arises for these desires to be expressed structurally in the exploitation of persons who, possessing limited economic power, are unable in truth to deal on fair terms with their employers regarding the contract of labour.

Barth here cites a violation of commutative justice that effectively treats the weak merely as means or instruments to the interests of others; appeal to the value of freedom in striking agreements and exchanges masks the fundamental unfairness of background conditions of power and resources.[17] While the same injustice applies to 'state socialism', Barth challenged Western churches to champion the weak against the strong through counter-movements that may not unfairly be described as 'socialist'; but these rely only on assessment of what is most helpful in a specific time and place. The church's 'decisive word' cannot be for socialism or any putatively plausible account of social progress, let alone the dubious recipe of state socialism. 'It can only consist in the proclamation of the revolution of God against "all ungodliness and unrighteousness of man" (Rom. 1:18), i.e., in the proclamation of His Kingdom as it has already come and comes' (*CD* III/4, p. 545).

Still the decisive word may include a political witness which, as here or there 'practically socialist', would correspond to the Kingdom by realizing to some greater degree the humanization and hence fellow humanity of work.[18] The call for counter-movements is especially 'for the championing of the weak against any kind of encroachment on the part of the strong', and this 'preferential option for the poor' completes and does not jeopardize the commended community of mutual assistance; for those who are most marginalized and powerless to take part in communal life are cherished and honoured as the human creatures they are through special efforts to enable and empower them to participate in this way. In a fashion again not alien to the arguments of the American Catholic Bishops, justice for Barth 'demands that social institutions be ordered in a way that guarantees all persons the ability to participate actively in the economic, political, and cultural life of society . . . Such participation is an essential expression of the social nature of human beings and of their communitarian vocation.'[19]

POLITICAL FORCE AND PRACTICAL PACIFISM

In a stunning comparative study of the political ethics of Barth and Paul Ramsey, Oliver O'Donovan persuasively suggests that:

[T]here is a central stream in Barth's thinking about the state which links his writings from about 1930 on, encompassing on the right hand the possibility of the state's use of force and on the left the abnormality of it . . . [I]n the wartime writings and those which shortly preceded and followed the war the stream flowed against its right-hand bank, and in the later post-war writings veered across to its left-hand.[20]

Adding that this 'vacillation' arises from Barth's own controlling dialectic between 'normal' and 'marginal' functions of the state, O'Donovan questions whether he 'leaves us with the gulf unbridged between an ideal, evangelical politics, grounded in the reconciling covenant of God with man in Christ, and actual political phenomena which we can only deplore and not interpret'.[21] In this section I want to investigate this criticism a bit more by commenting on Barth's major discussion of the morality of war in the *Church Dogmatics*. But I will also explore the way Barth's dialectic overlaps with a defensible 'practical pacifism' that may help to bridge the gap between gospel politics and political realities.

A reader of Barth on war in his 'special ethics' of creation would find it difficult not to conclude that he takes the practice of modern warfare to be utterly immoral. He contends that the 'real issue in war' is not really service to human needs, but just the possession and enhancement of economic power as its own end. War is, moreover, a matter of killing without restraint in which 'whole nations as such are out to destroy one another by every possible means'. These points are cast as prelude and warrant for Barth's statement that the possibility of Christian participation in a 'just' war must be determined with the greatest seriousness and with the prior assumption 'that the inflexible negative of pacifism has almost infinite arguments in its favour and is almost overpoweringly strong' (*CD* III/4, p. 455). Whatever may be Barth's rhetorical and stage-setting intentions regarding these remarks, they pose the problem O'Donovan sees; that is, if war idolatrously subordinates human persons to a quest for material possessions by way of indiscriminate killing, then it simply does appear 'with fairly little qualification, as the history of sin, but not as the history of grace abounding yet more'. So then how, as part of the latter history, can warfare be proclaimed 'just' at all? And how can participation in war witness to the gospel, looking at the good news from the vantage point of the *homo politicus* Barth presents?

Barth might add to the problem in declaring that not only war *but even the exercise of power* is an 'alien' and not 'proper' work of the state (*CD* III/4, pp. 456–7). On the face of it, the notion appears to contradict the definition of political systems quoted above; at best we find an instance of his 'vacillation', and a perspective that leaves little room for a 'gracious "you may!" in relation to the state's use of force'.[22] The redemptive grace of the sovereign God is put into question concerning the uses of power – and this is exactly what Barth sought to avoid in rejecting 'abstract' natural law and 'orders of preservation' conceptions of political life.

In any case, Barth opposes the doctrine of pacifism because it fixes itself to unyielding principles rather than the freedom of the gracious God. And wars may indeed be just, he says, to defend nations whose very existence and autonomy are threatened by aggression. The life of a people thus threatened, and to that extent their relationship to God, may need to be defended in self-defence and/or by way of intervention on behalf of the innocent. However well or poorly this case for 'just cause' fits the preceding analysis, Barth can continue to perplex readers with comments that urge that just wars be waged without concern for 'the anticipated success or failure of the enterprise', as if considerations of 'proportionality' or 'reasonable hope of success' are utterly irrelevant. One wonders whether the earlier concession to 'total war' is carried over inconsistently to the case of 'just war' as well (*CD* III/4, pp. 460–3).[23]

So much for a reading of Barth that fuels O'Donovan's criticisms. Consider another interpretation that does not escape the critique, but instead highlights other fruitful Barthian concerns. These revolve around exposing the self-congratulatory realities of war and statecraft which can be hidden within and behind ideologies that tend to render war ordinary, inevitable, righteous without qualification, and, in one case, not utterly horrible. So we *ought to stress* how killing in war challenges 'not merely for individuals but for millions of men, the whole of morality, or better, obedience to the command of God in all its dimensions' (*CD* III/4, p. 275). Christians ought to give *no aid and comfort* to the state with assurances that it 'may do gaily and confidently whatever it thinks is right'. They can in this context only make a 'detached and delaying movement' that calls for peace up to the last moment, that toils to fashion peace (in the direction of social democracy) more vigorously than states typically fashion war. Never counselling that war is absolutely avoidable, the church nevertheless opposes as 'satanic' that crude 'realism' which deems war inevitable and therefore justified, as unavoidable and therefore right. By refusing to howl with the pack, by seeking peaceably to keep war at bay, and more generally by trying in political life to construct true peace in international relations in conformity with normative humanity, Christians act also to enable discernment of when war is, tragically, morally necessary (*CD* III/4, pp. 453–60).

So the Christian ought to unmask false and inadequate reasons for war. He or she should contribute to a peace which does not lead to war, and to peaceable measures to restrain recourse to war when it threatens. Within this moral landscape, the Christian may well hear the divine command requiring a nation's recourse to war and one's own participation in it. By themselves, these recommendations do not save Barth from the problems just addressed. They could, however, outline a worthy vision of 'practical pacifism' for the church founded on a view of political life which (without vacillation) definitely establishes that the use of coercive power is of the essence of worldly politics, and that this coercive order is indeed in keeping with divine providence, employing violence against itself to clear a space for evangelization, and to protect the innocent and judge the guilty who threaten them. (If O'Donovan is right, Barth's dialectic of normal and marginal functions of the state does not do the trick.) Strategically the Christian community refuses to rule out war in principle, yet incessantly poses critical questions supporting genuine peace and opposing the ideology of war.

> Being against war . . . means opposing the idea that war is 'necessary' or 'inevitable', and that peace is not 'possible'. Finally, it means opposing the idea that wars are waged for noble motives: to restore a universal order of justice and peace or simply to make amends for injustices. For at most these noble motives – which some people do not lack – in most cases provide a juridical and moral cover for the true reasons of war: political domination and economic interest. In other words, to oppose the 'ideology of war' means to do what is needed to unmask war by showing it as it really is by uncovering its motives and results, by demonstrating that it is always the poor and the weak who pay for war, whether they wear a military uniform or belong to the civilian population.[24]

These last words belong not to Barth but to an influential Roman Catholic commentary on the Persian Gulf War. Needless to say, the resonances invite further study. The significant point is that our proposed 'practical pacifism' can connect evangelical politics and political realities by limiting war to its proper purpose, and extending political power's use short of war to effect forms of peace that meet more nearly the measure of creaturely humanity. Barth's unfinished ethics of reconciliation barely sketches a position on political power that is patient of this proposal. He states directly that government 'is not just the establishment and exercise of the right among men but also, for the sake of this, the establishment of sovereignty and dominion and the exercise of power and force by man over man'. The vain human struggle to live a lordless life, however, can find expression in the perversion and reversal of this order such that 'no state of any kind is or has or will be immune to the tendency to become at least a little Leviathan. The threat of a change from the might of right to the right of might couches at the door of every polity' (*ChrL* IV/4, pp. 220f.). 'Practical pacifism' figures as a response to this tendency in the light of a proper grasp of the human meaning of political power before God.

DISCIPLESHIP

In the last two sections, I have written of Barth's practical commitments to social democracy and pacifism. In both cases, the account appeals to the creaturely norm of fellow humanity as a kind of explanation or warrant for these recommendations in Christian political ethics. I need finally to caution that even this account becomes theologically abstract and unfair to Barth if it would substitute that 'norm' for God's freedom to act on humanity's behalf, or if it loses sight of the concretely redemptive and eschatological character of Christian political witness.

In their political activities, Barth makes clear, Christians witness to the grace of the sovereign God who in Jesus Christ looks to the cause of human beings made for covenant. They do not witness to an idea or programme of 'community' that becomes some first or final cause.

Barth also makes clear that Jesus Christ calls out disciples from the dominion of the orders or forces of the old aeon to which God's Kingdom stands in 'indissoluble antithesis'. If the gospel message is to be given, 'the world must see and hear at least an indication, or sign, of what has taken place. The break made by God in Jesus must become history. That is why Jesus calls his disciples' (*CD* IV/2, p. 544). However much our creaturely reality before God alerts us to the inhumanity of hostility or isolation, political witness also and always involves a definite movement out of conformity with the legalism determined by the dominion of worldly authorities. These include 'attachment to the authority, validity, and confidence of possessions' and 'the fixed idea of the necessity and beneficial value of force' (*CD* IV/2, pp. 548–50). Service of the neighbour, therefore, may and must witness to a genuine freedom from attachment to possessions and to the invalidation of the relationship between friend and foe. Work for social justice and peace is rooted in a revolutionary freedom that embodies and anticipates a new way of life that is faithful to God and embodied in Christian practices, rather than merely a 'better' or 'safer' life yet faithful to mammon or violent power. In this connection the terms of fellow humanity – merciful seeing, understanding, and solidarity – are made concrete in the divine permission 'to bid man hope, and thus to mediate to him the promise that he needs'. A credible Christian witness to Jesus Christ should give human beings 'the courage not to be content with the corruption and evil of the world but even within this horizon to look ahead and not back' (*CD* IV/4, pp. 270f.).

These last comments again reflect Barth's yoking of the necessarily political character of Christianity with God's utterly independent freedom to be for us in Jesus Christ. Corresponding to this, the Christian community is liberated from all worldly systems of political thought and action in political engagements for and with needy, suffering humanity.

Notes

1 Quoted by H. Gollwitzer in G. Hunsinger, ed., *Karl Barth and Radical Politics* (Philadelphia: Westminster, 1976), p. 99. Cf. editor C. Green's 'Introduction' in *Karl Barth: Theologian of Freedom* (Minneapolis: Fortress Press, 1991), pp. 43–5.
2 K. Barth, *God Here and Now* (New York: Harper and Row, 1964), p. 88.
3 A. C. Cochrane, *The Church's Confession Under Hitler* (Philadelphia: Westminster Press, 1962), pp. 207f.
4 K. Barth, 'The Christian Community and the Civil Community', in *Community, State, and Church* (Gloucester, Mass.: Peter Smith, 1968), p. 161.
5 *Economic Justice For All* (National Conference of Catholic Bishops: Washington, DC: 1986), p. 66.
6 K. Barth, 'The Church Between East and West', in *Against the Stream* (New York: Philosophical Library, 1954), pp. 136f.
7 Ibid., p. 143.
8 K. Barth, 'The Christian Community in the Midst of Political Change', in ibid., p. 80. In this and the next two sections, I rely on and develop ideas found in W. Werpehowski, 'Justification and Justice in the Theology of Karl Barth', *The Thomist* 50 (1986), pp. 623–42.
9 Barth, 'The Christian Community in the Midst of Political Change', pp. 80f.

10 Barth, 'The Christian Community and the Civil Community', p. 157.

11 See esp. K. Barth, 'Church and State', in *Community, State, and Church*, pp. 101–48.

12 Barth, 'The Christian Community and the Civil Community', pp. 150, 154f.

13 Ibid., pp. 163, 168, 170f.

14 Ibid., pp. 171–5.

15 Ibid., pp. 179f.

16 See W. C. Placher, *Narratives of a Vulnerable God* (Louisville, Ky.: Westminster John Knox Press, 1994), pp. 53–83.

17 J. P. Gunneman, 'Capitalism and Commutative Justice', in *The Annual of the Society of Christian Ethics 1985* (Washington, DC: Georgetown University Press, 1986), pp. 101–22.

18 See Green's parallel interpretation in his 'Introduction', p. 43.

19 *Economic Justice For All*, p. 40.

20 O. O'Donovan, 'Karl Barth and Ramsey's "Uses of Power",' *Journal of Religious Ethics* 19 (1991), p. 3.

21 Ibid., p. 14.

22 Ibid.

23 For an influential review of just war criteria, see National Conference of Catholic Bishops, *The Challenge of Peace* (Washington, DC: United States Catholic Conference, 1983), pp. 36–48.

24 La Civiltà Cattolica, 'Modern War and Christian Conscience', in P. T. Jersild and D. A. Johnson, eds., *Moral Issues and Christian Response*, 5th edn (Fort Worth, Tex.: Harcourt Brace Jovanovich, 1993), pp. 223f.

Further reading

Hunsinger, G., *Karl Barth and Radical Politics* (Philadelphia: Westminster Press, 1976).

Hunsinger, G., 'Barth and Liberation Theology', *Journal of Religion* 63 (1983), pp. 247–63.

Jüngel, E., *Karl Barth. A Theological Legacy* (Philadelphia: Westminster Press, 1986).

O'Donovan, O., 'Karl Barth and Ramsey's "Uses of Power"', *The Journal of Religious Ethics* 19 (1991), pp. 1–30.

O'Donovan, O., *The Desire of the Nations: Rediscovering the Roots of Political Theology* (Cambridge: Cambridge University Press, 1996).

Thiemann, R. F., 'The Significance of Karl Barth for Contemporary Theology', *The Thomist* 50 (1986), pp. 512–39.

Webster, J., *Barth's Ethics of Reconciliation* (Cambridge: Cambridge University Press, 1995).

15 Religion and the religions

J. A. DI NOIA, O.P.

Christian theology of religions is an area within systematic theology that has lately undergone considerable development. The area has taken on greater definition in recent years as Christian communities throughout the world come to grips with a heightened awareness of other religious traditions, and with a growing desire on the part of Christians to pursue interreligious dialogue and other forms of positive engagement with Jews, Muslims, Hindus, Buddhists, and others.

Theologians practising this sub-speciality commonly address such questions as these: Are any of the teachings of other religious traditions true? How should judgments about this issue proceed? Do other religions point their adherents in the right direction? Can Jews, Muslims, Hindus, and Buddhists be saved? Can they be saved by following the teachings of their religions? How should Christians relate to Jews, Muslims, Hindus, Buddhists, and others? Should they attempt to persuade non-Christians to become Christians? Should they engage in dialogue with the adherents of other religions? What purposes does such interreligious dialogue serve? Drawing upon a long and substantial tradition of inquiry about these issues within Christian doctrine and theology, the agenda of the theology of religions has taken on an increasingly systematic shape as more and more theologians within the Christian churches turn their attention to these questions.[1]

READING BARTH ON RELIGION AND THE RELIGIONS

Karl Barth's contribution to Christian reflection on these questions is considerable, but his writings on the theology of religion and the religions pre-date the development of this newly emergent sub-speciality. The failure to take this into account has sometimes led to misreadings and even caricatures of his treatment of religion and the religions in the *Church Dogmatics*. Readers who approach the volumes of the *Church Dogmatics* expecting to find therein a comprehensive theology of religions to guide Christian communities in their relations with the world of non-Christian religions will be disappointed.

Although Barth has some important things to say about other religions and their adherents, he does not undertake to provide a full-blown theology of religions of the kind we have come to expect from theologians in recent years. In fact, Barth has relatively little to say about particular *religions*, but a very great deal to say about *religion*. In his mature theology of religion and the religions in the *Church Dogmatics*, Barth is rather less concerned with what Christians should think about non-Christians than he is with how modern concepts of religion, religious experience, and religious conscious-ness have influenced what Christians think about being Christian. Because he believes this influence not to have been an entirely healthy one, a good deal of what Barth has to say about religion is critical.

The failure to recognize that Barth's chief interest is to provide a theology of *religion* rather than a comprehensive theology of *religions* has contributed to the widespread and now nearly entrenched misreading of his theology of religion and the religions, according to which he is alleged to have advanced an account of non-Christian religions that reflects 'sublime bigotry' and 'exclusivism'. It is further alleged that the Barthian account cannot support Christian communities in their efforts to pursue interre-ligious dialogue and other positive forms of engagement with Jewish, Muslim, Hindu, Buddhist, and other communities.[2]

The charge of 'exclusivism' must be seen in the context of a scheme for classifying positions in the theology of religions that has become standard for many practitioners in the field. According to this scheme, exclusivist positions are those which maintain that salvation and truth can be found only in Christianity. Such positions are to be contrasted, on the one hand, with inclusivist positions which maintain roughly that Christian salvation and truth are implicitly available in non-Christian religions; and, on the other hand, with pluralist positions which maintain that, given the radically transcendent character of the religiously ultimate, salvation and truth are diversely figured, and more or less equally available in Christian, Jewish, Muslim, Hindu, Buddhist, and other religions.

On a careful reading of the relevant sections of the *Church Dogmatics*, as we shall see, the charge that Barth's position with regard to non-Christian religions falls simply at the exclusivist end of this spectrum cannot be sustained. To be sure, Barth's analysis of modern concepts of religion and religious experience could be deployed in an effective theological critique of some pluralist positions. But, while Barth is clearly no pluralist, his theology of religion and the religions is too complex to be tracked on the standard grid in any straightforward way. As one recent survey of the field has it: 'Barth overturns these categories by being both exclusivist, inclusivist, and universalist!'[3]

Barth's theological approach to the topic of religion is typical of theologians during most of the twentieth century, and is already apparent in some of his earliest published papers where he addresses – still in the characteristic modalities of liberal Protestantism – the role of religious experience in theology and of the 'History of Religions' approach to biblical interpretation.[4] While the 1919 and 1922 editions of his commentary on the Epistle to the Romans mark a decisive shift away from liberal Protestantism, they nonetheless continue to reflect Barth's concern with what he will eventually term, in his mature treatment of these issues in the *Church Dogmatics*, 'the place of religion in theology'.[5]

The principal loci for Barth's theology of religion and the religions are found in *CD* I/2, paragraph 17, within the context of his discussion of the doctrine of revelation, and in *CD* IV/3, paragraph 69, within the context of his treatment of the doctrine of reconciliation. As we consider these sections in turn, we will be able to observe that paragraph 17 is chiefly, though not exclusively, concerned with the impact of the category of religion on Christian theology, while paragraph 69 touches more directly on the agenda we have come to associate with the theology of religions.

RELIGION AND REVELATION IN THEOLOGY

Barth's *CD* I/2, paragraph 17, is entitled in the English translation, 'The Revelation God as the Abolition of Religion'.[6] The rendering of the original German *Aufhebung der Religion* by the expression 'abolition of religion' has done a lot of mischief. In the words of Garrett Green, this misleading translation has played 'a major role in encouraging the caricatures of Barth's theology that have for so long distorted its reception in the Anglo-Saxon world'.[7] Green prefers 'sublation' – a term which, despite its unfamiliarity in English, at least avoids the almost entirely negative connotations of 'abolition', at the same time that it embraces the dialectical pairing of 'dissolution' and 'elevation' that the German *Aufhebung* entails.

The trinitarian context of Barth's treatment of religion is important to grasp. Within the grand scheme of the *Church Dogmatics*, the section entitled 'The Revelation of God as the Sublation of Religion' falls within Barth's treatment of the role of the Holy Spirit in the communication of divine revelation, which begins in paragraph 16 with a discussion of the

Holy Spirit as the subjective reality and possibility of revelation. Before he can proceed to describe in paragraph 18 how the Holy Spirit creates 'the life of the children of God' through the grace of revelation, Barth is obliged to dismantle an alternative account which locates the subjective reality and possibility of revelation not in the grace of the Holy Spirit, but in the dispositions of human religiosity. In effect, then, paragraph 17 constitutes an interlude in the unfolding trinitarian account of the doctrine of revelation in which Barth takes up the problem of the theological displacement of the grace of the Holy Spirit by the category of religion as the disposition for the communication and reception of divine revelation. Barth wants to reclaim for divine revelation itself a role in theology which the concept of religion and its cognates have usurped – to establish, as Garrett Green notes, 'the priority of revelation over religion without denying the religious nature of revelation'.[8] An authentically Christian theology must correct this 'reversal of revelation and religion' by affirming the work of the Holy Spirit in the sublation of religion by divine revelation.

This trinitarian context alerts the attentive reader to expect a properly theological account of religion. At the centre of attention is *religion* – or, perhaps more accurately, religiosity – as a structure or element in human personal existence. More to the periphery, but certainly present, are actually existing *religions* as social forms, comprising developed organizations and recognizable institutions (dogmas, rituals, and so on). Barth takes the basic forms of religion – a conception of the deity and the obligation to fulfil the law – to be more or less universal features of human existence. Although he assumes that religions are the 'externalization of religion' (*CD* I/2, p. 317), he does not field a complete theory, employing phenomenological, anthropological, or other standard methodologies to account for the connection of 'religions' with 'religion'. His most explicit discussion of this relationship occurs in regard to the Christian religion and takes a quite explicitly theological line. This is a further indication that what is at stake here is a strictly theological analysis of religion that has chiefly in view a problematic internal to Christian theology.

From the outset, it is clear that Barth is concerned to examine the singular prominence that the concept of religion has come to enjoy in Western theology in general and in neo-Protestant theology in particular. To be sure, the concept of religion, and, later, concepts like 'religious consciousness' and 'religious experience', would come to influence Christian views of the nature of actually existing religions. While maintaining an interest here in the impact of such concepts on Christian theology of religions and on Christian relations with other religions, Barth focuses on the impact of the category of religion on the theology of revelation and thus on Christian theology in its whole range.

In most theology prior to the seventeenth century, religion and Christianity were simply identified. What we might now call elements of a religious bent or interest that seemed to be intrinsic to human nature – the belief in the existence of God, the natural desire for God, the inclination to observe the natural law, the belief in an afterlife, and so on – were understood to have been taken up into the supernatural life of grace. Through theological analysis, such elements could usefully be distinguished as a *religio naturalis* and even systematized in a *theologia naturalis*. But the objective of such analysis was a properly theological one, based on revelation and arising from faith. Human nature and its religious inclinations were identified, not in order to define an independently existing set of intellectual and affective predispositions for revelation and grace, but in order to elucidate the internal structure of the 'theological' or godly life of communion with the Blessed Trinity. According to classical theology, this life is a strictly gratuitous new life that is made possible by the incarnation, passion, death, and resurrection of Jesus Christ. Since, according to revelation, human beings were created by God, and in the image of God, with a view to a gracious participation in the divine life, this supernatural life could not entail the suppression or destruction of human nature and its spiritual capacities but must involve what was variously described as their rectification, restoration, elevation, perfection, and/or fulfilment. Classical theology also recognized and exploited the apologetic potential of the identification of the religious elements intrinsic to human nature. Still, despite wide-ranging debates among Patristic and Medieval theologians, and even, during the Reformation period, church-dividing disagreements about the relationship of nature and grace, there was a shared presupposition about the object of the inquiry: human nature, not as an independently existing entity with self-defined ends and aspirations, but rather as the natural component within the supernatural life of grace.

Various developments contributed to the emergence of natural religion as a category independent of its setting in traditional theological anthropology. Prominent among them were the rise of rational religion in response to post-Reformation religious strife, and the emphasis on apologetics in response to sceptical critics of Christianity. Rationalists appealed to a natural religious core to counter religious factionalism, while believers appealed to inherent religious instincts to address religious scepticism. Together they succeeded in launching what might well be called the independent career of natural religion.[9]

Once it had come loose from its modest niche in classical, Medieval, and Reformation theology, the category of religion grew in significance throughout the seventeenth and eighteenth centuries until it was free, in the nineteenth and twentieth centuries, to mount what Barth calls 'that tumultuous invasion of the Church and theology ... whose astonished witnesses we have been in our day' (*CD* I/2, p. 290). In Barth's view, the difficulty here is not so much with the emergence of the category of religion as such, but with the normative role that this category has come to play in neo-Protestant theology (and, presumably, in cognate projects in other theological traditions). Where classical theology would require us to interpret religion and the religions in the light of revelation, neo-Protestant theology instead encourages us to regard 'the nature and incidence of religion ... as the norm and principle by which to explain the revelation of God' (*CD* I/2, p. 284).

It is this reversal of revelation and religion that Barth laments and, in paragraph 17, endeavours to correct. In part, the correction he advances is a methodological one that bears on all theological inquiries, including those conducted under the rubric of the theology of religions. In Barth's view, by exchanging revelation for the concept of religion, 'theology lost its object' (*CD* I/2, p. 294). As an inquiry arising from faith, theology has its distinctive character as an intellectual discipline precisely in virtue of the field of knowledge that is opened up for it by the grace of divine revelation. Human religiosity, natural religion, and the world of religions become objects of a properly (Barth would say 'uninterruptedly') theological inquiry only when they are viewed within the field or domain illumined by the light of revelation, and not vice versa.[10]

But it is clear that something more than methodological considerations is at stake here. For when Barth insists that religion be set within the properly theological context defined by divine revelation, it becomes clear that the grace of revelation entails the sublation of religion. The term 'sublation' – or 'taking up into' – may prompt the reader to think of the classical christological term, 'assumption'. And that is precisely what Barth has in mind. When the proper order of the concepts of revelation and religion is restored, then we see that 'the Christological doctrine of the *assumptio carnis* [assumption of the flesh] makes it possible to speak of revelation as the sublation of religion' (*CD* I/2, p. 297, English translation slightly modified). Barth's employment of the analogy of the incarnation to describe the proper order of revelation and religion hints at something that will emerge with increasing clarity as we proceed: sublation entails not only negation, but also rectification and elevation.

It is worth noting in passing that Barth's account of the place of religion in theology has important affinities with classical and Medieval understandings of the nature of theology, including, notably, that advanced by Thomas Aquinas and by many Thomists. It is true that, as we shall shortly see, in his theological description of religion and religiosity as *Unglaube* – faithlessness or unbelief – Barth betrays his preference for an account of the relationship between nature and grace whose provenance is in the Reformation tradition. Without denying the reality of sin and the human condition under divine judgment, Aquinas and his followers in Catholic theology would provide an account of human religiosity that is both more positive and less dialectically edged than the one advanced by Barth here. But, these weighty differences to the contrary notwithstanding, the overall logic of Barth's argument that the grace of revelation sublates – or takes up into itself – the natural components of human existence ('religious' and otherwise) is remarkably and unmistakably congruent with Thomistic (and generally Catholic) approaches to Christology, the theology of grace, and theological methodology.[11]

A THEOLOGICAL ACCOUNT OF RELIGION

Once the correct order of religion to revelation is established, two further assertions together comprise the heart of Barth's theology of religion and the religions as it unfolds in *CD* I/2, paragraph 17. The first is that, as we noted above, when religion is viewed in the light of divine revelation, it is revealed as *Unglaube*. The second is that, while this judgment falls on Christianity insofar as it is a religion, the Christian religion, in virtue of divine justifying grace alone, is nonetheless the true religion.

Readers of this *Companion* will not be surprised to learn that these assertions have given rise to heated controversy, and have even led some commentators to dismiss out of hand the suggestion that Barth's theology of religion could make any contribution to the theology of religions in its current form. In part, these reactions to Barth fail to recognize something to which our attention has been drawn at several points in this chapter: Barth's theology of religion and the religions is addressed primarily to Christians, and only secondarily to non-Christians. Beyond this, however, dismissive interpretations of Barth's theology of religion, and his potential relevance for current theology of religions, also fail to grasp the considerable subtlety and intrinsic interest of his theological account of religiosity and religion.

The English translation of the original German term, *Unglaube*, by 'unbelief' has not served Barth well. As Garrett Green has pointed out, *Unglaube* is perhaps best rendered in English by 'faithlessness' or 'unfaith'.[12] Human religiosity, according to Barth, is judged by revelation to be the absence or lack of faith: not simply an unwillingness to assent to certain truths, but an unwillingness to yield to the saving power of divine grace and revelation, and to surrender all those purely human attempts to know and satisfy God which together comprise human religion and religiosity.

Drawing upon the confessional and theological categories of the Reformation, Barth's account of religion views the human condition as being at once sinful and self-justifying. It is within this perspective that all religion, including the Christian religion, must be seen as *Unglaube* and thereby as falling under the judgment of revelation. For the truth about God can be truly known only when and insofar as God reveals himself, while the possibility of pleasing him can be realized only through his mercy, forgiveness, and grace. Conceptions of the deity and schemes of salvation – the bread and butter of human religion – have set their sights on an objective that is simply not within range: they can neither attain to a true knowledge of God nor deliver the salvation they promise. What God bestows as his gift – faith and justification – cannot be grasped as the accomplishment of human religion or religiosity. For, as Barth contends, the proper response to revelation is faith not religion (= unfaith).

It is crucial to observe that, for Barth, the judgment that all religion is unfaith is strictly a divine judgment rendered by revelation itself and knowable only by the grace of faith. This judgment is emphatically not one that is pronounced upon the world of non-Christian religions by Christianity nor its representatives. Nor is it an empirical judgment, such as might result from study and assessment of the various social forms and institutions in which human religiosity has expressed itself. Still less is this judgment one that is based on some definition of the essence of religion. Barth insists that 'it is only by the revelation of God in Jesus Christ that we can characterize religion as . . . unbelief' (*CD* I/2, p. 314).

In this context, the dialectical character of the *Aufhebung*, or sublation, of religion by revelation becomes apparent: religion is both negated (Barth says 'contradicted') and elevated (Barth says 'exalted') by revelation. Insofar as it clings to its conceptions of the deity and its pursuit of self-justification, religion can be seen actually to contradict revelation; insofar as revelation judges and negates this tendency, revelation can be seen to contradict religion. But the judgment of divine revelation does not sweep aside or destroy the world of religion. On the contrary, 'In his revelation God is present in the world of human religion' (*CD* I/2, p. 297) and enters 'a sphere in which His own reality and possibility are encompassed by a sea of more or less adequate . . . parallels and analogies in human realities and possibilities' (*CD* I/2, p. 282). The sublation of religion entails not only its negation by revelation, but also its exaltation by the grace of divine revelation. This exaltation occurs, according to Barth, at the point where God's gracious entry into the world of human religion renders the Christian religion the true religion of revelation. But this can be said of the Christian religion only by analogy with the justification of the sinner: 'We can speak of "true" religion only in the sense in which we speak of a "justified sinner"' (*CD* I/2, p. 325). In this perspective, we see that human religiosity is both negated and exalted, both judged and justified, by the grace of divine revelation.

Within this framework, the claim that Christianity is the true religion is not one that is based on an interior worthiness or excellence of the Christian religion *qua* religion, or even on the character of Christianity as a religion of grace. In one of his rare detailed references to a non-Christian religion, Barth invokes the presence of a well-developed doctrine of grace in Pure Land Buddhism to insist that to ground the truth of the Christian religion on grace is not equivalent to an appeal to 'the immanent truth of a religion of grace as such, but of the reality of grace itself by which one religion is adopted and distinguished as the true one before all others' (*CD* I/2, p. 339). Sacred Scripture makes it clear, Barth insists, that 'the religion of revelation is indeed bound up with the revelation of God: but the revelation of God is not bound up with the religion of revelation' (*CD* I/2, p. 329). The truth of the true religion must continually be attributed to the justifying grace of God. To do otherwise, Barth asserts, would be 'the dishonouring of God and the eternal destruction of souls' (*CD* I/2, p. 332).

The Christian religion is a religion like other religions; what makes it uniquely true is not that it is a religion, but that it is the religion that has been taken up by divine grace. It follows, then, that the claim that the Christian religion is the true religion is rooted in the reality of the divine action by which the church is continually created, elected, justified, and sanctified: (1) The Christian religion is the product of an act of *divine creation*, by the name of Jesus Christ, and it would not exist 'as a missionary and cultic and theological and political and moral force' (*CD* I/2, p. 347) apart from its relationship to the name of Jesus Christ. (2) This relationship to the name of Jesus Christ is one which the Christian religion did not choose for itself, but which is the result of *divine election*, in which the faithfulness and patience of God are enacted. (3) Furthermore, as we have already seen, the Christian religion is the true religion only in virtue of *divine justification* and the forgiveness of sins, which are the work of Jesus Christ. (4) Finally, by the continual act of *divine sanctification*, the Christian religion is 'the sacramental area created by the Holy Spirit, in which the God whose Word became flesh continues to speak through the sign of his revelation' (*CD* I/2, p. 359).

If Barth's insistence on the priority of revelation over religion can be construed in part as a correction of neo-Protestant theology's reversal of this order, then his account of the truth that can be claimed for the Christian religion might well be seen as a correction of older Protestant orthodoxy's straightforward identification of Christianity with the true religion.[13] Combined with his analysis of human religion as *Unglaube*, these themes are clearly addressed primarily to Christians. Without denying the reality of religion as an element in human existence and in human society and culture, Barth is concerned to advance a properly and consistently theological account of human religiosity which allows full scope to the doctrine of the gracious action of the triune God who draws human persons into the communion of trinitarian life through the saving work of Jesus Christ and the Holy Spirit.

TOWARDS A CHRISTIAN THEOLOGY OF RELIGIONS

While it is true, as we have seen, that Barth has primarily in view a Christian audience and a Christian theological problematic, his account of religion has important implications for Christian relations with non-Christians, and thus for the agenda we have come to associate with the theology of religions as it is currently practised.

Given prevailing misreadings of Barth's theology of religion, it may come as something of a surprise that the first of these implications follows directly from Barth's treatment of the *Aufhebung*, or sublation, of religion in *CD* I/2, paragraph 17. Where it is guided by an 'uninterruptedly' theological account of religion and of the truth of the Christian religion, the Christian approach to the world of non-Christian religions will be characterized by what Barth tellingly calls 'the forbearance of Christ': 'by great cautiousness . . . and charity' (*CD* I/2, p. 297) and by 'a very marked tolerance . . . a tolerance which is informed by the forbearance of Christ' deriving from the 'knowledge that by grace God has reconciled godless man and his religion' (*CD* I/2, p. 299).

Such modesty and tolerance are *theologically* required. Since Christians understand that the Christian religion is true only in virtue of the justifying grace of God, it would be a terrible error for them to adopt a superior or arrogant attitude towards other religions and their adherents. In his brief review of the history of the relations of Christianity with other religions, Barth complains that Christians have made just such a mistake when they have sought to demonstrate the truth of their religion by invoking its accomplishments whether as a successful institution, or a pious community, or a politically powerful society, on the one hand, or, on the other, because of the beauty of its liturgy, the consistency of its doctrines, or the wisdom and holiness of its adherents (see *CD* I/2, pp. 333–7). On the contrary, the truth of the Christian religion must be seen within the doctrine of the justification of sinners.

In this perspective, the situation of the Christian religion is, if anything, more serious and perilous than that of other religions. As Barth puts it in a striking passage, when Christians encounter other religions and their adherents, the question they must ask about themselves – 'Who are they in their naked reality before the piercing eye of God?' – stands over them like a sword: 'In the world of religions, the Christian religion is in a position of greater danger and defencelessness and impotence than any other religion. It has its justification in the name of Jesus or not at all' (*CD* I/2, p. 356). The judgment of revelation that religion is unfaith applies first and foremost to the Christian religion and to others only insofar as Christians recognize themselves in them, 'and anticipating them in both repentance and hope', Christians 'accept the judgment to participate in the promise of revelation' (*CD* I/2, p. 327).

Since the judgment of divine revelation on all religion cannot be translated into a human judgment – and hence into an ecclesiastical judgment – Christians 'should not become iconoclasts in the face of human greatness as it meets [them] so strikingly in the sphere of religion' (*CD* I/2, p. 300). Religion falls not under our judgment, but under the judgment of God. Barth's theology of the sublation of religion by divine revelation provides no purchase for the devaluation, destruction, or negation of the manifestations of human religion and religiosity. On the contrary, the appropriate attitude is one of reverence: 'In the sphere of reverence before God, there must always be a place for reverence of human greatness' (*CD* I/2, p. 301).

Such attitudes of tolerance, hope, and reverence – filling out the forbearance of Christ – are completed by the 'absolute self-confidence' with which the Christian religion confronts the world of religions as the true religion in faithfulness to its missionary commission and authority. This confidence is consistent with the forbearance of Christ, for these attitudes are all rooted in the same source. They rest in Christ and in confidence in him alone, 'not in ecclesiastical institutions, theological systems, inner experiences, moral transformation of individual believers or the wider effects of Christianity upon the world at large' (*CD* I/2, p. 357). One must conclude that a close reading of *CD* I/2, paragraph 17 gives the lie to the frequently voiced complaint that Barth's theology of religion fosters negative attitudes towards other religions and undermines positive engagement with their adherents. The failure of reading evident in this complaint is in the end a failure to grasp the properly theological character of the warrants which Barth advances for the central theses of his theology of religion and the religions. As we turn finally to a brief examination of the relevant portions of *CD* IV/3, paragraph 69 ('The Glory of the Mediator'), we will find this conclusion supported and confirmed by Barth's modest statements about what are generally regarded as two of the principal items on the current agenda of Christian theology of religions: the question of the presence of truth in other religions, and the question of the salvation of non-Christians.[14] As to the latter question, which arises towards the end of paragraph 69, Barth expresses a robust confidence in the possibility of the salvation of persons who do not yet know or acknowledge Christ. This confidence is warranted only and entirely because of the victorious reconciliation achieved by Christ. Barth affirms, in a strikingly worded passage, that in the end no refusal 'on the part of non-Christians will be strong enough to resist the fulfilment of the promise of the Spirit which is pronounced over them too . . . or to hinder the overthrow of their ignorance of Christ' (*CD* IV/3, p. 355).

As to Barth's statements about the presence of truth in other religions, their immediate context is his discussion of the role of Jesus Christ as the light, 'the one and only light of life . . . in all its fullness, in perfect adequacy . . . [with] no other light of life outside or alongside His' (*CD* IV/3, p. 86). A thesis like this would seem to offer little promise for our topic. Barth recognizes its offensiveness: there would be no problem in finding truth elsewhere if we were to say that Christ is one of the lights. But this is just what Christians cannot say if they want to account in a properly theological way for the truth they may discover outside the Christian ambit. Wholly consistent with the fundamental logic of his theology of religion is Barth's insistence here that to say that Christ is the one and only light is a necessary christological affirmation, having 'nothing whatever to do with the arbitrary exaltation and self-glorification of the Christian in relation to other men, of the Church in relation to other institutions, or of Christianity in relation to other conceptions' (*CD* IV/3, p. 91).

From the truth that Christ is the one light and the one Word, it follows, not that there are no other words, but that no other words can be set beside the Word of Christ. Barth deploys the metaphor of spheres or circles to account for the relationship of the one Word of God to all other words, or, as he calls them, 'parables of the kingdom'. At the centre, the innermost sphere is the Word of Christ. Radiating outward from this centre are three concentric circles containing: (1) the words of the Bible, (2) the words of the church, and (3) the words outside the church (Barth says, *extra muros ecclesiae*) by non-Christians and by Christians exercising their responsibilities in the world (*CD* IV/3, pp. 110, 122). Although these words are not identical with the Word of Christ, they can be neither ignored nor dismissed. Looking out from the smaller spheres of the Bible and of the church, and without invoking the 'sorry hypothesis of natural theology', Christians must expect that Christ can speak and that his speech will be attested in the spheres beyond their ambit (*CD* IV/3, p. 117). Barth insists that we must see these spheres as encompassed by an outer periphery which makes them part of the one circle, defined by the central core which is constituted by Christ's Word and revelation. In this sense, they are true witnesses and attestations to the Word of Christ.

It follows that a theology of religions can approach the study of other religions and that Christians can encounter the adherents of other religions in interreligious dialogue with the expectation that truth – what Barth calls Christ's 'free communications in parables of the kingdom' – will indeed be found there and that such truth is testable by reference to the criteria of agreement with Scripture and with church doctrine (which might entail development therein), as well as of the fruits this truth bears and its significance for the life of the community. For, 'why should it not be possible', Barth asks, 'for God to raise up witnesses from this world of tarnished truth?' (*CD* IV/3, p. 121). Such human witnesses will be shown to have 'their final origin and meaning in the awakening power of the universal prophecy of Jesus Christ himself' (*CD* IV/3, p. 129).

Notes

1 For a general orientation to this field, see J. A. Di Noia, *The Diversity of Religions: A Christian Perspective* (Washington: Catholic University of America Press, 1992).

2 For a sampling of typical misreadings and a discussion of their significance, see C. E. Braaten, *No Other Gospel: Christianity among the World's Religions* (Minneapolis: Fortress Press, 1992), ch. 3.

3 G. D'Costa, 'Theology of Religions', in D. F. Ford, ed., *The Modern Theologians*, 2nd edn (Oxford: Blackwell, 1997), p. 630.

4 See, for example, Barth's essays: 'Moderne Theologie und Reichsgottesarbeit', *Zeitschrift für Theologie und Kirche* 19 (1909), pp. 317–21; and 'Der Glaube an den persönlichen Gott', ibid., 24 (1914), pp. 21–32, 65–95. For a thorough discussion of these and other early essays, see B. L. McCormack, *Karl Barth's Critically Realistic Dialectical Theology: Its Genesis and Development 1909–1936* (Oxford: Clarendon Press, 1995), pp. 49–77.

5 In the 1922 edition of the Romans commentary, when treating Romans 7, Barth substitutes the category of 'religion' for the Pauline category of 'law' and advances the contrast between religion and revelation that would come to play a central role in his mature theology of religion. See *The Epistle to the Romans*, 6th edn., trans. E. C. Hoskyns (Oxford: Oxford University Press, 1933), pp. 229–70.

6 K. Barth, *Church Dogmatics*, eds. G. W. Bromiley and T. F. Torrance (Edinburgh: T & T Clark, 1956–75), vol. I, part 2, pp. 280–360.

7 G. Green, 'Challenging the Religious Studies Canon: Karl Barth's Theory of Religion', *Journal of Religion* 75 (1995), p. 477.

8 Ibid., p. 479.

9 For helpful discussions of these developments, see N. Wolterstorff, 'The Migration of Theistic Arguments: From Natural Theology to Evidentialist Apologetics', in R. Audi and W. J. Enright, eds., *Rationality, Religious Belief and Moral Commitment* (Ithaca: Cornell University Press, 1986), pp. 38–81; M. J. Buckley, *At the Origins of Modern Atheism* (New Haven: Yale University Press, 1987); and N. Lash, 'When Did the Theologians Lose Interest in Theology?' in B. Marshall, ed., *Theology and Dialogue* (Notre Dame: University of Notre Dame Press, 1990), pp. 131–47.

10 See I. U. Dalferth, 'Karl Barth's Eschatological Realism', in S. W. Sykes, ed., *Karl Barth: Centenary Essays* (Cambridge: Cambridge University Press, 1989), pp. 39–40.

11 For a Thomistic account of the nature and grace of theology, see J. A. Di Noia, 'Authority, Public Dissent and the Nature of Theological Thinking', *The Thomist* 52 (1988), pp. 185–207. On Barth and Aquinas, see B. Marshall, *Christology in Conflict* (Oxford: Basil Blackwell, 1987), esp. ch. 5; and E. F. Rogers, Jr., *Thomas Aquinas and Karl Barth* (Notre Dame: University of Notre Dame Press, 1995).

12 Green, 'Challenging the Religious Studies Canon', p. 480.

13 Dalferth, 'Karl Barth's Eschatological Realism', p. 39.

14 K. Barth, *Church Dogmatics*, eds., G. W. Bromiley and T. F. Torrance (Edinburgh: T & T Clark, 1956–75), vol. IV, part 3 (first half), pp. 3–367. The passages pertaining to the presence of truth in other religions are found chiefly in §69, 2 ('The Light of Life'), pp. 86–165; while those concerning the salvation of non-Christians occur in §69, 4 ('The Promise of the Spirit'), pp. 353 ff.

Further reading

Balthasar, H. U., von, *The Theology of Karl Barth*, trans. E. T. Oakes, S.J. (San Francisco: Ignatius Press, 1992).

D'Costa, G., 'Theology of Religions', in *The Modern Theologians*, ed. D. F. Ford, 2nd edn. (Oxford: Blackwell, 1997), pp. 626–44.

Di Noia, J. A., *The Diversity of Religions: A Christian Perspective* (Washington: Catholic University of America Press, 1992).

Green, G., 'Challenging the Religious Studies Canon: Karl Barth's Theory of Religion', *Journal of Religion* 75 (1995), pp. 473–86.

Griffiths, P. J., 'The Properly Christian Response to Religious Plurality', *Anglican Theological Review* 79 (1997), pp. 3–26.

Sullivan, F. A., *Salvation Outside the Church: Tracing the History of the Catholic Response* (New York: Paulist Press, 1992).

16 Barth and feminism

KATHERINE SONDEREGGER

Some years ago, the feminist critic Heidi Hartmann wrote an influential article entitled, 'The Unhappy Marriage of Marxism and Feminism'.[1] It was a brief against the easy assumption that feminism had natural and ready ties to Marxist theory, and that any feminist who thought the 'woman question' through to the end would become an 'historical materialist' – as Marx styled his own theory – and subsume the women's struggle into the class struggle. Hartmann hoped to put an end to such easy alliances; and a feminist approaching this chapter might hope to do the same. Feminism does not appear to be headed for a happy marriage to Karl Barth. Though comfortable in the presence of socialism, Barth was filled with misgivings about feminism. In the *Church Dogmatics*, Barth refers to feminism rarely, and then grudgingly. He appears suspicious of feminist claims to equality with men and reluctant to take up feminist theory into the work of dogmatic theology. Though he treats Jean-Paul Sartre with some seriousness in the third volume of his *Dogmatics* (*CD* III/3, §50), Barth gives only cursory attention to Simone de Beauvoir, and then only to *The Second Sex*, her major work on feminism (*CD* III/4, §54.1). His own relationships with women were complex and often painfully mis-matched. He was engaged to his wife, Nelly Barth, née Hoffmann, when she was not much more than a schoolgirl; she was not quite eighteen to his twenty-five, a student in his confirmation class at his congregation in Geneva. They married two years later. Theirs was not a happy marriage, but a lifelong one all the same. One complexity to this already burdened marriage was the presence of Charlotte von Kirsch-baum, a live-in secretary and intimate of Barth's. Mercifully, not much is known about their relationship; but it was known to have caused pain to all three, a pain Barth believed simply must be borne.[2] Recent scholarship has wondered whether von Kirschbaum, too, was not an injured party here: not simply her reputation, but her relation to her family was strained by her companionship to Barth, her original scholarship buried in Barth's own footnotes and analysis.[3] Such summary portraits of human lives, of course, are crude and cold. They cannot hope to do justice to the richness, depth, and ambiguity of Barth's personal life, nor capture the charisma that made Barth someone to risk one's life on. But if the personal is the political, as recent American feminists have argued, Barth's own intimacies with women do not make an alliance with feminism appear too promising.

More importantly, Barth held theological positions many feminists decry. He spent much of his early career attacking a theology that begins with human experience, a starting point Barth traced to Friedrich Schleiermacher, the greatest Protestant theologian of the nineteenth century and now associated with much feminist theology. Moreover, Barth maintained that dogmatic theology answered only to the call of Jesus Christ, heard in the words of Scripture, a position too exclusively biblical and ecclesiastical for many feminists today. Barth was also well known for advocating the writing of theology 'as though nothing had happened',[4] and considered too a-political and naive for liberation and feminist theologians today.

More famous still is the section of *CD* III/4, paragraph 54.1, 'Man and Woman', known in shorthand as the 'A and B' discussion. In this section of the doctrine of creation, Barth likens men and women to the letters, A and B:

> Man and woman are not an A and a second A whose being and relationship can be described like the two halves of an hour glass, which are obviously two, but absolutely equal and therefore interchangeable. Man and woman are an A and a B, and cannot, therefore, be equated. In inner dignity and right A has not the slightest advantage over B nor does it suffer the slightest disadvantage ... A precedes B, and B follows A. Order means succession. It means preceding and following. It means super- and sub-ordination. It does indeed reveal their inequality. But it does not do so without immediately confirming their equality. (*CD* III/4, pp. 169–70)

Barth considered this 'normal inequality' the teaching of the Apostle Paul, especially in the Corinthian correspondence, and held that it should not be set aside for modern concerns about equality which Barth considered both bourgeois and shallow.

And finally, Barth would show little patience, I think, for feminist theologians' preoccupation with what is called the 'problem of language' or the feminist critique of 'masculine God-talk'. His theological epistemology made the name of God – given in the Bible and creeds as Father, Son, and Holy Spirit – essential to and irreplaceable for genuine religious knowledge. 'To have experience of God's Word is to yield to its supremacy', Barth famously wrote in his first volume of the *Church Dogmatics*, a volume dedicated to the problems of religious knowledge and speech. 'Whether [God's Word] comes to us as Law or Gospel, as command or promise, it comes at any rate in such a way as to bend man, and indeed his conscience and will no less than his intellect and feeling. It does not break him; it really bends him, brings him into conformity with itself' (*CD* I/1, p. 206). Many feminist theologians flatly disagree.

So we may well feel discouraged when faced with the prospect of Barth and feminism; indeed many feminists are. Few write on Barth, and those who do rarely praise.[5] But appearances often deceive. Several American feminists have written appreciatively on Barth recently.[6] And examined more closely, the thought of Karl Barth echoes themes in contemporary feminist theory – in the understanding of the person and of humanity, in ethics, and in epistemology – that would make Barth attractive indeed. And, on closer study, his objectionable positions may appear not too far removed from some strands of current feminism and even some feminist theology. Differences will remain, especially in the commitment of theology to political action; but the similarities make Barth and feminism a more instructive alliance, perhaps even a happier one, than we might expect. Five areas deserve closer scrutiny: the theology of experience; language and the name of God; human essences and identity; the image of God; and the relation of ethics and politics. We begin where much theory begins, with the understanding of human experience.

Where should theology begin its work? That is the question a theology of experience raises at the beginning of its work. A seemingly simple question, this matter of theology's starting point has generated some of the most technical and daunting argument of the modern period. Much of the controversy in this area, and (to Barth's admirers) the innovation and renovation of it, can be attributed to the early work of Karl Barth.

Here, in fact, we find an odd meeting point for the criticism of Karl Barth and second-generation feminists. For both, the category of experience has become the problem, not the solution. For contemporary feminist theory, 'women's experience' has become a category plagued by the same ills that riddle most modern certainties. Postmodernism, a method so consciously eclectic it might better be called an 'anti-method', cannot accept the certainties earlier feminists advanced. Just what is 'women's experience'? postmodernism asks; just who are these 'women'? In the United States, African-American women have pointed out in trenchant criticism that the experience that would ground feminist thought in many fields has been, in fact, the fruit of reflection by white, bourgeois, educated women.[7] Indeed, the very efforts to overcome this blindness, bell hooks has written, demonstrate just how flawed the method is, root and branch.[8] For to 'include' the experiences of 'other women' is to betray the norm where one started, and to turn to the literary or autobiographical works of these 'others' is to assume their inwardness for one's own project, a kind of academic voyeurism. The more this problem is studied and repaired, the more the method of experi- ence appears doomed. Women are fundamentally diverse, the philosopher Elizabeth Spelman has written,[9] and attempts to find unity underlying diversity lead only to the unsurprising conclusion that the author finds her own face reflected in that glimmering ideal of oneness. Even the experience of a unitary feminism, a unity Hartmann herself could assume, falls under the weight of this challenge: there are only feminisms, not feminism.

Postmodern feminists have expanded this critique of women's experi- ence into a sustained attack upon another surety of modern thought, the concept of a given and universal human essence. 'Essentialism', as this surety has come to be known, holds that human beings – or any human or material reality – are constituted by essences, qualities that remain constant across time and place, or 'possible worlds' as analytic philosophers would have it. These creaturely essences have served to ground all other claims about human reality; they are 'foundations' of thought. Postmodern femin- ism rejects 'foundationalism' in thought and 'essentialism' in human ident- ity. Creaturely reality is a thoroughgoing historical, contingent, and 'con- structed' social product, as Sheila Devaney has argued.[10] We should not expect to discover what it is to be human, as we might discover, say, an axiom of geometry or a geological formation on the moon. Rather, we invent or construct human reality, much as we define an Elizabethan sonnet or refine the penalties for tax fraud. These constructed human practices are *real* – no one would deny the reality of a jail cell or its consequences – but they are the products of human minds and hands. They are 'webs of meaning we spin and are suspended in', in the memorable phrase of Clifford Geertz.[11] Feminists apply such postmodernism to our understand- ing of 'women's experience': we create what it is to be a woman; 'woman' can be made and remade. Indeed our deepest convictions about our inner lives – our private passions and certainties – are our most public and social experiences. Not only Freud teaches us to regard our experiences with suspicion; feminists too regard the personal and inward as the public, the political, the constructed. To be sure, for feminism this thoroughgoing anti-essentialism makes politics a difficult business. Without the certainties of women's essence and their common experiences, it is hard to know just what feminism advocates or just whom it exhorts. Ad hoc alliances among groups of women may generate some temporary commonalities, as

Spelmann and Sharon Welch have argued,[12] but the loss of certainty is just that: a freedom and a loss. Karl Barth would find much to agree with here.

Barth's theological argument often parallels these non-foundational and anti-essential themes of postmodern feminism. Barth does not *deny* human experience, its inwardness, piety, and self-certainty, but rather *unsettles* it: creaturely reality can reflect but cannot ground Christian knowledge of God. To *begin* with human experience of God, with faith, is to enter an airless room. We leave with what we took in – our own ideas, passions, and introspections. Barth does not mean to repudiate experience altogether: of course we must think of God through our own inwardness or 'hear God's word through our own ears', in Barth's more colourful language. But just as liberal feminism replicates its own starting point in its conclusions – unsurprisingly white and bourgeois – so a theology that begins in creaturely experience finds its Creator unsurprisingly familiar, an exalted version of ourselves, purified perhaps, but unmistakably ours. That is why, Barth would say, feminist theology that begins with women's experience longs to end with a God with a 'feminine face', a female Saviour who can save women. This method requires and rests upon likeness, for what is 'given' to experience takes on the character of the ones who receive it. This is the 'internal relational' or 'coherentist' nature of reality, the hallmark of idealism, and the danger to all theory that seeks an Other, apart from or beyond the self. It is sometimes said by Barth's critics that he did not understand that human experience shapes all our convictions, however objective we claim them to be,[13] but ironically this is just what Barth meant to underscore: we cannot escape the interior circle of our own experience. Indeed we cannot break out at all; we must be rescued from without. Barth's emphasis upon the doctrine of revelation – the knowledge of God that is disclosed by God alone – stems from his conviction that God alone can unsettle the closed world of experience:

> Karl Holl once formulated as follows the fundamental principle that is 'common to all men' and that constitutes 'the plumb-line of their religion'. 'Nothing', he said, 'is to be recognized as religiously valid but what can be found in the reality present to us and produced again out of our direct experience.' This principle is in fact the principle of Cartesian thinking, which is quite impossible in theology. On the basis of this principle there is no knowledge of the Word of God. For we do not find the Word of God in the reality present to us. Rather – and this is something quite different – the Word of God finds us in the reality present to us. Again it cannot be produced again out of our direct

experience. Whenever we know it, we are rather begotten by it according to Jas. 1.18.   (*CD* I/1, pp. 195f.)

A stark corollary follows, however. Just as the airless room of experience can be opened only from the outside, as it were, so too theology can draw its knowledge of the faith only from this Stranger who stands without. The sources of theology now are narrowed to Scripture, made living Word through the agency of the Holy Spirit. The tradition of the church – its dogmas, theologians, and saints – instructs the theologian but cannot bind; everything is made relative to the single divine starting point. So with an irony Barth himself would admire, this theology of revelation shadows the radical freedom of the modern theology of experience: it too makes the past serve the present.

But this theology of revelation, of course, is far from feminist theology's position on the sources of theology or, more pointedly, on Christian language about God – 'God-talk'. Feminist theologians, from Mary Daly to Letty Russell or Delores Williams, however dissimilar, agree that language about God reflects human ideals and ideologies. Divine names express, at least in part, the social relations of the theologian and the religious world he or she inhabits. They are 'models of' and 'models for' collective life – to borrow Clifford Geertz's shorthand[14] – and theologians as diverse as Gordon Kaufman, Judith Plaskow, Rosemary Ruether, and Susannah Heschel rely on this sociological and linguistic analysis.[15] Sallie McFague illustrates this conviction well: God as King or Lord reflects a feudal world of male honour and hierarchy in which subjects are protected, but ruled, and the royal realm is altogether different and majestically aloof from the commoner's hut. Such a kingly model of God creates passive Christians, childlike in their trust but also in their acceptance of evil and their easy accommodation to injustice. Another model – God as Mother, Lover, and Friend – may on one hand better reflect the moral adulthood of humanity, and on the other guide it to undertake the work for justice for which our culture cries out. So male names of God – Father, Son – reflect the patriarchy out of which they arose and reinforce in our culture the pseudo-divinity of men, the utter secularity of women. A male priesthood, these feminists argue, is the ecclesial confirmation of this linguistic projection. To be sure, this preoccupation with linguistic matters in feminist theology is not universal. As Susan B. Thistlethwaite, bell hooks, Katie Canon and others have argued, African-American women focus on practice above language; they are less apt to find male language confining or alienating.[16] But this heightened awareness about gendered language remains widespread in American feminism, and reflects some of the earliest convictions of the second wave of feminism.

Still, Barth's position on this linguistic turn in theology might be more differentiated than some feminists may realize. Like them, he was all too aware of the creaturely nature of theological language; he keenly knew the breadth and temptation of Feuerbach's analysis of religion as the projection of human desires and powers. But his pronounced taste for realism in theology, both in knowledge and in the nature of things – coupled with his conviction that revelation alone must disclose the true name of God – would make him reluctant, I believe, to alter the triune names or allow a sociological critique to prompt a massive theological change. Barth was not a traditionalist; he would rarely defend a doctrine on antiquity alone. But he believed the doctors and councils of the church were living voices, teachers, not texts. An ideological critique of gendered language, Barth might say, belongs to theologians' recognition of their fallen, worldly nature and must be applied radically to every human construction, whether patriarchal or feminist. But like human experience itself, God alone can liberate and make use of language; really liberate, really make use of it, not some but all of it.

Barth's analysis of human experience may surprise feminists in another way as well: Like feminists, Barth considers human beings 'made, not born', as de Beauvoir put it. Human beings, both agree, are thoroughgoing historical actors. In the *Church Dogmatics*, Barth is careful to follow what he understands to be a scriptural view of human nature. We are, he writes, composed of body and soul; indeed the soul directs, orders, and outranks the body (*CD* III/2, §§42.3, 4, 5). Yet we are a psychosomatic unity. Barth found much to dislike in dualisms, especially Cartesian dualisms. He did not consider the mind a distinct and opposing reality to body or 'extended matter', nor did he consider the 'mind–body problem' – so significant to modern philosophy – a puzzle Christian theologians must solve, much less adopt. No, the full human person, body and soul, is a creature of God, made rational, ready and able to serve the Creator. Because human beings find themselves called to this task – to be 'covenant partners with God' – their minds and bodies work together to achieve this end. Such transcendental arguments would appeal to Barth throughout his career. But we would mis-read Barth if we assumed that such traditional Christian anthropology blinded him to modern concerns in the field.

As Barth so often did, he here seamlessly wove together the claims from the theological past with the preoccupations of the present. Central to the university training he received was the conviction that historical consciousness transformed everything it touched. Not simply were fields of human inquiry, from the sciences to theology, subject to historical thinking – 'historicism' – but human nature itself was saturated by the historical. So thorough was this saturation that Barth, like Marx, was reluctant to speak of 'human nature' as though this were a timeless reality thrown into our sphere from beyond. In fact, Barth's dismissal of de Beauvoir, though often reactionary, shows a shrewd insight into de Beauvoir from this master reader and a pronounced flair for the concrete and embodied:

> If Simone de Beauvoir unmasks the myth of the woman and makes no use of the idealistic myth of the androgyne, it is plain that she proclaims another new myth so much the more powerfully and unreservedly – that of the human individual who in the achievement of freedom overcomes his masculinity or her femininity, mastering it from a superior plane, so that sexuality is only a condition by which he is not finally conditioned, with which he can dispense and whose operation he can in any case control. Even in the masculine form presupposed by Simone de Beauvoir, is not this individual a product of wishful thinking rather than a reality? Is he not more a man-God or God-man than a real human figure? . . . Why is it that the whole emancipation programme of this woman, who in her way fights so valiantly and skilfully, is still orientated on man, and particularly on this highly unreal man?   (*CD* III/4, p. 162)

Far better, Barth said, to speak of human beings as 'historical actors': they fashion themselves through their own actions. Now this is a far-reaching claim. Barth does not simply mean that 'human nature' is historical in a weak sense: that we can be understood only in the time and place in which we flourished. No, for that could allow for a substantial human nature simply to express its historicity rather as we express our membership in various societies by putting on this costume or that. Rather, Barth intended a stronger, more sweeping claim: that our very selves are constituted by history and historical action. Human beings are makers – *homo faber*, as Marx would put it – they decide, choose, affirm, repudiate, and join together. Their commitment to their own time and place, their linking of their own lives to others, their intimacies, their risks in work and politics; but also their suffering, their patience, their courage when nothing remains but hope: all these actions constitute historical being. Not just the heroic actor of Hegel's world-historical spirit – someone too 'titanic' for Barth's tastes – but everyone who determines his or her own life, from small preferences to great leaps of hope and trust, is historical in Barth's sense.

So strong is Barth's conviction that action is the centrepiece of the human that he focuses almost exclusively on Christ's agency, rather than his nature. This is not to deny what George Hunsinger has called the 'Chalcedonian pattern' in Barth's Christology;[17] Barth does affirm the traditional dogma of Christ's fully human and divine realities. But Barth makes new everything he receives; this is his hallmark as a theologian and not, as critics assume, his unflattering servility to the past. Barth casts the 'two natures' doctrine in terms of action: Christ is the 'man for others', the sole person whose life is completely absorbed into his agency on others' behalf. He *is* his vocation. His divinity is expressed as Lordship in service, the One who travels into the far or alien country. His humanity is expressed as another kind of Lordship, the royal man, the One who acts in obedience unto death. We would not be wrong to hear echoes of the 'teleological nature' of Christianity as Schleiermacher defines it, or the Christians' duty to vocation as Ritschl would have it. Barth repudiates these teachers from time to time, but only as one who learns much from them. But we would not be wrong, either, to hear echoes of a more contemporary debate in feminism over the place of the personal and private in human lives. It does not take Rosa Luxembourg, after all, to tell us that human beings who are only agents, only public actors, only servants of their vocation, are shells of the human. A private life, a recess away from public action and scrutiny, an inwardness of being and not doing, is essential to human flourishing, feminists argue. The Christ Barth portrays, especially in the early volumes of his *Dogmatics*, strikes a feminist as not quite human, a singular being, true enough, but hardly an ideal. If at any point, a critic is inclined to embrace von Balthasar's claim that Barth has no full theology of the creature,[18] she may be convinced to say so here. Historical being may be creaturely; historical act alone may be far less.

To be sure, Barth's claims for human historicity do not preclude a certain stability or uniformity in human beings. Though Barth was reluctant to use much philosophical or sociological work in his theology – and a glance at his brush with it in *CD* III/2 might convince us that his reluctance was well founded – Barth did recognize that human beings must have something like an abiding possibility or capacity for historical action. Human beings are not tortoises, Barth famously wrote to Brunner;[19] of course they have human bodies, little changed over centuries, and souls that can make decisions and in that act, recognize and accept them as their own. Most importantly, they were created as ensouled bodies so that they could stand in relation to their Creator: their enduring possibility or determination is as covenant partner to the Lord God of Israel. In another culture and place, Barth might have described this as Karl Rahner did: as the trans-cendental structure of human freedom. But as with Rahner, all such structuralism served only as a necessary, not sufficient, ground for human beings. They must still make themselves in history.

Two things follow from Barth's wide-ranging historicism, each of interest to feminists. Like many current feminists, Barth rejected ethical naturalism: he denied that the natural world contained our values and should teach us our duties (*CD* III/4, §§52.1, 54.1). There is no 'book of nature' in this sense, no law code embedded in the natural order that we must follow. This is not because we are radically free – Barth will have very interesting things to say about such Nietzschean daring – but because we are radically bound to history, to community, to the making of human lives and culture. We do not submit to our lives; we fashion them. In Barth's period, such claims were thrown in opposition to a widespread Lutheran commitment to a kind of ethical naturalism: the 'orders of creation'. According to Barth, opponents like Emil Brunner thought human beings were subject to certain natural, God-given orders or constraints:

> The man is the one who produces, he is the leader; the woman is receptive, and she preserves life . . . The man has to go forth and make the earth subject to him, the woman looks within and guards the hidden unity. The man must be objective and universalise, woman must be subjective and individualise; the man must build, the woman adorns; the man must conquer, the woman must tend; the man must comprehend all with his mind, the woman must impregnate all with the life of her soul. It is the duty of man to plan and to master, of the woman to understand and to unite.[20]

To our ears, these ideals of the orders of creation may sound like so many tired and tiring social stereotypes, rooted in a theological brand of biology as destiny. But to Brunner, as to many conservative Protestants today, these natural orders reflected a gracious and changeless will of the Creator for his creatures, revealed in the books of nature and of Scripture. For Barth, they represented a 'second source' of theology alongside the Word, a form of natural theology ruled out by his dogmatic method.

Even in his most traditional voice – in the A and B section, for example – Barth still repudiates the claim that gender roles are rooted in nature and given to the creature.

How are these rather contingent, schematic, conventional, literary and half-true indicatives to be transformed into imperatives? Real man and real woman would then have to let themselves be told: Thou shalt be concerned with things (preferably machines) and thou with persons! Thou shalt cherish the mind, thou the soul! Thou shalt follow thy reason and thou thy instinct! Thou shalt be objective and thou subjective . . . This is quite impossible. Obviously we cannot seriously address and bind any man or woman on these lines. They will justifiably refuse to be addressed in this way . . . [These typologies] may have value in other directions, but they are certainly not adapted to be a valid law for male and female, and we can only cause the greatest confusion if we try to exalt them into such a law and use them as such. (*CD* III/4, p. 153)

Men and women create themselves, including their social roles. And yet, Barth insists, men and women belong together. They are ordered, ranked and determined, as is everything in God's creation; indeed God himself is determined, both in the eternal Trinity and in the act of election. Men are determined for initiating fellowship; women for responding. But this ranking is purely formal or structural. 'The divine command permits man and woman continually and particularly to discover their specific sexual nature, and to be faithful to it in this form which is true before God, without being enslaved to any preconceived opinions' (*CD* III/4, p. 153). Only historical action can make concrete and living what 'super- and sub-ordina-tion' mean. Feminist theologians are unlikely to find Barth's analysis com-pelling here, however hedged about by cautions about 'orders of creation'.

But they will more likely approve of Barth's treatment of the image of God: human beings are made for God; they are made for each other. This is a claim contemporary feminists often extol as the 'relational self', but in Barth's hands it is a two-edged sword. The hallmark of Barth's mature work is the analogies found between the Creator and creature, first in the order of knowing, but then increasingly, in the order of being, in Christology and in the doctrine of persons. These two analogies have been designated in Barth scholarship as the 'analogy of faith' and the 'analogy of relation' although, as with many observations of scholars, Barth made far less use of these categories than do the critics. The analogy of relation, laid out in *CD* III/2, argues that the *imago dei* has been distorted in the tradition by assuming that it is a static, substantial property of the individual: the creature's intelligence, say, or freedom or obedience. To be sure, these are hallmarks of the human, Barth will say, but they do little to mirror the nature of God who is, above all, a divine act of freedom. The image of such a God in the creature must be an activity, a free activity, done with and towards another fellow creature. The *imago dei* must be life in relation or communion.

To be human is to be 'with another', *mitmenschlich*, a term rich with associations in the academic world of Barth's youth. Barth understands this analogy of relation, characteristically, in a radical sense. A weaker sense might be accepted universally: that human beings flourish in relation, and are lessened by isolation. But Barth means the stronger: human beings, as intended by their Creator, are constituted by their relation with another. Readers familiar with the work of Martin Buber will recognize the pattern here. I and Thou, Buber wrote in his famous essay by that name, not only belong together; they are in fact constituents of a single whole, the I-and-Thou. Barth comments on Buber in this section of the *Dogmatics*, not uncritically to be sure, but underscoring his relation to the dialogic thinkers all the same. Human beings, if faithful to their Creator, will find themselves in conversation and more, in solidarity with their neighbour; together they will make a human life. God is himself relational, Barth argued; in the eternal Trinity there is no solitude but rather free, rich, and intimate communion. Catherine LaCugna's recent work on the relational nature of the Trinity,[21] though critical of Barth, shows the continuing importance of relationality to both.

The prime example of such yoking, Barth thought, was the love match between male and female, husband and wife. Theirs is a relation of loving freedom. They are bound to one another, but bound principally by love. Barth could write lyrically about human intimacy; little in the early austerity of the *Epistle to the Romans* prepares us for the striking exuberance of Barth's praise here of erotic love. But Barth shows every sign of knowing firsthand what some feminists, inspired by French psychoanalysis, have called 'jouissance': the sheer delight in embodied love and life.

> Here [in erotic love] more than anywhere else man seems at least to stand on the threshold of a kind of natural mysticism. What else can stir him so much, bringing him as he thinks – whether he be a crude or a highly cultivated person – into such ecstasy, such rapture, such enthusiasm, into what seem to be the depths and essence of all being, into contemplation of the Godhead and participation in it, supposedly exalting him into the vicinity at least of another God and Creator – what else can do this like the primal experience of encounter between male and female? . . . It is obviously on account of the truly breath-taking dialectic which arises in this encounter – the dialectic of difference and affinity, of real dualism and equally real unity, of utter

self-recollection and utter transport beyond the bounds of self into union with another, of creation and redemption, of this world and the next. If humanity spells fellow-humanity and fellow-humanity is primarily experienced in this dialectic, how tempting it is to understand and experience this fellow-humanity as the bold and blessed intoxication of the deepest abasement and supreme exaltation of human essence, as its deification! (*CD* III/4, pp. 119–20)

To be sure, Barth is adamant that we resist just such an impulse to deification, and his criticism of Schleiermacher in this section reminds the reader strongly of his rebuke of Schleiermacher's eroticism in the *Epistle to the Romans*. But Barth gives every sign here of knowing firsthand what romantic, embodied love is all about, and why it is a great temptation, perhaps *the* temptation, to the religious person.

So too, contemporary feminists will recognize in Barth their claims that community, not solitude, makes for true humanity; and that intimacy is built on freedom and its risks, not security and control.[22] Barth's critique of Cartesian solipsism – capped by a provocative analysis of German high culture from Kant to Nietzsche – underscores his conviction that individualism is a modern disease, wasting away earlier ideas of interdependence and community and advancing corrupted notions of freedom as autonomy and invulnerability. Many contemporary feminists could only applaud.

But Barth, like many revolutionaries, retained an air of cultural conservativism, a trait he shared with other Ritschlians of his generation. He thought of the intimacy between men and women, their relationality, as principally expressed in indissoluble marriage between unequals. Compare Barth's account of human encounter in relation in *CD* III/2, where gender is unspecified – or more precisely, rendered in the generic male – to the encounter of man and woman in marriage in *CD* III/4. Worlds apart! And how poor the second in light of the first! In his discussion of the Sabbath, an earlier section in the same part volume, Barth casts a sidelong glance at couples, forced to push prams around idly, never working, never enjoying the Sabbath, a perfect example of that perfect misery, enforced rest. So here: marriage, in Barth's hands, is the duller affair, flatter and, one must admit, so primly conventional.

Not so in the account of general human relation. There, Barth speaks of an intellectual communion that crackles with electricity, and brings into its charge the physical and everyday; here is an I and Thou encounter that we would call a meeting of true minds, or in more feminist terms, a calling into speech. In marriage, Barth celebrates an intimacy of physical and emotional partnership – and it is a true celebration – but one without the sparkling warmth, depth, and searching devotion that intellectual or spiritual communion and equality provides. That Barth clearly had this kind of spiritual communion with Charlotte von Kirschbaum, a woman he calls in tribute his true 'partner', renders more eloquent his silence about such partnership in marriage. Here, perhaps, we see the limits of Barth's and many feminists' critique of mere or 'bourgeois' equality. It is not enough, we learn here, to proclaim mutuality as the goal of human intimacy; or better, mutuality without clear assumptions of equality. The risk is to strip marriage – and life partnerships of all kinds – of their powerful ground and spring in full, intelligent reciprocity and equal regard.

More important than divergence over marriage, however, is the gulf that divides Barth and Christian feminists over the place of social action in theology. Here Barth and feminism find no happy marriage at all. For feminist theology, both in its earliest and latest forms, joins together politics and theology, praxis and theory, into what may be called coinherence or synergy. Feminist theologians assume that feminist analysis and action will serve both as ground and critique of Christian theology: we may begin with the experience of women's oppression, as Rosemary Ruether does; or with communal understanding of Latinas, as Maria Asasi Diaz does; or the recognition of pluralism and particularity, as Sallie McFague does; or the analysis of womanchurch, as Elizabeth Schüssler Fiorenza does;[23] but in them all, we begin with an action and thought-world outside the realm of theology and approach theology from there. Theology then is an attempt to find usable traditions within the Christian past, and to fashion them in a coherent way to express and guide the movement of women toward full humanity and just social relations. It is, as was most liberal Protestant academic theology, a *moral* programme: it seeks a just society. Christianity can aid or hinder the quest for justice; feminist theology lives by the hope it can aid. Now the criterion for such a theology must be the lived experience, practice, or analysis of feminists, however postmodern the feminism may be. Christian theology is the refulgence of that emancipatory hope and practice, lived in small collectives of liberation, written out in books suffused with the joy and gritty determination of political activists.

This is cultural theology of a very high order indeed. And Barth, of course, is well known for his adamant opposition to cultural theology of any kind. Moral programmes, cultural ideals, ethics of all sorts cannot ground or constrain theology, Barth argued; it is disobedience of the highest kind for the creature to control and sanction the Creator, a disobedience particularly cunning and repellent because pious and so morally earnest. Notice here the full realist claims Barth quietly makes for theology: to dictate the terms of Christian thought is to attempt to dictate the terms of divine relation to creation. To be teachable in theology – to accept God's Word alone as necessary and sufficient for salvation – is to allow God to direct, command, and guide theology. From this commitment, Barth would not stray throughout his long career. His theological epistemology was grounded in revelation; his doctrine of Scripture grounded in the agency of the Holy Spirit, his ethics grounded in the living divine command. Now, cultural ideals, political activism, and acts of great personal risk and sacrifice may all follow from theology. Barth himself followed his theological convictions into opposition to the Third Reich and leadership of the Confessing Church. But such moral activism *may* follow. The entailment that feminist theology has proposed up till now cannot be accepted by Barth or Barthians: particular political actions do not follow from doctrine, nor doctrine from actions. The Christian must act: Barth was no quietist. But the Word of God, Barth would say, is free.

But women, feminists might add, are not. So perhaps it is too early to say just what the marriage of Barth and feminism might be like. Perhaps we can say now, as Hartmann did of Marxism, that like most things human, it would be a marriage of some sorrow, but also, of some real joy.

Notes

Thanks to Lynne Rudder Baker, Karen L. King, and Margaret Nelson for reading and improving this chapter.

1 H. Hartmann, 'The Unhappy Marriage of Marxism and Feminism', in L. Sargent, ed., *Women and Revolution* (Boston: South End Press, 1981), pp. 1–41.

2 E. Busch, *Karl Barth* (London: SCM Press, 1976), pp. 185f.

3 R. Köbler, *In the Shadow of Karl Barth. Charlotte von Kirschbaum* (Louisville, Ky: Westminster Press, 1989); S. Selinger, *Charlotte von Kirschbaum and Karl Barth* (University Park: Pennsylvania State Press, 1998).

4 K. Barth, *Theological Existence Today* (London: Hodder and Stoughton, 1933), p. 9.

5 R. Ruether, *Sexism and God-talk* (Boston: Beacon Press, 1983), pp. 97f.; S. McFague, *Models of God* (Philadelphia: Fortress Press, 1987), ch. 2, esp. pp. 44f.; A. Carr, *Transforming Grace* (San Francisco: Harper and Row, 1988); G. Kaufman, *In Face of Mystery* (Cambridge, Mass.: Harvard University Press, 1993), pp. 88–93; D. Hampson, *After Christianity* (Valley Forge: Trinity Press International, 1996), pp. 78f.; J. Ford Watson, *A Study of Karl Barth's Doctrine of Man and Woman* (New York: Vantage Press, 1995).

6 S. Jones, 'This God Which Is Not One', in C. W. M. Kim, *et al.*, eds., *Transfigurations* (Minneapolis: Fortress Press, 1993), pp. 109–41; E. Charry, *By the Renewing of your Minds* (New York: Oxford University Press, 1997), ch. 1; D. Hunsinger, *Theology and Pastoral Counselling* (Grand Rapids: Eerdmans Press, 1995); L. Russell, *Human Liberation in a Feminist Perspective* (Philadelphia: Westminster Press, 1974), pp. 159f.

7 A. Davis, *Women, Race and Class* (New York, Random House, 1981); C. Moraga and G. Anzaldua, eds., *This Bridge Called my Back* (Watertown: Persephone Press, 1981); D. Williams, *Sisters in the Wilderness* (Maryknoll: Orbis Books, 1993), ch. 7; E. Towns, *In a Blaze of Glory* (Nashville: Abingdon Press, 1995), Introduction, ch. 4.

8 b. hooks, *Yearning* (Boston: South End Press, 1990), chs. 2, 6, 15.

9 E. Spelmann, *Inessential Woman* (Boston: Beacon Press, 1988).

10 S. Devaney, 'The Limits to Appeal to Women's Experience', in *Shaping New Vision* (Ann Arbor: UMI Press, 1987), pp. 30–49.

11 C. Geertz, 'Thick Description: Toward an Interpretive Theory of Culture', in *The Interpretation of Culture* (New York: Basic Books, 1973), p. 5.

12 Spelmann, *Inessential Woman*, ch. 7; S. Welch, *A Feminist Ethic of Risk* (Minneapolis: Fortress Press, 1990).

13 See R. Bultmann, 'The Problem of Hermeneutics', in *New Testament and Mythology* (Philadelphia: Fortress Press, 1984), esp. pp. 88–90; M. Daly, *Beyond God the Father* (Boston: Beacon Press, 1973), pp. 7–11.

14 C. Geertz, 'Religion as a Cultural System', in *Interpretation of Culture*, pp. 93f.

15 Kaufman, *In Search of Mystery*; J. Plaskow, *Standing Again at Sinai* (San Francisco: Harper SanFrancisco, 1991); S. Heschel, *On Being a Jewish Feminist* (New York: Schocken Books, 1995).

16 S. Thistlethwaite, *Sex, Race, and God* (New York: Crossroad Press, 1989), ch. 7; b. hooks and C. West, *Breaking Bread* (Boston: South End Press, 1991), ch. 5; K. Canon, *Black Womanist Ethics* (Atlanta: Scholars Press, 1988).

17 G. Hunsinger, *How to Read Karl Barth* (New York: Oxford University Press, 1991).

18 H. Urs von Balthasar, *Karl Barth* (San Francisco: Ignatius Press, 1992), part II, ch. 4.

19 K. Barth, '"No!" Answer to Emil Brunner', in *Natural Theology* (London: Geoffrey Bles, 1946), p. 70.

20 E. Brunner, *Man in Revolt*, p. 358, as quoted in *CD* III/4, p. 152.

21 C. LaCugna, *God For Us* (San Francisco: Harper SanFrancisco, 1991).

22 Welch, *A Feminist Ethic of Risk*; S. Sellers, *Language and Sexual Difference* (New York: St Martin's Press, 1991); C. Gilligan, *In Another Voice* (Cambridge: Harvard University Press, 1982); N. Chodorow, *The Reproduction of Mothering* (Berkeley: University of California Press, 1978).

23 R. Ruether, *New Woman, New Earth* (New York: Seabury Press, 1975); M. Asasi Diaz, *En la Lucha/In the Struggle* (Minneapolis: Fortress Press, 1993); S. McFague, *The Body of God* (Minneapolis: Fortress Press, 1993); E. Schüssler Fiorenza, *Discipleship of Equals* (New York: Crossroad Press, 1993).

Further reading

Jones, S., 'This God Which Is Not One: Irigaray and Barth on the Divine', in C. W. M. Kim *et al.*, eds., *Transfigurations. Theology and the French Feminists* (Minneapolis: Fortress Press, 1993), pp. 109–41.

Köbler, R., *In the Shadow of Karl Barth. Charlotte von Kirschbaum* (Louisville, Ky.: Westminster John Knox Press, 1989).

17 Barth, modernity, and postmodernity

GRAHAM WARD

INTRODUCTION

There are several narratives of the years between our own and those of the thirteenth century, all of which have helped to produce the notions of 'modernity' and 'postmodernity'. A number of these narratives have a similar plot structure. For example: the dawn of modernity is evident in the seventeenth century; it arises from/with a new sensibility shaped by figures such as Galileo and Descartes, Hobbes, and Newton; it is characterized by a new confidence in the reasoning subject and by the establishment of a world order to be understood according to the laws of geometry, mathematics, and mechanics; and it is governed by secularized forms of power: nation states, social contracts, civic policing, and judiciary courts. This new sensibility gradually eclipses the *ancien régime* and fosters the Enlightenment. Romanticism, though in some ways a critique of the preceding rational utopias, shifted the way the world was modelled from mechanical to organic and immanently evolving orders. The anthropological centring of this world view remained, the sciences still offered their culturally significant account of Nature, and the realm of the theological became increasingly privatized as attention turned to interior, spiritual experience. Now two world wars, the genocidal projects of Hitler, the Khmer Rouge, and Idi Amin announce a new sensibility. Late capitalism, with its call for the value of goods to be regulated by the demands of the market, with its mass media promotions, and its fostering of virtual money (electronic banking and credit), produces the globalisms and eclecticisms of postmodernity. The old grand narratives, that gave the world and human experience of it its explanatory shape, have collapsed. Key figures in the promotion of this new sensibility are French and American: Michel Foucault, Jacques Lacan, Jacques Derrida, Jean Baudrillard, Stanley Fish, Charles Jencks, and Judith Butler.

What I wish to undertake in this chapter is an analysis of Karl Barth's work with respect to the metaphysics of modernity and postmodernism.

While accepting the shifts of sensibility narrated by cultural historians above, I wish to problematize them for reasons which do justice to the richness of historical particularity and which are, furthermore, theologically significant. In the opening sentence of his work of historical theology, *Protestant Theology in the Nineteenth Century*, Barth makes the point that he is not engaged in a historical exercise, but a theological one: attempting to trace in the voices of our theological forebears their struggle to hear and express the Word in their several generations. It is the same orientation which governs the concern of this chapter: not simply to contextualize Barth's work with respect to the historical criteria characterizing the era of modernity and its collapse or apotheosis (depending on who you read) in postmodernity. Rather, I wish to sketch a theology of history in which, first, we might understand why Barth's voice can resonate so insistently in contemporary culture and, secondly, we might hear the eschatological Word in the cultural tissue and textures of our time. For we too need to read the signs of the times, having recognized how Barth's work is woven into them.

STORIES

The story of modernity outlined above is concomitant with the rise of secularism and historicism itself. It is significant therefore that two Christian thinkers, the Swiss theologian Hans Urs von Balthasar and the French Jesuit historian Michel de Certeau, have told the story in a different way.

In volume five of *The Glory of the Lord*,[1] von Balthasar outlines what he terms a metaphysics of the saints in which theology and philosophy work together. Aquinas is cited briefly, but von Balthasar's attention is on the opponents against whom Aquinas debates: Averroes and his Parisian followers of the thirteenth century. These thinkers conflated the theological with the philosophical, forgetting the distance that always remained between the uncreated God and his creation. God as the highest being in the neo-Aristotelianism of their world-view collapsed the analogical relationality which had informed the liturgical cosmos into a new univocity. And in this univocity, von Balthasar hears the first notes of the confidence in present understanding rather than revelation and revelatory tradition. The univocity of being is developed more fully in the work of Duns Scotus: revelation and the natural world-order are fundamentally in agreement.

Von Balthasar's thinking was greatly indebted to the neo-Patristic and neo-Thomist teachings of the French *nouvelle théologie*,[2] and Certeau likewise. Certeau's focus, following Henri de Lubac's, is on the changing understanding of *corpus mysticum* (the hidden or mystical body), the eucharistic understanding of the body of Christ which related the Logos to *bios* (life) and *eros* (desire), the Word to rhetoric and facts, in the sacramental world-view prior to the thirteenth century.[3] This world-view collapsed, Certeau writes, because of a distrust that God spoke in the world. He cites the work of William of Ockham as the producer of a new linguistics in which word was separated from thing, and words could no longer speak to us of the ineffable God. With Ockham a new dualism rends the symbolic world order, making nature opaque, and separating the secular from the spiritual, the visible from the mysterious or hidden. Following the thirteenth century, Certeau notes, *corpus mysticum* no longer describes the eucharistic body but the visible church *as* the eucharistic body. Now what is visible is what is; perception governs what is known. For Certeau this is a streak of early light in what will become the dawn of modernity where seeing and believing become reciprocal. The dualism established here between word and thing, the divisions between what is seen, how it is represented and what it means, will found the dualisms of modernity itself: the private spiritual experience and the public practices; the soul and the body; the mind and the flesh; the seen and calculable and the unseen and miraculous; the subject and the object.

I cite these two genealogies because they extend the historicism of modernity/postmodernity theologically in terms of the ecclesial tradition (which is central to any understanding of a theology of history). As we will see, they enable us to position Barth with respect to this tradition, which is Catholic before it is Protestant. That may be important; for it will raise a question concerning the extent to which the Protestantism within which Barth situates his own work is embedded within the modernity which it fostered.

Two further accounts of modernity will help us to problematize the earlier narrative; these are not theological, but philosophical and historical accounts of the relationship between modernity and postmodernity. The first is Jean-François Lyotard's famous thesis: that postmodernism is the abjected (and therefore necessary) other of modernism.[4] Consequently, postmodernism does not simply follow and succeed modernity, but precedes and underwrites it. From this position it would follow that 'postmodernity' is a period concept, useful for both historiography and sociology. In fact, we are constantly being reminded that, as such, postmodernity is now *passé*. But 'postmodernism' concerns that which Lyotard terms the unpresentable, the repressed, the forgotten other scene that modernity both needs and negates in what Barth will call its 'will for form' (*PT*, p. 56), its absolutisms, its rational utopias. Lyotard writes that postmodernism 'is not a new age, it is the rewriting of some features modernity had tried or pretended to gain . . . But such a rewriting . . . was for a long time active within modernity itself'.[5] *Post* and *modo* are to be read, grammatically, as a future anterior. As such, postmodernism pre- and post-dates modernity.

Now, once again, this nuanced reading of the story of modernity is significant. For it points to the possibility of other so-called postmodern discourses continuing throughout modernity. The story of modernity is not uniform. Barth himself drew attention to this in the early chapters of his *Protestant Theology in the Nineteenth Century*. When discussing the absolutism of Enlightenment rationalism, and its metaphysical corollaries – natural theology and the exaltation of human reasoning – he points, first, to 'the pursuit of the mysterious' (*PT*, p. 35), and then to other (theological) currents which countermanded the conflation of revelation and reason, nature and grace. For him, reading these renegade voices theologically, a counter-tradition is evident, a gospel still present in the eighteenth and nineteenth centuries. Having outlined several of the categories ('moralistic, intellectualistic, individualistic') shaping Christian thinking in the eighteenth century and inventing 'the ghost of "dead orthodoxy"' (*PT*, p. 93), he concludes: 'It is impossible to read the documents without having to say that Christianity as it was really lived always went beyond the sphere marked out by all these categories' (*PT*, p. 24). Consequently, 'theology was never able to enjoy its modernity in peace, but willy-nilly went on becoming more out of date' (*PT*, p. 38). Thus in the maelstrom of secularization – when nature, reason, individualism, self-authorizing experience, and an identification of church and state infected the whole of European culture – a man like Hamann can nevertheless appear, counterpointing the Kantian critique with a theological metacritique of his own. This again is significant. For Barth, Hamann is the bearer of a tradition older than himself; his is a voice which reiterates an orthodoxy, a conservatism which stands opposed to the cult of the neo and the new (*PT*, p. 52). The great flagship of modern theology, for Barth, was a school who were called neologists, who prepared the ground (along with the Wolffians and Pietists) for the rampant theological liberalism of the nineteenth (and early twentieth) century. Barth stands in the tradition of Hamann (and Kierkegaard) – a theological conservatism opposed to the metaphysics of modernity as the gospel itself is opposed to the metaphysics of modernity. 'Modernity with its obtrusion of seemingly indispensable viewpoints and criteria is not the measure of all things' (*CD* III/3, p. 334).

It is important to register a distinction here between Lyotard's critique of modernity's 'grand narratives' and Barth's. For when Lyotard speaks of the unpresentable and allies it to the postmodern – whereas the beautiful, the ordered and the explicable all pertain to the modern – his understanding of that which pre-dates, disturbs, and post-dates modernity is both monistic and nihilistic. A vast and volatile flux of indeterminate becoming provides the background from which modernity's 'will for form' issues. It is this indeterminacy which modernity's Prometheanism represses or forgets. Barth, on the other hand, in his attempt to construct a theology of history – and therefore a theological account of modernity – speaks of the operation of the gospel or revelation or the Word as borne and attested by the church and by the tradition (from Paul and Tertullian through to Luther and Calvin). This, not nihilism, is for Barth the repressed other scene of modernity. In fact, as we will see, nihilism is not at all possible, for Barth, outside a theological world-view. What he detects in the eighteenth-century programme of the Enlightenment (and its Romantic reaction) is the constant secularization of theologically grounded truths. The absolutism of individualism – where the self-grounded and autonomous I makes its own judgments about the world and its experience of it – is a parody of the doctrine of the *imago dei*. Man now makes himself in the image of God. The proliferation of new societies and free communities, in which companions come together by choice and are united by some common feeling or aim, is a bastardization of ecclesiology. Before this time, Barth claims, 'there was in fact no such thing as a *societas*' (*PT*, p. 62). Now, as the church declines, mysterious groups appear, locked into private, non-political spaces. The freemasons (and others) become 'the real and true Church, the veritable Church of Humanity' (*PT*, p. 64). The all-seeing surveillance of the ever burgeoning state, like the attitude of detachment towards nature and history (which enabled these fields to develop as sciences), are all secularizations of divine attributes. For in the process of secularization, man 'places himself in an absolute position' (*PT*, p. 90). Furthermore, the authority of self-authenticating experience (a key concern of both Pietists and empirical scientists) required the collapse of temporal distance. There was a demand 'to experience . . . one's own present, indeed as one's own present, in a different way from the presence of the Holy Spirit, which is still an objective present' (*PT*, p. 115). Things must be fully present, the cult of the new becomes the worship of self-presencing. But this too is a secularization of a theological theme: the pseudo-realization of the eschatological vision in which all is fully revealed.

The contrast between Lyotard and Barth raises a certain question. Is Lyotard's monistic nihilism postmodern at all, or simply the logical corollary of the metaphysics of modernity? Could it be that only theology can be authentically postmodern in the Lyotardian sense, simply because it has never been modern at all? We will return to this question.

If Lyotard's philosophical analysis of postmodernism enables us to situate Barth's theological project, then Stephen Toulmin's historical analysis of postmodernity, in his book *Cosmopolis: The Hidden Agenda of Modernity*, enables us to situate Barth himself as the socially and historically embedded agent of this project. Toulmin emphasizes the secularization of theological projects (like Newton's view of the universe, for example). The changes in the understanding of what constituted matter, time, and space take place in the seventeenth and eighteenth centuries as a result of a fundamental uncoupling of Christian doctrine and experience accentuated by the wars of religion fought throughout the seventeenth century. The pursuit of peace required the separation of the state from religion, the state now guaranteeing religious tolerance, as an autonomous, if arbitrary, authority. But, and this is where Toulmin's thesis becomes important for our own, the modernity forged and founded here collapses in the early part of the twentieth century. As Toulmin writes: 'By 1914, then, all the material was ready to hand to justify dismantling the last timbers of the intellectual scaffolding that had, since the late 17th century, established the parameters of established thought.'[6] Postmodernity is fostered by the collapse of the Newtonian, stable universe (the uniformity of which guaranteed Nature as modernity had come to understand it rationally), by Einstein and Planck; and the Freudian calling into question of rationality itself (and the new focus on what rationality had suppressed, *eros*). Both the unity of the objective world and the unity of the subjective *cogito* dissolved. The garden of liberal humanism was rank and rotting. By 1914, Toulmin claims, there was 'an acceptance of pluralism in the sciences, and a final renunciation of philosophical foundationalism and the Quest for Certainty'.[7] Nevertheless, Toulmin writes, the nascent change was forestalled. '[T]he greater part of the European *avant garde* chose to revive the rational dream of a clean slate and a return to abstract fundamentals' – Berg and Bauhaus, Mondrian and Le Corbusier.[8] 'The same move away from the historical, concrete, or psychological, towards the formal, abstract, or logical is evident in natural science in the 1920s and '30s.'[9] Postmodernity was deferred.

The significance of this thesis for our own lies in the way it identifies the proto-postmodernity in the early part of the twentieth century. Among those Barth scholars who have argued for Barth's relevance to any discussion of postmodernism or postmodernity, a difference of opinion has arisen. There are those scholars such as Richard Roberts in Britain, and

David Klemm, Walter Lowe, and Stephen Webb[10] in the States, who, in drawing attention to the similarities of world-view operative in some post-modern thinking and the second edition of *The Epistle to the Romans*, wish to limit such observations to that early work. The Barth of the *Göttingen Dogmatics* and onward cannot so easily be compared with the rhizomatic logics[11] evident in postmodernity. On the other hand, other scholars such as Isolde Andrews, William Stacy Johnston, and myself[12] have insisted that Barth's work throughout betrays strong affinities with postmodernism. For some this is argued on the basis of rejecting the influential theses of Balthasar, Torrance, and Frei: that a radical change took place in Barth's thinking some time in the late 1920s and early 1930s, effecting a move away from dialectical theology and towards a theology founded upon the *analogia fidei* (analogy of faith) or *analogia Christi* (analogy of Christ). To limit the postmodernist tendencies in Barth to his early work does not do justice to the nature of his theological critique. To see it simply as culturally located in, and limited to, the nihilistic *avant garde* of the early Weimar period overlooks the fact that the theological critique is itself already postmodern (as it was postmodern in Hamann and Kierkegaard) in the Lyotardian sense of the term. In fact, we might wish to argue that only theology can be postmodern in this way. The corollary of this is that the orthodox and traditional teaching of the Christian church has always been and will always necessarily be a critique of modernity, an unveiling of that which modernity forgets, polices, or suppresses.

BARTH'S CRITIQUE OF MODERNITY

It is time now to outline the nature of Barth's theological critique of modernity. I will do so with reference to Barth's late, not early, work; in particular to the analysis, which is part of his unfolding doctrine of creation in *CD* III/1, of the Cartesian *cogito* and to his discussions of nihilism in Heidegger and Sartre in his treatment of 'Nothingness' (*das Nichtige*) in *CD* III/3. I will bring out the affinities and differences between Barth's theological analysis and postmodernism's critique, bearing in mind that these are pieces of work executed by Barth throughout the middle to the late 1940s. I will outline this critique and comparison through its three determinative positions: nonfoundationalism, non-realism, and post-humanism.

Nonfoundationalism

In foundationalism, what is understood as an account of what is known or knowable is that which can be rationally justified. Nonfoundationalism accepts that there can be true knowledge beyond or outside of rational justification. The basis of Barth nonfoundationalism is the mystery of the triune God. Because human beings are brought into existence and sustained by God's gracious will, no position is naturally available to us from which to understand ourselves or the world in which we live. 'Always beneath our feet there yawns the gulf of the possibility that our healthy opinion might be deceiving us, that it might actually turn out that nothing is real' (*CD* III/1, pp. 345f.). We mis-read what is real, and begin to construct a whole range of world-views when we take the contents of human perception and consciousness as a self-evident basis for reasoning about what is. For our knowledge of the world and ourselves within it has to be given to us by revelation. Only in the divinity and humanity of Christ are we 'to recognize the *maxima ratio*' (*CD* III/1, p. 413).

Barth's nonfoundationalism is a form of philosophical scepticism made possible by a theological realism. Philosophically, nonfoundationalism announces that no final justification or explanation is available for certainties to be established; there is no ground for apodictic truths. *Über Gewissenheit* (*On Certainty*) by Wittgenstein is a classic text in philosophical nonfoundationalism. It is important to distinguish this form of nonfoundationalism from the nonfoundationalism of those convinced there is nothing outside the words we employ to bring something into existence. This second form of nonfoundationalism is linguistic idealism. Neither Barth nor Wittgenstein were linguistic idealists. To clarify the nature of his own position, Barth has both to advance this scepticism concerning our judgments about the world – and develop his critique of rationalist systems built in the air (*CD* III/1, p. 341) – and to define its consequent nihilism, with respect to the reality of nothingness *à propos* of God's Yes to creation. This is the burden of paragraphs 42 and 50 of *Church Dogmatics*. He is able to proceed by first demonstrating how the secularizing of the theological in modernity – which manufactured the book of nature, the authority of the human senses and human reasoning – stands on the edge of an abyss. The atheism – as the denial of the Lordship of God – intrinsic to modernity's project leads inexorably not only to nihilism, but to the power-broking and totalitarian politics made inevitable when 'the world which is present . . . [is] but as an objectification of will and idea, of human will and human idea' (*CD* III/1, p. 339). Having concluded that all human wisdom is bound for and bound up with nothingness, Barth then proceeds to circumscribe this nothingness theologically: 'The existence, presence and operation of nothingness . . . are also objectively the break in the relationship between Creator and creation' (*CD* III/3, p. 294). Philosophical scepticism and its nihilistic consequences are thus swept up into the distance separating the uncreated God from his creation.

We need to examine this more closely, for it will become an important argument in my proposal that only theology can be truly postmodern. In his analysis of Descartes's work, what strikes Barth is the way Cartesian doubt defines the project such that 'the proof of the divine existence is no more than a buttress for the proof of the self-existence of the thinking subject' (*CD* III/1, p. 351). The world-view that Descartes announces – based upon relating perceptions of the external world to mathematics and geometry – in which the coherence of created nature becomes the basis for scientific analysis, is founded upon, first, a radical dualism and, second, self-assertion. These are the bases for Enlightenment thinking: the distinction between consciousness and being, mind and world, and the will for form (Nietzsche's will to power). And both these axioms are the consequence of doubting. 'All the wretchedness of human life is bound up with the fact that sound common sense and the *natura docet* have no power at all firmly to plant our feet on the ground of the confidence that the created world is real' (*CD* III/1, p. 362). Barth concludes his analysis with a thought experiment: what if Descartes had fully faced the doubt he never seriously engaged? Then the insubstantial nature of modernity's foundations would have presented itself and Descartes would have fallen into despair, having recognized 'his own nothingness, and then also the nothingness of his own thinking and of the whole external world' (*CD* III/1, p. 362).

Dualism and absolutism (in which the omnipotence of God is reconceived as the omnipotence of human creativity) make possible modernity's project; a project masking a nihilist metaphysics. Theology, as such, becomes culturally irrelevant; for the God who now arises in the work of Descartes, Leibniz and Wolff is a God set in place by the metaphysics of modernity. And since these metaphysics are themselves founded upon nothing, then the death of such a God (suggested by Hegel, endorsed by Schopenhauer, and propounded by Nietzsche) is implicit in the world-views of modernity from their inception. Wolff's development of Leibniz' monadology employs the idea of God as perfection, but 'He does not need this, of course' (*CD* III/1, p. 394) because his idea of perfection is based upon the mutual relationship and harmony of all things in the world. 'Atheism', Barth concludes, 'is lurking somewhere at the doors' (*CD* III/1, p. 409). With Schopenhauer, God is excluded from creation (*CD* III/1, p. 339). Barth admires the honesty of Schopenhauer: '[F]or an honest gaze the creation from which God is excluded can only be evil' (*CD* III/1, p. 340). The alternative to such honesty is to seek refuge in 'an aesthetic world-view' (ibid.), which will be Nietzsche's response.

Barth's genealogy[13] betrays a tension in the metaphysics of modernity which he himself does not draw out further. If modernity is founded upon dualism and an absolutism based in nothing but language's facility to assert, then from quite early on the project is already under threat from the instability of those foundations. For the absolutist position is at odds with the imposed limits of the subject with respect to the object in the dualist position. The tension can only be erased by allowing the absolutist pole to consume the dualist world-view: I make the world. Dualism is constantly threatened by monism. Barth points out that in Descartes the horizontal dualism (between mind and world) is held in place by a vertical dualism between the finitude of being human and the infinite, transcending God. A cross-hatch of dualisms kept the world from being conceived as merely secular. Barth is also aware that within Descartes's lifetime, Spinoza was already countering the dualisms and propounding God as one substance of which all things, intellectual and corporeal, are modifications: in other words a radically monistic (and atheistic) world-view. Spinoza, as Barth notes, does not have his day until 'the more sublime humanism of the period of Goethe' (*PT*, p. 131); nevertheless, in his discussions of the movement of ideas from Leibniz to Schopenhauer, Barth reveals the developing immanentism that increasingly guarantees and completes the secular world picture. With radical immanentism not only does dualism, and therefore transcendence, disappear, but also all notions of difference, of alterity, of otherness. Barth writes: 'Indifference alone . . . would be genuine ungodliness' (*CD* III/1, p. 378). And so we arrive at the philosophical analysis of nothingness, indifference, in the work of Heidegger and Sartre:

> Their thought is determined in and by real encounter with nothingness . . . nothingness has ineluctably and unforgettably addressed them, the question of nothingness has emerged from the plenitude of problems and . . . has become for them the real problem. We can certainly learn from them . . . And their positive value is to direct their age to this outstanding opportunity, to introduce the subject of nothingness with such urgency. (*CD* III/3, pp. 345f.)

In the work of Heidegger and Sartre, modernity faces its own non-foundationalism and the 'new gospel of the free sovereignty of man' collapses (*CD* III/3, pp. 399f.).

Barth traces, then, the way in which what is done in secret (modernity's ignorance about its own metaphysics and their theological implications) is finally announced from the rooftops. He traces the positive, theological value in the movement of human (far too human) thinking from Descartes to Sartre. But what becomes evident, for us who follow in the wake of Barth, is that the founding voices of postmodern thinking are, in fact, none other than those voices which brought about the apotheosis of modernity's metaphysics: Nietzsche, Heidegger, and Sartre. In other words, the appeal by many postmodern thinkers to nihilism is the advanced development of modernity, not modernity's repressed and forgotten scene. Barth embraces what is positive for theology in such an unmasking of the modern; this is part of his eschatological reading of culture. He embraces this nonfoundationalism so fundamental to the post-structuralist programme. Earlier, he had gone further and applied this nonfoundationalism to theological discourse itself: 'We do not know what we are saying when we call God "Father" and "Son"' (*CD* I/1, p. 433); 'We do not know what we are saying when we call Jesus Christ the eternal Word of God' (*CD* I/1, p. 436). But his nonfoundationalism is a rejection of modernity's thesis of the sovereignty of man. It emerges as a consequence of his insistence that any knowledge we have of God is given to us through God's revelation of himself in Christ. And this insistence re-establishes difference, alterity, otherness; reaffirms transcendence. But it is at this point that a question remains that we shall need to examine later: whether, despite Barth's critique of modernity, he remains caught within its logics because he reifies another dualism – between creation and Creator, between this world and that which is wholly other.

Non-realism

The basis of Barth's non-realism lies in his refusal to accept anything as true or real outside of the knowledge given to human creatures through Christ. Jesus Christ is the ontic and noetic possibility for any true and objective understanding of what we, other people, and the things of our world are as created. Therefore, in his critique of Nature (the universe rooted in itself and maintained by its own dynamic), Nature constructed outside the Christian knowledge of the covenant and outside the Christian knowledge of creation, Barth writes:

> Our consciousness of ourselves and the world, i.e., our awareness and conception of our ego, and of people and things existing outside ourselves, might well be a matter of mere supposition, of pure appearance, a form of nothingness, and our step from consciousness

to being a hollow fiction. It is not true that we have an immediate awareness of our own or any other reality. It is only true that we immediately suppose that we have such an awareness.   (*CD* III/1, p. 345)

Barth, following Kant, accepts that we cannot know 'things in themselves'; we work with the mediated representations of these things and, on this basis, we live in the world 'as if' we had immediate awareness.

Philosophical non-realism developed as a critique of realism as realism came to be understood in modernity; but its roots lie in the quasi-mechanical link between mental language, spoken language, and the referent in William of Ockham's analysis of the relationship between truth and propositions.[14] There are forms of realism covering Hobbesian materialism, Lockian and Humean empiricism, the naturalism of Rousseau, and the positivism of Comte. But, fundamentally, the realist bases knowledge on experience or sense data – for these present the realist with the world as it objectively stands outside of any subject – and trusts that language more or less accurately mirrors that experience of the world. Space is filled with numerous bodies, each of which has an autonomous, discrete existence. Each body is made up of its substance and its predicates. Each body can be identified, named and catalogued and the world, as such, stripped of mystery and miracle. It is a form of realized eschatology: all things appear fully and manifestly as they are. Realism endorses, then, presence and the self-validating experience. The immediacy of the experience fosters discussions about representation or the role of language with respect to the experience. Some form of correspondence theory of language facilitates the realist position: i.e., sensation produces thought and that is then named in such a way that the word stands for and corresponds to the experience.[15]

CD II/1 explicitly critiques the correspondence view of language, working within a neo-Kantian framework.[16] Barth understands language as picturing the world such that human consciousness of the world and what the world is in and of itself are distinct. Only the noetic operation of the Spirit of Christ, establishing *analogia fidei* or *analogia Christi*, can enable us to have some understanding of the world as it is. Only God sees things as they are. This theological position, as I pointed out, critiques notions of 'presence' and 'identity', for the world (and God's unveiling of himself within the world) is always and only mediated to us. This position is reiterated and developed in *CD* III/1 with respect to countering naturalism and emphasizing the unreality of human constructions of creation (which are, after Kant, 'world-views', *Weltanschauungen*). Rather than immediately apprehending creation, world-views 'take their departure within the circle of perception and being' (*CD* III/1, p. 340). It is the circularity that is significant here for Barth's non-realism. The circularity guarantees both a subjective perspectivalism and the self-verifying character of that perspectivalism: 'It must be viewed independently if it is to escape the suspicion that it has not really been viewed at all' (*CD* III/1, p. 341). Nevertheless, the relativism of perspective and the constructive nature of consciousness (always historically, linguistically, and culturally embedded) is denied by the realists in a move which turns the observer into God himself. The realist's naturalism implies that he sees the world as it is, and his experience is objective evidence of that fact. Barth ridicules this notion of objectivity – and the priority it gives to the visual, the spectacle – in a manner which leads directly to Foucault's work *Discipline and Punish* and Zygmunt Bauman's work on postmodernity as a surveillance society:

> They sit at their telescope . . . observing and then reflecting upon what they have seen. They do not allow themselves to be personally affected, for all their interest in these things. It is they who decide and regulate the distances and relations between themselves and things. It is they who observe and experiment and note the interconnexion of things and their detailed and general harmony and usefulness. They are the masters who are able to put everything to rights . . . Things do not really touch them, either for evil or for good. And so they cannot really make contact with things or be sure for evil or for good. Everything remains in the sphere of views and opinions and persuasions. Everything is a *panopticon*. (*CD* III/1, p. 411)

Barth demonstrates his awareness here of the relation between knowledge and power; the absolutist ambitions of a metaphysics of objectivity and the way in which such a metaphysics relegates ethics to social mores; and the internal incoherence of the realist position, which does not really have contact with things, trades only in 'views and opinions and persuasions' so that if 'the glasses were different, everything would change' (ibid.), and yet they 'are masters'.

Barth attacks the two fundamental axioms of the realist position: its belief in the immediacy of experience and the correlative of that position, its conviction that language mirrors the world. He does this by emphasizing the social, historical and political investments in knowledge, and by drawing attention to the way language does not mirror but create fictions of our world. His non-realism is dialectically necessary in order to open a space for what Ingolf U. Dalferth has termed 'eschatological realism'. But it differs from certain post-Heideggerian forms of non-realism (though not, I would argue, Derrida's), insofar as it does not posit an indifferent flow of atoms and a linguistic idealism ('moving energies, formed into words, are what everything's made of'[17]). For these post-Heideggerians, we have only 'reality effects' given by the language which constructs the real from the flux and reflux of energies. For Barth, like Kant, there is a real world and a created order out there as gifted to us and sustained by God; we simply have to be taught how to read it in Christ: 'It is not nothing but something; yet it is something on the edge of nothing, bordering it and menaced by it, and having no power of itself to overcome the danger. . . . It has subsistence [*Bestand*]; yet it does not have such subsistence as it can secure and maintain for itself' (*CD* III/1, p. 376).[18]

POST-HUMANISM

Barth's post-humanism is a theological reaction to the Pelagian heresies underwriting modernity. Recognizing that these spring from roots in Renaissance thinking (*PT*, p. 176), Barth traces the extent to which they are the product of Descartes's 'asserted existence of myself as thinking subject' (*CD* III/1, p. 358) and a new self-confidence and optimism evident in Leibniz, and coming to full flower in Rousseau: 'Nature, which Rousseau so often pointed out as the true source and eternal law of human life, is very simply man himself, as distinct from man as he is in his circumstances, as he is in his works, and as he is determined by other people' (*PT*, pp. 227f.). Man is essentially good and would remain so if left to follow the natural inclinations of his own heart. In this, the ideology of natural law again reasserts itself. To access and evaluate the workings of this natural law one has to look inside oneself, and so an individualism is reinforced by 'the *culte intérieur*' (*PT*, p. 205) and the appeal to one's experience. With Rousseau, and the age of Goethe which followed him, feeling was 'considered to be the true organ of the human mind' (*PT*, p. 229). In *CD* III/1, Barth will call this 'abstract this-worldliness and anthropocentricity' (*CD* III/1, p. 408). This is absolute man and, as this figure enters Romanticism through Lessing's work on the education of 'historical humanity' (*PT*, p. 263), he constitutes the basis for nineteenth-century liberal humanism with its educational ideologies and its doctrines of progress and freedom.

Earlier in *CD* III/1, in an exegesis and discussion of the Genesis account of Adam and Eve, and later in *CD* III/2, discussing 'The Basic Form of Humanity', Barth outlines a theological anthropology which decentres this notion of selfhood. Human beings are not nomads capable of determining their own freedom because their existence lies within a cosmic chiasmus: a covenant with God in which man is 'commissioned to serve and work' (CD III/1, p. 237) and a covenant to each other (figured in Genesis as the sexually differentiated other). And so, 'Man is no longer single but a couple' (CD III/1, p. 308); no longer in the nominative case (as Emmanuel Levinas would put it), but the accusative. The solitariness of Rousseau's *promeneur* is, therefore, not fulfilling what it is to be human. This solo-supremacy has the same structure, for Barth, as homosexual relations: in closing itself to a relation with what is other, it embraces a narcissism. This is contrary to the external and internal covenants: 'If man were created solitary, creation as a whole would not be good, because it would then lack its internal basis in the covenant' (CD III/1, p. 290). The self is always incomplete, for Barth, nurtured in dependency – upon the grace of God and upon the society to which he or she belongs – and its subsequent responsibilities. As incomplete, this self, to become authentic (for it never *is* authentic, always *coming* to its authenticity in Christ) must live beyond itself in service to God and in relation to other people.

The nature of the self, outlined here, has similarities to post-structural ecstatic models of selfhood propounded by Emmanuel Levinas and Julia Kristeva, among others. For these models too challenge modernity's sovereignty of the self – its self-justifying autonomy. For Levinas and Kristeva, subjectivity is not a given; there is no essential self. Furthermore, their models of the self are also models of subjects-in-process, subjects acting in the unfolding of time and, in acting, always coming into an identity, a self-understanding, which is never complete. Where Barth differs from them is in his conception of the origins and *telos* of this selfhood. For Barth, human beings were always so constituted by God; only as such can personhood be caught up in eschatological performance – moving to the fullness of the stature of Christ. Modernity's absolutism is a result of a fall. Hence the irony, to which Barth is sensitive, that modernity's Pelagianism is not the eradication of original sin but its radicalization. Both Levinas and Kristeva locate the origin for this ecstatic self in secularized versions of this fall.

Outside God man makes himself and, as Barth notes, the ungrounded nature of this making becomes conscious of itself in existentialism. Sartre's conviction that man can be as he wills to be and imagines himself to be is another version of modernity's will for form. This is the apotheosis of the human, and its nihilism and its pessimism are evident. For Sartre (and Heidegger), according to Barth, 'our existence itself is a projection into nothing and is constituted by our enquiry into it; how to be open to nothing is the fundamental virtue of existence' (CD III/3, p. 343). The road to humanism leads to nihilism; a theological anthropology must therefore be post-humanist. But the value of existentialism lies precisely in showing that humanism is, ultimately, inhuman. For the ego is an arbitrary centre; it has to manufacture its values. Like any other object in the capitalist market-place, it has no intrinsic value; it is given value by those who wish to buy. Now figured, by postmodern thinkers such as Lyotard, Certeau and Braidotti, as a nomadic, deterritorialized self, it can, therefore, be all too easily erased.

NIHILISM

Barth's critique of modernity – which draws him close to postmodern espousals of nonfoundationalism, non-realism and post-humanism – moves, in *CD* III/1 and *CD* III/3, from a critical examination of the Cartesian *ego cogito* to the nihilisms of Schopenhauer, Heidegger, and Sartre. His critical examination of Nietzsche appears in *CD* III/2. These are volumes written between 1942 and 1949. In 1942, we find him writing to an American inquirer: '[S]o much nihilism has accumulated in all possible forms throughout the world that finally it had to come to an explosion in the anarchy and tyranny of Hitler's Germany'.[19] The analysis of modernity culminates in Barth's analysis of 'God and Nothingness' – for its founda-tions, naturalism, humanism, will for form and social contracts are parodies of revealed truths about God and 'counterfeits of nothingness' (*CD* III/3, p. 359). The 'of' there is both a subjective and an objective genitive. Modernity manufactures both counterfeits which have only virtual reality and counterfeits of the nothingness itself. And it is at this point that Barth's recognition of the truth and reality of the Nihil obtains a theological reorientation. For the nihilisms which surface as modernity comes of age – and therefore the nihilistic fluxes, abysses, chaoses, and *choras*[20] – are also virtual. 'From the standpoint of the *ego cogito* true nothingness cannot be discerned, no matter how powerful the impression of its presence and operation may be' (*CD* III/3, p. 346). Because of this, as Barth repeatedly observes, in all the metaphysics of modernity a place for true evil (and sin and the devil as corollaries of that evil) cannot be found. For Barth, then, modernity's (and postmodernity's) nihilism is itself ideological – manufac-tured by the will for form. True nothingness is a consequence of God's Yes to creation, for the Yes implies a No: 'Only with the operation of His election and grace, and only as its converse, is His *opus alienum* also performed, and the sovereign No pronounced by which nothingness is granted its distinc-tive form and existence' (*CD* III/3, p. 355). Nothingness is unthinkable and inexplicable. Our only insight into its nature is by what is revealed about it through Christ as judge: the 'sickness unto death' which Kierkegaard describes (*CD* III/3, p. 348). In Christ this nothingness is also deprived even of its temporary, transient, and impermanent purchase upon what is (*CD* III/3, pp. 362f.).

IS POSTMODERNISM POSTMODERN ENOUGH?

In my analysis of Barth's three fundamental critiques of modernism – nonfoundationalism, non-realism, and post-humanism – I have pointed to the similarities between these critiques and those proclaimed by post-modernism. I have also pointed to the differences. In each case the post-modern critique does not exactly counter the modern, but propel the trajectory of the modern towards its ultimate conclusions. The nonfoundationalism and non-realism of much postmodern thinking – the world is an indifferent flux of energies to which our language gives the effect of reality – are developments from Cartesian self-reflexivity and self-assertion. They are consequences of the absolute I. Barth recognized the fragility of this 'circle in which my thinking has moved' (*CD* III/1, p. 361). The self, grounded on itself, proving its own existence endlessly to itself, is a self which has to deny its own fallibility, its own susceptibility to both evil and the shadow side of creation: pain, sickness, death. The absolute I is a creation *ex nihilo* and always a virtual reality or simulacrum. Furthermore, the exaltation of the I is, simultaneously, making each I an object in a world full of other objects. Cartesian humanism leads to perspectivalism and the devaluation of humankind. Sartre's repudiation of subjectivity and an essential human nature are, therefore, workings within the logics of modernity. Hence, post-modernism's posthumanism – even with its rejection of a unified self and its analysis of a performative, relational, and processive concept of identity – pursues the modern notion of freedom (now termed *jouissance*[21]); the endless freedom of consumer choice. The world Barth shares with these postmodern thinkers is a world of hybrids, ambivalence, and uncertainties; a world perched on the edge of nothingness. Hence Barth can resonate in postmodernity. But resonance is not enough. Theology cannot confirm the logics of postmodernity, because postmodernism is the ultimate triumph of secularism – hence its marketable appeal and its strong affiliations with late capitalism.[22] Theology has to show postmodernism that it is not postmodern enough. One of the most provocative cultural historians, Bruno Latour, in a book which challenges whether we have ever been modern at all – for we have always lived with hybrids, ambivalences, and uncertain identities – points out: 'The postmoderns retain the modern framework by dispersing the elements that the modernizers grouped together in a well-ordered cluster.'[23] The postmodern critique of modernity, therefore, is not sufficiently postmodern at all.

My thesis is that Barth's critique of modernity is more fundamentally postmodern. For only theology can provide the postmodern critique of modernity by repudiating the secular and the metaphysics of nihilism intrinsic to secularism. The secular is itself Nothingness. Post-secularity, then, is only conceivable within a doctrine of creation. That is why Barth's analysis of nothingness is so significant. 'The ontic context in which nothingness is real is that of God's activity grounded in His election, of His activity as the Creator, as the Lord of His creatures, as the King of the covenant between Himself and man which is the goal and purpose of His creation' (*CD* III/3, p. 405). This is a truly postmodern statement within Lyotard's terms: that which comes before, constitutes the other scene of and follows after the modern. In fact, this statement (and theology's postmodern status) pitches Christianity outside the stories of pre-modernity, modernity, and postmodernity. Christianity, the movement of its traditions, the processes of its salvation within time, while always being historically embedded and historically specific also transcends our history-making with its epochs and periodizations. My only question now is whether Barth's theology is sufficiently 'postmodern', whether it too needs to be rethought or reworked because of the shadows cast by modernity across his own work.

DUALISMS

In an essay published in 1973, the German scholar Dieter Schellong describes Barth as 'a theologian of modernity'. Schellong's account of modernity focuses upon certain of its emphases, particularly history, praxis, and transformation. He observes how these same characteristics are fundamental for Barth.[24] I do not wish to take issue with Schellong, only to point out that on the basis of the doctrines of soteriology, incarnation, and Christology theology has always to do with history, praxis, and transformation; and that the distinctiveness of Barth's reworking of each of those three categories lies exactly in the way he returns these categories to their orthodox Christian inspiration. He desecularizes modernity's concerns with time, action, and progress. In doing this he is not a theologian of modernity, though the question remains as to whether other characteristics of modernity do not affect Barth's project.

One of the fundamental aspects of modernity was its emphasis upon dualism. Dualism enabled modernity to constitute a world as separate from the sovereignty of God as its creator. Dualism establishes secularism; just as monism becomes the triumph of the secular. We can view dualism as doing one of two things. First, we can read it as necessary for an appreciation of God as omnipotent and wholly Other. (We can discern the outlines of this thesis in late Medieval thinking and Reformation theology.) Or, secondly, we can read it as necessary in order to define a domain in which the human and the natural operate, outside of God. (We can recognize this thesis within and as a consequence of Cartesianism.) Either way, a maze of dualisms develops. From the first thesis there arise the oppositions grace/nature, revelation/reason, Creator/creation, God/man, soul/body, eternity/time, infinite/finite, transcendence/immanence, etc. From the second thesis there arise the oppositions private/public, mind/world, reason/passion, internal/external, reflection/praxis, passive/active, absence/presence, mediation/immediacy. Many of these oppositions become mapped on to the concept of sexual difference, male/female, which develops from the seventeenth century onward. Now from what we have understood so far, in Barth's rejection of foundationalism, realism and humanism, he seeks to overcome the second, secular, series of binaries in terms of a new relationality. The body and the soul are co-implicated and, similarly, the private has public consequences; the female is the helpmeet of the male and so forth.[25] But the question of the extent to which Barth's thinking is implicated in the logics of modernity lies more with the first set of theological oppositions. Many critics have pointed specifically at the way these theological binaries frame Barth's thinking. Some critics, following in the line of Balthasar and Frei, have suggested a move towards a greater theological holism in Barth's later work, emphasizing how the earlier dialectic method accentuated the binary oppositions. Some more recent studies have emphasized a co-creativity between the divine and the human as it is expressed in the *Church Dogmatics*, if only in the later sections.[26] Some have declared Barth's project fundamentally flawed because of the revelation/reason, Creator/creation, grace/nature, eternity/time dualities which render the operation of the former category – revelation, God, grace and eternity – punctiliar and arbitrary. If these judgments upon Barth's theology stand, then they situate Barth within an Ockhamist world-view, and committed to a nominalism that can, all too easily, ignore the psychological, the social and the political aspects of embodiment. To be theologically postmodern requires a strong doctrine of participation in the operations of the triune God, through the Spirit, in creation and the church as the body of Christ. Nominalism bars the doors to such a doctrine and in this way (as I have shown) invents the secular. The question is whether Barth's theology hypostasizes difference – trinitarian difference, ontological difference, and sexual difference – such that participation is enfeebled. These criticisms of Barth's theology are, therefore, important for determining just how postmodern Barth's theology is.

Theologically, there are four fields of inquiry central to resolving the issue; fields which, traditionally, have been characterized by equivocation and dualism. They are: Barth's doctrine of analogy, Christology, pneumatology, and creation. The extent to which Barth's theology moves beyond modernity is the extent to which it is coherent with respect to: his *analogia fidei* (analogy of faith, or, elsewhere, analogy of relations or analogy of Christ); his teaching on the humanity and divinity of Christ such that, on the one hand Christ is coequal and not subordinate to a Father-God, and, on the other, he embraces the full nature of what it is to be human; the operation of the Spirit such that the Spirit constitutes a true second difference within the Trinity and not simply the relationship between Father and Son; and the relationship between the Trinity and creation such that the Spirit of Christ as Word informs (in a strong sense of that word) the world, humankind, and history. It would seem to me that Barth has the potential to present a radically orthodox voice that is genuinely postmodern and, therefore, post-secular – a voice we need in the turmoil of today's nihilistic indifference. But these are the doctrinal fields which have to be both examined critically and redefined if we are to move beyond Barth's theological resonances with contemporary society to challenge effectively that society's floating margins and foundations. Barth's theology, too, now has to be read eschatologically. His work is not timeless. There is no original Barth that can be recovered. Barth's theology is part of our theological legacy: to be read in the light of our present but also future condition in Christ.

CONCLUSION

In critiquing modernity Barth, unlike postmodern thinkers, returns to these fields of theological inquiry and demonstrates that what we called modernity issued from these fields and from the changes within theological investigation that affected orthodoxy in the seventeenth century. He does so not in a way which totally denigrates the modern – viewing the modern as a time when God was no longer active – and not in a way which is nostalgic for the past. Rather Barth points the way beyond modernity, because theology has no place for the ideologies of the modern. It is in this respect that he is postmodern and his theological inquiry likewise.

Notes

1 H. von Balthasar, *The Glory of the Lord*, vol. V: *The Realm of Metaphysics in the Modern Age*, trans. O. Davies *et al.* (Edinburgh: T & T Clark, 1991), esp. pp. 9–29.

2 *Nouvelle théologie* was a movement in French Roman Catholic theology in the middle decades of the twentieth century. It is marked by a return to Patristic and Medieval sources.

3 M. de Certeau, *The Mystic Fable*, trans M. B. Smith (Chicago: University of Chicago Press, 1992), pp. 79–94.

4 J.-F. Lyotard, *The Postmodern Condition: A Report on Knowledge*, trans G. Bennington and B. Massumi (Manchester: Manchester University Press, 1984); J.-F. Lyotard, *The Postmodern Explained*, trans. J. Pefanis and M. Thomas (Minneapolis: University of Minnesota Press, 1993); and *Le postmoderne expliqué aux enfants* (Paris: Galilee, 1986).

5 Lyotard, *The Postmodern Condition*, p. xxv.

6 S. Toulmin, *Cosmopolis: The Hidden Agenda of Modernity* (Chicago: University of Chicago Press, 1990), p. 150.

7 Ibid, p. 159.

8 Ibid, p. 153.

9 Ibid.

10 R. Roberts, *A Theology on its Way? Essays on Karl Barth* (Edinburgh: T & T Clark, 1991); D. Klemm, 'Towards a Rhetoric of Postmodern Theology through Barth and Heidegger', *Journal of the American Academy of Religion* 55 (1987), pp. 443–69; W. Lowe, *Theology and Difference. The Wound of Reason* (Bloomington, In.: Indiana University Press, 1993); and S. Webb, *Re-Figuring Theology: The Rhetoric of Karl Barth* (Albany, N.Y.: State University of New York Press, 1991).

11 A rhizoma is a subterranean root which grows in several arbitrary directions. In the work of Gilles Deleuze and Felix Guattari, it became a metaphor for a post-structural thinking.

12 I. Andrews, *Deconstructing Barth. A Study of the Complementary Methods in Karl Barth and Jacques Derrida* (New York: Peter Lang, 1996); W. S. Johnson, *The Mystery of God. Karl Barth and the Postmodern Foundations of Theology* (Louisville, Ky.: Westminster John Knox Press, 1997); G. Ward, *Barth, Derrida and the Language of Theology* (Cambridge: Cambridge University Press, 1995).

13 I employ a Nietzschean term here, but Barth is not systematic in his attempt to trace the paths which lead to atheism in *Church Dogmatics*. The closest he comes to being systematic is in his piece of historical theology, *Protestant Theology in the Nineteenth Century. Its Background and History* (London: SCM, 1972).

14 Ockham: 'The concept truth, in addition to the proposition it signifies, connotes that things are such in reality as they are conveyed to be by means of the proposition' (*Quodlibet* VI, q. 29). In turn, Ockham is indebted to, though he did not espouse, the materialistic particularism of Duns Scotus. See A. Gibson, 'Ockham's World and Future', in J. Marenbon, ed., *Mediaeval Philosophy* (London: Routledge, 1998), pp. 329–67.

15 There are a variety of correspondence theories of language. For a more detailed discussion see my article, 'Theological Materialism', in C. Crowder, ed., *God and Reality: Essays on Christian Non-Realism* (London: Mowbray, 1997), pp.144–59.

16 For two excellent discussions of Barth's neo-Kantian framework see S. Fisher,

Revelatory Positivism? Barth's Earliest Theology and the Marburg School (Oxford: Oxford University Press, 1988); and J. F. Lohmann, *Karl Barth und der Neukantianismus: Die Rezeption des Neukantianismus im 'Römerbrief' und ihre Bedeutung fur die weitere Ausarbeitung der Theologie Karl Barths* (Berlin: de Gruyter, 1995).

17 D. Cupitt, *The Last Philosophy* (London: SCM, 1995), p. 47.

18 Hence science is possible and informative: *CD* III/2, pp 12–13.

19 K. Barth, 'Brief an einen amerikanischen Kirchemann', in *Theologische Fragen und Antworten*, 2nd edn (Zurich: TVZ, 1986), p. 279.

20 This term is taken – by Derrida and Kristeva, in particular – from Plato's *Timaeus* where he names a dark, motile space from which all things emerge.

21 Often translated 'delight' or 'bliss'. In French it has sexual overtones.

22 See F. Jameson, *Postmodernism, or the Cultural Logic of Late Capitalism* (London: Verso, 1991); and T. Eagleton, *The Illusions of Postmodernism* (Oxford: Blackwell, 1996), especially pp. 20–44. Capitalism thrives on the atomism that nominalism invokes. As Slavoj Zizek writes, 'A capitalist is a common-sense nominalist.' See *The Plague of Fantasies* (London: Verso, 1997), p. 6.

23 B. Latour, *We Have Never Been Modern*, trans. Catherine Porter (London: Harvester Wheatsheaf, 1993), p. 74.

24 D. Schellong, 'Karl Barth als Theologe der Neuzeit', in K. G. Steck and D. Schellong, eds., *Karl Barth und die Neuzeit* (Munich: Chr. Kaiser Verlag, 1973), pp. 35–102.

25 For an analysis of Barth's work on sexual difference, see my 'The Erotics of Redemption After Karl Barth', in *Theology and Sexuality*, June 1998.

26 See J. Webster, *Barth's Ethic of Reconciliation* (Cambridge: Cambridge University Press, 1995); and W. S. Johnson, *The Mystery of God: Karl Barth and the Postmodern Foundations of Theology* (Louisville, Ky.: Westminster John Knox Press, 1997). Significantly, Johnson, while concluding that '[d]ivine and human co-agency is at the heart of Barth's theology' (p. 95), has had to admit that 'Barth does not say explicitly in the texts we have been summarizing' (p. 87) and that 'Barth does not spell it out clearly' (p. 88).

Further reading

Andrews, I., *Deconstructing Barth. A Study of the Complementary Methods in Karl Barth and Jacques Derrida* (Frankfurt: Lang, 1996).

Johnson, W. S., *The Mystery of God. Karl Barth and the Postmodern Foundations of Theology* (Louisville, Ky.: Westminster John Knox Press, 1997).

Lowe, W., *Theology and Difference. The Wound of Reason* (Bloomington, In.: Indiana University Press, 1993), pp. 33–47.

Roberts, R. H., *A Theology on its Way? Essays on Karl Barth* (Edinburgh: T & T Clark, 1991).

Smith, S. G., *Argument to the Other: Reason Beyond Reason in the Thought of Karl Barth and Emmanuel Levinas* (Chico, Calif.: Scholars Press, 1983).

Ward, G., *Barth, Derrida and the Language of Theology* (Cambridge: Cambridge University Press, 1995).

Webb, S., *Re-figuring Theology. The Rhetoric of Karl Barth* (Albany, N.Y.: State University of New York Press, 1991).

18 Karl Barth

A personal engagement

ALASDAIR I. C. HERON

Assessments of significance depend at least in part on the standpoint of the observer and the context of interpretation. The more prominent the object, the more perspectives are likely to be available. That is certainly the case with Barth. He still stands out in the history of theology in the twentieth century both as a major figure – to put it no more strongly – and also as a disputed figure. He has been hailed by some as the modern church father, and dismissed by others as out of touch and out of date even in his own day, to say nothing of *trente ans après*.

These thirty years have been the period of my own involvement in theological research and teaching – a period in which a not uncritical engagement with Barth has been one recurrent activity. It was within a few weeks of beginning my doctoral study in Tübingen in 1968 that I heard from Jürgen Moltmann of Barth's death the day before. That puts me in the generation of those who began theological work to some degree under Barth's shadow and in awareness of his impact, but who never actually met or heard him in the flesh. My acquaintance with him is strictly either literary or second-hand through my contacts and friendships with many who did know him or studied with him. This limitation has perhaps both a negative and a positive aspect. The negative aspect is that we increasingly have only a truncated Barth before us – the work rather than the man. The positive aspect is that this puts me in the same boat as those for whom this collection of studies is being written – and that Barth himself would have insisted that the work he attempted to do, especially in dogmatic theology, was his primary commitment and main contribution.

What then was Barth's contribution to dogmatic theology and what is likely to be its enduring significance? The first question is easier to tackle than the second; indeed the second faces us with all the buzzing and blooming confusion of contemporary theology – and that is a much harder field to survey than, say, the shift from German liberal theology to the new theological climate of Barth and his 'dialectical' allies in the 1920s. It is further complicated by the fact that the question of Barth's likely lasting importance tends to look very different depending on the setting in which it is posed, whether in Germany or Switzerland, in Britain or in America. Another complicating factor is ecclesiastical or confessional: the process of 'reception' of Barth's theology tends to be rather different in Reformed, Lutheran, Anglican, Catholic, or Orthodox traditions. Perhaps, however, we can seek some leverage on the second question by focusing on the first.

Let me begin with a little autobiographical retrospect, an attempt to think back on how Barth entered my own field of view. It must have been some time in the late 1950s that my father – a Scottish parish minister with a great interest in doctrinal theology – mentioned the name of Karl Barth and on my asking who he might be replied simply, 'The greatest theologian of the first half of this century.' For a schoolboy, that was an impressive testimony from an unimpeachable source. My father was not uncritical of Barth – particularly on the subject of infant baptism – and found the few volumes of the *Church Dogmatics* that he had been able to afford excessively lengthy and wordy, comparing Barth here unfavourably to Emil Brunner; but he still regarded Barth as the greater of the two, as the *doctor ecclesiae* of his day, the towering figurehead of dogmatic theology. In this, as I later found, my father was representative of many of the ablest Scottish theological students of the 1930s – the years when Barth was really beginning to become well known in Britain, especially in Scotland.[1]

As time passed I went on to study divinity at New College, Edinburgh, and came under the aegis of Thomas F. Torrance, the most redoubtable and most massively learned of all Barth's disciples in that generation. Two abiding memories are of learning German using *Dogmatik im Grundriß*[2] as the reading text and of compiling a précis of *Church Dogmatics* I/2, paragraph 15: 'The Mystery of Revelation' – that being the prescribed exercise to introduce us to dogmatic theology. It was an exercise that could, and in my case probably did, mark one for life. Having previously studied classics and philosophy, I had a largely exegetical, liturgical, and homiletical conception of theology: here I was confronted with tough, biblically, and historically shaped theological ideas and questions demanding thorough and serious discipline in their handling – a handling intended to think through and, if possible, beyond positions attained in the past. In my own small way, I was making a similar discovery to that which Barth describes in his foreword to Ernst Bizer's revision of Heppe's *Reformed Dogmatics*: that theology is a serious and responsible intellectual discipline with its own proportions, symmetry, and elegance, no less demanding than the questions of contemporary philosophy which had occupied me in the previous years.[3]

At the same time, I became well aware that 'Barthianism' was often more a term of opprobrium than of praise in the British and American context. Barth's frontal attacks on natural theology were a thorn in the flesh of a style of philosophical theology which had a venerable tradition in Britain in both Anglican and Reformed dress. Similarly, Barth's critique of 'religion' could not but be found unsympathetic by the advocates, coming to prominence in Britain in the 1960s, of 'religious studies' rather than 'confessional dogmatics'. In both respects, I soon found that much criticism and rejection of Barth was based more on ill-informed caricature than on any real attempt to understand him, and that the points he was making deserved to be taken more seriously and grasped in a more differentiated way; but, of course, substantial issues remained (and still remain) in these areas. On another tack, we knew even in Edinburgh that the postwar generation of German theological students was much more deeply coloured by the Bultmann school than by Barth, though a certain reaction associated with names such as Pannenberg, Moltmann and Jüngel was beginning to make itself felt. We did not on the whole hear anything very much about the Barthian theologians still active in Germany – Otto Weber, for example, or Walter Kreck. If anything, the greatest impact out of Germany (apart from Bultmann's) came from Gogarten via Harvey Cox's popularization of the theme of secularization. Yet there was also Barth's *Dogmatics*, complete in English by the end of the 1960s, a monument that could not be overlooked, and a mine of information and argument on all kinds of theological issues – which is how, like many others, I tended to use it. '*Da magistrum!*' meant not, as when Cyprian said it, 'Give me Tertullian', but 'Look up Barth!'

Edinburgh dogmatics under Torrance was not, however, characterized by any kind of uncritical Barthianism. In the theology I learned at New College in the 1960s (and taught there in the 1970s), Barth was an important source and a significant authority, but one with whom one had a perfect right to disagree and who was certainly not to be regarded as having said the last word on any subject. It may seem banal to say so, but we were not 'Barthians' in any narrow sense of the word at all, in spite of the respect in which we held him. My own special subjects in the final honours examination in dogmatics were Calvin and Tillich; I went on at Torrance's encouragement to do research in Patristics; and my first published article ventured to attempt to correct Barth on the *filioque* question with the help of Anselm, Augustine, and Vladimir Lossky! That was characteristic of Torrance's influence. A number of factors probably contributed to this. One was

Torrance's critical loyalty to the tradition of Scottish Reformed theology, with which Barth not surprisingly had only very sketchy familiarity. Another was the much greater breadth of Torrance's own historical and ecumenical theological studies from his student days onward, as compared with Barth's relatively late entry into the scene of academic theological teaching as a virtual autodidact in his mid-thirties. Perhaps most significant of all was Torrance's deliberate pushing far beyond Barth on the interface between theology, specifically *dogmatic* theology, and the thinking of natural science.

After moving to Erlangen in 1981, I found myself in a rather different setting. On the one hand, the general retrospective view and evaluation of Barth current in German theology tended to approximate to what I had first heard in my father's study more than twenty years before: Barth had been the most significant single figure in evangelical theology in the first part of the century. The emphasis was on the 'had been'. A generation of younger systematic theologians, some of them virtually unknown outside central Europe, were busily working away in research and teaching in the field of dogmatic theology. Some were conscious of a debt to Barth, others were more inclined to pass him by. I began to see more clearly what it meant that Barth had been Swiss, not German; that he had been Reformed, not Lutheran; that he had been clearly identified with the Confessing Church, which had never been more than a minority in the German Evangelical Church in the Nazi period; that after the war he had been prominently allied with the continuing representatives of that strand – for example, Martin Niemöller – in their opposition to the restoration politics of other church leaders; and that his vocal criticism of German rearmament and his rejection of the politics of the Cold War had not made him popular everywhere in the German church. In much the same way, his public opposition to fascism had made him politically suspect in Switzerland before 1945, his refusal equally to condemn communism in the years thereafter. The more I learned about all this personal history, the more I began to appreciate Barth's only half-humorous complaints in later years about being excluded from the company of respectable theology; complaints which hardly make any sense to anyone who has only heard of Barth that he was 'the greatest theologian of his age' or the leader of 'neo-orthodoxy' – a term incidentally at which Barth could only laugh.[4] In many ways, Barth was made to feel and felt himself to be an outsider, albeit one who was content to go his way as 'God's cheerful partisan'.

An observation may perhaps help to illustrate this. I was fortunate in arriving in Erlangen in 1981 in time to become a close friend of two of the

Bavarian Lutheran ministers who had been most active in the Confessing Church: Karl Steinbauer and Walter Höchstädter. Both published their memoirs before they died, which are powerful testimonies.[5] More powerful still was their personal witness to a time when, as Arthur Cochrane has said, the Confessing Church had nothing but the Word of God by which to live.[6] Both men had the highest regard and appreciation for Karl Barth for his role in Germany in the years before his expulsion from his chair in Bonn in 1935, and for his encouragement from Basel in the years following. Witness and faithfulness were what they had learned, not *only* from Barth, but *also* from Barth. The theology represented in my own faculty of Erlangen in that period – that of Werner Elert and Paul Althaus – was, to put it mildly, of a very different stamp and *that* was the official theology of the Lutheran Church in Bavaria.[7] All in all, a reflection *in nuce* of the situation in which Barth found himself as a Swiss Reformed theologian in a context dominated by German Lutherans.

That is perhaps enough of personal retrospect, though all the themes touched upon could be developed at much greater length. It is time to look more closely at Barth's contribution to dogmatic theology.

Other contributions in this collection deal in detail with various aspects of Barth's work; here, I can do little more than list those points which seem to me of abiding importance and relevant for the future orientation of theology. These concern, first of all, Barth's impulses for the discipline of dogmatics as such; second, particular developments and directions to be seen in his work which represent an advance on what had gone before; and third, critical reservations where it might seem better that theology should *not* follow Barth.

It was no part of Barth's original intention to become a dogmatic theologian. His *Romans* commentary grew out of frustration with a purely objective, distanced, historical approach to the understanding of biblical texts which left them having nothing to say to preacher and congregation in their contemporary context. Barth attempted to listen out of that context to what he could hear in Paul addressing Barth's own time as the Word of God. Lively and relevant theology was what he was after, as opposed to archaeological study of documents from the past. This applies to both the first and second editions of Barth's *Romans*, though the theological and hermeneutical perspectives had changed fairly radically between them. The heavy existentialism, the echoes of Overbeck and Dostoyevsky and, above all, the Kierkegaardian emphasis on the 'absolute qualitative difference' and 'vertically from above' are features of the second edition rather than of the first, though it was the first – today almost totally forgotten – which led to Barth's call to the professorship of Reformed theology in Göttingen.

This concern to practise a relevant and lively theology of the Word of God remained central to Barth's work for the rest of his life, but he was compelled by the circumstances and responsibilities of his new position as an academic teacher to expand his arsenal of resources and his stock of information. This involved him in the years in Göttingen in continuing and extending his biblical work, in deepening his acquaintance with early Reformed theology – notably Zwingli, Calvin, and the Heidelberg Catechism, all themes of lectures in Göttingen – and in making a first effort at writing a dogmatics.[8] A few years later in Münster, intensive if critical dialogue with Roman Catholic theology and with the heritage of scholastic Medieval theology, especially Anselm and Aquinas, was added. Here too in 1927, the first volume of his *Christian Dogmatics* was published – only to be radically recast and massively expanded as *Church Dogmatics* I/1 and I/2 in the 1930s. With that, the course for his future work was set and work on the *Dogmatics* became the main – though never the only – priority in the remaining decades of his life.

Barth's dogmatics, for all the modernity of much of the content, belongs to a *genre* and reflects a tradition and style of lecturing, teaching, and writing which is scarcely practised today and arguably is no longer effective as a pedagogical method. The obverse of that coin, however, is that it was probably only because he was prepared to take such a long breath, to reflect at such length and detail, to argue from this side and from that, to go round and round questioning and rethinking, that Barth was able to reformulate and cast fresh light upon many of the central themes and issues of Christian dogmatics and to re-establish dogmatic thinking as a dynamic and creative inquiry at the heart of Christian theology, indeed as an instrument of theological and ecclesiastical self-correction, and as such as a discipline pointing forward rather than backward. That is why it is still worth the effort and trouble of going to school with him and reflecting with him, instead of succumbing to the temptation of simply picking up his main conclusions and going on from there.

Space permits here only the briefest mention of some of the issues radically recast and freshly illuminated by Barth. Much could be said of other themes, such as the integration of trinitarian thinking with the understanding of revelation, the dynamic combination of the traditional doctrines of the person and work of Jesus Christ, and the unifying of dogmatics and ethics. The same style of integrating and unifying reflection is splendidly demonstrated in two chapters of Volume II: the doctrine of

God as 'the One who loves in freedom', and the reworking of the theme of the divine election. This latter is sometimes (wrongly) seen as merely a problem for Reformed, specifically Calvinist theology; in fact it is a problem for the entire Augustinian tradition of Western theology, both Roman Catholic and Protestant, though more often ignored than addressed. Barth's detailed treatment of it – including perhaps some more than adventurous biblical exegesis! – may be open to criticism; but in one fundamental correction of virtually the entire previous tradition, he is surely right: that both election and reprobation (God's 'Yes' and 'No') must first of all be understood *christologically*, in the light of the cross and the resurrection. In a similar way in Volume IV, Barth departs from the tradition of developing the understanding of the Fall and sinfulness as a prolegomenon to and precondition for the doctrine of reconciliation, and treats them instead as a reflex of the achieved reality of reconciliation. In between these, in Volume III, it is above all Barth's exposition of the topics of creation and covenant which reflects the same concern to unify and integrate themes more traditionally dealt with separately. One may add that Barth's daring handling of 'God and Nothingness' in this volume – however problematic the exegetical basis may be here too – is a *tour de force* of sustained theological and philosophical reflection which shows the formerly so existentially influenced Barth countering such thinkers as Heidegger and Sartre as an intellectual equal.

In ways such as these, the judgment seems justified that Barth has set new directions for dogmatic theology; that, at any rate, it cannot afford to ignore or retreat behind the challenge he represents. But are there respects in which it would do better not to follow him – or, at any rate, to do so only with critical caution? I believe there are.

First, Barth's rejection of natural theology, his dislike of the discipline of defensive apologetics, his concern for the authenticity of dogmatics as a subject with its own task, questions and methods free from any subservience to or dictation from other disciplines, are all in their own way not only understandable but justifiable. They do not, however, necessarily make dogmatic theology easily capable of entering into dialogue with these other disciplines. The clearest case is the sense of relief shown by Barth when he discovers in Volume III of the *Church Dogmatics* that he can handle the dogmatic theme of creation quite adequately *without* entering into any discussion with natural science, which has quite simply a different job to do. Torrance has certainly been right in seeing that dogmatic theology cannot allow itself to be bound by this restriction, that indeed impulses in Barth's own style of theological work and argument already strain against it. There is a tightrope to be walked here; but proper insistence on the independence and integrity of dogmatics should not be pushed to the point of leaving it in a ghetto.

Second, it is a commonly voiced complaint that Barth pays too little attention and does too little justice to the justifiable claims and necessary insights of the historical-critical approach to biblical exegesis. The criticism is sometimes driven to the point of crass misrepresentation, but it is not entirely lacking in basis. Barth's use of biblical material is sometimes distinctly idiosyncratic – or, one might say, more artistic than scientific. Huge hermeneutical questions arise here and it must be admitted that Barth's exegesis, even when problematic, is at least very often provocative and interesting – which is not always the case with professed historical-critical exegesis. There is, however, room for the suspicion that Barth was not always sufficiently aware or critical of his own hermeneutical perspectives when drawing on biblical texts for dogmatic construction. That does not necessarily make his arguments and contributions invalid, but it does demand further consideration of the interpretative principles involved in dogmatic theology. In this connection, I should perhaps add a word on the topic which is sometimes seen (I believe, incorrectly) as the paradigm case for this problem in Barth: his disagreement with Bultmann. That disagreement was not, however, about the principles of historical-critical exegesis, nor even primarily about Bultmann's programme of demythologization. Barth himself testified clearly enough that his problem was Bultmann's reduction of *theo*logy to *anthropo*logy[9] – a dogmatic, not an exegetical issue.

Third, Barth's ecclesiology and sacramental theology betray a tendency towards individualism and congregationalism, which culminates in Barth's rejection of the whole concept of *sacrament* in favour of the idea of 'free, obedient response' with the consequent reduction of the *sacramental* to the *ethical*.[10] Barth's argument to this end, developed most finally in the fragment, *Church Dogmatics* IV/4, is in its own way coherent and conclusive, consistent and programmed to come to no other result so that readers can be sucked along it, much like travellers in the Channel Tunnel who have no choice other than to be carried on to the end. Just this, however, highlights the necessity of reading Barth not only sympathetically but also critically; and in particular looking out for the places where the very consistency and apparent compelling necessity of the train of argument demands that one ask about the hidden presuppositions which are steering it.

It shows no lack of respect or appreciation for Barth's achievement to raise such questions. The massive scale of the *Church Dogmatics* can evoke the impression that they were intended to be a final word, a last statement, in the words of Thucydides, a *ktema es aei*, a 'possession for ever'. Yet they were not. They were the product of engaged and lively theological and dogmatic reflection deliberately undertaken as a critical task in the service of the church and its witness; and as such the product of a theology *in via*, theology on the road. Barth never had the idea that he could sum up, let alone incarcerate, the whole scope of the divine revelation and invitation in Jesus Christ even in many thousands of pages. He simply went to work, day by day, week by week, and year by year in the conviction that the great themes of dogmatic theology are only taken seriously when they are also thought through as deeply and carefully as possible. Barth applied himself to this task with an energy and a manifest enjoyment which – whether we follow him in this point or that – is a standing challenge to understand the work of dogmatics as he described it in *Evangelical Thelogy*: as a 'modest, free, critical and – above all – happy science'.[11]

In June 1964 Barth drafted a brief *Selbstdarstellung*, in anticipation of the sixtieth anniversary of the beginning of his theological studies. In closing, he hazarded a glimpse into the future; perhaps these last two paragraphs can best sum up what he believed to be his legacy and his challenge to those who would come after.[12]

> I won't risk even a guess at the prospects for what I have undertaken in theology. 'For everything there is a season'.[13] I am well aware of at least some of the weaker aspects of my capacity and achievement. I am indeed very far from imagining that my achievement of what I wished and presented cannot be surpassed. From the start I have reckoned with the likelihood that one day with other means and methods everything might be done better than was possible for me. What possible right could I have to object – should I not rather rejoice for the sake of the cause,[14] were I yet to see my advocacy of it overtaken and superseded?
>
> Admittedly I could only regard myself as legitimately overtaken in this sense under the following conditions. A fresh theological programme must (1), however emancipated from my sketches, not betray their fundamental intention regarding the source, object and content of all theology worth the name, but carry it through in a better form. It must (2) prove itself to be a fresh programme by developing that fundamental intention in a way that points and leads forwards rather than backwards – inviting and encouraging the continuing Exodus from Egypt rather than something like the programme of the Jews back to that land in Jeremiah's later years. And it cannot (3) be

just another mere 'project' announcing itself ever and again in fresh garb. It must be brought under way in a reasonably consistent and complete form corresponding formally to what I have attempted to offer. I may have become hard of hearing, but so far the new song to be sung to the Lord that would meet these conditions has not yet reached my ears. Thus with all modesty I would provisionally regard myself as not yet overtaken and superseded. However that may be: *Dominus providebit.* It only remains for me to wish for systematic theology (whatever may become of my contribution) in the nearer and further future that it may remain (or become again) the modest yet free, critical yet joyful enquiry which has become dear to me through all wanderings and temptations – and well worth all the trouble.

Notes

1 See A.-K. Finke, *Karl Barth in Großbritannien. Rezeption und Wirkungsgeschichte* (Neukirchen: Neukirchener Verlag, 1995).

2 K. Barth, *Dogmatics in Outline* (London: SCM Press, 1949).

3 H. Heppe, *Reformed Dogmatics* (London: George Allen and Unwin, 1950), pp. v–vii.

4 See Barth's dismissal of the term 'neo-orthodox' as 'simply comical' in *Letzte Zeugnisse* (Zürich: EVZ, 1969), p. 34.

5 W. Hochstädter, *Durch den Strudel der Zeiten geführt* (Bubenreuth: privately printed, 1983); K. Steinbauer, *Einander das Zeugnis gönnen*, vols. 1–4 (Erlangen: privately printed, 1983–7).

6 See A. C. Cochrane, *The Church's Confession under Hitler* (Philadelphia: Westminster Press, 1962).

7 See R. P. Ericksen, *Theologians under Hitler. Gerhard Kittel/Paul Althaus/ Emmanuel Hirsch* (New Haven: Yale University Press, 1985); B. Mensing, *Pfarrer und Nationalsozialismus. Geschichte einer Verstrickung am Beispiel der Evangelisch-Lutherischen Kirche in Bayern* (Göttingen: Vandenhoeck & Ruprecht, 1998); B. Hamm, 'Werner Elert als Kriegstheologe. Zugleich ein Beitrag zur Diskussion "Luthertum und Nationalsozialismus"', *KZG* 11/2 (1998), pp. 206–54.

8 See here M. Freudenberg, *Karl Barth und die Reformierte Theologie* (Neukirchen: Neukirchener Verlag, 1997).

9 Barth states this quite explicitly in the *Selbstdarstellung* of 1964 from which I quote below: 'Was mich ihm [sc. Bultmann] gegenüber zur Zurückhaltung nötigte und noch nötigt, ist viel weniger seine von der Mehrzahl seiner Gegner beanstandete "Entmythologisierung" des Neuen Testaments, als sein "Existentialisierung" von dessen Aussagen, in der ich die Theologie nur eben neu in die Sackgasse einer philosophischen Anthropologie laufen sehe . . .'

10 On these issues, see P. D. Molnar, *Karl Barth and the Theology of the Lord's Supper* (New York: Peter Lang, 1996).

11 K. Barth, *Evangelical Theology* (London: Weidenfeld and Nicolson, 1963), pp. 1–12.

12 I am grateful to Dr Drewes of the Barth Archive and to the members of the Barth Legacy Commission for permission to quote from this as yet unpublished text. It will eventually appear in the complete edition of Barth's writings.

13 Eccl. 3:1. Barth quotes in the form 'Alles Ding hat seine Zeit', perhaps with Paul Gerhardt's hymn in the back of his mind:

Sollt ich meinem Gott nicht singen?
Sollt ich ihm nicht dankbar sein?
Denn ich seh in allen Dingen,
Wie so gut er's mit mir mein.
Ist doch nichts als lauter Lieben,
Das sein treues Herze regt,
Das ohn Ende hebt und trägt,
Die in seinem Dienst sich üben.
Alles Ding währt seine Zeit,
Gottes Lieb in Ewigkeit.

14 'For the sake of the cause' renders Barth's 'Um der Sache willen'.

Further reading

Barth, K., *The Humanity of God* (London: Collins, 1961).
Barth, K., *Evangelical Theology* (London: Weidenfeld & Nicolson, 1963).
Barth, K., *How I Changed my Mind* (Richmond, Va.: John Knox Press, 1966).
Barth, K., *Fragments Grave and Gay* (London: Collins, 1971).
Barth, K., and Bultmann, R., *Letters 1922–1966* (Edinburgh: T & T Clark, 1982).

Index

Achelis, Ernst Christian, 19
Age of Absolutism, 197
Althaus, Paul, 301
Amsterdam Assembly of the World Council
    of Churches, 7
analogia Christi (analogy of Christ), 280,
    285, 293
analogia entis (analogy of being), 46, 108–9,
    167, 266
analogia fidei (analogy of faith), 46–7, 53,
    108, 167, 266, 280, 285, 293
Andrews, Isolde, 280
anhypostasis, 44, 55–6, 56n.8, 163
Anselm of Canterbury, 5, 28–9, 298, 300
Anselm. Fides Quaerens Intellectum, 28
Aquinas, Thomas, 123, 184, 208, 249, 275,
    301
ascension, 138, 153–4
Athanasius, 76
atheism, 159–61, 282
atonement, 149, 151
Augustine of Hippo, Augustinian, 80, 162,
    145, 180, 183, 298, 302
Averroes, 275

Balthasar, Hans Urs von, 108–9, 206, 266,
    275, 280, 292
baptism, 80, 156, 195–209
    see also infant baptism
Barmen Theological Declaration, 6, 200,
    229
Barth, Fritz, 2
Barth, Nelly, 258
Baudrillard, Jean, 274
Bauhaus, 279
Bauman, Zygmunt, 286
Beauvoir, Simone de, 258, 264, 265
Berg, Alban, 279
Berkouwer, G. C., 154
Bethge, Eberhard, 228
'biblicist', 58–9, 60
Bizer, Ernst, 297
Bonhoeffer, Dietrich, 84, 161, 220

Brennan, J. M., 220
Bromiley, Geoffrey, 74, 81
Brunner, Emil, 4, 6, 92–3, 183, 220, 266, 267,
    297
Buber, Martin, 269
Buddhists, 243, 244, 251
Bultmann, Rudolf, 4, 5, 84, 153, 160, 298,
    303
Busch, Eberhard, 1
Butler, Judith, 274

Calvin, John, 3, 12, 13, 27, 34, 82, 88, 92,
    102, 278, 301, 302
    Barth's lectures on, 12
    doctrine of election, 93–8, 145
Canon, Katie, 263
casuistry, 220–2
Certeau, Michel de, 275, 276, 289
*Christian Dogmatics in Outline: The Doctrine
    of the Word of God*, 4, 25, 27, 301
Christliche Welt (Christian World), 3, 17,
    23
Christology, 27, 88, 93, 130–9, 154, 207–8,
    216, 266, 302
    Alexandrian, 129–32, 134, 139
    and doctrine of creation, 120–1
    and pneumatology, 181–2
    Antiochian, 129–32, 134, 139
    Chalcedonian, 127–30, 139, 140n.2
    dogmatic ground for ethics, 222–5
    Logos Christology, 95–101
    relation to soteriology, 144, 146
    see also ethics, and Christology
Christus Praesens, 181–2
church, 66, 73, 79, 128, 173–4, 303, 278
    and doctrine of creation, 112, 115, 118,
    126
    and event of revelation, 46–9
    and theology, 10
    as community, 190–2
    doctrine of (ecclesiology), 152, 195–6,
    199–209
    political responsibility, 228–41